THE FUTURE OF M   ₊NANCE

The

FUTURE

of

MICROFINANCE

———

Edited by
IRA W. LIEBERMAN
PAUL DILEO
TODD A. WATKINS
ANNA KANZE

BROOKINGS INSTITUTION PRESS
Washington, D.C.

Copyright © *2020*
THE BROOKINGS INSTITUTION
1775 Massachusetts Avenue, N.W., Washington, D.C. 20036
www.brookings.edu

The Brookings Institution is a private nonprofit organization devoted to research, education, and publication on important issues of domestic and foreign policy. Its principal purpose is to bring the highest quality independent research and analysis to bear on current and emerging policy problems. Interpretations or conclusions in Brookings publications should be understood to be solely those of the authors.

Library of Congress Control Number: 2020936117.

ISBN 978-0-8157-3763-6 (pbk)
ISBN 978-0-8157-3764-3 (e-book)

9 8 7 6 5 4 3 2 1

Typeset in Granjon and Avenir Next

Composition by Westchester Publishing Services

To the memory of Marguerite Robinson

Contents

Section III
The Challenge of Technology and New Product Innovation and Development

Section IV
A Geographic Perspective

Foreword

Should proponents of microfinance claim victory and go home? This seemingly innocent question has sparked much discussion. For some of the early supporters of microfinance, mostly donors and economic development agencies, the "fairy dust" is gone. Many have gone on to other endeavors such as working on financial inclusion, which is closely related to microfinance, but not quite the same thing. If microfinance is a thing of the past to some, this volume clearly establishes that microfinance is not only alive, but it is still growing dynamically and is relevant to the working poor, the clients of microfinance institutions.

Many issues remain to be addressed:

- Why has product diversification—into areas such micro-savings, insurance, housing, education and money transfers—not become more important as sources of growth for the sector?

- How are mobile or digital finance and fintech challenging the way microfinance institutions operate? Are they an existential threat to the sector?

- What is being done to mitigate the effect of over-lending and over saturation of MFIs in some countries, particularly in urban areas?

- With the early pioneers of microfinance now retiring, many MFIs having grown exponentially, and risks also expanding, how will MFIs and the sector overall address the changes in governance required to ensure that the industry continues to grow soundly? How can the risks be mitigated?

■ Academic assessments of microfinance have raised doubts on its role in poverty alleviation. Unrealistic expectations may have been created early in the development of the sector, how is this issue being addressed?

These and other pertinent questions are addressed in the chapters that follow, not only in a general way, but by a series of in-depth chapters that address these and other issues in specific geographic markets such as Asia, particularly in some depth in India and China, in Latin America and in Africa.

Alex Silva, Executive Director
Calmeadow Foundation

Preface

IRA W. LIEBERMAN AND PAUL DILEO

This book was written before the outbreak of the COVID-19 virus. As it nears publication, microfinance institutions, their staff, and clients are facing this additional enormous challenge. While we maintain our optimism about the future of microfinance, with all of the opportunities and challenges discussed in the book still in place, the immediate task is to preserve as many of the capabilities and as much of the value of the industry as possible in the face of the crisis.

By the time you read this, the scale of value destroyed by the COVID-19 pandemic and the related economic crisis will be clearer: savings depleted, plantings and harvests missed, schooling suspended, lives lost. Even countries relatively unaffected in health terms will have suffered the effects of lockdowns, financial and economic contraction, and disruption in global supply chains that will shut factories and the suppliers and service businesses that surround them. As you read this volume, you will know how successful the industry has been in minimizing the damage.

Crises are complex: a real estate or stock market bust often turns into a financial crisis, which turns into an economic crisis, which in turn can lead to devaluations and a sovereign debt crisis. Crises move around the world and can become global in nature—what used to be referred to as "contagion" before we were faced with actual contagion. Governments find themselves needing to address all of these issues at the same time. This means they need robust institutional capacity deployed with speed and agility, substantial financial and fiscal resources, a national lender of last resort, and frequently an international lender of last resort such as the IMF, World Bank, regional development banks, and G-7 nations.

Understandably, government efforts in this crisis must focus first and foremost on the immediate health impact. Only when this is addressed, and lockdowns and social distancing have been relaxed, can comprehensive efforts to address the economic damage take center stage. But even in the best such rescue programs, many MFI "core" clients—those who work in informal and seasonal businesses, in home-based business, or as smallholder farmers—will be bypassed by national efforts. These clients often cannot access or will be overlooked by many of the measures governments are employing to give relief and stability to individuals and families: mortgage and debt relief, cash grants through provident fund systems, wage and salary support to formal businesses.

This situation casts into sharp relief both the unique capabilities and the vulnerability of microfinance. For many of their clients, MFIs are the best available channel for support, with established, trusted relationships, last-mile infrastructure, and decades of experience in innovating solutions for poor and otherwise excluded populations. The role that MFIs play in normal times—smoothing income through loans and savings, providing emergency funds, disseminating relevant information and guidance—now mean the difference between life and death for many families.

But many MFIs—particularly smaller companies in rural areas, with a larger proportion of small, informal, and women borrowers—are themselves in danger of being overlooked as rescue efforts focus on larger institutions with stronger links to the financial system and macroeconomy. Just as governments are likely to focus their attention on the most visible participants in the real economy—large corporations, state or privately owned, that are "too big to fail," and to a more limited extent SMEs—the microfinance sector will most likely get little formal attention and support. Banking supervisory agencies and central banks are likely as always to focus their attention on bigger institutions, those that pose a systemic risk and are likewise considered too big to fail.

This is, therefore, the moment that the industry's networks, associations, and lead investors exist for, even if it was unanticipated and unprepared for. Leaders in the microfinance sector will need to engage one another and develop a strategy for crisis resolution and rescue of MFIs in distress, putting aside business as usual. They will need to resist the understandable impulse to free-ride and instead step up to collectively act as lenders of last resort to inject liquidity into the sector to assist their clients during this most difficult time.

Unlike the financial sector—banks, nonbank financial institutions, and capital markets—the microfinance sector has not previously experienced a systemic or global crisis. There have been individual failures of MFIs, country crises such as in India, Nicaragua, and Bosnia usually triggered by political interference or overlending, but no systemic crises.

Nevertheless, the decades of work and accomplishment summarized in this volume have placed the industry in a unique and critical position: to ensure that the world's most vulnerable are not, once again, left to fend for themselves. The industry's leaders and core supporters need to step up and support MFIs in devising solutions to the challenges they face. The physical distancing that characterizes this crisis poses a severe challenge to those MFIs that are not yet well along in incorporating digital services into their offerings. Preserving the "high touch" that is so central to their client relationships will test their resolve and their creativity. This is the worst possible moment for investors and funders to increase the pressure on MFIs to abandon the distinguishing social ambitions that will ensure their financial stability and indeed, their survival. "Solutions" can't sacrifice lower-density rural populations, or smaller-ticket women borrowers. In all these and other areas, the industry has a critical role to play in ensuring that the "rescue" preserves the future depicted in this book.

That future is still achievable, but requires that the industry come together quickly, comprehensively, and coherently as it has not had to do before, to focus its resources and influence on preserving its unique capability to support vulnerable populations, and to advocate tirelessly for them through the ultimate resolution of the crisis and the long rebuilding that follows.

The future of microfinance will be in this rebuilding of families and communities. We hope this volume clearly articulates how and why microfinance will play such an essential role in this rebuilding and in the years that follow. We hope that, as you read this, you will be able to see that the microfinance industry has risen to the challenge.

Acknowledgments

This book had its origins in a workshop on the future of microfinance held at Lehigh University March 30–April 1, 2017. The editors of this book were the primary organizers of the workshop, which was sponsored by the Calmeadow Foundation and the Martindale Center for the Study of Private Enterprise at Lehigh. Following the workshop, the editors published a white paper based on the discussions held during the workshop: "Microfinance: Revolution or Footnote? The Future of Microfinance Over the Next Ten Years." This current volume is a detailed follow-up to the workshop and the white paper, and contains the contributions from a number of authors who have deep expertise in the microfinance sector as well as the related financial inclusion and impact investing sectors.

I want to thank my co-editors for their efforts in organizing this volume and for the chapters they contributed. I also want to thank the other authors who have contributed their time and knowledge. Matt Colyar served as an able and thoughtful research associate throughout the process, despite finishing a graduate degree at Lehigh University and having a full-time job thereafter. My thanks go to Matt.

We cannot thank Richard Rosenberg sufficiently for reviewing the book. Rich spent years in the microfinance sector; his writings and his work in Bolivia and at CGAP constitute a major contribution to the field.

I want to thank the Calmeadow Foundation, above all Alex Silva, for funding and supporting our efforts in organizing this book. I also want to thank the Martindale Center, and my co-editor Professor Todd A. Watkins for his support and funding for the conference and book.

The editorial team at Westchester Publishing Services did an outstanding job in editing the manuscript. My deep thanks to Angela Piliouras and her colleagues. Any mistakes are those of the authors.

I also want to thank the team at Brookings Institution Press led by Bill Finan, Elliott Beard, Steve Roman, and Cecilia González for providing their input and expertise in preparing the book for publication and its subsequent marketing and distribution.

Ira W. Lieberman

The editors dedicate this book to Marguerite Robinson, who was a scholar at the Harvard Institute of Development. Marguerite spent considerable time in the field, above all in Asia and in particular Indonesia, working with Bank Rakyat Indonesia in its formative stages. She was an anthropologist who called herself a financial anthropologist, an unusual combination. From her experience with Bank Rakyat, Marguerite gained an in-depth knowledge of savings programs for the poor and subsequently advised a number of microfinance institutions around the world on their savings programs. She also wrote extensively on microfinance, including a seminal work, *The Microfinance Revolution*. Marguerite gave generously of her time to mentor many of us who worked in the sector. She is missed.

Abbreviations

ABC	Agricultural Bank of China
ADBC	Agricultural Development Bank of China
AUM	assets under management
BOP	bottom of the pyramid
BRI	Bank Rakyat Indonesia
CBFO	community-based financial organization
CBIRC	China Banking and Insurance Regulatory Commission
CFI	composite financial index
CFPA	China Foundation for Poverty Alleviation
CGAP	Consultative Group to Assist the Poor
CMEF	Council of Microfinance Equity Funds
DFI	development financial institution
DFS	digital financial services
FSP	financial service provider
IBA	Indian Bankers Association
IDB	Inter-American Development Bank
IFC	International Finance Corporation
ILO	International Labour Organization
IMF	International Monetary Fund
IPO	initial public offering
LAC	Latin America and the Caribbean
LDC	least-developed countries

LGOP	Leading Group Office on Poverty Alleviation and Development (China)
MCC	microcredit company
MDI	microfinance deposit taking institution
MFI	microfinance institution
MFS	mobile financial service
MIV	microfinance investment vehicle
MNOs	mobile network operations
MOF	Ministry of Finance
MSEs	micro and small enterprises
NABARD	National Bank for Agriculture and Rural Development (India)
NBFC	nonbanking financial company
NBFI	nonbanking financial institution
NGO	nongovernmental organization
NPL	nonperforming loan
PAR	portfolio at risk
PBOC	People's Bank of China
PSBC	Postal Savings Bank of China
PSP	payment service provider
RBI	Reserve Bank of India
RCB	rural commercial bank
RCC	rural credit co-operative
RCOB	rural co-operative bank
RCT	randomized controlled trial
RFC	rural fund company
RFI	rural financial institution
RFM	rural financial market
ROSCAs	rotational savings and loan schemes
SDG	Sustainable Development Goals (United Nations)
SHG	self-help groups
SME	small and medium-sized enterprise
SOCB	state-owned commercial bank
SOE	state-owned enterprise
UFA	Universal Financial Access Plan (World Bank)
UIDAI	Unique Identification Authority of India
UPI	unified payment interface
USAID	United States Agency for International Development
WBG	World Bank Group

THE FUTURE OF MICROFINANCE

Introduction

PAUL DILEO AND JOSE RUISANCHEZ

This volume brings together the perspective of twenty longtime participants in the "microfinance revolution." Some have been engaged with the sector since its earliest days, and together the chapters reflect hundreds of years of cumulative experience. The essays paint a picture of where microfinance (MF) is now and how it got here, before turning to the contributors' multiple perspectives and visions for how we move on from here.

How has the evolution of MF from nonprofit, grant-funded programs to regulated institutions fully integrated into mainstream capital markets been navigated? How has assessment of the social bottom line evolved from counting women to mapping against the United Nations Sustainable Development Goals (SDGs)? How have incumbent microfinance institutions (MFIs) reached out to partners from elsewhere in the financial sector and beyond to introduce new products and enhance outreach and efficiency? What is the special role of governance in a double-bottom-line financial intermediary in an environment of rapid technological change? Amid all the hype and frenzy, what can be expected from financial technology (fintech), and what is required to ensure that it delivers? What does the latest research tell us about how microfinance benefits the poor and what is required to do this more and better?

We also take a regional perspective, looking at key markets to discern how they share features, how they diverge, and their possible trajectories. Do India and China have lessons for the rest of the world, or are they each so extraordinary as to be forging unique paths? How can all the experience of the past thirty years be constructively brought to bear in Africa, where the poorest are now concentrated? And is Latin America, where microfinance was first and most successfully integrated into financial systems, continuing to lead the way or falling behind?

Finally, we have asked several observers from a range of perspectives to share their visions for the future, assembling a Roshamon-type view of what lies ahead.

One threshold question arises at the outset of this discussion and relates to terminology: What are we talking about when we talk about "microfinance," and how does it differ from "financial access," which itself is not the same as "financial inclusion"? How do we distinguish a "microenterprise" from a small business? Is the "bottom of the pyramid" equivalent to the "poorest," or does it encompass a broader range of the population? Even a few years ago, it seemed easy to distinguish MFIs from other companies, and in the absence of textured data documenting who was borrowing and what they were doing with the money, trying to distinguish among businesses and borrowers or locate borrowers within the right quintile of the income distribution seemed a not particularly good use of limited resources.

But today, between financial inclusion, mobile money, downstreaming banks, fintechs, and specialized finance companies targeting education, solar power, or small and medium-sized enterprises (SMEs), it is not at all clear how to delineate the microfinance industry. And within the sector, whatever that is, how is one to distinguish those institutions targeting the "poor," however defined, with a meaningful commitment to a double bottom line from those that pay lip service, at most? If corporate structure, scale, loan size, and client base are no longer distinguishing features, what differentiates the "microfinance industry"?

The chapters reflect this diversity, and we have made no attempt to impose a common terminology; any such attempt would be doomed. The reader is therefore alerted to read each chapter with discernment, and to be sensitive to the likelihood that the "microfinance industry" cited in one chapter or one set of data may well differ significantly from the same category cited by another author. Caveat lector! Nevertheless, we hope that readers will come away with a sense of the trajectory and key trends of microfinance, where it fits in the world of financial inclusion, and toward which clients it orients the bulk of its energies. We would also note that the very diversity and resistance to clear delineation that have emerged in recent years are, in fact, markers of the success and maturation of microfinance.

Just as we have not attempted to enforce a common terminology, neither have we tried to forge consensus among the many views and perspectives represented in this volume. Nevertheless several themes can be extracted. Among the most provocative are these:

The Gap Remains

Over a quarter century of commercial microfinance has provided financial services to hundreds of millions of previously excluded low-income persons the world over. In spite of this unique progress, 1.7 billion adults are estimated to still remain excluded, many or most of them poor. While MFIs continue to grow, and while fintech has the potential—but not the certainty—for a breakthrough in outreach and increasing client value, the gap in financial inclusion remains, along with doubts that technology alone will close it. The challenge is for further innovation to do the job, through a combination of high-tech and high-touch initiatives.

Should the Bar Have Dropped?

We have moved from "microfinance ends poverty" to a much weaker, more oblique (and less catchy) "financial inclusion is correlated with economic growth and development, which under some circumstances can reduce poverty." But this move away from microfinance is too hasty: recent research has undercut press reports of widespread harm and the highly publicized early studies that found little benefit from MF. The more recent research summarized by Timothy N. Ogden in chapter 7 finds that while the average impact of borrowing is modest at best, there is significant benefit for some, and little evidence of borrowers being significantly harmed. And the cost-benefit case for continued investment in microfinance from a social and development standpoint seems solid; there are few pro-poor initiatives that provide better bang for the buck. Thus the challenge is not to move on to other interventions in pursuit of greater impact, but to recognize the value of the infrastructure that microfinance represents, understand the nuances of what microfinance does well, and build on that.

The move from microfinance, which from inception has had a core focus on poverty, to the more anodyne "financial inclusion" also warrants scrutiny because delivering value to the poor is much more challenging than setting up a mobile phone wallet and payment service. Financial inclusion may sound more fashionable than microfinance, but it also has no particular focus on or accountability for reducing poverty. The bar should be raised, not lowered, and complementary services should be developed to more effectively reduce poverty. With financial inclusion we should not repeat the original mistake of microfinance, *assuming* that it is equivalent to poverty reduction. Rather, the specific ways that financial inclusion does and does not improve the circumstances and opportunities of the poor must be rigorously demonstrated.

A few of the contributors to this volume have broadened their chapters to include financial inclusion, with microfinance as a subset of that discussion.

Mission Drift Is Inevitable, Will Be Sidestepped by Fintech, Won't Happen Because Profit Maximization and Social Impact Are Mutually Reinforcing, or None of the Above

The debate over mission drift has been under way at least since significant amounts of commercial and quasi-commercial capital began to flow into MFIs in the very early 2000s, but that extended discussion does not seem to be nearing any conclusion. The chapters in this volume explicitly or implicitly advance a full range of views on the subject. In chapter 3, Ogden points to the history of efforts to target excluded populations over the past several hundred years and notes that almost inevitably the life cycle of such efforts includes a move away from the original goals. But he (like Ira W. Lieberman in chapter 1) goes on to argue that, with the continued engagement of insistent social investors, drift can be avoided. Others, such as Momina Aijazuddin and Matthew Brown in chapter 8, expect that advances in technology will reconcile serving the most recalcitrant pockets of exclusion with the expectations of commercial investors. Still others, as in Renée Chao-Beroff and Kimanthi Mutua's chapter 15 discussion on Africa, observe that some of the better-performing MFIs with respect to "client centricity" are the most commercially funded and managed, although the relationship of client centricity to social performance and the pro-poor mission is a debate of its own. Compromising the whole debate is that the most commonly used metrics for determining whether or not mission drift has occurred remain what they were two decades ago: loan size, percent women, borrower attrition. Ultimately, though, while the persistently inconclusive debate about mission drift may seem like an especially unentertaining version of the movie *Groundhog Day*, it serves a purpose: reminding all concerned that the core ostensible purpose of microfinance has never been to maximize shareholder value, but to better the lives of the poor.

Fintech Is No Magic Bullet

Much of the excitement in recent years has centered on fintech as the magic bullet that will leapfrog microfinance and effortlessly eliminate financial inclusion barriers, which is assumed to benefit the poor. But much of the feedback from the field is nuanced, and even the fintech poster children in East Africa are attracting closer scrutiny with respect to both real inclusion and client benefit. What is the differential relevance of fintech to rural, female, and elderly clients? What is the real value of "client loyalty" to the MFI and of "high touch" to the client? Just as we have learned that the value of microfinancial services is not the same for all clients, fintech requires the same scrutiny before we redirect our resources on a large scale. After thirty years, traditional microfinance is still learning how to best design and deliver products for the poor; fintech is in the early stages of that journey.

People at the bottom of the pyramid are not all tech savvy, which helps explain why in many countries most persons have a mobile phone and even a mobile wallet yet they continue to use the services of the neighborhood informal lender. The temptation among many MFIs is to spend on technology rather than on high-touch, bottom-up research. As Greta Bull points out in her vision piece after chapter 8, the challenge is how MFIs can thoughtfully and selectively invest in fintech in ways that actually enhance their performance and better reach their poor clients.

Will Microfinance and the Microenterprise Lose Out to SMEs and Higher Profitability?

The trend is toward a slower rate of growth in microfinance outreach. Increasingly, the leading MFIs prefer to aim their financial services at SMEs rather than focusing on microenterprises and financial services for the poor. Underlying this trend is the contentious question of profitability, on which a diversity of views are amply represented in this volume. Some contributors emphasize the critical role that the achievement of reliable profitability has played in the success of microfinance. Others caution that profit maximization is fundamentally at odds with the double-bottom-line character of microfinance and starves microfinance of the capital it needs to finance pro-poor innovation and outreach. Clearly we need financial institutions serving not just SMEs, but also the entrepreneurs and others at the bottom of the pyramid. The issue is how to preserve focus on the poor rather than on the more affluent clients. In this regard, Latin America may once again point the way, demonstrating that both highly commercial MFIs and nongovernmental organizations (NGOs) are holding their own—against each other as well as new entrants. Both are serving a purpose and finding viable niches.

The Way Forward

At the end of the day, it is clear that the path out of poverty is through a combination of a good job or enterprise and access to the right nutrition, health, and education services. Having access to financial services no doubt helps, but only together with gainful opportunity, good education, and health. Institutions that continuously research and innovate how financial services can best play a role in this combination are essential. Whether these will continue to be MFIs is the question for the future.

But as the pioneer and poster child of a successful pro-poor "impact business model," microfinance has a rich trove of experience and a solid infrastructure to help shape its next phase as well as new impact businesses, and to define criteria that can distinguish true double-bottom-line enterprises from the greenwashed and the marketing hype.

A system that has created certain problems—of extreme poverty, exclusion, economic injustice—cannot be expected to remain intact and meaningfully contribute to solving these problems. This volume presents a view of the most successful poverty-focused efforts based on market instruments. The readers can decide for themselves whether they represent a sufficiently significant systemic change to solve these problems, or will ultimately help perpetuate them.

Section I

BACKGROUND

Photo by Alice Young on Unsplash

ONE

The Growth and Commercial Evolution
of Microfinance

IRA W. LIEBERMAN

Defining Microfinance

Microfinance seeks to provide *financial services* for that segment of the population in the developing world that does not have ready access to formal financial services. This population is often called the *underserved*. These are primarily the working poor, many of whom live on one or two dollars a day and are either self-employed or operate a microbusiness. Many wage earners are also very poor, and though not self-employed or operating a microbusiness, also need such financing. The working poor also need a safe place to save. Most of these people work in the informal sector, which in poorer countries may comprise 80 percent or more of employment. Poor people have a number of ways to secure financing—from family and friends, from money lenders, and from traditional financing schemes such as ROSCAs (rotational savings and credit associations, which are well known in Africa). However, they usually have not had access to formal financial institutions such as banks either for borrowing or, perhaps more important, as a safe place to save.

With few exceptions, microfinance has not served the very poor or the poorest of the poor living below two dollars a day. Some institutions such as the Bangladesh

Rural Advancement Committee (BRAC) have experimented with programs that assist the poorest to move this population up the poverty scale to the point where they become more self-sufficient and can then draw down microloans.

Microentrepreneurs are often self-employed with very few employees or unpaid apprentices. They are also characterized as family businesses; that is, the family is dependent on them for housing, food, health care, education, and other basic services such as electricity and water, if they are available. If the business has employees, it is likely to employ family members.

Microfinance has traditionally referred to microcredit or small working capital loans delivered to the working poor by community-based financial institutions known as microfinance institutions (MFIs). MFIs can be not-for-profit or nongovernmental organizations (NGOs), the majority of which are credit and savings co-operatives, credit unions, nonbank financial institutions, or commercial banks, the latter as a result of NGOs transforming into commercial banks. In recent years, larger commercial banks have downstreamed into microfinance and have become active in the sector, particularly in Latin America. While microfinance has traditionally been credit driven, as MFIs have transformed and become regulated they have increasingly attracted savings deposits. It turns out that the poor may need to save as much as or more than they need loans.[1] In addition to working capital loans, borrowers have also tapped microloans for other purposes—for example, to smooth erratic cash flows or to finance a family wedding or funeral.

In time, MFIs that have scaled up have also provided other financial products and services such as money transfers, remittances, housing finance, loans for education and microinsurance, and small-business loans. Because these diverse products and services, other than savings, constitute at present only a small part of the portfolios of most MFIs, donors and other funders are talking increasingly about financial inclusion as more relevant to the needs of the working poor. Financial inclusion seeks to extend financial services for the poor to include bank accounts, digital payment systems, loans for poor rural populations for water and irrigation, and solar energy, as examples. As such, microfinance is increasingly viewed by donors and investors as a subset of financial inclusion. Chapter 13 by Jennifer Isern discusses financial inclusion and the rapid expansion of financial services to India's poor. Several other chapters in this book also address financial inclusion.

Four Main Phases of Development

The forty-year path of microfinance to its current position encompasses four key phases with several critical components: (1) developing the business model and demonstrating profitability and scalability; (2) developing a deep supporting ecosystem and institutional capacity; (3) "cracking" mainstream international capital markets; and (4) transformation and commercialization—for example, NGOs converting to commercial MFIs such as nonbank financial institutions and commercial banks; the latter are largely regulated and licensed to mobilize deposits. Understanding this path and these factors can help highlight what features must be protected and preserved and what may be required for other aspiring social impact business models to gain traction, whether in deepening and leveraging microfinance itself or outside the sector.

A main leitmotif throughout has been the importance of targeted subsidies. More than the success of microfinance on purely commercial terms, the role of subsidies— not for market-distorting price reductions, but rather for innovation, benchmarking, and infrastructure and capacity building—is perhaps the most salient feature of microfinance in fostering emerging business models that aim for social impact. Over time, however, the subsidy element in microfinance has diminished considerably, and most commercialized MFIs operate at present without substantial subsidies.[2]

Developing the Business Model and Demonstrating Profitability at Scale

In the 1980s through the mid-1990s, when microfinance spread throughout the developing world as well as the transition economies of Eastern and Central Europe, the former Soviet Union, the Balkans, Vietnam, and China, microfinance was provided largely by NGOs. Muhammad Yunus, the founder of Grameen Bank in Bangladesh, is credited as being the founder of the industry or sector.[3] If the public knew anything about the sector, it knew of or had heard of Grameen Bank. Industry insiders talked about the potential of the industry based on the experience of three prominent institutions: Grameen, Bank Rakyat Indonesia, and Banco Sol in Bolivia. Most of the other microfinance institutions were relatively small not-for-profit or nongovernmental institutions operating in a particular region of a country.

During this initial phase, few institutions were taking what Marguerite Robinson called a "financial systems approach" to microfinance.[4] But a few pioneering MFIs began charging fees and microcredit interest rates that, together with keeping loan losses in check, brought in enough revenue to cover all their costs—this was defined as self-sufficiency—while simultaneously ensuring affordability for their clients. In the 1980s, the state-owned Bank Rakyat Indonesia (BRI), was the first to profitably operate a large-scale microfinance banking system, through some 3,000 *uni desas* (village units) with millions of clients, without relying on donors. BRI succeeded by leveraging its ability to take deposits from its clients and turning its clients' deposits into microloans.[5] These institutions at the forefront proved that MFI financial viability was possible without the charity of donors, laying the basis for commercialization of the industry to truly take off by the mid-1990s.

MFIs are the retailers of financial services to the working poor. They provide loans, primarily working capital loans, in small amounts and of relatively short duration to their clients. Regulated MFIs, which operate largely as commercial banks or nonbank financial institutions, are able to attract savings. This has two important advantages: it lowers the cost of capital for MFIs, and it provides a safe place for the poor to save. Credit unions and co-operatives also attract deposits (especially in West Africa, where they are modeled on the French financial system and the massive credit union system in Canada).

An important feature of the microfinance industry is its appeal to social entrepreneurs who have focused on building their institutions. Microfinance is a bottom-up initiative, begun for the most part by social entrepreneurs such as Muhammad Yunus. Many others have been instrumental as well, including Faisal Abed, who created BRAC in Bangladesh, one of the largest and most successful MFIs as part of one of the most successful national NGOs in the world; Ella Bhatt of SEWA Bank in India; Carlos Daniel and Carlos Labarthe of Compartamos in Mexico; and Kimanthi Mutua of K-Rep Bank and James Mwangi of Equity Bank in Kenya.

What Is Commercial Microfinance and How Has It Evolved?

Throughout the late 1990s and to the present, MFIs have commercialized and have also become regulated by national banking supervisors. They may fall under general banking regulations or special regulations governing the microfinance sector.

By commercial microfinance, we mean MFIs that meet the following criteria:

- They are structured as shareholder-owned institutions.

- They seek to and in time do operate profitably, offering their investors an acceptable return on investment.

- They raise their funds in commercial markets in a variety of ways.

- They operate as regulated nonbank financial institutions or commercial banks.

- They are increasingly expanding their product offerings to such products as savings, insurance, money transfers, housing improvement loans, and small-business loans.

- Successful MFIs have been able to scale up and serve increasing numbers of the working poor, while also operating profitably. That is what we call the double bottom line: serving the poor while also operating in a sustainable manner. Some institutions now talk of the triple bottom line, which means being ecologically sustainable as well.

Once they were able to demonstrate profitability, MFIs such as Banco Sol in Bolivia, K-Rep in Kenya, and Acleda in Cambodia took the next step, transforming from charitable NGOs into commercial banks. Gaining access to deposits and attracting commercial investors resulted in explosive growth for many MFIs. See box 1-1 on the transformation, commercialization, and explosive growth of Acleda Bank in Cambodia.

In 1994, the U.S. Agency for International Development (USAID) commissioned a team to prepare an assessment of leading microfinance institutions. The resulting report was a seminal work on microfinance that examined eleven leading MFIs at the time. The study asked a series of questions about microfinance, several of which continue to be examined by the industry as it focuses increasingly on commercialization.

- How are outreach and financial viability related? Does serving the poor preclude achievement of financial self-sufficiency?

- If we wish to ensure that micro-enterprise finance reaches even the very poor, must we expect to support institutions that cannot become financially independent of donor subsidies?

- How financially viable can micro-enterprise finance institutions be? Can they reach commercial standards? Consistently or only in limited settings?

- What factors are necessary for the achievement of strong outreach and financial viability?

- What are the challenges facing frontier institutions, as well as the challenges facing institutions that have not yet reached the frontier?[6]

BOX 1-1. Acleda Bank Plc., Cambodia: Transformation to a Commercial Bank

"Acleda Bank's vision was to be Cambodia's leading commercial bank, providing superior financial services to all segments of the community." Acleda originated from the tragedy that befell Cambodia with the assumption of power by the Khmer Rouge in 1975. The International Labour Organization (ILO) and Care International recruited the company's management from refugee camps on the Thai-Cambodian border. The program's initial aim was to develop local economic development agencies (LEDAs). Acleda was the association of these independent regional agencies. In 1996 a liquidity crisis forced Acleda to decide between providing business development services and financial services—microfinance—to its constituency. The General Assembly of the association (made up primarily of employees) decided to merge Acleda's agencies into a single unified institution. Acleda began transforming itself into a bank in the mid-1990s and finalized the legal transformation in 2000. Since then, both the loan portfolio and savings have grown at a rapid pace: savings at a cumulative growth rate of 137 percent and loans at a cumulative growth rate of over 50 percent a year. The bank has expanded its base to almost all of Cambodia's provinces. Its growth and transformation were driven largely by its success in securing funding. As an NGO, the MFI would have quickly outpaced its ability to secure donations and even subordinated debt; savings deposits offered an attractive source of leverage that also provided an important service to clients. As an NGO, the organization enjoyed a strong sense of employee ownership. When managers and directors began considering the transformation, they took time to explain the process and motives to all employees. Part of this transformation included the creation of an investment company, owned by the employees, that would hold shares in the bank, thus making the employees real owners. The MFI then handpicked the future external investors to ensure that mission was not an issue. Acleda Bank purchased the NGO's portfolio, and the NGO received both shares (a 45 percent stake in the bank) and a subordinated loan for the value of the portfolio. The institution invested heavily in the training of the management team and ultimately retained most of the key managers.

Source: Pasquale di Benedetta, Ira W. Lieberman, and Laura Ard, "Corporate Governance in Microfinance Institutions" (Washington: World Bank, 2015), pp. 24-25.

The study went on to indicate that the best programs had made large advances in outreach and financial viability over five years (1990–94). Many of the institutions had sustained very high growth rates over three years. Ten of the eleven were fully self-sufficient operationally (meaning that they covered all of their operational costs, but not necessarily their financial costs, especially when the financial costs were adjusted for subsidies such as grants from donors). Five had crossed the hurdle to full self-sufficiency (meaning that the institutions covered both their financial and operational costs, with the former adjusted for subsidies or grants from donors, inflation accounting, and their cost of capital to the extent that they received subsidized loans from donors), generating returns that reflect banking standards.

Six years later, in 2001, Marguerite Robinson, in her seminal book on microfinance, *The Microfinance Revolution*, defined the microfinance revolution in terms of commercial microfinance: "The microfinance revolution is a commercial revolution based on new financial technology and greatly accelerated by the information revolution that developed concurrently. It began in the 1970s, developed in the 1980s, and took off in the 1990s. . . . These combinations enabled institutional profitability and long-term viability, making possible large-scale formal-sector financial outreach to low income segments of the population."[7]

In 2005, with the commercialization of microfinance well advanced, Beatriz Marulanda and Maria Otero (Otero was president of Accion International, an important microfinance network with headquarters in the United States but with strong affiliated MFIs primarily in Latin America) examined the future of microfinance in Latin America. Their study projected that:

Two approaches to the provision of financial services to the region's low-income people have consolidated in the last years. They both have commercial criteria, which we think will prevail as a model in Latin America in the next ten years. Firstly, the microfinance institutions, as yet primarily operating as NGOs, will undergo "up-scaling," or transformation into regulated entities, while at the same time commercial banks entering the microfinance sector will adopt "downscaling" to provide a range of financial services to the poor.

The authors concluded that:

The ability of some of the leading microfinance institutions in the region to sell bonds successfully on their local capital markets is leading the way to the ever-increasing availability of private capital funding. With such funding, microfinance in the region will see the elimination of what in past years was the key constraint to growth of the industry, that of access to sufficient capital.[8]

The study identified seventeen commercial banks and forty-seven nonbank regulated MFIs in Latin America that represented some US$2.4 billion of a total of US$3.3 billion in microlending (73 percent of the total) among reporting MFIs, with some fifty-six NGOs providing US$868 million in loans to the region. Clearly, regulated and commercially oriented MFIs had taken the lead in the industry.[9] The report also cited eight institutions each with over US$100 million in lending.

In two papers published in 2006—one by Elisabeth Rhyne and Brian Busch, and a second by Elisabeth Rhyne and Maria Otero, the authors further confirmed the exponential growth of commercial microfinance.[10] In the Council of Microfinance Equity Funds (CMEF)–sponsored study by Rhyne and Busch, the authors compared growth of commercial microfinance as of 2006 with an earlier CMEF-sponsored study in 2004. Of 120 institutions, the 2006 study found sufficient comparable data on seventy-one commercial MFIs. The loan portfolios of these institutions grew 231 percent over the three years in question (an average of 77 percent per year), reaching almost US$5 billion from US$1.5 billion three years earlier. The number of borrowers had increased by 73 percent (24 percent a year) to some 4.1 million borrowers, up from 1.7 million borrowers in 2004. Moreover, this growth was widespread globally, with portfolio growth at 119 percent in Africa, 249 percent in Asia, 396 percent in Eastern Europe, and 169 percent in Latin America over the same period.[11] The authors concluded that the 199 MFIs in the study provided a snapshot of shareholder (commercial) microfinance throughout the world in 2006. Together they accounted for a combined portfolio of 11.5 million borrowers and US$8.7 billion in portfolio assets.[12] The number of large MFIs—portfolio over US$100 million and clients in excess of 100,000—also increased; twenty institutions had over 100,000 borrowers and twenty had assets over US$100 million.[13]

The Rhyne and Otero study was more qualitatively oriented. It looked at the drivers of success in microfinance and the quality gap, which goes beyond massive outreach by large MFI to the quality of services offered beyond credit such as, for example, savings, insurance, housing rehabilitation, and education loans. The authors noted that one of the drivers is commercial entry:

> The entry of commercially oriented providers will substantially change the microfinance field. . . . The right conditions for rapid entry by new commercial players are now present in the marketplace: demonstrated profitability,

business models that can be copied, and competencies for working with low-income populations. The history of financial innovation suggests that once such conditions are present, spread can be very rapid.[14]

In 2007, I wrote a paper with a small research team for CMEF on the initial public offering and listing of four MFIs: Bank Rakyat Indonesia (BRI), BRAC Bank in Bangladesh, Compartamos in Mexico, and Equity Bank in Kenya.[15] Each of these institutions scaled up to reach a very large number of microfinance borrowers, and three of them (the exception being Compartamos) reached a very large number of savers. These institutions were highly profitable and provided good returns on equity and on assets. They also benchmarked more than favorably with the banks in their respective countries.

Our study further confirmed the rapid progress made by commercial MF and the potential for the industry to reach a new takeoff stage in growth and outreach to the poor, while maintaining the profits, return on assets (ROA), and return on equity (ROE) necessary to attract private equity investors on a substantial scale. This new stage of development in the industry would not necessarily come from the ability of institutions to do IPOs, but rather from the signals these successful IPOs send to commercial investors, such as private equity investors or venture capitalists, and their ability to eventually exit investments they make in MFIs or microfinance equity funds. The study also focused on what made these MFIs excellent institutions.

How Did Microfinance Succeed?

Any analysis of how microfinance emerged as fully attractive to commercial investors and mainstream financial institutions, even while remaining today's leading impact investment, must look back, to the 1980s and 1990s, when the initial experiments and pilot projects providing credit to the poor were undertaken. These pilots were largely funded by subsidies (grants); "investments," largely donor soft loans, were on subsidized, noncommercial terms. Retained earnings also allowed successful MFIs to expand. This extended period of experimentation, during which several billions of dollars were devoted to microfinance projects, resulted in solid business models and an ecosystem that supported a transition of that model from substantial reliance on subsidies to a more diverse funding base, and eventually to an ongoing absorption into mainstream commercial finance.

For example, in June 1995, the Consultative Group to Assist the Poor (CGAP) was established by the World Bank and eight other donor institutions to begin scaling up funding for the sector largely directed to MFIs. Three years later, CGAP's membership consisted of twenty-six donor institutions plus the Ford Foundation, representing some US$300–500 million a year in annual funding.[16] The CGAP Secretariat was housed in the World Bank and, working with an advisory board that represented the leading institutions in the sector, began to define good practice for MFIs. CGAP also quickly became a knowledge center for the sector. The objective of this funding was twofold: one, to build the capacity of MFIs so that they could scale up their funding to their clients; and two, to provide funds for on-lending (when an organization lends money that it has borrowed from another organization or person) to these clients. CGAP became de facto the world secretariat for the sector.[17]

In addition to donor support, other forms of institutional support emerged in the 1990s to propel growth in the sector. Networks, mostly operating as NGOs, formed "holding groups" to support MFI operations globally. In time, although the networks were NGOs, many of their operating subsidiaries or affiliates became commercialized for-profit MFIs. Most of these networks were based in the United States, such as Accion International, initially focused on Latin America but in time expanded more globally; FINCA; Opportunities International; Women's World Banking; and Pro Mujer, the latter solely focused on Latin America. In Germany, operating initially as a consulting firm, the ProCredit Group operated a holding company, supported by an investor consortium of both public and private investors; it opened some twenty "greenfield" (startup) banks, many of which were located in transition economies such Serbia, Georgia, and Kosovo. A number of these networks in time formed investment funds to inject equity into their affiliates.

In addition, charitable or social funders also began to operate microfinance institutions allied with their social mission. Groups such as Care International, Save the Children, Oxfam, GRET, and faith-based groups such as Catholic Relief Funds all operated successful microfinance programs.

Microfinance gained widespread attention during the 2000s, as it began to reach beyond a small group of government agencies and philanthropies to develop new sources of capital to support growth. Microfinance in this period was characterized by very rapid growth, a focus on institutional sustainability (including positive return on equity and assets), and the development of a diverse set of institutional structures.

MFIs that transformed and attracted both equity investors and deposits soon represented the majority of both clients (savings accounts and borrowers) and the vast majority of assets in the sector. The largest MFIs had in excess of a million clients, and there were many with more than 100,000 clients. Reaching scale meant that these MFIs could begin to develop other financial products and services such as housing

TABLE 1-1.   Measures of Outreach, Concentration, and
Efficiency, by MFI Scale

Active borrowers	*Small (less than 10,000)*	*Medium (10,000 to 100,000)*	*Large (100,000 to 1 million)*	*Very large (more than 1 million)*
Share of total number of MFIs (%)	41	41	16	2
Share of all borrowers (%)	1.3	12.0	38.2	48.6
Share of all savers (%)	2.6	20.5	48.1	28.8
Median real interest rate + fees (as % of loan, inflation adjusted)	22.2	20.6	17.8	13.0
Median profit margin (% of revenues)	8.8	9.4	17.1	22.8

Source: Modified from Todd A. Watkins, *Introduction to Microfinance* (Singapore: World Scientific, 2018). *Data source:* Microfinance Information Exchange (themix.org); data for December 2015.

Note: Interest and fees row reports "Yield on Gross Portfolio," using real rates, adjusted for inflation.

finance, education, transfers, remittances, and microinsurance. Expectations that these large MFIs would rapidly scale these other services have not been met for a variety of reasons, and that challenge remains for the sector, as discussed in the chapters that follow. Getting to scale meant that formerly regional or village NGOs began to develop widespread branch networks spreading their operations throughout their country. Table 1-1 demonstrates the degree of portfolio concentration in the sector in MFIs that have over 100,000 borrowers and those that have over 1 million borrowers. It also shows that larger institutions can be much more profitable than smaller ones.

In addition to scaling within their respective countries, some of the leading MFIs began to emerge as multinational NGOs operating in a variety of countries. For example, Grameen Bank, based primarily in Bangladesh, operates Grameen USA in various cities throughout the United States; Bangladesh-based BRAC operates a debt fund in Africa; the Association for Social Advancement (ASA), also in Bangladesh, operates in other Asian countries as well; Compartamos, a Mexican MFI, owns and operates MFIs in Peru and Guatemala; and Kenya-based Equity Bank owns and operates in several other countries in Africa, including Uganda and Rwanda.

Finally, national commercial banks in these markets and major international commercial banks began to see microfinance as an opportunity and began to downstream into microfinance. Banco Viscayo Bilbao (BBVA) used its foundation to acquire MFIs in Peru (see chapter 5, which discusses the BBVA Foundation in Peru), Panama, and the Dominican Republic; Scotia Bank operates MFIs in the

Caribbean; Commerz Bank in Germany became part of the ProCredit investment consortium; and Citi Corp set up a microfinance division in London to support its operating units in several countries engaging in microfinance and to fund other initiatives in the sector.

Developing a Supporting Ecosystem and Institutional Capacity

Demonstrating profitability was a necessary condition for engaging new sources of funding. But many other pieces needed to come together to form the ecosystem of infrastructure to support investors looking for return on capital as distinct from donors providing outright grants or with a high tolerance for and expectation of loss. Much of this ecosystem was supported or encouraged by donors. Key components were:

- standardized financial performance metrics;

- longitudinal databases and peer-group analysis; the MIX affiliated with CGAP became the standardized worldwide database for the sector based on self-reported information from MFIs throughout the sector globally.

- specialized institutional rating agencies with trained analysts such as MicroRate and M-Cril, the latter focused on Asia;

- training of human resources, particularly the development of managerial talent; including a training institute. The Boulder Institute, organized and operated by a social entrepreneur, initially attracted some 250–300 students each summer from around the world to Boulder, Colorado. In more recent years the Boulder Institute has operated from the International Labour Organization's training center in Turin, Italy.

- the emergence of supervisory and regulatory frameworks that would allow MFIs to take on shareholder structures and, in some cases, access public deposits;

- industry associations and collaboration networks at both the national and international levels;

- persistent outreach to and education of new investors;

- the creation and maturation of specialized commercial investment managers and microfinance investment vehicles (MIVs) that could underwrite and monitor diversified pools of microfinance assets (see box 1-2 for a discussion of the first investment fund dedicated to funding MFIs), enabling channeling large volumes of investments into MFIs;

- the creation of a facility, the MFX, to offer hedging services for microfinance investment funds and others providing loans to MFIs in local currencies.

BOX 1-2. ProFund: The First Microfinance Investment Fund

ProFund, launched in 1995, was the first private, profit-seeking venture capital fund that exclusively targeted microfinance. ProFund proved that private investment in commercial MFIs could be profitable over the long haul. Before then the sector had no commercial investment track record. Most of the sector's funding came from nonprofit, government, or similar development-related sources with social missions. Looking to fill that gap, ProFund sought to demonstrate to others that providing financial services to the poor could not only sustainably pay for itself but also return a profit. The main original sponsors were the nonprofit Accion International, two private foundations (Calmeadow of Canada and FUNDES of Switzerland), and the French social business SIDI—in other words, subsidized, patient, impact investment capital. Other socially oriented investors soon joined. Through investment and advising, ProFund fostered numerous high-profile successes, demonstrating profit and commercial potential via several different mechanisms: transformations from NGOs to banks; public-private partnerships (e.g., MiBanco in Peru); commercial downscaling of mainstream banks into microfinance (e.g., Sogesol in Haiti); and even public stock offerings (e.g., Compartamos in Mexico). When ProFund liquidated after ten years, as planned, it generated a 6 percent average annual return for its investors, which was especially notable given the political instability and currency volatility in Latin America during the period. More important, the demonstration effect clearly worked. Within a year after ProFund closed in 2005, at least twenty other private microfinance funds were actively investing in Latin American microfinance.

Source: ProFund International, S.A., 2005 report on the history of the fund (Costa Rica: ProFund International, 2005).

This complex support ecosystem for microfinance, painstakingly put in place in many cases by social entrepreneurs and supported by substantial donor funding, succeeded in promoting industry transparency and establishing and spreading best practices.

Experimentation and demonstration were central.

Cracking Mainstream International Capital Markets

The result of such pioneering proof-of-concept efforts in the 1990s was an explosion in the 2000s of fund managers and microfinance investment vehicles (MIVs) seeking to intermediate private investment in microfinance. The 2017 Symbiotics report surveyed ninety-three MIVs with a combined market size estimated at US$12.6 billion out of a total estimated asset base of US$13.5 billion. The market size had more than quintupled since 2006, representing a compounded growth rate of 20 percent for total assets and 22 percent for microfinance portfolios. Debt represented the majority of the investments (82 percent), with equity at 16 percent. By the end of 2016, more than half (58 percent) of total MIV investment had gone to the largest MFIs, those with more than US$100 million in assets.[18]

In terms of sources of funding, while early investments were largely from public, development-related sources, commercial interests now dominate. As of December 2016, private institutional investors financed 52 percent of MIVs' capital while public funders contributed 20 percent. Financing from institutional investors has grown the fastest since 2006, at a rate of 26 percent annually (see figure 1-1).

As many managers established a track record, and more data accumulated on loss rates, exits, and secondary market liquidity, purely mainstream investors increasingly turned their attention to the sector. Commercial MFIs can now access mainstream international capital markets through all the usual international financial channels, such as the interbank market, corporate debt issues, and both private and public equity financing. Global banks now make substantial microfinance investments directly themselves, with acquisitions and mergers accelerating, and global investment firms provide services to help MFIs issue debt and sell shares. More than a dozen MFIs have now had IPOs, some (for example, Compartamos Banco, SKS, Equity Bank, Equitas Holding, Ujjivan Financial) establishing shareholder valuations in the billions of dollars.[19]

In short, the top-tier MFIs have full access to international financial tools. As in any industry, only the most successful firms with long-term growth potential can

FIGURE 1-1. Trend in Microfinance Investment Vehicle
Funding Sources, 2006–16

US$ millions

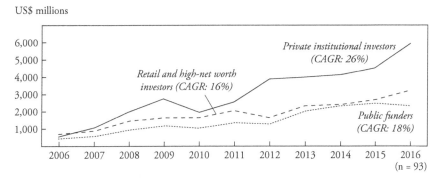

Source: Symbiotics, "2017 Symbiotics MIV Survey: Market Data and Peer Group Analysis, 11th Edition" (Geneva, 2017) (https://symbioticsgroup.com/wp-content/uploads/2017/09/Symbiotics-2017-MIV-Survey.pdf).
Note: CAGR = compound annual growth rate.

climb into that rarified tier, attractive to global capital markets. Inevitably, many firms never achieve track records that are attractive to purely commercial investors. But the top MFI performers have done so.

Transformation and Commercialization

Initially, when most MFIs were NGOs, the emphasis of MFIs and the sector at large was on poverty alleviation and social impact. Over the decades, as many MFIs transformed into commercialized institutions with external investors, there was much more emphasis on operational performance and financial sustainability. Commercialization fueled a schism in the sector, with Muhammad Yunus, for example, criticizing the high interest rates charged to poor clients and the focus on profitability for investors. This split was openly debated when Compartamos launched its IPO. Its high interest rates and return on assets and equity were publicly disclosed, and the founders and early investors, such as the nonprofit Accion International and the World Bank's International Finance Corporation, reaped substantial rewards from modest financial investments in the institution.

Perhaps the strongest argument of proponents who believe microfinance is working is that hundreds of millions of clients are voting with their feet, suggesting they value MFI services. Whether microfinance helps large fractions of them escape poverty remains an open question. In recent years, the work of leading academic researchers has called into question the role of microfinance in alleviating poverty. At best, their research seemed to suggest that, for the majority of clients, microcredit supported income smoothing and had the ability to prevent the working poor from falling into deeper poverty in the event of a costly crisis in the family such as a death or illness, or even a joyous event such as a wedding. Only a minor fraction of clients saw substantial positive impact on various measures of their well-being.[20] This research largely focused narrowly on micro*credit,* not microfinance more broadly or financial inclusion. The literature is thinner on microsavings or microinsurance. Yet many commercialized MFIs now offer microsavings services, often together with microinsurance and other services, most often built on the infrastructure made possible by scaling microcredit. Microsavings is recognized by practitioners as being as important as microcredit for MFI clients—perhaps even more important—and so far the limited academic evidence generally supports that conviction. Nevertheless, the lack of clear evidence of impact on poverty reduction has contributed to dampening enthusiasm from a number of investors, donors, and development finance institutions, who now conceive financial inclusion investment opportunities more broadly. Robert Cull and Jonathan Morduch conclude that, with respect to impact: "These results, taken as a whole, suggest that the average impacts of microfinance are modest. Still, target populations are liquidity-constrained, and getting the right product to the right population can yield substantial impacts."[21]

Similarly, detrimental to the sector's attractiveness to some investors, individual country crises have suggested that MFIs risked overlending, causing some clients to fall deeply into debt and inextricably into arrears. In addition, prevailing high interest rates rationalized by the need to be sustainable have led many external analysts to question the commitment of commercial MFIs to their social missions. Microfinance has experienced individual institutional crises and some country crises, notably in countries such as Bosnia, Pakistan, India (state of Andhra Pradesh), Morocco, and Nicaragua. None of these crises have been systemic or caused contagion in the sector internationally, and overall losses in the sector have remained below 1 percent, which is extraordinary given that many pundits in the financial sector felt that the sector would never succeed because the poor would not repay their loans.[22] Most cases in the sector have been the result of poor institutional performance. But in a few cases crises in individual countries have been caused by political intervention in the sector, such as in the state of Andhra Pradesh in India, leading the State Bank of India (the central bank) and the government to adopt new policies governing the sector. In Nicaragua, the president's instruction to farmers in the north of the country not to pay their loans led to a payments crisis and the failure of a microfinance bank, Banex, which had attracted substantial international investment capital—both equity and loans (see box 1-3).[23]

While knowledgeable insiders recognize that microcredit on its own cannot eradicate poverty, nor serve the very poorest who need comprehensive forms of poverty intervention, most would argue that together with other areas of support—education, health care, sustainable agriculture, infrastructure—microfinance and MFIs can

---

BOX 1-3.   Banex and the No-Payment Movement in Nicaragua

Background: Banex began as Finde, a very successful, rapidly growing NGO in Nicaragua. In 2002 it converted to a nonbank financial institution, Findesa, and in October 2008 it changed its name to Banex (Banco del Exito, or "Success Bank") when it received its full banking license. Starting with a loan portfolio of US$7 million in 2002, Findesa soon had thirty branches throughout the country and also began to attract deposits. By 2008 the bank had 68,000 clients and a loan portfolio of US$125 million. Banex began to move upstream to offer small-business loans, cattle-raising loans, and agricultural loans, all of which had distinctly different risk profiles than the plain vanilla working capital loans that were the staple of MFIs. Banex's success allowed it to attract both domestic and international equity investors, including a large bloc owned and controlled by the bank's chairman and managing director. International equity investors were primarily microfinance investment vehicles (MIVs). Banex also attracted a number of MIVs as lenders, as well as development finance institutions (DFIs)—the Inter-American Investment Corporation (IIC) at the Inter-American Development Bank (IDB)—and a local and regional development bank, which provided lines of credit to the bank. As of year-end 2008, the bank had mobilized some US$100 million in loans and over US$30 million in deposits and was profitable. Local investors owned 57.8 percent of shares and foreign investors 42.2 percent. Of the eight board members, four represented local investors, three were international investors, and one board member was independent.

The No-Payment Movement: In response to aggressive legal action by one MFI (not Banex) against its clients for nonpayment of loans, a local protest

(continued)

BOX 1-3.   Banex and the No-Payment Movement in Nicaragua
(continued)

movement began in the summer of 2009 accusing all the MFIs of usurious interest rates. This protest soon evolved into a no-payment movement, supported by the populist president of Nicaragua, Daniel Ortega, a former
Sandinista.

Banex in Crisis: The initial reaction by Banex was to assure its investors
and creditors that the no-payment movement would slow and that Banex had
ample liquidity and capital to withstand the crisis. By May 2009, Banex's board
had grown increasingly concerned. Performance had begun to deteriorate,
and the board asked management to consider a US$3 million recapitalization
plan. Management resisted, expressing confidence that beef prices had bot-
tomed out and that cattle loans, perhaps the riskiest segment of the portfolio, would be safe. In September 2009 the shareholders met in Managua.
Performance had continued to deteriorate. Lack of agreement between international investors on the size of the investment needed, resistance by local
investors who lacked the resources to participate in the rights movement,
and a legal agreement with a lender that required majority local ownership, all
made the recapitalization process difficult and less timely than it needed to
be. In addition, creditors, who had to be part of the solution, had not yet been
approached. A large number of loans were maturing in the first quarter of
2010, and it was clear that Banex would face difficulty replacing those loans
with new loans or having the creditors roll over their loans. Not only did Banex
need more equity, but perhaps more important, there needed to be a debt
restructuring as well, with creditors converting a percentage of their loans to
subordinated loans that would serve as tier-two capital and equity. In September 2009 MicroRate (an MFI rating agency) was retained to do a special portfolio audit. Its audit showed clearly that provisions for bad loans were significantly understated. At the time of the MicroRate audit, the company was
reporting PAR (portfolio at risk)>30 days at 19 percent, while MicroRate projected PAR>30 days at 30 percent. A financial advisory team was hired just
before the MicroRate report was finalized. It soon became clear to the advisers
that the capitalization plan was in trouble. There was no agreement between
international and local shareholders. Local shareholders severely resisted the

(continued)

BOX 1-3. Banex and the No-Payment Movement in Nicaragua
(continued)

dilution that a large equity investment would mean. They also objected to the valuation of the bank by international investors, which would further dilute their holdings. In addition, the bank lacked any form of forward projections as a basis for negotiating with creditors. A meeting of the investors, the creditors, and the advisers in Geneva seemed to offer some hope for a debt restructuring, but this was conditional on the equity investors recapitalizing the bank in the interim to prevent intervention by the banking supervisor, who was pushing the company hard to recapitalize to maintain capital adequacy. Under Nicaraguan banking law, if capital adequacy fell below 10 percent, the supervisor was obliged to intervene in the bank. With a very diverse group of some thirty creditors and investors spread across three continents, getting agreement was not going to be easy under any circumstances. Following a meeting between the investors, creditors, management, and the banking supervisor in Managua on December 1, 2009, negotiations between the creditors and the investors went on for an extended period as the bank deteriorated. A restructuring plan was agreed to in principle, with the creditors agreeing to restructure 13.6 percent of their senior debts to subdebt and equity and the equity investors agreeing to inject some US$8 million in new funds into equity, a package of some US$20 million. Unfortunately, the debt restructuring was too little and too late. The restructuring called for an eighteen-month agreement, rather than an intermediate-term agreement of five to six years as recommended by the advisory team. The major creditors, who controlled the creditors committee, were hoping that the market would turn around and that they would be able to get paid since their loans were among the first due in the original maturity schedule. Creditors also indicated that the nature of their debt funds, special-purpose vehicles (SPVs), made it very difficult for them to get agreement on a restructuring. As part of the recapitalization agreement the managing director was replaced, and the board composition was changed. Nevertheless, losses continued in 2010, and the state eventually intervened to protect the depositors. Its portfolio was allocated to Nicaraguan banks, and both investor and creditor losses were substantial.

Source: Pasquale di Benedetta, Ira W. Lieberman, and Laura Ard, "Corporate Governance in Microfinance Institutions" (Washington: World Bank, 2015), p. 28.

contribute to poverty alleviation.[24] Thus, as discussed in the chapters that follow, MFIs should, to the extent they are capable, continue to offer an increasingly diverse array of financial services to their clients and continue innovating in order to deepen their impact.

In part as a result of these concerns about social impact, the microfinance industry itself has taken social impact and attention to clients ever more seriously. In the past decade, focus groups, financial diaries, and the Smart Campaign's Client Voice Project,[25] together with standardized indicators and transparent reporting like the Social Performance Task Force and MIX, have helped measure, track, and report the social performance of MFIs. MFIs' boards of directors and senior management are creating specialized impact departments and bringing in external advisers to assist in developing social impact goals, analyzing performance, and strategizing to enhance future impact. It is increasingly clear that MFIs recognize the need to continuously and convincingly demonstrate that they are meeting social missions and benefiting clients.

Technology: A New Opportunity to Expand or an Existential Challenge

Technology is a powerful driver of access to finance, especially to rural populations. Over the past ten years or so, in several developing countries mobile phone providers and networks are working with large MFIs to bring mobile banking to the poor. Kenya is the outstanding example of how this can work to facilitate payments, lending, savings, and money transfer. Safaricom, a subsidiary of Vodafone, has some 20 million clients using its services to facilitate financial services without a bank in the middle. Both K-Rep Bank (now Sidian Bank) and Equity Bank, the largest microfinance or small-business bank in the country, the latter with branches throughout the country, have joint ventures with Safaricom to further extend their penetration. Supporting this effort are networks of agents developed by each of the banks.

Financial technology companies (fintechs) are also rapidly emerging both in the advanced economies and in developing economies to challenge traditional financial institutions. Fintechs are developing proprietary models or platforms that will allow these institutions to rapidly scale up their lending to microfirms and small and medium-sized enterprises (SMEs).[26]

The existential question discussed herein by Renée Chao-Beroff in "The Future of Microfinance in Africa" is whether the "low-touch, high-tech" approach to financial services through mobile lending or by fintechs will erode the value added of the "high-touch, low-tech" approach of microfinance. If commercialized MFIs of scale are able to adapt and venture successfully with mobile networks or fintechs, the sector will likely grow over the next ten years. The technological opportunities and challenges are discussed in greater depth in various chapters in this book.

Governance

Governance is one of the least-discussed and written-about topics in microfinance,[27] but it has become increasingly important as MFIs have scaled up and diversified and are now being forced to adapt to new technologies. These present an important opportunity for the sector to grow or, alternatively, present an existential threat. In today's expanded and more commercialized environment, several factors give rise to governance concerns:

- **Growth and scale of MFIs.** In several poorer countries, such as Mexico, Bolivia, Peru, Cambodia, Bangladesh, and Kenya, MFIs have become systemically important in serving the poor and underserved.

- **Emergence of legal and regulatory gaps.** Many MFIs have transformed, becoming microfinance banks that mobilize deposits. Banking supervisors need to understand how best to regulate these institutions to ensure sound governance practices, to safeguard the safety and soundness of these institutions, and to protect depositors.

- **Succession.** Many of the original entrepreneurs who founded and managed MFIs for an extended period of time have begun to retire. Also, during MFIs' transformation to commercial banks, many change management because investors view the managers of the transformed NGOs as inappropriate managers of a commercial bank. For whatever reason—retirement, change in status, death, or illness—succession is one of the most critical governance issues and it is the responsibility of boards of directors to plan for it and to oversee it when required.

- **National crises.** In Nicaragua, India, Morocco, Nigeria, and Bosnia existing overcrowding and overlending are beginning to elevate risks for the industry.

- **Increasing industry risks.**

  - *Foreign exchange risk.* Some commercial MFIs are borrowing from international debt funds in dollars or euros at relatively high costs and are bearing the attendant foreign exchange risk in the event of a devaluation of their local (national) currency.

  - *Product-diversification risk.* MFIs are adding new product lines and are moving away from "plain vanilla" working-capital loans with typical maturities of twelve months or less. They are adding small-business loans, housing-rehabilitation loans, and agricultural loans, for example, that may carry different maturities, different payment terms, and different associated risks, hence different risks. Services such as insurance, money transfers, remittances, and even mobile banking are also becoming part of the mix. MFI boards need to be able to evaluate the strategic fit, investment requirements, potential returns, and risks—that is, the cost-benefit of product diversification of such products and services.

  - *Political and operational risk.* Political risks, such as state intervention and nonpayment movements, as seen in India and Nicaragua, have damaged the sector's reputation. In Nicaragua, one of the important microfinance banks became distressed and was forced to accept intervention by the banking supervisor. In India, several large MFIs were left barely functioning and financially at risk, putting millions of clients temporarily without access to services.

  - *Client risks.* Overlending, high interest rates, and crises have increased the demand for client protection and transparency in the sector. The Smart Campaign is one of the best examples of an effort to improve client protection while raising awareness of social impact. The Smart Campaign was launched by several leading institutions, such as Accion, to focus on client protection and improved transparency and disclosure to clients on topics such as, for example, effective interest rates charged by the MFI. The boards of MFIs are feeling pressure to oversee the performance of their organizations more closely with respect to client protection, pricing transparency, and social impact, as well as operating and financial performance.

- **Diversification of MFI structure and type.** Several groups and networks have expanded substantially to the point where they are systemically important to the sector. Normally governance should be critically examined at the level of the individual institution, but in several countries, groups have expanded and become transnational institutions. This is the case for NGO networks such as the Foundation for International Community Assistance (FINCA, today a holding company) and Accion International (USA); bank holding groups, such as ProCredit Holding (Germany); and previous national banks or NGOs, such as the Bangladesh Rural Advancement Committee (BRAC) and Equity Bank (Kenya); social-sector-based institutions, such as Care International, Save the Children, and Oxford Committee for Famine Relief (Oxfam), have developed substantial microfinance activities. How the latter separate social services from financial services and how they manage these distinct lines of business is important. How these diverse groups provide governance support to their large network of affiliates or subsidiaries and how they, in turn, govern themselves is important not only for their clients, but also for the sector as a whole.

■ **Entry of new institutional investors.** Some seventy debt funds and thirty equity funds, primarily with a mix of public development finance institutions (DFIs) and private investors, have emerged and are paying more attention to the quality of governance in MFIs in which they invest or to which they lend. These institutions frequently take a seat on the boards of directors of the institutions in which they invest. This means that the quality of their nominees and the ability of these nominees to represent the MFI as a whole is critical to the governance of these institutions.

■ **The double bottom line.** Microfinance is viewed as having an important social purpose, providing the resources for the working poor to pursue self-employment opportunities or to build microenterprises that provide basic support to their families. Regulated microfinance banks also give clients a safe place to save. As such, the performance of MFIs should not be judged only by their finances and operations, but also by their social impact on poverty alleviation and creation of employment opportunities. MFIs thus have a double bottom line, and boards of directors need to oversee MFIs' finances and their performance with respect to its social impact.

Chapter 9 by Lory Camba Opem, "Governance in the Digital Age," discusses these issues in more depth.

Conclusions

Microfinance has moved almost irretrievably toward a commercial model, as a segment of the financial inclusion sector while also supporting niches of the impact investment sector such as loans and investments in solar energy, irrigation, the agricultural value chain, education, and affordable housing. As such, microfinance represents an important niche sector in the emerging markets financial industry and not as a charitable endeavor through MFIs operating as NGOs. There are still thousands of MFIs operating as NGOs, from very small self-help groups in India to NGOs in Tajikistan, Bosnia, and Albania to the very large MFIs in Bangladesh such as BRAC and Grameen Bank, though Grameen now holds a banking license. I believe that the industry will largely continue to try to self-regulate against commercial abuse by promoting consumer protection and disclosure to clients of effective interest rates. Also, countries such as Bolivia and Ecuador are beginning to cap interest rates, which may either pose a threat to the sector or moderate excessive rates if their capping policy is done appropriately. MFIs now reach some 200 million borrowers, up from 10 million in 1995 and far exceeding the goal of 100 million set at that time by industry leaders and donors.[28] The only way to finance the capital needs of this growth is to commercialize. Scaling up through access to savings and capital markets, introducing new technologies, and developing new products all rely on MFIs commercializing, generating a profit, and producing an acceptable return on investment to attract private investors.

This statement by MicroRate in 2011 after the end of the international financial crisis, or Great Recession, on the state of the microfinance sector perhaps best sums up where the sector is at present:

> The microfinance market today looks much different from 2007. Despite the worldwide financial crisis, the sector has doubled in size, transformed from mostly an NGO driven market to one increasingly dominated by regulated institutions, experienced a strong expansion of savings services, and held its first public listings and mergers. Microfinance is displaying the signs of a maturing industry. It has also weathered its first global downturn, lived through several major market crises, and is currently living through a crisis of perceptions and confidence on whether microfinance actually helps alleviate poverty in the first place. None of these issues existed in 2007.[29]

Notes

1. See Stuart Rutherford with Arora Sukhwinder, *The Poor and Their Money*, 2nd ed. (Warwickshire, U.K.: Bourton on Dunsmore, 2009) for a discussion on the importance of savings by the poor. See also Marguerite S. Robinson, *The Microfinance Revolution: Sustainable Finance for the Poor*, vol. 1 (Washington and New York: World Bank and Open Society Institute, 2001).

2. For a balanced discussion on subsidies, see Robert Cull and Jonathan Morduch, "Microfinance and Economic Development," Policy Research Working Paper 8252 (Washington: World Bank, November 2017), pp. 30–32.

3. The year 2005 was called the Year of Microfinance by the United Nations, and Professor Yunus was awarded the Nobel Peace Prize in 2006 for his work. See Muhammad Yunus, *Creating a World without Poverty: Social Business and the Future of Capitalism* (New York: Public Affairs, 2008).

4. Robinson, *The Microfinance Revolution*.

5. Robinson, *The Microfinance Revolution: Lessons from Indonesia*, vol. 2 (Washington: World Bank and Open Society Institute, 2002). For an analysis of BRI's performance before its initial public offering, see Ira W. Lieberman and others, "Microfinance and Capital Markets: The Initial Listing/Public Offering of Four Leading Institutions" (Boston and San Jose, Costa Rica: Council of Microfinance Equity Funds [CMEF] and Calmeadow, December 2007).

6. Robert Peck Christen, Elisabeth Rhyne, and Robert C. Vogel, "Maximizing the Outreach of Microfinance: The Emerging Lessons of Successful Programs" (Washington: IMCC, September 1994).

7. Robinson, *The Microfinance Revolution*, vol. 1, pp. 28–29.

8. Beatriz Marulanda and María Otero, "The Profile of Microfinance in Latin America in 10 Years: Vision & Characteristics" (Washington: Accion International, April 2005).

9. Ibid., p. 6, table 1.

10. Elisabeth Rhyne and Brian Busch, "The Growth of Commercial Microfinance, 2004–2006" (Council of Microfinance Equity Funds, September, 2006) (https://centerfor financialinclusionblog.files.wordpress.com/2011/10/the-growth-of-commercial-microfinance -2004-2006.pdf); Elisabeth Rhyne and Maria Otero, "Microfinance through the Next Decade: Visioning the Who, What, Where, When and How" (Washington: Accion International, November 2006).

11. Rhyne and Busch, "The Growth of Commercial Microfinance," p. 6.

12. Ibid., p. 9.

13. Ibid., pp. 11–12.

14. Rhyne and Otero, "Microfinance through the Next Decade," p. 17.

15. Lieberman and others, "Microfinance and Capital Markets."

16. Donors or funders were the World Bank, bilateral funding agencies such as USAID, KfW (Germany), FMO (Holland), CIDA (Canada), regional development banks such as the Inter-American Development Bank and the Asian Development Bank, and various UN agencies.

17. Ira Lieberman, the author of this chapter, was the founding CEO of the CGAP Secretariat at the World Bank. He managed CGAP for five years, from 1995 through 1999.

Ismail Serageldin, vice president for sustainable development at the World Bank, was responsible for oversight over and managing the consultative group of donor institutions.

18. Symbiotics, "2017 Symbiotics MIV Survey: Market Data and Peer Group Analysis, 11th Edition" (Geneva, 2017) (https://symbioticsgroup.com/wp-content/uploads/2017/09/Symbiotics-2017-MIV-Survey.pdf).

19. See Lieberman and others, "Microfinance and Capital Markets."

20. Cull and Morduch, "Microfinance and Economic Development," pp. 20–30, discuss the economic literature with respect to the economic impact of microfinance.

21. Ibid., p. 30.

22. For a discussion of the causes of crises in microfinance, see Daniel Rozas, "Weathering the Storm: Hazards, Beacons and Life Rafts," Publication 11 (Washington: Center for Financial Inclusion at Accion International, July 2011).

23. The author of this chapter headed an advisory team that tried to resolve the Banex crisis, and one of the editors of this book, Paul DiLeo, represented the equity investors in trying to resolve the crisis. See also Shawn Cole and Baily Blair Kempner, "BANEX and the 'no Pago' Movement," *Harvard Business Review*, April 21, 2011.

24. Robinson, *Microfinance for the Poor*, argues that poverty intervention requires an array of support mechanisms and that loans are inappropriate for those in abject poverty. Muhammad Yunus, on the other hand, has argued that microfinance should serve the poorest of the poor. Indeed, as chairman of CGAP's advisory board, he pushed to have CGAP named the Consultative Group to Serve the Poorest of the Poor. Other advisory board members generally advised against this name change, as did management.

25. The global Smart Campaign is committed to embedding client protection practices into the institutional culture and operations of the financial inclusion industry. Since 2009, the Campaign has certified more than 80 global institutions in Client Protection and worked with industry leaders to amplify the importance placed on "doing no harm." For information on their Client Voice Project, see http://smartcampaign.org/tools-a-resources/1075.

26. On Deck Capital, a publicly traded company in the United States, has joint venture agreements with JP Morgan Chase and BBVA of Spain to analyze and underwrite micro- and small-business loans in the United States, with the banks utilizing their balance sheet to finance these loans and their branch structures and market penetration to maintain the client relationship.

27. The Council of Microfinance Equity Funds (CMEF) published governance guidelines for its member funds in 2005 and updated these guidelines in 2012 in light of changes in the industry such as increased emphasis on transparency and social protection for microfinance clients. See CMEF, "The Practice of Corporate Governance in Shareholder Owned Microfinance Institutions," Consensus Statement of the Council of Microfinance Equity Funds, May 2005, revised in 2012. The author was a contributor to these guidelines. This summary on the importance of governance is largely derived from the introduction to the paper by Pasquale di Benedetta, Ira W. Lieberman, and Laura Ard, "Corporate Governance in Microfinance Institutions" (Washington: World Bank, 2015). Also, the International Finance Corporation has published a paper, "Corporate Governance for Financial Inclusion, Guidance for Board Members of Microfinance Institutions, September 2017," to which this author was a contributor.

28. Cull and Morduch, "Microfinance and Economic Development," p. 6. In 2013, MFIs attending the Microfinance Summit, an event organized by Yunus and others starting in 1997, self-reported reaching some 211 million clients. There have been seventeen such summit meetings since 1997.

29. "Role Reversal II Learning to Wield the Double Edged Sword," MicroRate, October 2011, p. 4.

Section II

WHERE WE ARE NOW–WHAT
IS NEEDED IN THE FUTURE

Photo by Tiago Rosado on Unsplash

TWO

The Changing Face of Microfinance and the Role of Funders

Financing the Future

PAUL DILEO AND ANNA KANZE

In 2001, Marguerite Robinson summarized the defining trajectory of the sector in her seminal book, *The Microfinance Revolution: Sustainable Finance for the Poor*:

> The microfinance revolution is a commercial revolution based on new financial technology and greatly accelerated by the information revolution that developed concurrently. It began in the 1970s, developed in the 1980s, and took off in the 1990s. . . . These combinations enabled institutional profitability and long-term viability, making possible large-scale formal-sector financial outreach to low-income segments of the population.[1]

Growth

In the years since Robinson saw the pieces falling into place, microfinance successfully achieved the milestones its proponents set and achieved meaningful scale:

- Outreach far surpassed the original—wildly optimistic—goal of 100 million clients.

39

FIGURE 2-1.   Trends in Numbers of Borrowers Reported to MIX, 2001–15,
by MFI Regulatory and Profit Status

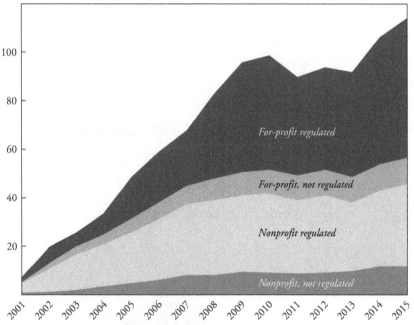

Number of Active Borrowers (millions)

Source: Data from Microfinance Information Exchange (themix.org).

■ The trajectory of the sector has been dramatic. In 1997 the Microcredit
Summit Campaign estimated there were 13 million clients of microfinance
institutions. By the start of 2014 the most recent campaign estimate available showed a sixteenfold increase, to 211 million clients worldwide.[2] As
figure 2-1 illustrates, from a different source of data on microfinance institutions (MFIs) reporting to the Microfinance Information Exchange, as
the industry expanded rapidly after 2000, it evolved from one dominated by
nonprofit, often unregulated institutions to one where the majority are now
regulated for-profit MFIs. Still, a number of the largest MFIs continue to
operate as nonprofits.

■ Commercial investment in the sector expanded rapidly as well, with assets of
microfinance investment vehicles (MIVs) growing at a 20 percent annual clip
on average for more than a decade through 2017.[3]

As David Roodman noted in his book *Due Diligence*, "The existence of major microfinance institutions—competing, innovating, employing thousands, serving millions in ways once thought impossible—embodies the essence of development."[4] In this view, microfinance has succeeded, not by turning clients into entrepreneurial heroes, but by building institutions and industries that compete and innovate, cater to poor people, create jobs, and enrich the national economic fabric.

Capital Markets

A key feature of this success was the effort to enable microfinance institutions to "crack the capital markets" and attract investment capital to supplement the limited donor funds on which they were founded. The first targets were social or impact investors, initially official institutions that provided loans and occasionally equity. The results of this effort were dramatic. Microfinance and other financial services investments taken together have consistently attracted the largest share of "impact investments" according to annual surveys by the Global Impact Investing Network (GIIN); taken as a whole, such "financial inclusion" investment represents roughly a quarter of the total and dwarfs any other impact sector (table 2-1).[5]

According to the GIIN surveys of impact investors, microfinance and financial services represented 16 percent and 9 percent, respectively, of total reported assets under management (AUM) in 2014 and 13 percent and 11 percent in the most recent survey covering 2018. Two developments suggest that some meaningful portion of the "financial services" category is microfinance. First, in a number of countries, leading providers of microfinance have transformed into banks (India), have been acquired by banks (Peru), or have been banks for many years (Bolivia, Africa). Second, many MFIs have moved away from the classic small-group loan toward loans to individuals and small and medium-sized businesses. In both cases many of these institutions are no longer categorized as MFIs, although microfinance may remain a large part or even the bulk of their business.

If assets in North America and Northern, Southern, and Western Europe are excluded, microfinance alone, which is almost entirely concentrated in emerging countries, is the largest impact sector. Its continued heavy weight in impact investment portfolios reflects the fact that microfinance benefits from a robust track record of returns on debt instruments, and a steady flow of equity exits, including of entire fund portfolios, which provide investors with a more accurate sense of expected returns than one-off exits. A number of high-profile microfinance initial public offerings in the period 2016–18 also contributed to confidence in the sector.

TABLE 2-1.   Global Impact Investing Network

Annual Impact Investing Survey 2019, Figure ii
Sector Allocations % of AUM
n = 259, AUM = $131B

Energy	15%
Microfinance	13%
Financial services (excl. microfinance)	11%
Food and Ag	10%
WASH	7%
Housing	7%
Healthcare	6%
Forestry	5%
Infrastructure	4%
Education	4%
Manufacturing	2%
ICT	2%
Arts and culture	0.10%
Other	15%

While below-market-rate capital is a declining proportion of total impact AUM, it remains substantial, representing 36 percent of the total in 2017, or over US$80 billion. But anecdotal evidence suggests that there is a desire to shift this capital away from microfinance, which has a proven investment proposition and reliable access to capital markets, and toward more "innovative" and untested sectors.

While the steady dominance of microfinance in impact portfolios is noteworthy, however, the real story is that, on an aggregate basis, cross-border investment in the sector, which includes most impact investments, plays a diminishing role in the microfinance balance sheet. The Consultative Group to Assist the Poor (CGAP) estimates total cross-border investment in "financial inclusion" at US$37 billion,[6] but this is overstated since microfinance and financial inclusion institutions account for a subset of this universe. The CGAP estimate is roughly consistent with the 2017 GIIN survey, which reports impact investment in microfinance of US$21 billion and in other financial institutions of US$43 billion; and the 2018 Symbiotics microfinance investment vehicle (MIV) survey, which found 111 MIVs managing US$15.8 billion.

In another study, Symbiotics found that its 139 borrowers had a total loan portfolio of US$114 billion. Applying an 80 percent loan-to-total-assets ratio yields total assets of US$140 billion. Even assuming that the Symbiotics portfolio covers the entire microfinance sector, impact investments account for only 25 percent of estimated total assets. Additional data from the Symbiotics study[7] are roughly consistent with this finding: the weighted average of savings deposits in the liabilities of Symbiotics borrowers was 49 percent as of December 2017, and local currency liabilities were 73 percent. Although the latter number may include some hedged cross-border liabilities, the bulk are presumably sourced in the home market.[8]

Taken together, these accomplishments with respect to growth in clients and balance sheets place microfinance as the only pro-poor "impact" business model that has achieved an extended track record of solid profitability, meaningful scale, liquidity for investors, and capacity to understand client needs and continue innovation to reach deeper into poor and excluded populations.

Corporate Form

The change in balance sheets has paralleled a shift in corporate structure. Although a number of important "legacy" MFIs, particularly in South Asia, are still structured as nonprofits, for-profit shareholder MFIs provide the majority of microcredit and other microfinance services, including the vast majority of microsavings accounts. The increase in scale has required large amounts of capital, much more than could be obtained solely from donors, which in most cases were best mobilized by shareholder companies demonstrating a track record of profitable operation.

In 2015, as shown in figure 2-2, nearly eight in ten MFIs operated profitably.

In 2016 there were at least twenty-five MFIs with 1 million borrowers or more (table 2-2). Nearly all have healthy returns on equity and have been growing rapidly, with sustained double-digit annual growth rates for a decade or more. Nineteen of these 25 million-plus borrower MFIs are for-profit. About half of all borrowers do business with these largest MFIs. Three-quarters of all other microcredit borrowers are clients of MFIs with over 100,000 clients. A similar pattern emerges for savings: about two dozen MFIs have more than a million depositors. Table 2-3 also analyzes the performance of MFIs by size, demonstrating the advantages of scale in serving a larger number of poor clients and in increased sustainability and profitability, as well as lower prices for clients.

As tables 2-4 and 2-5 highlight, MFIs have been able to reach scale and sustainability largely regardless of legal structure or geography. Table 2-4 summarizes key performance metrics of MFIs from 2009 through 2016 by legal type (nongovernmental organizations, credit unions, nonbank financial institutions, and banks) and according to whether or not they are regulated institutions. The growth rate data for assets and loan portfolios represent the median compound average annual increases

FIGURE 2-2.   Distribution of Profit Rates for Microfinance Institutions
Worldwide, 2015

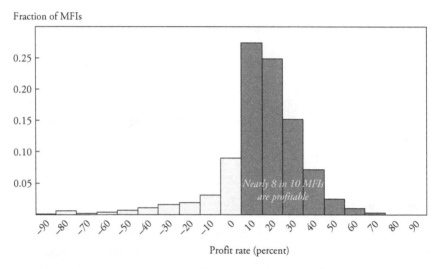

Fraction of MFIs

Profit rate (percent)

Source: Modified from Todd A. Watkins, *Introduction to Microfinance* (Singapore: World Scientific, 2018).
Data from Microfinance Information Exchange (themix.org).
Note: For clarity, excludes MFIs in the extreme tails, reporting profits (losses) exceeding 100 percent
(–100 percent).

for MFIs of each type over the period, while portfolio at risk (PAR), write-off ratio,
and return on equity (ROE) represent the seven-year average of the median annual
rates. The rate of MFI nonperforming loans (for example, PAR90, open loans whose
principal is overdue by ninety days or open loans on which no repayment has been
made for ninety days) have been, except for MFI rural banks, generally comparable
to or better than mainstream commercial banks. For example, according to International Monetary Fund data, the average median annual PAR90 for all banks worldwide during that same period was 3.9 percent.[9]

The median ROE performance has been similarly comparable to that of mainstream commercial banks; average return on equity for all U.S. banks, for instance,
has hovered between 7.5 percent and 10 percent since 2010.[10] The share of loan portfolios that need to be written off as unrecoverable remains low, with median rates at
1 percent or below for all types of MFIs.

Table 2-5 suggests that MFI growth and performance has been healthy across
most geographic regions as well. Double-digit annual growth in the number of active
borrowers for the median MFIs in all regions continued during the period 2009–16,
and the median MFI loan portfolio in all regions also outperformed the 3.9 percent

TABLE 2-2. Million-plus Borrower MFIs

MFI name	Country	Active borrowers	As of date	Annual growth % (2007–16)	Return on equity (%)	Profit status	Legal status
BRI	Indonesia	8,900,000	12/16	9.6	20.3	Profit	Bank
Grameen Bank	Bangladesh	7,180,000	12/15	1.9	–1.8	Profit	Bank
Bandhan	India	6,525,623	3/16	28.2	16.0	Profit	Bank
ASA	Bangladesh	6,207,689	6/16	1.5	17.2	Non-profit	NGO
BRAC	Bangladesh	5,356,521	12/16	–2.0	26.7	Non-profit	NGO
Bharat Financial (SKS)	India	5,323,061	3/17	14.1	13.7	Profit	NBFI
Janalakshmi	India	4,622,578	3/16	68.1	13.9	Profit	Bank
Share	India	3,771,000	3/16	16.0	18.1	Profit	NBFI
Ujjivan	India	3,625,000	3/17	58.1	11.9	Profit	Bank
SKDRDP	India	3,612,431	3/16	22.7	3.6	Non-profit	NGO
Capitec Bank	South Africa	3,507,819*	2/17	22.1	25.7	Profit	Bank
Compartamos Banco	Mexico	2,835,127	3/17	14.5	30.2	Profit	Bank
PROSHIKA	Bangladesh	2,770,106*	12/16	5.2	n/a	Non-profit	NGO
Equitas	India	2,744,336	3/16	76.9	19.8	Profit	Bank
Satin	India	2,300,000	3/17	68.8	5.1	Profit	NBFI
Caja Popular Mexicana	Mexico	2,271,299*	7/17	12.6	18.4	Non-profit	Credit Union
Asmitha	India	2,150,000	3/16	16.0	n/a	Profit	NBFI

(continued)

TABLE 2-2. (continued)

MFI name	Country	Active borrowers	As of date	Annual growth % (2007–16)	Return on equity (%)	Profit status	Legal status
CrediAmigo	Brazil	2,030,821	12/15	27.0	11.1	Profit	Bank
African Bank	South Africa	1,500,000	3/16	n/a	6.7	Profit	Bank
ASA Philippines	Philippines	1,273,136	12/16	39.1	98.1	Non-profit	NGO
Asirvad	India	1,193,328	3/17	79.7	13.3	Profit	NBFI
Grameen Koota	India	1,153,000	3/17	28.9	12.8	Profit	NBFI
Spandana	India	1,060,000	3/17	−1.3	−65.3	Profit	NBFI
AgroAmigo	Brazil	1,037,554	12/16	14.7†	n/a	Profit	Bank
Utkarsh	India	1,010,208	3/16	91.1†	18.5	Profit	NBFI

Notes: Annualized growth rate is CAGR for number of borrowers. Table does not include the Vietnam Bank for Social Policies or the Postal Savings Bank of China, large but essentially government run subsidized banks. *Capitec Bank is number of loans; Caja Popular Mexico and PROSHIKA is number of members. †AgroAmigo annual growth rate from 2008; Utkarsh from 2009.

Data sources: Microfinance Information Exchange (themix.org); Bank Rakyat Indonesia, Annual Report 2016; Capitec Annual Report 2016.; Capitec Annual Report 2016, cpm.coop/solidez -empresarial; proshika.org/what-proshika-docs.html.

TABLE 2-3.   **Measures of Outreach and Efficiency, by MFI Scale**

MFI scale	Small (less than 10,000)	Medium (10,000 to 100,000)	Large (100,000 to 1 million)	Very large (more than 1 million)
Active borrowers				
Share of total number of MFIs (%)	41	41	16	2
Share of all borrowers (%)	1.3	12.0	38.2	48.6
Share of all savers (%)	2.6	20.5	48.1	28.8
Median real interest rate + fees (as % of loan, inflation adjusted)	22.2	20.6	17.8	13.0
Median profit margin (% of revenues)	8.8	9.4	17.1	22.8

Source: Modified from Todd A. Watkins, *Introduction to Microfinance* (Singapore: World Scientific, 2018). *Data source:* Microfinance Information Exchange (themix.org); data for December 2015.

Note: Interest & fees row reports "Yield on Gross Portfolio," using real rates, adjusted for inflation.

TABLE 2-4.   **Performance Metrics for Median MFI, by Legal Structure, 2009–16**

	Bank	Credit union/ Co-op	NBFI	NGO	Rural bank	Regulated	Not regulated
Assets compound annual growth rate (CAGR, %)	20.4	24.6	30.7	29.9	37.1	29.5	23.8
Gross loan portfolio CAGR (%)	23.4	29.4	34.8	29.4	47.7	35.1	20.8
7-year average of annual:							
PAR90 (% of loan portfolio in arrears >90 days or restructured)	2.7	4.1	2.2	2.2	5.1	2.7	2.2
Write-off ratio (% of gross loan portfolio)	0.9	0.5	1.0	0.7	0.7	0.7	1.0
Return on equity (%)	10.4	5.8	7.5	9.3	11.4	8.3	8.9

Data source: Microfinance Information Exchange (themix.org).

median bank PAR90 worldwide. Only in Africa did returns on equity significantly underperform worldwide mainstream banking. Median write-off ratios are remarkably low for MFIs in Asia, while the median African and Latin American MFIs were closer to the average 1.3 percent loan charge-off rate of all U.S. banks during the same period.[11]

TABLE 2-5.   Performance Metrics for Median MFI, by Region, 2009–16

	Africa	East Asia and the Pacific	Eastern Europe and Central Asia	Latin America and the Caribbean	Middle East and N. Africa	South Asia
Active borrowers CAGR (%)	21.5	10.9	29.7	19.8	22.4	16.4
7-year Average of annual:						
PAR90 (%)	3.8	1.4	2.7	3.4	1.5	0.9
Write-off ratio (%)	1.3	0.2	0.5	1.6	0.6	0.1
Return on equity (%)	4.6	10.6	8.0	7.7	10.3	11.1

Data source: Microfinance Information Exchange (themix.org).

This dramatic growth has taken many different forms regionally and institutionally. In Latin America, many MFIs are regulated, deposit-taking institutions, and the line between MFIs and commercial banks is blurring. In Asia, India is becoming the center of microfinance, and the sector is evolving rapidly, most recently with the licensing of the new small finance banks that are aiming at the small and medium-sized enterprise (SME) sector. Microfinance is becoming part of the mainstream financial sector both in India and elsewhere in the region, such as Cambodia. In China, the lack of a reliable regulatory framework is an impediment. Meanwhile Bangladesh, while perhaps less focused on financial product innovation, remains a leader in scale, penetration, and coordination of microfinance with nonfinancial interventions. Africa is building on the microfinance revolution with a mobile banking revolution, still very much a work in progress. A high-tech, low-touch model of offering some bottom-of-the-pyramid (BOP) financial services is showing efficiency gains, but for many clients it seems that access to knowledge and a trusted counterparty is an essential complement to better access to capital.

These shifts in structure and in the volume and type of capital have enabled MFIs to expand rapidly and completely changed the industry, in both hopeful and troubling ways. A persistent concern has been the possibility of "mission drift": a loss of an MFI's priority commitment to improve the lives and prospects of its clients and home communities in favor of generating high returns to attract and reward investors.

By one crude but widely used measure, this fear is not being realized. The sector has largely preserved its focus on the BOP with the median average loan balance at MFIs holding at well below 30 percent of per capita income (figure 2-3).[12] Recent research has also found that in one respect at least, fears of mission drift due to the

FIGURE 2-3.   Median of MFI Average Loan Balance as Percentage
of per Capita Income, 2005–15

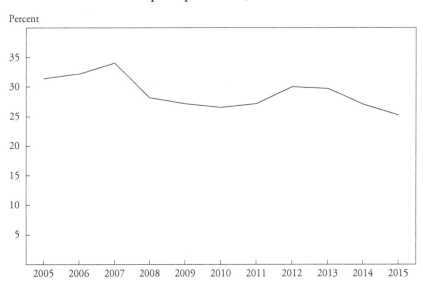

changes in the profile of the sector are unfounded. A 2018 study by Calmeadow[13] finds
that corporate structure—in other words whether an MFI is structured as a nonprofit
or a for-profit company—bears no clear relationship to how well the institution responds and adapts to clients: many for-profit MFIs rate highly in catering to clients'
needs while nonprofits can be unresponsive and rigid.[14] (Although many for-profits
also charge lower interest rates on loans to clients, this is more related to scale than to
corporate structure.)

Disquiet

But these positive signals do not seem to allay persistent concerns that the sector is
losing its social mission as it attracts mainstream, conventional capital. At a session
at the 2018 European Microfinance Week (EMW) where the Calmeadow study was
presented, attendees were quite willing to grant that corporate structure was not the
determining factor in whether MFIs were committed to client benefit, but noted that
some MFIs, regardless of structure, were more committed than others. This disquiet
was loudly reiterated at the EMW plenary session, which debated whether there is
still room and a role for smaller tier 2 and tier 3 MFIs, usually defined as having less

than US$100 million in assets. Their continued importance was resoundingly confirmed.

To some extent, this presumably reflects the resentment of incumbents as new-comers crash their cozy club. But MFIs do confront the unique challenge that faces double-bottom-line businesses that achieve financial success and capital market access. On one hand, impact investors, donors, and the broader public, in part echoing the sector's poverty-alleviation messaging, continue to challenge MFIs to preserve the priority of benefiting poor clients. On the other hand, growing, financially success-ful MFIs are perceived as golden geese, tempting targets for takeover by unscrupulous or merely profit-maximizing operators with no particular interest in client outcomes one way or the other.

Fintech

A particularly topical illustration of why this disquiet is so persistent is financial tech-nology, or fintech. In recent years, fintech, loosely defined to encompass mobile money, cashless operations, algorithmic scoring, and fully machine-driven credit decisions, has obsessed the microfinance industry as simultaneously its greatest competitive challenge (with new and more nimble entrants luring away their best clients or over-indebting the rest) and its greatest opportunity (a chance to reduce costs and improve outreach to heretofore inaccessible or costly clients). The 2018 Banana Skins report, an annual survey of microfinance risk, finds that "technology risk" overwhelms all other risk cited by market participants, the first time any risk was so dominant.[15]

To date, the threat has not materialized to the extent feared, and many MFIs are steadily incorporating aspects of fintech into their operations. But notably, the ben-efits of fintech are not materializing either. In an analysis of the results of the 2017 World Bank Global Findex, the Center for Financial Inclusion (CFI) finds that after correcting for account dormancy in developing countries, account growth has slowed, the access-usage gap is widening, credit is flat, and savings is declining. A bright spot, however, is the proliferation in the use of digital payments.[16]

The disappointing results beg the question of why such powerful new tools seem to be accomplishing so little. Part of the answer is that in some countries, such as India, greater penetration by fintech has been driven by government fiat rather than care-fully designed with an eye to commercial, much less social, implications. But the prev-alence of the disappointing results suggests that this lack of attention to client needs and client benefit is not just a feature of a heavy-handed government but a more gen-eral phenomenon. Even institutions ostensibly dedicated to financial inclusion and client benefit are engaging with fintech primarily as a cost-cutting effort, driven by the need to sustain profitability.

Lost in the hurry is attention to such considerations as value of the traditional "high-touch" microfinance model to some clients, or the differential impact of fintech on different types of clients: young and old, rural and urban, men and women. Thus while the potential of fintech to increase outreach and enable MFIs to deliver better, more effective products more cheaply appears huge, it is not being realized. These results are not inconsistent with a shift away from the hard, expensive work of designing and delivering products and services to hard-to-reach, low-margin populations.

Role of Impact Capital

So is there a common thread between the changes in the balance sheets, declining interest by impact investors, persistent fears of mission drift, disproportionate importance assigned to small MFIs, and the disappointing early results of the fintech revolution?

The changing composition of the balance sheet, and specifically the decline or disappearance of social investors in shareholding and governance, particularly in larger MFIs, is an obvious candidate. This is not to disparage the motivations and good intentions of all mainstream investors that have piled into the space. Many of them genuinely appreciate and respect the commitment of MFIs to client benefit. But they are ultimately in the game to do well by doing good, with an emphasis on doing well.

In this picture, we would argue that to declare victory and conclude that the job of impact capital in microfinance is done is an enormous error. Just as politicians and foundations are often justly criticized for losing interest after the ribbon cutting and failing to provide ongoing guidance and operating support, so too impact investors have a critical ongoing role to play in ensuring that the machine they have built continues to innovate and address the unsolved challenges, and should bear in mind that the objective is not financial inclusion for its own sake, but a meaningful shift with respect to economic justice and opportunity. The CFI analysis of the Findex results is a clear example that, in the absence of committed oversight, MFIs and other financial institutions will use their market knowledge and available technologies in the time-honored pursuit of profits rather than to achieve social objectives.

Many analysts and observers have found that the impact of microfinance on the poor or on women has fallen far short of what was promised. But analysis also seems to find that with careful targeting, microfinance can indeed have a meaningful benefit for many. This will require innovation, trial and error, and the sacrifice of financial results at times—just as the creation of the original microfinance model required many years to financially stabilize.

In short, the microfinance sector overall is healthy and profitable, continues its several-decades-long robust growth trajectory, has proven attractive to commercial capital providers, and at the same time remains the largest element of impact investing portfolios. Microfinance remains a compelling investment proposition, both for commercial investors and for investors seeking social impact, not only directly, but also—importantly, as impact investors appear to be increasingly attracted to other opportunities—in lessons drawn from the long history of how the industry was built so successfully.

At the same time, the composition and alignment of shareholders and board members of MFIs around a coherent social mission is crucial to the continued relevance of microfinance as an impact investment, and this will require the continued active and disproportionately influential engagement of social investors who prioritize impact.

Notes

1. Marguerite S. Robinson, *The Microfinance Revolution: Sustainable Finance for the Poor* (Washington and New York: World Bank and Open Society Institute, 2001), pp. 28–29.

2. Microcredit Summit, State of the Campaign Report, 2015, http://stateofthecampaign .org/2015/12/09/read-the-full-2015-report/.

3. Symbiotics, "2018 MIV Survey: Market Group and Peer Analysis, 12th Edition" (Geneva: 2018), p. 13 (https://symbioticsgroup.com/wp-content/uploads/2018/10/Symbiotics-2018 -MIV-Survey.pdf).

4. David Roodman, *Due Diligence: An Impertinent Inquiry into Microfinance* (Washington: Center for Global Development, 2012), p. 12.

5. Global Impact Investing Network, "Annual Impact Investor Surveys," 2018 and 2019, Figure ii: AUM by sector. New York.

6. Consultative Group to Assist the Poor (CGAP) 2017, "International Funding for Financial Inclusion," cited in Symbiotics, "Banking for Impact," White Paper, November 2018, p. 9.

7. Symbiotics, "Banking for Impact," White Paper, November 2018, p. 13.

8. These findings are consistent with those of Matthew Soursourian, Edlira Dashi, and Eda Dokle, who found that by the end of 2015 microfinance had attracted an estimated US$34 billion in cumulative investments across international borders, about a third from private sources ("Taking Stock: Recent Trends in International Funding for Financial Inclusion," CGAP Brief [Washington: World Bank Group, December 2016], p. 1).

9. See World Bank, "Bank Nonperforming Loans to Gross Loans" (https://data.worldbank .org/indicator/FB.AST.NPER.ZS/?end=2016&start=2009).

10. Federal Financial Institutions Examination Council (FFIEC), "Consolidated Reports of Condition and Income" (www.federalreserve.gov/releases/chargeoff/chgallsa.htm).

11. Federal Financial Institutions Examination Council, "Consolidated Reports of Condition and Income."

12. Data presented here and elsewhere below are derived from the MIX Market database. The MIX database represents most of the sustainable MFIs internationally by region, by network, and at the level of the MFI. The MIX is the primary source for investors to analyze MFIs and for other analytical and research work in the sector.

13. R. Quiros, C. Gonzalez-Vega, and P. Fardella, "Do Clients Still Matter?" (San José, Costa Rica: Calmeadow, 2018).

14. Of course, being responsive to clients may simply be good business in a competitive environment, whether the product is beneficial or deleterious, and does not necessarily indicate a priority on client and community well-being.

15. Center for Financial Inclusion, "Finance for All: Wedded to Fintech, for Better or Worse: A CSFI 'Banana Skins' Survey of the Risks of Financial Inclusion," August 2018, p. 1.

16. Elizabeth Rhyne and Sonja E. Kelly, "Financial Inclusion Hype vs. Reality: Deconstructing the 2017 Findex Results" (Center for Financial Inclusion, 2018), pp. 2–3.

Fifteen Years of Financing MFIs

From Microcredit to SDG Integration

ROLAND DOMINICÉ

At Symbiotics we believe in pushing money to where it normally doesn't flow. Putting our beliefs into action, we have built the leading market access platform for impact investing.

Hindsight: A Sense of Purpose

After almost fifteen years of practice, Symbiotics can claim US$5 billion of investments into eighty low- and middle-income countries that are largely outside the scope of traditional investment portfolios, reaching as far as possible into least-developed economies. And in those markets we have pushed our capital as far as possible to the bottom of the pyramid. Over that period we have analyzed more than 1,000 local financing intermediaries, all focusing on financial inclusion for microbusinesses, small and medium-sized enterprises, and low- and middle-income households. We ended up investing in more than 400 of them, enabling them to service the financial needs of millions of small businesses and families. With average financing fluctuating between US$1,000 and US$1,500, this capital has empowered over 3 million borrowers, as well as their employees and relatives, providing them with the credit they needed to further their livelihoods. It represents over 4,000 transactions that we sourced, structured, and pushed out in capital markets across Europe, as well as in North America and East Asia. On average, that's about one debt transaction issued every business day since inception. Today these are split equally between single loans to about twenty-five investment funds and syndicated impact bond issuances, bringing a much larger crowd of professional investors on board.

The intent was clear from the start, but the magnitude of the output, and the operations built to sustain it, have grown beyond our wildest dreams. Could we have known fifteen years ago that, with a simple idea, we would get caught in a much larger tide beyond our control? It became clear early on that we were at the right place at the right time with the right proposition. During this period, we became aware of investors of all kinds who were unhappy with the disconnect between socioeconomic dynamics at home and abroad, the way their money was managed and put to work by their bankers, and the scandals they were exposing them to. We have seen these change-making investors, conscious of the power of their capital and asset allocation decisions, come to us, test our products, enjoy them, and return. They have grown with us and, unsurprisingly, asked for more. We knew that our promise to expose their portfolios to simple, tangible, transparent, and effective value propositions outside of known territories and in the real economy, where the capital needs are strongest, made sense. We were fulfilling the basic social function of finance, taking excess savings and putting it to work.

We started in 2005 with a large Swiss bank onboarding retail investors, a European Union fund, a German development bank, a Dutch nonprofit co-operative, a Swiss government fund and several Swiss pension funds, and both Austrian and German private clients. Soon thereafter, we engaged with private banks in Geneva, Luxembourg, Vaduz, and Zurich, with specialized funds in France, Germany, the Netherlands, the United Kingdom, and the United States, and with a dozen development banks across Europe and North America. Today our largest exposure is to pension and insurance beneficiaries, predominantly in Scandinavia. Recently, some of our banking clients have experienced growing traction from private clients in Hong Kong and Singapore, and a few in Tokyo.

Symbiotics is just an intermediary, bringing wealth managers with new aspirations in the North together with inclusive bankers in the South. We simply lend into their operations, sustaining their growth. We do not claim credit for the success and courage of their hardworking outreach at the bottom of the pyramid in their domestic markets. But we are amazed and thrilled by their capacity to innovate and be restless as they confront the complexity and go the extra mile to increase access to basic goods and services, ground finance in the real economy, act as responsible bankers, create lasting business models, and connect them to a multiplicity of networks across the globe. Our work and journey is dedicated to them, their diversity, depth, success, and sense of purpose. They teach us every day what banking should be about.

Outlook: SDG Integration

In the development aid and policy space, multilateral banks initiated the microfinance movement in the 1980s as an alternative to the massive government indebtedness programs in the South following the decolonization era of the 1960s. It was seen as a bottom-up private sector solution meant to complement, or maybe one day replace, top-down public aid while finding ways to service the needs of low-income households and their livelihoods in high-population-growth countries that were both underdeveloped and underserved. The value chain has remained unchanged since then but has evolved quite a bit in its underlying framework, which can sometimes be confusing to the outside observer.

By the time the United Nations celebrated the industry in 2005, the narrative had moved from an initial focus on microcredit in the 1990s—a small loan to a poor individual engaged in small income-generating activities with little or no collateral to offer and usually jointly bound to self-selected peers to raise his or her credit profile—to microfinance. The focus then moved to bankers—successful microfinance institutions that offer small loans and, increasingly, savings, insurance, and payment systems of all kinds. After the first microbank IPOs in India and Mexico, policymakers shifted to a more systemic course of *building inclusive financial systems.* When the global financial crisis hit in 2007–08, the underlying framework evolved again, to a focus this time on outcome or impact. While industry experts eventually settled into using the term "impact investing," it remains somewhat of an abstract idea to everyday savers and pensioners. More recently, focusing on the themes and activities in which money is put to work, the model is increasingly viewed through the lens of the United Nations' seventeen Sustainable Development Goals (SDGs) to be achieved by the year 2030.

Microcredit, microfinance, inclusive finance, impact investing, and SDG financing are all about doing the same thing: reaching far into low- and middle-income economies and investing at the base of their social pyramid, in microbusinesses, small and medium-sized enterprises, and low- and middle-income households. Whether we look at it from a development-aid lens of addressing the needs of individual life stories in poorer households, or from a venture capitalist's view of stimulating wealth, employment and success through self-entrepreneurship, or from a policy lens of financial sector development and bank institution-building; or whether we take an economist's systemic approach to global capital flows and interventions needed to make them more inclusive; whether we focus on academic outcome measurement corroborating positive outcome assumptions, or just simply explaining how money is put to work and enhances access to goods and services of first necessity: each approach and narrative is a variation of the same story and value chain, just looked at from a different lens.

Offering the development aid and policy space as an investment opportunity to foreign wealth managers, private banks, and asset managers requires organizing and structuring the investment strategy and value chains in an intelligible manner for financial professionals, making the experience as normal as possible for traditional investment portfolios. At Symbiotics we have strived to organize this market evolution into a new investment strategy for impact investors (see table). We see the current landscape or investment universe as split into three parts: households, small businesses, and larger projects and corporations. The first two are approached by foreign investors through local financing intermediaries; the third can be invested in directly. We thus refer to (1) household finance, (2) small-business finance, and (3) project and corporate finance. They all follow the same value proposition of investing in the real economy at the bottom of the pyramid in underserved economies, or put more simply, "pushing money to where it normally doesn't flow."

SDG Integration Investment Strategy for Impact Investors

Investing in the real economy at the bottom of the pyramid in underserved economies

Financial institutions		Direct investing
Household finance (SDGs 1, 5, and 10):	*Small-business finance* (SDGs 8 and 12):	*Project and corporate finance*:
Commercial banks	SME banks	Food and agriculture (SDGs 2, 14, and 15)
		Climate and energy (SDGs 7 and 13)
Microfinance institutions	Finance companies	Housing and infrastructure (SDGs 6, 9, and 11)
Fintech companies	Investment funds	Health care and education (SDGs 3 and 4)

Household Finance: Consumption and Security

Our portfolios are domi-
nated by financial inclusion
models delivered through
microfinance institutions—
increasingly commercial

banks and more recently fintechs. Backed by their various income streams, all of
them seek to address the financial security needs (through savings, payments, insurance, and credit line products) and consumption needs (through consumer, working
capital, and fixed-asset loans) of low- and middle-income households at the base
of the pyramid. Most financial institutions active on this value proposition are taking a multisector approach, but some specialize in specific themes and segments
such as education finance, housing finance, or even energy financing. They distinguish themselves by offering capital that is usually not formally secured or collateralized, in very small amounts, from as little as US$100 up to a maximum of
US$10,000 in certain countries, and as low as a couple of dollars for some mobile
fintech solutions.

The low-income household financial inclusion models primarily address Sustainable Development Goals 1 (no poverty), 5 (gender equality), and 10 (reduced in-
equalities). Our local partner financial intermediaries tend to focus on the poorest
categories of clients, have been largely biased toward women, and have by design an
intent to reduce the income, consumption, and access to finance gaps.

Small-Business Finance: Employment and Entrepreneurship

With a slightly up-market portfolio strategy
in comparison with that of household finance,
the focus of small-business finance is on formalized shops, which require different lending methodologies that are more concerned

with the collateral and security their cash flow can offer. Here too, most financial
intermediaries and models take a multisector approach, but some do focus on specific
themes, such as agricultural value chains, energy solutions, or small infrastructure
projects. They can be split between SME banks (with a majority of small-enterprise
clients), specialized financial intermediaries (such as leasing, factor, or lending operations), and local investment funds. While the underlying investments normally

range from US$10,000 to US$100,000 per small business for the first two, they can be as large as US$1–10 million for the third.

The small-business finance strategy primarily addresses SDGs 8 (decent work and economic growth) and 12 (responsible consumption and production). Small-business finance is principally about employment and entrepreneurship as vehicles of growth and economic development. Formalized companies are also the best means to address new normative developments in responsibly producing goods and services for public consumption.

Project and Corporate Finance: Food, Homes, and Energy

The third set of investment strategies are direct investments in businesses that serve the bottom of the pyramid, whether through project finance or private debt or equity. Experienced impact investors are moving beyond household and small-business finance into a wider spectrum of risk and return, taking on, for instance, local green bonds for infrastructure and energy projects, with sizes of US$10–50 million a piece or, at the other end of the spectrum, venture capital focused on impact and technology starting at US$100,000.

Historically, our impact theme has ranged beyond microcredit, and the financial security and consumption impact promise it put forward, to address *jobs, food, homes, and energy*. Some of our partner lending institutions have developed new credit products addressing these four issues in their portfolios: small-business finance (jobs), but also agricultural lending and trade finance (food), housing finance and real estate or infrastructure projects (homes), and energy-saving credit solutions or new renewable and clean-tech leasing schemes (energy). We have also seen more new intermediaries entirely dedicated to these core impact issues. Some have also offered health and education credit, which is considered a public good and government prerogative in many economies but has emerged as a valid private market complementary offering in some underserved economies. Symbiotics has thus recently also adopted health and education as a fifth theme. Systematically incorporating employment dynamics into our impact management and measurement, we have organized our direct project and corporate finance segments with the four other core themes: (a) food and agriculture; (b) housing and infrastructure; (c) climate and energy; and (d) health and education.

If they are often addressed indirectly through multisector or dedicated financial institutions loan portfolios, they are more directly addressed through dedicated business models. They go beyond financial security, household consumption, and employment and entrepreneurship to allow for a more comprehensive integration of the SDG issues into investment portfolios.

Food and Agriculture

Agricultural value chain financing, whether production, trade, distribution, or other models, focuses on businesses that are adopt-

ing a sustainable approach to extraction and harvesting of natural products from the planet, whether crops, cattle, fish, or other plants and animals; these efforts extend to mining and forestry, as well as land use and conservation. With sustainability intentionality in mind, the businesses engaged in these sectors address SDGs 2 (zero hunger), 14 (life below water), and 15 (life on land).

Housing and Infrastructure

Community development financing involves housing, utilities, and infrastructure investments, and the industries that develop, support,

and construct them. Sustainable innovations include, for instance, those that provide green buildings, clean energy, transportation, and water systems that are accessible and affordable for those at the base of the pyramid; they also address rapid urbanization and congestion, as well as rural exodus and scarcity of services. This investment segment best aligns with SDGs 6 (clean water and sanitation), 9 (industry, innovation and infrastructure), and 11 (sustainable cities and communities).

Climate and Energy

Energy financing with a sustainable bias will include strategies to reduce and save energy use in a more efficient manner or use of new renewable energy and clean technologies for alternative production and consumption

schemes, or a combination of both. Initially split between hydro, solar, wind, and waste topics, our more recent activities have segmented these issues more narrowly (into about twenty segments and fifty subsegments) for the purpose of working with a dedicated fund established by a Nordic bank and policymaker. The multiplicity of models and businesses in this segment best address SDGs 7 (affordable and clean energy) and 13 (climate action).

Health Care and Education

These two issues are deeply rooted in the public good and government prerogatives in the most advanced economies but increasingly present private sector opportunities in some low-income economies. Health care is-   sues, addressing SDG 3 (good health and well-being), encompass hospitals and clinics, health care plans, services and insurance, and the production and distribution of health products and solutions. Education, addressing SDG 4 (quality education), refers mostly to student and school loans but integrates a wider training realm, including innovative knowledge learning, transfer, and management of digital solutions.

We do not believe SDGs 16 (peace, justice, and strong institutions) and 17 (partnerships for the goals) are measurable investment topics for wealth management portfolios. We assume that by furthering SDG integration strategies, either via the three pillars or specific subsegments, investors contribute to fulfilling goals 16 and 17 as well.

It is with this framework in mind that we have designed our investment strategy going forward, structuring our client offerings as a toolbox for market access that they can tap into à la carte. When we started, the impact investing markets did not offer this variety of choice; the investment universe has widened, matured, and diversified to offer all types of investors the opportunity to engage in this space in ways that meet their needs and expectations. We believe emerging and frontier markets are singling themselves out today by their advanced and leading financial services industries, driven by modern and innovative bankers, and are offering an impressive avenue for SDG integration into northern traditional investment portfolios.

In January 2019 we successfully helped launch our first institutional investor fund using this SDG integration framework, with about US$50 million in seed capital, a structure that we are replicating with all new global banks and large asset manager prospects. Unsurprisingly, the bulk of the portfolio is going to microfinance institutions, or new types of financial institutions launched by former microbankers; they are implementing a larger variety of products and services that fit well with the SDG integration framework, still focusing on low-income households and small businesses at the base of the pyramid, with the same DNA and vision that inspired the industry fifteen years ago.

THREE

The Future of Microcredit Depends on Social Investors

TIMOTHY N. OGDEN

The modern microfinance industry styles itself as something new and different from both financial services and antipoverty efforts that came before. It is not. Matt Levine, a Bloomberg columnist, frequently teases the fintech industry with the (paraphrased) line: the fate of fintech is to relearn all the lessons of financial history, painfully, and in public. Although that would be an overstatement of modern microfinance's situation, the industry has in fact been repeating history and relearning lessons.

Historically, the evolution of consumer banking followed a predictable pattern. The exclusion of a certain group—whether farmers, working-class urban dwellers, immigrants, or low-income households—led to the creation of financial institutions, often subsidized by philanthropic capital, specifically to serve that population.

But serving a particular population is hard—there is almost always a reason that a population is excluded. The challenges of reaching the population—for instance, lots of small transactions, high customer acquisition costs, high risk due to social exclusion—require the financial institutions to get creative with their business model and strategy. But once established, these new financial institutions often do quite well. Pent-up demand for basic financial services leads to growth and initial success. Eventually, though, a crisis occurs. Sometimes it is a macroeconomic shock (such as a depression or war), sometimes a natural disaster, sometimes a debtors' rights movement. But in any case, the strategic choices these new financial institutions for the excluded made in order to overcome barriers common to providing financial services make them especially vulnerable to particular kinds of shocks.

For instance, limiting geographic scope to contain costs makes an institution more vulnerable to regional shocks such as natural disasters or local recessions. Drawing customers from an existing network (or creating a network of customers) to make outreach and customer acquisition easier makes an institution more vulnerable to runs or repayment strikes. Structuring products to minimize risk of loss limits the gains that are possible for both customers and the institutions, and encourages successful customers to defect to other providers.

When the crisis hits, these institutions often struggle or fail. When they do, surviving financial institutions take the cream of the customer crop—the group that the upstarts proved was most profitable to serve—while jettisoning the less-profitable and harder-to-serve segments. Those on the margins are excluded once again, until a new effort at serving these customers comes along.

Though highly stylized, this is the story of countless banks and countries: the credit unions of Germany, the mutual aid societies of Britain, the local savings banks in the United States. The modern microfinance movement has largely, though inadvertently, followed this well-worn path. Today there are a number of "crises" that are putting pressure on the global microfinance movement. The two most significant, the two that have the potential to affect the broadest set of institutions and countries, are questions about the impact of microfinance and the emergence of digital financial services.

Whether the evolution of the modern microfinance movement will shift toward irrelevance or extinction, as has happened to so many other efforts to extend financial services to excluded communities, or toward innovation, reinvention, greater impact, and a permanent place in the global financial services landscape depends almost entirely on social investors.

The Innovation Investment Imperative

Understanding of microfinance's impact and limitations grew by leaps and bounds in the second decade of the twenty-first century. More will continue to be learned. But, as I discuss in chapter 7, "Understanding the Impact of Microcredit," the current research is remarkably consistent, given the controversies over the years about the "true" impact of microfinance, both across studies and after a century of economic theory on financial systems. The average impact of microfinance is modest but beneficial, with benefits spreading well beyond customers to broader communities. And while the truly self-sustaining microfinance institution (MFI) is rare, on average subsidies to deliver this modest benefit are quite low.

But the world does not stand still. Social investors were promised, by some industry leaders, not modest benefits at low cost, but an end to poverty *and* market-rate investment returns. As reality has undermined those claims, social investment in general has taken off, and investors now have a much broader range of choices if they believe that microfinance does not deliver. Meanwhile, technology is rapidly changing the infrastructure of delivering financial services with uncertain effects on impact, and especially on microfinance business models. Will digital transformations allow MFIs to cut costs, increase outreach, boost impact, grow, and reduce subsidies? Or will they allow other players to disintermediate MFIs and put them out of business?

The only thing that is certain is that the status quo in microfinance is unlikely to hold. Business as usual is not likely to appeal to social investors for long. Dollars will flow elsewhere, as will customers (at least the most profitable ones), if MFIs fail to adopt and incorporate digital financial tools.

If the microfinance industry does not innovate, rapidly, it will lose relevance, subsidies, impact, and independence (by being absorbed by other financial institutions, most of which will not have any pro-poor mandate, or by shutting down).

Innovation does not happen just because of desire or urgency. Innovation requires investment. It is inherently risky and almost always involves multiple rounds of experimentation and failure (meaning no profits or even losses) before profitable processes, products, or practices are discovered and refined.

Social enterprises in general and microfinance institutions in particular are ill-suited for organically funding innovation. Profit margins, usually by design, are not sufficient to cover most organizations' true cost of capital. Profits are certainly not enough to fund serious innovation—particularly in an industry where even the existence of profits is controversial. It may not be logical that charging interest is more controversial than other fees, but the fact is that lending has been controversial in almost all societies dating back to ancient Mesopotamia. Raising interest rates enough to generate the surplus needed for risk-taking innovation is simply not in the cards for most microfinance institutions.

Significant innovation will only happen if it is funded by social investors. Social investors also have a role to play in driving innovation in microcredit beyond just providing cash. It will also be necessary to change the norms of the social investment infrastructure. One of the reasons the microfinance industry has been able to attract so much capital is that there are widely accepted rules of thumb for judging the quality of institutions. Ranging from the cost of loans to operational ratios to repayment ratios, the conventional wisdom rewards avoiding risk and limiting costs. In other words, the prevailing practices of microfinance institutions send a very clear message to MFI executives: do not invest in risky innovation.

Increasing the impact of microfinance will require new products, new operational procedures, and perhaps even new business models. Testing these new products, procedures, and business models will almost inevitably lead to higher default rates, higher operating costs, and lower sustainability ratios in the short term.

Social investors will have to adapt their mindset these new circumstances in order to drive innovation in microfinance.

A Mindset for Driving Innovation in Microcredit

- Drop the "no trade-offs" myth—outreach to poor customers is always going to be more expensive.

- Drop the "no subsidy" myth—see previous item.

- Explicitly fund innovation—set specific innovation-related targets and hold organizations accountable.

- Blow up the theory of change—the standard microcredit approach is not going to yield large gains for the average borrower.

- Choose new theories of change to test.

Promising Channels for Innovation

While we waited many years for rigorous evaluations of microcredit impact, there was a great deal of other research being done on microcredit specifically, and microfinance in general, in an effort to understand demand for and use of financial services, and borrowers' needs and preferences (see chapter 1 for an overview of some of this work). Impact evaluations indicate that a subset of borrowers see large gains from microcredit and suggest one promising channel for innovation; but the impact evaluations have overshadowed other research that also can inform innovation. Since MFIs generate the vast majority of their revenue from lending, the focus of innovation should remain on lending operations.

Research points to five promising channels for innovation to increase the effectiveness of microfinance. They are:

1. *Targeting*. This is the most obvious channel, but that makes it no less challenging. Targeting loans to borrowers most likely to achieve high returns is the goal of every business lender (and venture capitalist for that matter) in every market. Still, there are a number of possibilities that bear exploring, from the mundane to the more speculative. Across studies, the impact of microcredit is found to be heterogeneous. Borrowers who were operating businesses before the arrival of microcredit, and those that were more profitable before borrowing, among other characteristics, had significantly higher returns from borrowing. If such borrowers had been the initial target of microcredit, the average impact of expanding access would have been much higher. Similarly, targeting loans to particular industries that are likely to benefit from increased capital investment, while less exact, may also be a useful approach. Understanding local market dynamics and small-business operations has been a staple of local business lending for hundreds of years, but has been largely ignored in microfinance business models.

Another possibility is outsourcing targeting to third parties who have tacit knowledge of potential borrowers. For instance, one study found that using agricultural brokers to identify farmers most likely to use credit well worked better than traditional group lending models.[1] Another experiment that polled community members about who in the community was most likely to run a successful business found that their responses were accurate.[2]

Several service providers now provide a different approach—using psychometric profiles to evaluate borrowers. Others use transactional data gathered from digital platforms or from other sources. It may also be the case, as is documented in developed countries, that a single question, such as asking a small-business owner how much she plans to grow, is a good predictor of which small businesses will grow. Small-business owners who are able to answer the question with specific detail are much more likely to grow and hit those targets than people who are not.

It is important to note that innovation around "alternative data" needs to be conducted with great care. For instance, it is not clear what psychometrics are measuring. Are these inborn traits? Or are they the result of context? Regardless of the answer, important questions about equity and inclusion must be asked. Similarly, data on call patterns or school test results or social media contacts (all of which have been proposed) may accurately predict likelihood of default. But those factors are likely not much more predictive than income—and so may simply re-create patterns of exclusion in less obvious ways.

2. *Product design*. One of the best kept secrets in microcredit is that the core product, a small loan that requires steady repayment beginning one week after disbursement, is unsuited for business investment. At the very least it requires the borrower to generate free cash flow immediately. Another secret is that takeup rates for microcredit are quite low: less than 30 percent of eligible borrowers actually take out a loan. These two features go hand-in-hand. It is likely that the product design of microcredit loans discourages many potential borrowers who could generate higher returns if they did not have to begin repayment immediately after taking out a loan.

In one test of a new loan product, borrowers were allowed a few weeks before beginning repayment. Those borrowers' profits were higher and they invested more in their business than borrowers who were required to begin repayment immediately. The product was canceled, however, because although it was profitable for the MFI, default rates exceeded the thresholds set by investors.[3] Additional recent studies have backed up the initial finding. Allowing borrowers more flexibility in repayment has small effects on default, but meaningfully positive effects on borrowers' returns.

Other product design innovations supported by research include working capital loans—perhaps delivered in-kind rather than in cash—and loans with payment cycles geared toward production cycles such as agricultural loans that defer repayment until harvest, or provide a grace period during planting season.

Outside the microenterprise lending space, making loans specifically for the purchase of useful consumer goods has shown promise in a number of areas, including loans for solar power generation equipment, for agricultural product storage, for more efficient engines for motorbikes, and for indoor plumbing.[4]

3. *Lines of credit*. Many of the people microfinance targets do not have reliable and predictable incomes or expenses. Traditional microcredit is built on the opposite premise, with rigid rules about when customers can borrow and when they must repay. More flexibility could be better for customers. Instead of providing a one-time loan, providers could offer lines of credit that allow customers to borrow quickly or delay payments during an emergency. Lenders who have experimented with more flexible borrowing and repayment terms have not seen defaults rise but have seen happier customers.[5]

4. *Business consulting and services*. Running a business of any size is hard—and learning to run one efficiently via trial and error is unlikely to happen in many parts of the world. There are big potential gains from helping microentrepreneurs run their businesses better. Recent research has documented that some business practices make a large difference in microenterprise performance and are useful in predicting survival rates and sales growth in several countries. Helping firms adopt these practices could have significant effects.

One study found large gains for shopkeepers from reminding them to keep enough change on hand; another from encouraging them to invest in more inventory. Another study found promising business benefits from teaching shop owners simple accounting rules of thumb.

To be clear, traditional business training—a few hours of instruction in a classroom—does not work. The traditional model can, though, suggest ways to adopt new approaches such as setting up peer-to-peer learning opportunities, deploying "business extension agents," or helping borrowers set up supply chain cooperatives; or even offer traditional business practice consulting.

Finally, there is emerging evidence that one factor holding back borrowers is aspirations. Borrowers do not plan to grow their businesses because they do not think it is possible. Working with these clients to raise their aspirations can induce them to take more steps to grow and generate higher returns.[6]

5. *Hybrid products.* We usually think of financial products in distinct buckets: savings, credit, insurance. But customers do not really think this way. They are trying to solve problems, not provide consumer financial services. The first day of business school, marketers learn that no one wants a 3/8-inch drill bit—what they want is a 3/8-inch hole.

It is clear from in-depth studies of households, like those conducted by U.S. Financial Diaries, that households do not think about financial products.[7] A simple rubric is that customers are trying to manage liquidity, manage investment, and manage risk. Most financial products can be used to meet any one of these goals. Assuming that a loan is going to be used to invest, rather than to smooth liquidity—as with a postal savings account or insurance, for example—will inevitably mislead.

Microfinance could benefit from innovative packaging of financial products that are more closely attuned to customers' needs: a postpaid savings account; a virtual rotating savings and credit association (ROSCA); a permanent weekly payment that may be a savings deposit, a loan repayment, or an insurance premium in any given week—or all three.

Lessons on Investing in Innovation

Investment necessarily involves risk. That fact has far too often been papered over by rhetoric in the social investment industry, and especially in the microfinance industry. Even if social investors take on the need to invest and support innovation, and even if the required capital is made available, there is no guarantee that the social returns—even the limited returns of boosting innovation—will materialize. There are, however, things social investors can do to increase the likelihood that investment in innovation accomplishes the goal.

Use of the term "corporate finance" today is likely to call to mind complex financial instruments, credit default options, derivatives, initial public offerings, and Goldman Sachs. Particularly in the social sector, many participants think of their activities as an antidote to the perceived evils wrought by corporate finance in recent decades. Misconceptions and ignorance of the origins and foundations of corporate finance come at a significant and increasing cost for the social sector, however.

Social investment in innovation raises important questions that all too often go unasked. How can investors ensure that MFIs will live up to their promises of innovation? How can entrepreneurs protect their vision if it clashes with that of funders? When conflict between double-bottom-line goals occurs, do managers or investors have the final say? When innovations deliver gains, who reaps the benefits?

Such questions all boil down to principal-agent problems, which are the foundations of corporate finance. How do investors ensure that executives use capital to further the goals of the investors? How do executives ensure that managers serve the goals of the enterprise?

There is a rich corporate finance literature that explores how various forms of financing influence the behavior of executives and firms. There are compendiums of studies of the effects of debt versus equity financing, the role of metrics and reporting, the role of governance and so on—all written about for-profit firms, but now clearly relevant to innovation in the social sector. Unfortunately this literature and knowledge has largely been neglected in social investment.

A short summary necessarily obscures nuance and details, but a quick overview of the options and considerations that social investors must consider may be useful.

In general, equity is used when an investor wants more direct oversight of strategy and the ability to directly enforce accountability. By owning shares, and especially by joining a board of directors, an investor has some measure of authority and ability to challenge executives' decisions or ensure that plans are being followed. The trade-off is that the equity holder can lose all of her money if things go wrong, with very limited recourse. Making equity investments also requires paying more attention to the goals of other equity investors—who likely do not share exactly the same goals and timelines. When multiple investors providing "oversight of strategy" have mismatched goals, innovation efforts (and even operational survival) can be hamstrung.

Debt allows more discretion to executives—the executives' responsibility is to ensure loan repayments are made in full and on time, but the social investor trusts that the executives' methods for generating surplus for debt payments will be in accord with stated goals without needing additional oversight (or the lender simply doesn't care what methods executives use). The upside of this lack of authority over executive actions is that the providers of debt financing usually hold a binding claim on the assets of the firm and are somewhat protected from losses.

Grants, of course, provide neither the direct nor indirect check on executive actions that equity or debt provide. Grants do have some ability to compel action, however. First, there is the "dynamic incentive" of grants if there is the possibility of future funding—executives know if they fail to take agreed actions they will lose access to the future funds. Often grantmakers use this dynamic incentive within a single grant, by dividing it up into tranches with the release of additional funds dependent on the grantee reaching defined milestones. The effectiveness of dynamic incentives is entirely dependent on the availability of alternative sources of funding. And grantmakers who ex ante make it clear that further funding will be unavailable essentially give up any power they have to hold grantees to account. Second, large grantmakers can insist on being named to an organization's board, which gives them the opportunity to conduct oversight that is similar to that provided by equity. Finally, particularly in the microfinance sector, there is another form of social financing that can resemble any of the three main forms, depending on how it is structured: loan guarantees. A loan guarantee, by absorbing risk, is usually used to lower the cost or increase the amount of debt financing available from other investors. Terms of loan guarantees vary widely and may resemble equity, debt, or grants. Loan guarantees typically offer less influence or protection than equity or debt, but allow smaller investors to leverage limited funds and influence larger investors.

Four Types of Smart Subsidies

A subsidy can be considered "smart" if it supports one or more of the following four kinds of activities: experimenting, extending, multiplying, and demonstrating.[8]

Experimenting: Developing New Models

Subsidy is critical to experimentation and innovation in the social sector. Research and development (R&D) is challenging for nonprofits and social businesses to self-fund: the benefits of R&D are enjoyed widely while the costs are borne by the innovator alone (in economic jargon, investment in innovation has a strong positive externality). This externality weakens any one institution's incentives to invest in research and new product development, which leads to inefficiently low levels of R&D.

Funding for this type of work is almost never available from commercial sources, as the risks seem too high and the financial returns too uncertain (or impossible, given regulations around various corporate forms). Subsidy is particularly important when piloting new—and then expanding the scope of—products or services.

> Example: Piloting new credit products such as agricultural cycle loans, or water and sanitation loans

> Subsidy form: Equity or grant, not debt

> Metrics: Operational data

Extending: Scaling Successful Models

When experimentation proves successful—when new models have been developed, tested, and piloted with seemingly positive results for the targeted clients—an institution will usually seek to expand its operations. Expansion may be to new clients in the same markets, or to new locations. Scaling up both provides valued services to more clients and generates more income, serving both sides of the double-bottom-line ledger.

> Example: Providing business training consulting in additional, or underserved, areas

> Subsidy form: Debt, equity

> Metrics: Operational data, quality measures, client outcome measures

Multiplying: Attracting Additional Investment

As already noted, the infrastructure of investment in microfinance has created pronounced rigidities that discourage innovation. Subsidy for innovation can be directed specifically to helping demonstrate the concept, capacity, and impact on innovation in ways that attract additional social investors and help break down those rigidities.

Attracting additional social investors to fund innovation in microcredit—equity as well as debt—will allow innovation (and funding) to go much further.

Example: Investment in MFI with successful new products or models

Subsidy form: Equity, loan guarantees, grants

Metrics: Finance measures

Demonstrating: Documenting and Disseminating Lessons from Successful Innovation

Maximizing the gains from supporting innovation requires deliberate steps to evaluate and communicate lessons. Too often these steps are incomplete. To derive the full benefit of a subsidy invested to develop public goods, the lessons learned (positive and negative) must be captured, analyzed, and disseminated to the broader field.

Example: Funding an MFI operations team to train other MFIs

Subsidy form: Grants

Metrics: Takeup measures

Conclusion

The future of microfinance is decidedly unclear. After forty years, the claims that it can eradicate poverty are no longer tenable. There is little remaining question that the average impact of microfinance is modest. Similarly, the enduring presence of subsidy makes it clear that the rhetoric around fully self-sustaining institutions targeting excluded populations was a mirage. At the same time, the technology landscape is evolving very rapidly. It is clear, however, that microfinance provides a low-cost platform for providing useful services to many formerly excluded communities, those communities benefit, and some customers benefit a great deal. So what comes next?

There are patterns in the historical record of the development, success, and failure of consumer financial services. Which of these patterns the industry follows will depend primarily on the social investors who propelled microfinance to its present state as the only social investment with global scale and a fully functional investment and operational infrastructure.

If there is no significant investment in innovation, then MFIs will gradually (and in some cases rapidly) cease to be a meaningful part of the global financial services landscape. MFIs that survive will pursue wealthier customers and end up indistinguishable from traditional banks. Others will be absorbed by larger financial services institutions and again focus on the most profitable customers in their portfolios and steadily lose their focus on inclusion and outreach. Many will simply have to cease operations as they lose access to subsidy and customers to digital competitors.

If there is principled and focused investment in innovation, then the microfinance industry has the potential to build on the foundation it has created, increase impact, serve more customers, and serve them better. And the long-hoped-for impact of reducing poverty may yet come to pass.

Notes

1. P. Maitra and others, "Financing Smallholder Agriculture: An Experiment with Agent-Intermediated Microloans in India," *Journal of Development Economics* 127 (2017): 306–37, doi: 10.1016/j.jdeveco.2017.03.001.

2. R. Hussam, N. Rigol, and B. Roth, "Targeting High Ability Entrepreneurs Using Community Information: Mechanism Design in the Field," Working Paper (https://economics.mit.edu/files/14591).

3. Erica Field and others, "Does the Classic Microfinance Model Discourage Entrepreneurship among the Poor? Experimental Evidence from India," *American Economic Review* 103, no. 6 (2013): 2196–226.

4. M. Burke, L. Bergquist, and E. Miguel, "Sell Low and Buy High: Arbitrage and Local Price Effects in Kenyan Markets," Working Paper 24476 (Cambridge, Mass.: National Bureau of Economic Research, 2018) (www.nber.org/papers/w24476).

5. P. Agarwal and G. Barboni, "Knowing What's Good for You: Can a Repayment Flexibility Option in Microfinance Contracts Improve Repayment Rates and Business Outcomes?," Working Paper, 2018 (www.giorgiabarboni.com/home/Research_files/Barboni_JMP.pdf).

6. F. Campos, "Teaching Personal Initiative Beats Traditional Training in Boosting Small Business in West Africa," *Science* 357, no. 6357 (2017): 1287–90. doi: 10.1126/science.aan5329.

7. D. Collins and others, *Portfolios of the Poor: How the World's Poor Live on $2 a Day* (Princeton University Press, 2010).

8. This model of smart subsidy was first proposed by Jonathan Morduch and developed with Tony Sheldon.

FOUR

Microfinance Industry Concentration and the Role of Large-Scale and Profitable MFIs

TODD A. WATKINS

The large majority of microfinance institutions are too small. Most serve too few clients, with too narrow a scope of services to be efficient and stable, as is, over the long haul. If institutions offering microfinancial services ever hope to approach serving anywhere near a majority of the world's billion extremely poor people, they need to find more ways to serve mass markets and drive costs per client down. The microfinance industry's trends in practice and the empirical evidence in academic research on the sector together suggest that the future of microfinance will involve continued quests for scale, scope, and consolidation.

The first and perhaps most obvious indication of the inevitable consolidation wave in microfinance comes from mainstream commercial banking. Fueled by technological and regulatory changes, U.S. banks, for example, have been consolidating—remarkably steadily—for more than three decades. In 1984 there were 14,400 commercial banks chartered in the United States; by the middle of 2018 that number had shrunk by 67 percent, to fewer than 4,750.[1] In the 1990s there were on the order of 500 bank mergers annually. There is little indication that the microfinance sector should be immune to economic and technical pressures driving consolidation in mainstream financial services. As explored below, the economies of scale and scope, coupled with incentives for profitability and sustainability, are too compelling.

The discussion here begins with industrywide descriptive statistics in order to illustrate the broad patterns of scale and scope. It then moves to a nontechnical overview of some of the central findings in the academic literature that uses more complex statistical modeling to account for mitigating factors that could affect the nature of potential economies of scale and scope. The final sections turn to consolidation trends in several of the more competitive and increasingly saturated microfinance markets, such as Peru and India.

Many Serving Few, Few Serving Many

It may border on tautological to say that deepening financial access for the poor means reaching more poor clients; but most microfinance institutions (MFIs) are small, and small MFIs simply do not reach many clients. At all. Reliable, globally comprehensive data on the size of MFIs is dated. But as table 4-1 shows, 41 percent of MFIs self-reporting to the MIX Market by 2015 (the most recent year with comfortably high numbers of reporting institutions) had fewer than 10,000 borrowers.[2] In total, those two-fifths of all MFIs served only a minuscule 1.3 percent of borrowers. Another 41 percent of MFIs had 10,000–100,000 borrowers. Together, those more than four-fifths of MFIs across the MIX Market globe—with all their staff, CEOs, infrastructure, computers, donors and investors, logos and letterhead—served few clients, a

TABLE 4-1. Measures of Outreach and Efficiency, by MFI Scale

| | MFI Scale (number of active borrowers) | | | |
	Small (less than 10,000)	Medium (10,000 to 100,000)	Large (100,000 to 1 million)	Very large (more than 1 million)
Percent of total number of MFIs	41	41	16	2
Percent of all borrowers	1.3	12.0	38.2	48.6
Percent of all savers	2.6	20.5	48.1	28.8
Median real interest rate + fees[a] (percent annual)	22.2	20.6	17.8	13.0
Median profit margin (percent of revenues)	8.8	9.4	17.1	22.8

Source: Modified from Todd A. Watkins, Introduction to Microfinance (Singapore: World Scientific, 2018). Data are from Microfinance Information Exchange (themix.org) for December 2015.

a. Yield on gross portfolio, using real rates, adjusted for inflation.

13.3 percent share. That entire market sliver equals what essentially amounts to some single year's growth of the largest MFIs.

By contrast, almost 87 percent of microfinance clients were banking with just a few hundred MFIs, those with hundreds of thousands or millions of clients. Worldwide by 2015, 368 MFIs reported serving at least 100,000 or more depositors and savers.[3] Of those, only two dozen MFIs—mostly in South Asia—each served more than a million borrowers. As table 4-1 shows, nearly half of all borrowers did business with those two dozen million-plus-club MFIs; 18 of those 24 were for-profit. Nearly three-quarters of all other microcredit borrowers were with MFIs above 100,000 clients. A similar pattern emerges for savings. About two dozen MFIs had more than a million depositors. The global leader in microsavings, Bank BRI in Indonesia, alone claimed 50 million customers, mostly poor savers, in 2017.[4]

Economies of Scale Are Strong

Among the largest MFIs, the advantages of scale and scope are particularly notable. Compare MFI costs per borrower—at a median of US$250—for the half of MFIs in the MIX Market database that have fewer than 10,000 clients with the US$17 for those few very large MFIs with millions of clients (figure 4-1). With lower costs come higher profits. As shown in table 4-1, the median large and very large MFIs operate with profit rates two to more than two and a half times higher than small MFIs. Outside of specialized markets or niches, MFIs that remain small will be unsustainably cost-uncompetitive or require ongoing subsidies.

The pattern of strongly declining costs with scale is also evident in a different and more recent data source, the Symbiotics MFI investment portfolio.[5] In 2017, Symbiotics, among the top global microfinance investment firms, held investments in 240 individual MFIs and banks serving financial-inclusion markets. They reported summary performance statistics segmented into four categories by size of the institutions.

- The smallest, tier 3 institutions are those with total assets below US$10 million, most of them nongovernmental organizations (NGOs), small cooperatives, small nonbank financial institutions (NBFIs), and startups. They average roughly 5,000–13,000 clients, depending on the reporting year.

- Tier 2 institutions have assets in the range of US$10 million–100 million. Most are NBFIs (often regulated) or cooperatives whose client numbers average from around 25,000 to 60,000.

FIGURE 4-1.   MFI Costs Fall with Scale

Median cost per borrower (US$)

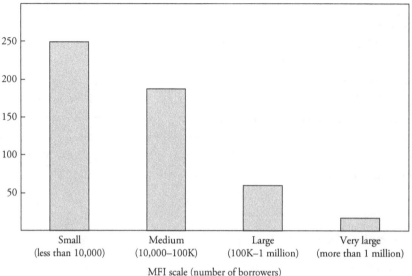

MFI scale (number of borrowers)

Source: Todd A. Watkins, *Introduction to Microfinance* (Singapore: World Scientific, 2018). Data from themix.org, data for FY 2014.

- Tier 1 institutions are large, with assets of US$100 million–1 billion. Symbiotics says, "They are likely to be banks or upper scale NBFIs that have grown and transformed from lower scale operations. In some specific cases, they can also be large credit and savings cooperatives, often in countries with strong regulatory supervision of cooperatives." They average on the order of 150,000–300,000 clients.

- The largest 20 or so firms in the Symbiotics portfolio, tier 1+, each has total assets above US$1 billion and include a mix of commercial banks that have moved downmarket to serve the poor and "pure financial inclusion banks" that have scaled up in large markets. They average above 600,000 clients.

The Symbiotics data are not only more recent than much in MIX Market, but may be more reliable (and audited) than the self-reported information in MIX Market. Moreover, because these are international-investment-attracting institutions, they are among the top-performing MFIs globally. Yet even among these top performers, small MFIs are by far the least cost-efficient.

FIGURE 4-2.   Lending Expense Ratios by Institution Size,
Symbiotics Portfolio, 2017

Expenses as % of gross loan portfolio

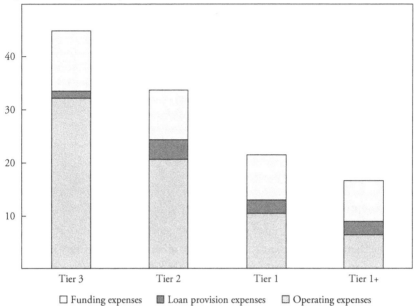

☐ Funding expenses   ■ Loan provision expenses   ☐ Operating expenses

Source: Modified from Symbiotics, "Banking for Impact: A Historical Review of Our Partner Financial Institutions, Their Business Models and Key Developments," White Paper, November 2018, figure 21.

Symbiotics reports three subsets of average costs: operating expenses (including personnel and administrative); loan provision set-asides for future defaults and other loan losses; and funding expenses related to interest payments to debtors and depositors. As illustrated in figure 4-2, overall total expenses in Symbiotics' portfolio institutions in 2017 fell from an average of nearly 45 percent for the smallest institutions, tier 3, to below 17 percent for the largest, tier 1+. The cost ratio decrease is primarily driven by operating efficiencies. Average operating expense ratios fell more than threefold, from above 32 percent of gross loan portfolios in tier 3 to less than 7 percent in tier 1+. Larger institutions also have substantially lower relative costs of obtaining funds; costs fell by a third, from about 11.5 percent in tier 3 to well below 8 percent in tier 1+.

In short, larger institutions benefit from a lower cost of funds, and they can operate substantially more efficiently via likely advantages in maturity, infrastructure, technologies, management and human resources systems, attractiveness to top-tier talent, access to service providers, and presumably learning-curve economies via their broader or longer experience than smaller institutions (though learning efficiencies are understudied in the literature and challenging to disentangle from scale).

For Symbiotics' institutions, just like those in the MIX Market, lower operating costs and larger scale are directly related to higher profits. Tier 1+ had average profit margins of 13.3 percent in 2017, tier 1 averaged 9.3 percent, followed by 7.3 percent for tier 2. For its smallest institutions, tier 3, Symbiotics reports average negative profit margins for five consecutive years through 2017. With investors seeking social impact together with financial return, Symbiotics acknowledges the attractiveness, despite the losses, of investments in tier 3 NGOs and others that particularly target those with the very lowest incomes.

Clients Benefit from Cost Efficiency Too

Institutional efficiency, while good for the MFI, is also good for the clients. There is a clear link between operational efficiency and benefits to borrowers. As table 4-1 shows, the pattern of increasing profit with scale occurs despite the larger institutions charging lower average interest and fees on loans, a benefit for their customers. Small MFIs averaged nearly 29 percent rates of interest and fees, adjusted for inflation, in comparison with 13.5 percent for the very largest. The Symbiotics portfolio demonstrates the same inverse relationship between the prices microfinance clients pay and the scale of the financial institution they do business with. The portfolio yield of interest, fees, and other charges for tier 1+ was only about 16 percent in 2017, 21 percent for tier 1, and more than 32 percent for both tiers 2 and 3.[6] Higher volumes in the large tiers more than make up for lower pricing-above-cost unit margins, driving profit margins the opposite way.

Figure 4-3 shows the relationship more granularly between MFIs' operating efficiency and interest rates and fees charged to microcredit customers. Highly subsidized small NGOs complicate and cloud the basic pattern because they can decouple prices from operating costs and are numerous yet serve few. Hence the figure includes only MFIs in the MIX Market database that show an operating profit. Among those, the most cost-efficient MFIs charge their clients much lower real yield premiums—that is, the inflation-adjusted rate of interest and fees the MFI gets paid for loans above their financial costs of funds. MFIs with higher operating costs tend to charge higher interest rates and fees.

The overall effect of all these advantages of scale for the clients shows up in outcomes. Figure 4-4 shows that the large-scale MFIs in India charge, on average, 6 to 8 percentage points lower rates of interest on microcredit than MFIs that remain

**FIGURE 4-3.   Loan Interest Rates and Fees Charged Rise
with Operating Costs**

Interest rate premium (% above financial expense)

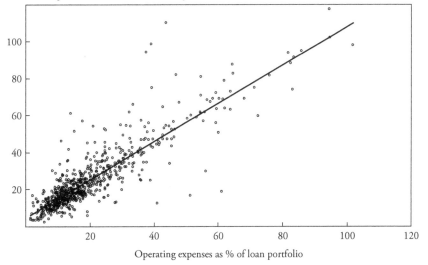

Operating expenses as % of loan portfolio

Source: Todd A. Watkins, *Introduction to Microfinance* (Singapore: World Scientific, 2018). Data from mixmarket.org for profitable MFIs only.

small-scale, except on the smallest microloans (those below 5,000 rupees, roughly US$75). The figure also shows that bigger microloans incur lower rates no matter what size the MFI is.

Although figures 4-3 and 4-4 provide a simplistic picture of the relationship because they do not control for any differences among MFI situations, organizational maturities, competitive market conditions, national environments, and the like, more complex models do show similar qualitative patterns. For instance, Darrell Glaser and coauthors explore the impact of competition and MFI costs on fees paid by clients, while controlling for differences among MFIs in legal structures, region, rural vs. urban settings, and lending methodologies.[7] They find on average that each 1 percent increase in operating expenses as a fraction of loan portfolio raises interest rates and fees for an MFI's customers by about half a percent. In addition, they also find fees for an MFI's direct customers rise as well via an indirect cost-associated route, when competitors' costs rise. Potential social impact is also affected. Higher fees mean fewer clients served: each 1 percent increase in interest rate and fees paid by microloan customers was associated with an estimated average decrease of 0.33 percent in the number of borrowers.

FIGURE 4-4.   Average Loan Interest Rates Fall with MFI Scale,
India, 2010–14

Average loan interest rate (%)

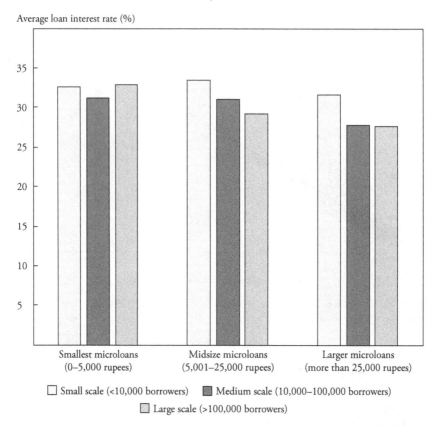

Smallest microloans   Midsize microloans   Larger microloans
(0–5,000 rupees)   (5,001–25,000 rupees)   (more than 25,000 rupees)

☐ Small scale (<10,000 borrowers)   ☐ Medium scale (10,000–100,000 borrowers)
☐ Large scale (>100,000 borrowers)

Source: Todd A. Watkins, *Introduction to Microfinance* (Singapore: World Scientific, 2018). Data from Microfinance Transparency, India Country Data (www. MFTransparency.org); average interest rate is the effective annual percentage rate (APR), including all fees (not inflation-adjusted).

Scale and Mission Drift: Weighing Risks and Benefits for the Poorest Clients

The bigger-loans-get-lower-interest-rate pattern highlights a central concern in the vigorous debate over the risks of mission drift in the quest for returns for investors via market scale and profitability. Despite the cost advantages of scale and maturity, might transformed commercial MFIs and mainstream banks moving down into financial inclusion markets lose sight of serving the poorest? Those at the very bottom of the pyramid are rarely the most profitable customers. Even though the successful scaling of the largest and most-mature commercial institutions has expanded their outreach to tens (likely hundreds) of millions of more customers than the smallest MFIs, have they done that mostly by targeting somewhat higher-income clients who need larger loans and keep larger deposit accounts, leaving the poorest without access? On the other hand, the counterargument often put forward is that larger and mature institutions could use their resources and infrastructure, and lower costs from economies of scale and learning efficiencies, to better serve the poorest clients, perhaps even cross-subsidizing.[8]

Critics of commercialization often point to data on average loan size. The average size of clients' loans is one of the main indicators of potential mission drift—indeed too often the only one—used in much of the literature by both academics and practitioners. As discussed in more detail below, there are many reasons average loan sizes might rise over time. Yet the literature unfortunately has largely ignored most, rather focusing on one: poorer clients on average take out smaller loans; those with less income have lower ability to pay back larger loans. In the MIX Market data, the average loan from for-profit MFIs in 2014 (US$855) was nearly 60 percent higher than from nonprofit MFIs (US$537), a gap often used as direct evidence that for-profits target higher-income clients. Indeed, the family of for-profit MFIs in the Pro-Credit Group in 2009, seeking better returns for investors and concerned about the increasing competitive pressure to focus on consumer lending—and aggressive microlending sales practices—that ProCredit considered not only potentially harmful to poor clients but also less likely to drive economic development than business lending, deliberately shifted toward larger loans for relatively higher-income small-business clients, withdrawing from the lowest-income markets.[9]

Because larger loans are more cost-efficient to manage, effective interest rates tend to average a bit lower on larger loans. Figure 4-4 shows this for loans in India, and a similar trend occurs in Kenya. Figure 4-5 compares the average percentage rate (including fees) on various loan products from 26 MFIs in Kenya. Rates vary widely, from 10 percent to 70 percent, for many reasons, such as loan term and purpose. But the smallest loans are on average about one-third again costlier than the largest. The pattern of rates falling with loan size is true both in nonprofit and for-profit MFIs. This means that the relatively better-off clients with the larger loans tend to face lower microcredit interest rates than the poorest clients. Yet does larger loan size mean that the poor are being abandoned by MFIs? Far from it. Indeed, if anything, the empirical evidence points the other way.

Larger average loan size in and of itself is not necessarily a sign of mission drift. As Claudio Gonzalez-Vega and his colleagues point out, loan sizes could rise for at least five different reasons, only the first of which is mission drift away from the poorest.[10] Other possible explanations have to do with the maturity of the MFIs and the

FIGURE 4-5.   Annual Percentage Rate (APR) by Loan Size, Kenyan MFIs

Annual percentage rate (including fees)

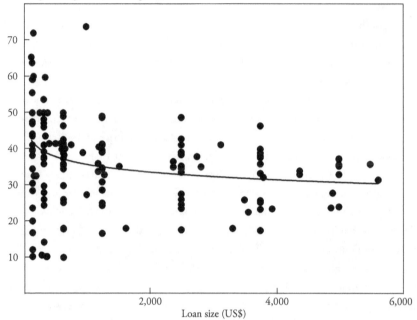

Source:* Todd A. Watkins, *Introduction to Microfinance* (Singapore: World Scientific, 2018). Data from Microfinance Transparency, Kenya Country Data (www. MFTransparency.org).

learning effects that come with accumulated experience. Because it is generally the more experienced MFIs with demonstrable track records of success that can attract the resources to commercialize and scale, and that can benefit from learning-curve efficiencies over time, analyses that point to loan size alone as prima facie evidence of mission drift tend to conflate explanations and miss the potential advantages of maturity, learning, and scale for the poorest clients. Unfortunately, learning-curve effects in particular are a somewhat neglected issue in the literature. Two notable exceptions are studies that both find older institutions more efficient, after controlling for scale, and that larger institutions are more efficient after controlling for age.[11]

One (second) possible reason well-established MFIs may drift statistically—but not by mission—toward larger average loans is the widespread use of progressive lending. Clients with good track records qualify for progressively larger loans. A closely related third explanation without mission drift has to do with the evolving structure of an MFI's customer pool even as the MFI continues to serve the poorest. Young MFIs have mostly new clients. For established MFIs, if customers remain loyal, the

FIGURE 4-6.   Mission Drift

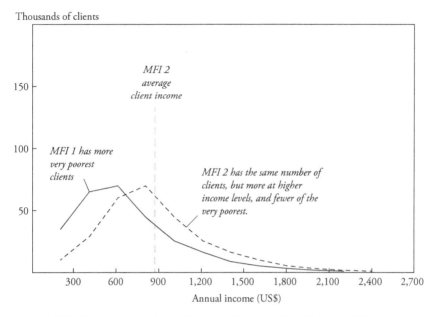

Source: Todd A. Watkins, *Introduction to Microfinance* (Singapore: World Scientific, 2018).

fraction of clients with experience and who qualify for larger and longer-term loans could grow. Indeed, this is exactly the statistical outcome expected if microfinance works to improve livelihoods. It is not mission drift; it is mission in progress.

A fourth possibility related to learning-curve efficiencies is reduction in information asymmetries: with experience, an MFI gains better information on its clients and—particularly with greater scale—a better handle on likely risks spread across its target customer base more generally. To the extent that learning and scale enable better risk management, more experienced or larger MFIs may be more willing to offer bigger first loans or accelerate progressive growth for subsequent loans even among the poorest clients.

Figures 4-6 and 4-7 differentiate pure mission drift in theory from the other explanations, and in particular highlight the potential advantage of scale and learning economics for outreach to the poorest clients. Figure 4-6 shows pure mission drift. Hypothetical MFI 1 serves large numbers of very poor clients, those with incomes below US$2 a day. For MFI 2, the income distribution of its customers has shifted higher, leaving many fewer of the poorest clients. Figure 4-7 similarly compares two MFIs, but relative to MFI 1, MFI 3 not only has a higher average income clientele but also has twice as many of the poorest clients below US$2 a day. MFI 3 grows its

FIGURE 4-7.   Not Necessarily Mission Drift

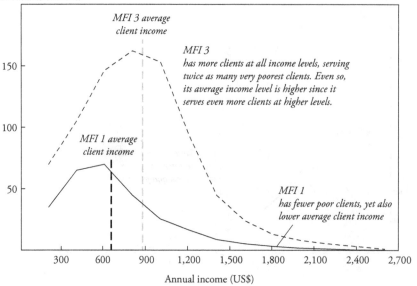

Thousands of clients

Source: Todd A. Watkins, *Introduction to Microfinance* (Singapore: World Scientific, 2018).

client base across the whole range of income. It could be adding many new clients with very low incomes, existing poor clients could be progressing to higher levels, and perhaps new better-off clients are joining the mix as well, all helping the MFI gain economies of scale and scope.

Which alternative dominates in practice? The evidence is mixed; both clearly happen. Substantial mission drift is very real for some MFIs. ProCredit was a longtime champion of the power of commercial investment to expand financial access for the poor, yet essentially abandoned all microloans and instead focused on lending to not-so-small and medium-sized businesses where ProCredit saw greater demand, greater potential for economic impact, and better potential returns for investors.

By contrast, evidence points the other way at Bolivia's Banco Sol, today one of the largest MFIs in Latin America. Average loan balances increased from about US$125 when the MFI started as a small nonprofit NGO in 1987, to double that by 1992 when Banco Sol became a commercial bank, and doubled again to about US$500 by 1995. Yet Claudio Gonzalez-Vega and colleagues concluded that the increase was "consistent with sustained attention to the same market niche," not mission drift away from the poorest clients.[12]

FIGURE 4-8. Median Loan Size at Banco Sol, by Loan Cycle, 1987–95

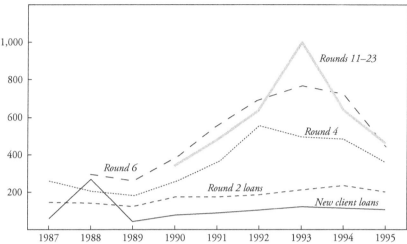

Average loan size (US$)

Source: Todd A. Watkins, *Introduction to Microfinance* (Singapore: World Scientific, 2018). Data from Claudio Gonzalez-Vega and others, "BancoSol: The Challenge of Growth for Microfinance Organizations," Economics and Sociology Occasional Paper 2332 (Ohio State University, Rural Finance Program, Department of Agricultural Economics, 1996).

Most of the increase was due to better information about clients—that is, learning effects, and existing clients advancing through progressive lending to increasingly larger loans. As figure 4-8 shows, the median size of loans to new clients and to second-round borrowers, though slightly higher by 1995 than in 1987, was fairly stable and remained small. Half of new borrowers in 1995 took loans below US$107, about 12 percent of per capita income in Bolivia at the time. Loans for continuing clients became progressively larger in later cycles. Second-round loans averaged 70 percent larger than loans to new clients; third-round loans 58 percent larger than second-round, and so on, with growth slowing through about the sixth round, then leveling off. (Some clients by 1995 were on their twentieth loan cycle or more.) Some upward drift in later-cycle loan size happened around 1992–93, as the NGO transformed into a commercial bank, but then dropped again as management adjusted lending policies.

A more general noteworthy trend is the average loan size over time in the industry overall. As Richard Rosenberg and colleagues at the Consultative Group to Assist the Poor (CGAP) found, at nonprofit MFIs around the world, average loan size measured as a fraction of per capita income fell slightly to 23 percent in 2011, from 25 percent in 2004—in other words, fairly steady targeting of the poor with no mission drift evident.[13] For-profit loan sizes have remained higher than for nonprofits. Yet in for-profit MFIs the change over time has been far larger, dropping from an average of 55 percent of per capita income in 2004 to only 30 percent in 2011, significantly closing the gap with nonprofits. The for-profit MFI sector expanded rapidly during that period, but on the whole grew by moving downward on average, consistent with learning economies and industry scale effects, not upward as mission drift would imply.

Finally, declining MFI loan discipline, pushing loans bigger than clients can handle, is an unfortunate fifth possibility for loan sizes rising as MFIs pursue scale, even in the absence of mission drift. Evidence that such discipline was deteriorating led Banco Sol to rein back loan sizes after 1993 (figure 4-8). More broadly, systematic lending discipline risk has fueled occasional microfinance market crashes in some countries, including short-term crises in India, Bosnia and Herzegovina, Nicaragua, and several other nations.[14] In such cases the short-term incentive structures for lending staff may not align with the interests of poor clients. However, long-term incentives for sustainably managing risk at scale do.

Scale Expands Scope Too, Broadening Clients' Access to Services

Ongoing debate and academic investigation about the impact of microfinance has for the most part centered on microcredit. Well reviewed elsewhere, the findings in that literature suggest more limited impact of microcredit on the incomes or consumption patterns of the poor than proponents of the industry had hoped—indeed perhaps not any, statistically. The emphasis on increasing the (formal) debt of the poor while collecting paid interest and fees from them also remains controversial. Although not much research has been done exploring the benefits of alternatives to debt, many believe the poor might benefit more from expanded access to other financial services like microsavings and microinsurance, as well as nonfinancial services such as business training and health care. Larger MFIs are more likely to offer much wider suites of services, broadening access for poor clients who do business with them rather than with smaller MFIs.

The regulatory ability to take deposits is one of the most fundamental differences between those MFIs at the small end—typically NGOs, co-operatives, and small NBFIs—and those at the large end, such as big banks that have come downmarket or MFIs that have scaled up and transformed into banks. The median small MFI in the MIX Market database had zero depositors in 2015. Among MFIs with more than 100,000 borrowers, the median number of depositors was more than 156,000.

FIGURE 4-9. Ratios Comparing Credit and Savings Levels,
Symbiotics Portfolio, 2017

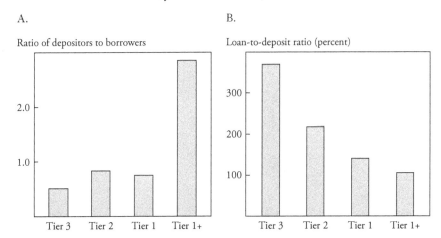

A.

Ratio of depositors to borrowers

B.

Loan-to-deposit ratio (percent)

Source: Data modified from Symbiotics, "Banking for Impact: A Historical Review of Our Partner Financial Institutions, Their Business Models and Key Developments," White Paper, November 2018, figures 11 and 15.

Symbiotics' portfolio institutions show similar scope advantages in deposit-taking in the larger tiers. Indeed, the very largest firms have far more deposit customers than loan clients. In 2017, Symbiotics' tier 1+ institutions, the large banks and transformed MFIs, had slightly shy of three times more depositors than borrowers, while the small tier 3 had only about half as many depositors as borrowers (figure 4-9A). The ratio was half-again higher, about three to four, both in the large tier 1 and also in mid-sized tier 2, with its co-operatives, which tend to have high ratios of savers. This increase in deposits with scale also has advantages for reducing the overall risks the institutions carry in financing their loan portfolios. The ratio of outstanding loans-to-deposits fell from about 3.7:1 for tier 3 to nearly 1:1 for tier 1+ (figure 4-9B). It is evident that the regulatory and infrastructure advantages of larger institutions facilitate deposit-taking.

The scope advantage also extends to a wider portfolio of services. Figure 4-10A shows the percentage of the Symbiotics portfolio institutions offering their clients non-credit financial products, including not only savings but also insurance and payments services. The increasing product-scope diversity with scale is clear. All tier 1+ firms offer savings and payments services, whereas only 60 percent or fewer tier 2 and 3 firms do. Fewer than half of tier 3 institutions offer insurance of any sort, compared to roughly three-quarters across the larger three tiers. Because Symbiotics also reports the availability of nonfinancial services offered to clients, such as training and

FIGURE 4-10.   Symbiotics' Institutions Offering Noncredit Services, 2017

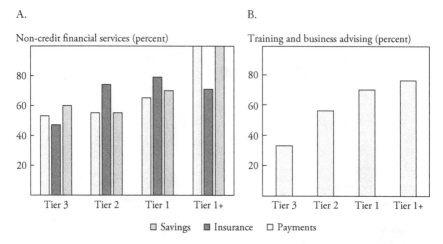

A.

Non-credit financial services (percent)

B.

Training and business advising (percent)

☐ Savings   ■ Insurance   ☐ Payments

Source: Data are modified from Symbiotics, "Banking for Impact: A Historical Review of Our Partner Financial Institutions, Their Business Models and Key Developments," White Paper, November 2018, figures 13 and 14.

business advising, an even broader take on the scope-of-service advantages of scale is apparent (figure 4-10B). Only one-third of the small tier 3 institutions offered nonfinancial training or business advisory services, in comparison with 70 percent or more of the largest, in tiers 1 and 1+.

Academic Literature: Complex Modeling, Similar Qualitative Takeaways

While the average trends illustrate the potential relationship between efficiencies and scale, the academic literature digs much deeper than averages, controlling statistically for myriad factors that might affect scale-and-scope economies, such as institutional maturity, country or regional differences in things like population density and regulatory regimes, strategic and institutional choices (for example, profit vs. nonprofit, emphasis on the poorest, focus on women's empowerment, tolerance for portfolio risk, NGO vs. co-operative). Disentangling the complex interactions among factors like these is important work in progress in the literature because of the very wide contextual variations, as table 4-2 shows for just one variable. Note how vastly different the scales of the very largest MFIs in different regions can be. The largest in South Asia in particular have roughly 20 times as many borrowers as the very largest in

TABLE 4-2.   Largest MFIs in Each Region by Number of Borrowers, 2015

Region	MFI	Country	Number of borrowers
East Asia and Pacific	BRI	Indonesia	7,850,000
	ASA Philippines	Philippines	1,073,580
	Card NGO	Philippines	816,619
Europe and Central Asia	UniBank	Azerbaijan	447,918
	Khan Bank	Mongolia	358,914
	CREDO	Georgia	196,947
Latin America and Caribbean	Compartamos Banco	Mexico	2,861,721
	CrediAmigo	Brazil	2,030,821
	AgroAmigo	Brazil	1,097,759
Middle East and North Africa	Al Amana	Morocco	328,361
	ABA	Egypt	283,979
	Enda	Tunisia	270,563
Sub-Saharan Africa	Capitec Bank	South Africa	3,684,000
	African Bank	South Africa	1,500,000
	LAPO	Nigeria	800,6111
South Asia	Grameen Bank	Bangladesh	8,806,779
	Bandhan	India	6,717,331
	ASA	Bangladesh	5,362,966
	BFIL (formerly SKS)	India	5,325,244
	BRAC	Bangladesh	4,923,936

Source: Todd A. Watkins, *Introduction to Microfinance* (Singapore: World Scientific, 2018). Data are from Microfinance Information Exchange (www.mixmarket.org); Bank Rakyat Indonesia, Annual Report 2015; Capitec Annual Report 2016; Grameen Bank Monthly Report, December 31, 2015.

Notes: Clients as of 2015, except Capitec, February 2016; UniBank and LAPO, December 2014; and African Bank Ltd. as reorganized, April 2016. For consistency, the table does not include the Vietnam Bank for Social Policies or the Postal Savings Bank of China, large but essentially government-run subsidized banks. In late 2018, BFIL was in the process of being acquired by IndusInd Bank.

Europe and Central Asia. Potential markets in the latter are simply relatively much smaller.

For instance, Amy Eremionkhale and I use stochastic frontier analysis to investigate the degree to which MFIs in six regions approach the economies of scale levels seen in the most cost-efficient institutions.[15] After controlling for country, region, and institutional choice variables, we find that more than three in five MFIs in all six regions have not yet fully achieved available economies of scale. Roughly two-thirds of the world's MFIs are too small, in the sense that their unit costs of providing the loan

TABLE 4-3.   Estimated Percentage of MFIs Operating below
Minimum Cost-Efficient Scale

Region	2005–09	2010–15
Sub-Saharan Africa	84.5	77.1
East Asia and the Pacific	92.9	74.4
Eastern Europe and Central Asia	73.2	62.7
Latin America and the Caribbean	73.6	61.1
Middle East and North Africa	83.2	61.2
South Asia	80.6	70.8

Source: Amy Eremionkhale and Todd A. Watkins, "The Effect of the Global Financial Crisis on the Cost Structure and Double Bottom Line Goal of Microfinance Institutions," Working Paper (Lehigh University, Martindale Center, 2017).

and social outreach services they offer would fall (usually substantially) if they grew. We estimated that MFIs' unit costs are on average nearly 300 percent higher than they would be if all MFIs were large enough to be as cost-efficient as those on the frontier. The good news is that through a combination of MFI growth and consolidation the proportion that have achieved efficient scale has improved over time in every region (table 4-3). This suggests some progress toward broader achievement of the cost benefits of scale, but also that there remains considerable room for consolidations, mergers, and acquisitions across the global microfinance industry essentially everywhere.

One of the major complicating factors explored in the academic literature is the double-bottom-line interaction and tension (or not) between MFIs' financial performance and social impact missions. Related to the question of financial incentives for mission drift away from serving the poorest, we also find that MFIs on the cost-efficient frontier can achieve those cost efficiencies while providing loans on average as small as less than 1/11 of the gross national income per capita. This would represent loans on the order of US$50 in Afghanistan, US$100 in Bangladesh, or US$150 in Ukraine. Serving very poor clients with loans this small can be cost-efficient for firms on the cost frontier, but the majority of firms are not close to there. Average loans are substantially larger, which suggests there is potential for greater depth of social impact if efficiencies improve.

These findings on scale economies in terms of the financial performance of microfinance institutions are quite consistent with a growing assortment of economic literature using different methodologies. In the most comprehensive review yet available of the related literature, Niels Hermes and Marek Hudon identify 169 academic articles published through August 2017 on topics related to MFI efficiency. Fully two-thirds of these were published between 2013 and 2017, when serious academic interest significantly ramped up. Of those 169, 48 articles address the relationship of efficiency to MFI-specific characteristics such as scale, age, and type of institution. Hermes and Hudon conclude that among those studies that specifically explore scale (usually measured either as numbers of clients, total assets, or total loan portfolios), scale is nearly uniformly found to help efficiency or overall financial performance.[16]

One of the earliest (2007) multivariate modeling studies, by Adrian Gonzales using data from 1999 to 2006, found economies of scale only for very small MFIs.[17] Operating cost efficiencies improved substantially with size, but only up through 2,000 clients before leveling out. However, most of the literature since, across various methodologies, has found stronger scale effects. For example, Valentina Hartarska, Xuan Shen, and Roy Mersland suggest that, after controlling for other differences (including institutional age), depending on the model, costs would fall 11–24 percent for each doubling of scale, measured by numbers of clients or by total portfolios.[18] Similarly, Md Aslam Mia and V. G. R. Chandran estimate that the mean Bangladeshi MFI is 40 percent below the most efficient, after controlling for regional and other differences.[19] This pattern is consistent whether the underlying data are broadly global[20] or country-specific (for example, in Peru, India, Bangladesh, or Pakistan).[21] Interestingly, Hartarska and colleagues conclude that the only category of MFIs that on average have managed to achieve the full benefits of scale are "profitability-focused deposit-mobilizing MFIs."[22]

In related work, Hartarska and other colleagues have also found scope economies when MFIs provide both microsavings and microcredit.[23] They estimate that MFIs could save from 10 percent to more than 60 percent, depending on region (and on how efficiency is measured), by offering both loans and deposits jointly rather than operating as microcredit-only institutions. Evidence of economies of scope also comes from Steven Caudill and coauthors who, after controlling for other variables including scale and age of the institution, show better cost efficiencies among deposit-taking MFIs and those that are less reliant on subsidies.[24] Similarly in the line of inquiry regarding scope of services, at least two studies have explored factors that influence how MFIs perform well on environmental issues like providing green loans, doing environmental risk assessment, and offering other environmental nonfinancial services.[25] Scale helps again: both studies find larger MFIs do better.

Findings on the influence of scale on social impact are more mixed and often troublingly contradictory. Hermes and Hudon highlight Patrick Reichert's[26] meta-analysis synthesis of 623 econometric models in the literature addressing the trade-off or complementarity of MFIs' double bottom lines of financial performance and social impact. Overall, the relationship appears to be substantially dependent on how performance is measured. Trade-offs are likely to turn up when cost performance measures are the focus, but not when models use profit or portfolio risk. Moreover, as noted earlier, the metric usually used to proxy for social impact, average loan size, has serious limitations in conflating potential explanations. So too, most studies have focused on microcredit, while emerging evidence hints that savings services might be substantially more important for social impact. The state of this social impact literature is certainly unsatisfactory. Much work remains in exploring whether there is double-bottom-line complementarity or trade-off in scale with scope of services.

Consolidation Under Way in Competitive Markets

While smaller and relatively inefficient institutions appear to be the norm, and can succeed in markets that are growing and relatively underserved, the strong and consistent evidence suggests that industry consolidation via mergers and acquisitions seems inevitable wherever markets become more competitive. Indeed, consolidation is well under way in several of the world's most competitive microfinance markets. Although a complete accounting of all consolidation activity globally so far is well beyond the scope of this chapter, the most competitive markets include Peru and India. Both in recent years have consistently ranked among the top handful of widely acknowledged most well developed microfinance markets, for example in the Economist Intelligence Unit's annual *Global Microscope* of financial inclusion.[27]

Figure 4-11 shows a timeline of consolidation activity in Peru since 2005. The activity includes major international banks coming downmarket by acquiring and merging multiple MFIs into microfinance subsidiaries: for example, BBVA combining multiple MFIs in creating Financiera Confianca; CreditCorp similarly using its BCP subsidiary to merge serval MFIs into MiBanco; and the Bank of Nova Scotia's subsidiary ScotiaBank acquiring an MFI to form Crediscotia Financiera. Other MFIs have consolidated as they seek scale, new markets, operating efficiencies, and healthier balance sheets: for example, Mexico's Compartamos created a Peruvian subsidiary; CMAC Arequipa absorbed the assets of the failing CRAC Senor de Luren; and CRAC Chavin merged with Edpyme Raíz to form CRAC Raíz.

FIGURE 4-11. Microfinance Mergers and Acquisitions in Peru, 2005–17

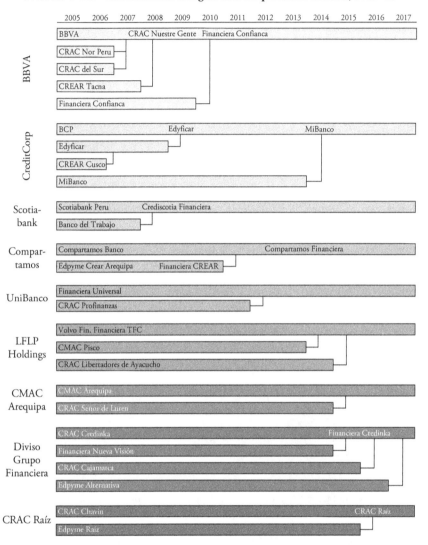

Source: Author's graphic; list updated from Hilbert Chen, "Peruvian Microfinance: Mergers and Acquisitions and Industry Outlook," *Perspectives on Business and Economics* 35 (2017) and Banco Central de Reserva del Perú, Reporte de Estabilidad Financiera May (May 2018).

TABLE 4-4.   Mergers and Acquisitions in Indian Microfinance, 2007–19

Year	Acquirer	Target	Notes
2007	Sonata Finance	Jeevika Livelihood Support Organization	Acquired portfolio of nonprofit MFI
2008	Hand in Hand (NGO)	Belstar NBFC	Became Belstar Investment and Finance
2012	IntelleCash Microfinance	Arohan Financial Services	Acquired retail lending operations in 2012; merged merchant cash operations in 2017; Arohan in 2018 announced considering IPO
2015	Manappuram Finance	Asirvad Microfinance	Gold-loan moneylender diversifies
2016	Muthoot Finance	Belstar Investment and Finance	
2016	IDFC Bank	Grama Vidyal Microfinance	First bank in India to take over an MFI
2016	Kotak Mahindra Bank	BSS Microfinance	Another large bank entering microfinance segment
2017	IIFL Finance	Samasta Microfinance Ltd.	
2017	Centrum Capital	FirstRand Bank's microfinance business	Became Centrum Microcredit
2018	Svatantra Microfinance	Micro Housing Finance Corporation (MHFC)	Diversifying into microhousing
In Progress (2019)			
2019	IndusInd Bank	Bharat Financial Inclusion (BFIL, formerly SKS)	In final stages early 2019
2019?	Federal Bank or other offers	Madura Microfinance	Talks under way; multiple bidders

Source: Author's compilation from press releases.

Merger-and-acquisition momentum grew more recently in India, ramping up in earnest in 2016 (table 4-4). But now, similar active consolidation is ongoing in the wake of substantial changes in regulation driven by the 2010 sectorwide crisis originating in Andhra Pradesh. The new regulations create incentives for MFIs to scale up and also to apply for licenses to transform into banks. MFIs seeking scale and scope by merging with other MFIs include the earliest microfinance consolidation in India among for-profit firms, IntelleCash Microfinance and Arohan Financial Services. IntelleCash in 2012 acquired a majority stake and the retail lending operations of Arohan. Then in 2017 the two organizations merged their lending operations and merchant services into Arohan; Arohan now offers IntelleCash merchant services as a branded business line. Leveraging the potential attractiveness to investors of its increased scale and breadth of services, in 2018 Arohan announced it was considering raising substantial capital in an initial public offering (IPO).

Muthoot Finance took a very similar path, acquiring Belstar Investment and Finance as a subsidiary in 2016. Then it later announced it was considering an IPO, spinning out of its parent holding company. Belstar itself was the result of an acquisition in 2008, when Belstar NBFC was acquired by the NGO Hand in Hand, combining Hand in Hand's self-help-group lending with Belstar's joint liability lending and other services.

Existing large banks (such as IDFC Bank and Kotak Mahindra Bank) are also acquiring MFIs as they move downmarket, seeking to diversify and improve competitiveness in the evolving regulatory landscape by taking advantage of expanding microfinance markets. By far the biggest acquisition along these lines is IndusInd Bank's move to merge with Bharat Financial Inclusion (BFIL, formerly SKS Microfinance), the leading MFI in India. Initiated in 2017, the deal has been approved by regulators and shareholders and should be fully completed in 2019. In 2010, SKS was the very first Indian MFI to go public in an IPO, so its merger with a large bank is a milestone in the consolidation trend. With many hundreds of small MFIs, nonbank financial institutions, and banks in India, and with the new regulatory regime, the landscape is increasingly competitive. Add in the compelling economic incentives outlined here, that trend will surely accelerate.

Conclusions

With many hundreds of millions of poor worldwide still unbanked, considerable opportunities remain for organic growth among MFIs. New and emerging small and midsized MFIs can yet take advantage of serving greenfield market niches, just as the early innovators and later imitating legions of MFIs have done since modern microfinance began in the 1970s.

Nevertheless, the trends and economic forces discussed here, the inexorable advantages of scale and scope for both MFIs and their clients—in costs, services, marketing, infrastructure, technology, governance, regulatory compliance, partnerships, innovation, and most important, sustainability and profit—are steering the future of microfinance. Boundaries between mainstream commercial banking and microfinance, already blurry, continue to erode. And where mainstream banking treads in search of scale and scope, microfinance is sure to follow. Consolidation within and between both sectors continues apace. Consolidation is most notably accelerating in the most competitive and saturated microfinance markets like Peru and India, but is very likely inevitable everywhere. The world has too many small MFIs costing too much to do too little. The world's poor—banked and yet-unbanked alike—will be better served by the fewer, bigger, broader ones the future will bring.

Notes

1. Federal Reserve Economic Data, Economic Research Division, Federal Reserve Bank of St. Louis (www.fred.stlouisfed.org).

2. The following scale, client advantages, and mission drift discussions draw extensively on, expand, and update Todd A. Watkins, *Introduction to Microfinance* (Singapore: World Scientific, 2018), specifically chap. 8, "The Evolution of Commercial Microfinance."

3. Data are from themix.org.

4. BRI, *Annual Report 2017* (http://ir-bri.com/misc/AR/AR-BRI-2017-English-new.pdf).

5. Symbiotics, "Banking for Impact: A Historical Review of Our Partner Financial Institutions, Their Business Models and Key Developments," White Paper, November 2018.

6. Ibid., figure 20.

7. Darrell Glaser and others, "Product Differentiation and Consumer Surplus in the Microfinance Industry," *BE Journal of Economic Analysis and Policy* 13, no. 2 (2013): 991–1022.

8. For example, see Beatriz Armendáriz and Ariane Szafarz, "On Mission Drift in Microfinance Institutions," in *The Handbook of Microfinance*, ed. B. Armendáriz and M. Labie (Singapore: World Scientific, 2011).

9. See ProCredit Holding Annual Reports at www.ProCredit-Holding.com. Also see ProCredit Bank, "Where We've Come From: History of the ProCredit Group" (www.procreditbank.de/en/procredit-bank/where-we-ve-come-from-history-of-the-procredit-group.html).

10. Claudio Gonzalez-Vega and others, "BancoSol: The Challenge of Growth for Microfinance Organizations," Economics and Sociology Occasional Paper 2332 (Ohio State University, Rural Finance Program, Department of Agricultural Economics, 1996).

11. See Valentina Hartarska, Xuan Shen, and Roy Mersland, "Scale Economies and Input Price Elasticities in Microfinance Institutions," *Journal of Banking and Finance* 37, no. 1 (2013): 118–31; and Steven B. Caudill, Daniel M. Gropper, and Valentina Hartarska, "Which Microfinance Institutions Are Becoming More Cost Effective with Time? Evidence from a Mixture Model," *Journal of Money, Credit and Banking* 41, no. 4 (2009): 651–72.

12. Gonzalez-Vega and others, "BancoSol," p. 21.

13. Richard Rosenberg and others, "Microcredit Interest Rates and Their Determinants: 2004–2011," Access to Finance Forum Reports by CGAP and Its Partners 7 (Washington: Consultative Group to Assist the Poor, 2013).

14. Greg Chen, Stephen Rasmussen, and Xavier Reille, "Growth and Vulnerabilities in Microfinance," Focus Note 61 (Washington: Consultative Group to Assist the Poor, 2010).

15. Amy Eremionkhale and Todd A. Watkins, "The Effect of the Global Financial Crisis on the Cost Structure and Double Bottom Line Goal of Microfinance Institutions," Working Paper (Lehigh University, Martindale Center, 2017).

16. Niels Hermes and Marek Hudon, "Determinants of the Performance of Microfinance Institutions: A Systematic Review," *Journal of Economic Surveys* 32, no. 5 (2018): 1483–513.

17. Adrian Gonzales, "Efficiency Drivers of Microfinance Institutions (MFIs): The Case of Operating Costs," *MicroBanking Bulletin* 15 (Autumn 2007): 37–42.

18. Hartarska, Shen, and Mersland, "Scale Economies."

19. Md Aslam Mia and V. G. R. Chandran, "Measuring Financial and Social Outreach Productivity of Microfinance Institutions in Bangladesh," *Social Indicators Research* 127, no. 2 (2016): 505–27.

20. Robert Cull, Asli Demirgüç-Kunt, and Jonathan Morduch, "Financial Performance and Outreach: A Global Analysis of Leading Microbanks," *Economic Journal* 117, no. 517 (2017): F107–F133; Caudill, Gropper, and Hartarska, "Which Microfinance Institutions Are Becoming More Cost Effective?"; Hartarska, Shen, and Mersland, "Scale Economies"; Thomas Bolli and Anh Vo Thi, "Regional Differences in the Production Processes of Financial and Social Outputs of Microfinance Institutions," *Economics of Transition* 22, no. 3 (2014): 461–95.

21. See, respectively, Jorge R. Gregoire, and Oswaldo Ramirez Tuya, "Cost Efficiency of Microfinance Institutions in Peru: A Stochastic Frontier Approach," *Latin American Business Review* 7, no. 2 (2006): 41–70; Abdul Rashid and Koire Twaha, "Exploring the Determinants of the Productivity of Indian Microfinance Institutions," *Theoretical and Applied Economics* 20, no. 12 (2013): 83–96; Nisha Bharti and Asmita Chitnis, "Size and Efficiency of MFIs: A Data Envelopment Analysis of Indian MFIs," *Enterprise Development and Microfinance* 27, no. 4 (2016): 255–72; Mia and Chandran, "Measuring Financial and Social Outreach Productivity of Microfinance Institutions in Bangladesh"; Rahell Gohar and Amna Batool, "Effect of Corporate Governance on Performance of Microfinance Institutions: A Case from Pakistan," *Emerging Markets Finance and Trade* 51, no. sup6 (2015): S94–S106.

22. Hartarska, Shen, and Mersland, "Scale Economies."

23. Valentina Hartarska and others, "Economies of Scope for Microfinance: Differences across Output Measures," *Pacific Economic Review* 15, no. 4 (2010): 464–81; Valentina Hartarska, Christopher F. Parmeter, and Denis Nadolnyak, "Economies of Scope of Lending and Mobilizing Deposits in Microfinance Institutions: A Semiparametric Analysis," *American Journal of Agricultural Economics* 93, no. 2 (2011): 389–98; Michael S. Delgado and others, "Should All Microfinance Institutions Mobilize Microsavings? Evidence from Economies of Scope," *Empirical Economics* 48, no. 1 (2015): 193–225.

24. Caudill, Gropper, and Hartarska, "Which Microfinance Institutions Are Becoming More Cost Effective?"

25. Marion Allet and Marek Hudon, "Green Microfinance: Characteristics of Microfinance Institutions Involved in Environmental Management," *Journal of Business Ethics* 126, no. 3 (2015): 395–414; Davide Forcella and Marek Hudon, "Green Microfinance in Europe," *Journal of Business Ethics* 135, no. 3 (2016): 445–59.

26. Patrick Reichert, "A Meta-analysis Examining the Nature of Trade-offs in Microfinance," *Oxford Development Studies* (2018): 1–23.

27. Economist Intelligence Unit (EIU), *Global Microscope 2018: The Enabling Environment for Financial Inclusion* (New York: EIU, 2018).

FIVE

The Future of Microfinance as Knowledge Management

The Experience of the BBVA Microfinance Foundation

CLAUDIO GONZALEZ-VEGA

In his book *The Great Escape*, Angus Deaton, 2015 Nobel laureate in economic sciences, claimed that, over the past three centuries, the amazing progress of mankind has been due to a great extent to the invention and diffusion of *useful knowledge.*[1] Indeed, swift progress has been the outcome of the harnessing of the scientific method for the solution of concrete problems. A central claim of this chapter is that microfinance is a type of useful knowledge, capable of contributing—under certain circumstances—to the alleviation of poverty and the reduction of the vulnerability of populations still excluded from access to the institutional financial system, goals associated with the mission of the BBVA Microfinance Foundation.

Microfinance is an activity intensive in the efficient acquisition, handling, accumulation, and application in decision making of useful knowledge about the concrete realities where this endeavor is deployed. Such knowledge is indispensable for: (1) the design, at a reasonable cost, of high-quality financial services (means of payment, deposit facilities, various types of credit and insurance, among others) that respond to the circumstances and legitimate demands of those populations, thereby facilitating improvements in their living conditions, and (2) the reduction of the costs and mitigation of the risks that microfinance institutions encounter in their efforts to broaden the supply of services and enhance the financial inclusion of these populations.

Financial inclusion—the expansion of the frontier in the provision of institutional financial services beyond their current outreach in order to cover populations still excluded—requires sustained innovation, namely, the creation of new useful knowledge through experimentation and learning, mostly through learning by doing. Further, microfinance inescapably requires two types of knowledge: *universal* knowledge (such as conceptual approaches, methods of analysis and control, managerial best practices); and *local* knowledge (about the circumstances of the environment, economic circuits within the locality, the potential clients' cash flows, their business habits, the risk aversion and time discounting of agents, the varied preferences of households, social connections, and the cultural traits that determine the behavior of the population).[2]

The BBVA Microfinance Foundation (BBVAMF) represents a quite successful attempt to combine these two types of knowledge. The efforts of the BBVAMF have ensued from the recognition that the exclusion of broad segments of the population from institutional financial markets has been mainly the outcome of the formidable barriers that block the emergence of financial transactions.[3] Key among these barriers are diverse information imperfections (that is, incomplete knowledge about reality, which is asymmetrically possessed by various market agents), as well as incentive incompatibilities among the diverse participants in financial transactions (which may lead to opportunistic behavior and moral hazard).[4] In general, incomplete and asymmetric information and the insufficient or inadequate alignment of incentives make credit decisions—or the decisions to deposit a portion of one's wealth in a savings account or the decisions to supply some type of insurance—too costly and too risky, frequently prohibitively costly, in particular when the resulting services must be delivered to marginal and vulnerable segments of the population. These transactions will not emerge unless such challenges are resolved at a reasonable cost. A solution requires innovations with respect to both the *financial technology* (that is, the production function of the desired transactions) and the *organizational design* used to deploy the new technology. As a collection of such innovations, microfinance has been one of these solutions.[5]

To overcome these barriers, the BBVAMF has designed and implemented an institutional structure capable of achieving two things: (1) the confluence of the diverse knowledge from four different sources, which it has incorporated in its lending technology and in the provision of other financial services; and (2) the alignment (compatibility) of the diverse objectives of the four types of actors, to ensure that each one of them, from their own particular interest, contributes to the ultimate goal in the mission of the foundation: the socioeconomic development—comprehensive, inclusive, and sustainable—of household-firms in conditions of poverty or vulnerability that possess a productive opportunity undertaken on their own (self-employment).

From the perspective of the innovations about the management of diverse types of knowledge, the BBVAMF institutional structure encompasses:

- the BBVA financial group, an internationally leading entity with broad experience (over 150 years) in the banking business, able and ready to transfer, at a sunk cost, valuable universal knowledge, in particular about managerial practices, tools of analysis, internal control methods, information systems, and the digitalization of operations as well as intelligence about how to access capital markets at a low cost

- the BBVA Microfinance Foundation itself, as an intermediary between the knowledge of its founder, the BBVA financial group, and that of the six entities in the foundation's group of microfinance institutions in Latin America, which is capable of:

  - adapting, relying on its economies of scale, the universal banking knowledge of its founder to the peculiarities of the environments where those local entities operate and to the specific market segments that they serve—the poor and vulnerable household-firms that manage businesses on their own

  - developing tools to overcome new challenges and resolving, at the lowest cost possible, key dilemmas that the entities in the group face, such as achieving an adequate combination of personal and digital contact with the clients

  - innovating in social performance measurement methods and making both the methods and the results of their application available, as a semi-public good, to the entities in the group and to the industry at large

  - collecting, adapting, and transferring, along the system resulting from this institutional structure, the lessons learned in each local environment where the entities of the group operate, in order to transform the group into a large laboratory of innovations in financial inclusion, and using those lessons for the design of products and choice of channels

- the current system of six microfinance institutions, in five Latin American countries (Chile, Colombia, Panama, Peru, and the Dominican Republic), which contribute the local knowledge needed for an effective operation. This intangible asset is an outcome of their history (since the buildup of knowledge is *path dependent*) and is already incorporated in their experienced human capital and in the social capital that ensues from their networks of alliances and connections.

- the multitude of (over 2 million) individual clients, owners of a great wealth of knowledge and a variety of experiences, including:[6]

  ◦ value expectations and service attributes that are important to them

  ◦ new ideas about products and channels

  ◦ information about local market trends

  ◦ product comparisons across the market

  ◦ their individual preferences as well as their willingness to pay market prices for various types of services

  ◦ their repayment capacity, given diverse loan terms and conditions, which emerges from the nature of their productive activities and the risks that they face

  ◦ their risk-coping strategies and the demand for insurance services that would help them mitigate those risks

  ◦ their savings capacity, the ways in which they accumulate their wealth, and their demand for payments and deposit facilities

It is widely accepted that it is critical for MFIs to know their clients in order to place the "client at the center" of their operations.[7] For this reason, the BBVAMF not only tries to learn about the clients in ways that are reasonably cost-effective, but it also attempts to learn from the clients—that is, to learn from the inexhaustible source of heterogeneous and idiosyncratic knowledge that they represent. Thus, for the foundation, to be centered on the client mostly requires tolerance and a respectful attitude, a willingness not only to learn *about* the clients and their individual beliefs and preferences (in order to respond to these preferences and demands, rather than to impose terms and conditions of the services from above), but also to learn *from* the clients, to understand their individual dreams and expectations, and to gain insights about ways to improve the delivery of the services offered.

In sum, each of these four groups of actors possesses some useful knowledge that is indispensable in meeting the goals proposed in the foundation's mission. Separately, however, each group of actors possesses very little power to generate a substantial impact. The central challenge for the BBVAMF has been to find the most efficient combination of these diverse stocks of knowledge. It is only when they operate *jointly* that success in the struggle against poverty and vulnerability can be achieved. To implement this approach, after the acquisition of the institutions that led to the creation of the group, the BBVAMF retained several of the outstanding board members and managers who had founded and until then had managed the original institutions acquired to create the group. Similarly, the foundation has shown great appreciation for the local human capital and has attempted to retain and further train the entities' original staff.

The goals of institutions like the BBVAMF cannot be reached through individual, isolated efforts. They require the coherence, combination, and coordination of the efforts of teams, within the organization and across the whole spectrum of stakeholders. These efforts must be grounded on cooperation and on the creation of useful collective know-how.[8] In the BBVAMF, this outcome is achieved through the coordinated efforts of specialized teams, which include participants both from the foundation's headquarters in Madrid (some formerly with BBVA) and the entities in the field. These teams sustain their efforts via regular communication through weekly video conferences, field trips, and annual meetings (*jornadas*) where lessons and experiences are exchanged and shared by all.

Recognizing that knowledge management and the construction of collective know-how would be most successful in organizations that value all dimensions of diversity, the BBVAMF has been keen to listen to a variety of voices and has recruited staff members from different fields and many nationalities. In particular, it has adopted a strong commitment to gender parity across the organization, from the board of trustees, managers, and staff at the Madrid headquarters to the members of local management teams.[9]

Further, the BBVAMF has developed alliances and partnerships in order to: (1) share new knowledge and encourage the adoption of good practices across the microfinance industry, (2) have a voice in major international development forums that is based on lessons from actual experience, (3) jointly create public goods when the social gains exceed social costs, (4) generate economies of scale and scope in joint interventions, and (5) induce the synergies that emerge from well-designed complementarities. Thus the BBVAMF has entered into numerous alliances with multilateral and bilateral international organizations, local providers of complementary services (such as technical assistance agencies), and academic institutions.

Among prominent partners in some of these alliances have been the United Nations, which granted the BBVAMF special consultative status in its Economic and

Social Council (2016), the UN Sustainable Development Goals (SDG) Fund, UN Women (to promote the development and inclusion of low-income women entrepreneurs in Latin America), the UN Environmental Program (UNEP) to promote sustainability, the Food and Agriculture Organization of the United Nations (FAO) to seek solutions for the inclusion of rural household-firms, the World Bank–IFC (since 2008, including the foundation's adherence to the Universal Financial Access 2020 initiative), Habitat for Humanity (to seek housing solutions for the poor and vulnerable), several Spanish international cooperation programs, the Inter-American Development Bank (to promote microfinance in the region), CAF Development Bank of Latin America, USAID (for the expansion of rural finance in Peru and Colombia), and Microsoft (on innovation).

Both information and incentives matter. In addition to a confluence of diverse types of knowledge, in order to effectively achieve the proposed goals it has been necessary to align the objectives of the diverse actors that participate along the chain of transactions. Each type of participant responds to a diverse set of objectives incorporating a different mix of philanthropic and profit motives within the framework of a common mission.

A first actor is the BBVA. The creation of the BBVA Microfinance Foundation and its endowment of resources as received from the BBVA financial group responded to a purely philanthropic objective. In effect, in 2007, as an initiative within its social responsibility strategy, a for-profit bank, the BBVA made the unrestricted transfer—except for the pursuit of a well-defined mission—of a fund, in perpetuity, of 200 million euros, as the founding endowment for the achievement of the goals of the BBVAMF. No pecuniary returns have been expected by the BBVA from this generous endowment.

Indeed, except for the expectation of a positive impact on its reputation, no consolidation of results between the foundation and the BBVA is allowed (by the Spanish regulator of foundations—Protectorado—or by the foundation's own independent governance); nor is there any financial gain for the BBVA, which could result from the autonomous operations of the foundation. Neither is there any process of client development, with the expectation of the eventual graduation and transfer of clients to any of the BBVA banks in Latin America, nor any exchange of information about individual clients other than what is available in a country's credit bureau. Rather, the creation and endowment of the BBVAMF was a reciprocity deed by the BBVA, a sort of devolution—giving back—to the countries where the bank has operated of a "good," created in the same sector of activity where the bank participates, but directed at a segment of the population where traditional banking operations would be completely infeasible.

In effect, at the same time that it was granted full autonomy from its founder, the BBVAMF invested its endowment in acquiring, merging, transforming, and strengthening existing local organizations into the current six microfinance institutions in Chile (2009 and 2011), Colombia (2008), the Dominican Republic (2012), Panama (2010), and Peru (2008 and 2010).[10] The clearly defined mission of the BBVAMF, adopted by the entities in the group, of promoting the socioeconomic development of household-firms in conditions of poverty and vulnerability has, at least so far, reasonably differentiated the markets where the two groups of entities (BBVA and BBVAMF) operate, in some cases within the same country.

This purely philanthropic initiative is uncommon, for at least three reasons. First, the exceptional magnitude of the endowment (combined with the prudential regulation of its largest entities) has allowed the group to rapidly expand into one of the largest microfinance portfolios in the world (US$1.1 billion).[11] Only the Gentera Group (Compartamos) from Mexico reaches a larger number of clients in Latin America. It is further important to recognize that the BBVAMF manages a *group*— namely, that it is a holding with controlling participations in the equity of each of the local entities—rather than being a collection of organizations that belong to a particular network (with or without equity stakes in the participating entities), as for example in the cases of Accion International or Women's World Banking. As a controlling partner, the BBVAMF assumes ultimate responsibility for the performance of each of the entities in the group while, at the same time, allowing a substantial input from the local partners in the the governance structure.

Second, the creation of the BBVAMF has been an intervention in the same area of undertaking as the BBVA banking group, namely the financial sector, although the target market segments have been clearly differentiated. This is also uncommon. On the one hand, commercial banks have typically shied away from operations at the bottom of the pyramid. Instead, usually foundations created by banks have directed their attention to the arts, science, education, or purely philanthropic charities.[12] On the other hand, an initiative in the same area of operations might have added to the founding bank's reputational risk. Indeed, while any misstep might have had negative reputational effects on the bank, nevertheless, the foundation's robust governance structure, its adoption of top-level internal control systems (inherited from the BBVA and similarly applied to all of the local entities), and a strong performance have minimized this threat. Instead, the stream of very positive reputational returns has been a valuable intangible asset for the BBVA.

This concern about reputation matters, given the importance of trust, image, and public perceptions for the stability of financial institutions. In this sense, the creation of the BBVAMF was an act of supreme trust, in that it placed the reputation of the

BBVA in "other hands," not just those of the autonomous foundation itself, but in the hands of all the actors along the entire transactions chain that has linked the philanthropist bank with local financial intermediaries and their clientele. Indeed, the choices and actions of all of these actors along the chain will, in the end, influence the BBVA's reputation. So far, the results have been outstanding at all levels of the chain, given the performance and sustainability of the entities in the group and the substantial improvements in the living standards of large proportions of the clientele.

Third, as an act of uncommon reciprocity, the creation of the BBVAMF reflects a strong social commitment and the BBVA's desire to give back to some of the countries where it has profitably operated. The initiative acknowledges the value of a mutually beneficial relationship, where the contribution of the bank exceeds the intrinsic value to society in the provision of its own services through the transfer of some fruits of the knowledge that it has acquired in its own operations. This knowledge, about the production of financial services, has been rechanneled to the promotion of the financial inclusion of segments of the population that the bank itself has not been able to reach, given the peculiarities of this clientele and of its own operations.

A second actor along the chain has been the BBVAMF. It was created as a nonprofit entity that nevertheless seeks to become sustainable with the returns earned from the investment of its endowment. Its nonprofit constitution has given it the ability to engage, in addition to the management of the entities acquired with the endowment, in the creation of several public goods (training, measurement tools, publications), which would be underprovided by a purely profit-maximizing entity, and which have been directed at the improvement of the entire microfinance sector.

In turn, the pursuit of the foundation's own sustainability reflects acknowledgment of a long-term horizon in its efforts as well as a concern with the extent of the financial exclusion found in the developing world.[13] This raises an interesting patience paradox. On the one hand, the mission and interventions of the BBVAMF have been prompted by impatience about the limited rates of financial inclusion found in many countries, coupled with unacceptable poverty levels, despite important recent gains in both areas.[14] This impatience would trigger a desire for rapid expansion and the high profits needed to grow fast. On the other hand, the BBVAMF is a perfect example of a *patient* investor, more interested in long-term results than in immediate profits.

A third set of actors are the local entitities in the group. The foundation's endowment has been invested in the acquisition, merging, consolidation, upgrading, and management of the group of six microfinance institutions in five Latin American countries. These institutions are operated under a common governance structure.[15] From their NGO origins, they have been transformed into for-profit corporations, as is required in the countries of their operation by the corresponding prudential authorities for them to be managed as regulated financial intermediaries, which as such are authorized to offer the full range of financial services.[16] From the BBVAMF's perspective, a broad supply of services (various types of loans, deposit facilities, money transfers and remittances, insurance, and other products) are critical tools in the financial management and improvement of the living conditions of the clients among the vulnerable population. Further, the BBVAMF values the discipline required by an external prudential regulator and the accountability that is demanded by being regulated as additional components of a good governance structure.[17] If repressive policies prevail, however, the undertaking would not be successful, and the BBVAMF has chosen not to work in countries where the regulation is not conducive to achievement of the mission.

Despite being chartered as for-profit corporations, the objective functions of these entities do not entail unrestricted profit maximization. Rather than their ultimate goal, the generation of surpluses as a result of the excellence in their management is a means to allow the sustained scaling up of their operations and expansion of their breadth of outreach, incorporating large numbers of those so far excluded into the institutional supply of financial services.

Fourth, at the center of the stage are the clients as key actors: vulnerable microentrepreneurs, their families, and their communities. Individually as well as collectively, they possess large reservoirs of latent entrepreneurship, usually constrained by barriers that include, very noticeably, their lack of access to a key range of institutional financial services. The BBVAMF sees its mission as contributing to the unlocking of this entrepreneurship, so they can improve their lives through their own efforts. The intent is for these improvements to be: comprehensive, leading to socioeconomic development in its multifaceted dimensions; inclusive, such that the provision of its services benefits very large numbers of people; and sustainable, not transitory interventions that are eroded over time.

In pursuit of these objectives, the financial institutions in the BBVAMF Group offer a broad range of financial services as well as advice, training, and support to vulnerable household-firms, provided that they possess a sufficiently profitable productive opportunity such that, when they receive financial services for a sufficiently long period of time, they are able to improve their living conditions in a sustainable fashion. These clients pursue a combination of profits from their enterprises as well as other nonpecuniary objectives in the implementation of their private livelihood strategies, according to their own needs and preferences.

The multiple components of the objective functions of these household-firms (their preferences, dreams, and aspirations) are extremely heterogeneous (as are the ways in which they can employ the increased purchasing power and other financial tools provided by the intermediaries in the group), but they all possess a productive opportunity that promises a high probability of earning sufficiently high incomes to allow them to repay loans with interest (at market terms) and to earn surpluses that improve their lives, according to their own choices. Establishment of the existence of this opportunity at the start of the client relationship is a key condition in the implementation of the BBVAMF's technology of "productive finance."

The accumulation and productive use of these surpluses would allow the clients to increase the net income from their businesses and improve the welfare of their household members. They seek to improve their living conditions in a sustainable manner and to gradually alleviate their condition of poverty or vulnerability as they develop a long-term relationship with the financial institution. Therefore, among these four groups of actors, more than anything else, the clients must seek high returns from their productive efforts that will allow them to improve their lives according to their own preferences—as specified by BBVAMF's mission—within a framework of freedom.

In summary, the undertaking of the BBVAMF spans the entire spectrum of the individual private activities of hundreds of thousands of clients, the constrained profit maximization of several microfinance institutions, the nonprofit activities and semi-public goods contributions of the BBVAMF, and the purely philanthropic initiative of the BBVA. Despite this diversity (and quite possibly because of it), this combination of objective functions creates a complex structure of compatible incentives that govern the choices and actions of the four types of actors and contribute to the achievement of the goals of the whole undertaking.

The BBVAMF represents, therefore, an unusual instance of the ability to manage, combine, and coordinate diverse layers of knowledge along a multiparty chain of diverse actors, in order to address the complexities of a particular challenge: to foster the inclusive and sustainable socioeconomic development of financially excluded and vulnerable segments of the population in low-income countries, through an expansion of the supply of "productive and responsible financial services." The expectation is that these outcomes will emerge in the process of building long-term personalized relationships with the clients. It is the creation of these relationships that is at the heart of the microfinance revolution.[18] From this perspective, the BBVAMF Group is a factory of relationships.

The accomplishments of this complex undertaking have been, so far, impressive. The consolidation of the group of six microfinance institutions, by attracting international impact investors, various types of debt, and the deposits of thousands of savers, allowed the BBVAMF to leverage its initial endowment into an outstanding loan portfolio of US$1,155 million by the end of 2018.[19] In turn, the flow of credit disbursed during 2018 by the entities in the group amounted to US$1,469 million (US$5.5 million per day). This resulted from the disbursement of over 1.1 million loan transactions during the year (4,240 per day). The average loan disbursement was US$1,298, in itself an indication of the success of the BBVAMF in reaching its target clientele (table 5-1).

The six institutions range broadly in size, with the outstanding portfolio of Financiera Confianza in Peru being almost thirty-five times larger than the portfolio of Emprende Microfinanzas in Chile. Moreover, in terms of the flow of annual disbursements, Financiera Confianza is almost fifty-three times larger than Emprende. These differences are mostly a consequence of their diverse status within the prudential regulation framework of the respective countries, which reflects the importance of regulation in facilitating microfinance operations, but they also reflect differences in market size and the maturity and saturation of the microfinance sector as well as the institution's history.

The ability of the three largest entities to mobilize deposits from the public not only leverages their own equity but also creates an organizational structure and corporate culture that promote portfolio growth, while at the same time offering their clients a valuable service that is in high demand.[20] Moreover, by being part of the group, the smaller institutions gain access to tools and innovations that would be too expensive or unreachable for them on their own. These economies of scale give the group an important competitive advantage in markets characterized by a few large entities competing with a multitude of very small microfinance organizations. The largest are precisely those institutions that have obtained charters that authorize them to mobilize deposits from the public. By December 2018, the total outstanding deposits in these three institutions amounted to US$616 million (table 5-1). Over half the loan portfolios of Colombia (54.2 percent), Peru (65.8 percent), and the Dominican Republic (53.7 percent) are being funded with deposits mobilized by the group's institutions in those countries.

There are also some differences in lending technology, reflecting their different histories and the nature of the local markets. In particular, Fondo Esperanza in Chile specializes in village banking, while all others have focused mostly on individual loan technologies. These local differences offer a quasi-laboratory for experimentation and learning. As a result of the different technologies used, average loans disbursed ranged from US$762 (Adopem in the Dominican Republic) to US$1,644 (Emprende in Chile).

Their breadth of outreach is admirable. With a staff of 8,022 collaborators and a network of 515 branches, complemented by a growing number of corresponding agents (21,447) and other third-party points of attention (21,600),[21] these entities have

TABLE 5-1. BBVAMF: Financial and Operational Data and Numbers of Clients, December 31, 2018

	Group	Bancamía	Financiera Confianza	Banco Adopem	Fondo Esperanza	Emprende	Microserfin
Financial data							
Gross outstanding portfolio (000 USD)	1,155,141	404,991	494,446	132,054	81,947	14,194	27,508
Amount disbursed in 2018 (000 USD)	1,468,643	352,874	668,555	143,927	271,074	12,677	19,535
Number of disbursements in 2018	1,131,583	280,814	325,193	188,901	316,374	7,711	12,590
Average Disbursement in 2018 (USD)	**1,298**	**1,257**	**2,056**	**762**	**857**	**1,644**	**1,552**
Outstanding deposits (000 USD)	616,390	219,868	325,585	70,938	...	...	...
Operational data							
Number of employees	8,022	3,373	2,173	1,449	615	138	274
Number of branches	515	200	154	74	56	18	13
Net number of clients	**2,085,945**	**1,016,625**	**524,750**	**393,924**	**124,530**	**8,788**	**17,328**
Number of credit clients	923,615	339,386	217,669	215,914	124,530	8,788	17,328
Credit clients in the BBVAMF Group (%)	100	37	24	23	13	1	2
Number of deposit clients	1,828,750	999,784	455,485	373,481	...	...	...
Deposit clients in BBVAMF Group (%)	100	55	25	20	...	...	...
Number of clients with only deposits	1,162,330	677,239	307,081	178,010	...	...	...
Number of clients with only loans	257,195	16,841	69,265	20,443	124,530	8,788	17,328
Clients with only loans/ credit clients (%)	28	5	32	9	100	100	100
Number of clients with voluntary insurance	567,568	341,420	157,288	68,860	...	...	...

Note: . . . = not applicable.

been able to reach and include in the supply of institutional financial services large numbers of (mostly) previously excluded and vulnerable household-firms. Indeed, as of December 2018, these institutions were serving almost 2.1 million *net* clients (table 5-1).[22] Among these clients, over 1.8 million owned a deposit account in one of the three institutions authorized to offer this service. This has been an important achievement, reflecting the trust of a multitude of small savers in these institutions and the value that these segments of the population place on access to deposit services. In addition, over half a million of the total clients acquired insurance policies, a service that allows them to reduce their vulnerability to adverse shocks. Further, more than half a million clients have benefited from financial education initiatives to assist them in making better financial decisions and understanding the challenges of financial market participation.

In turn, almost 1 million clients (923,615) had loans outstanding with the institutions in the group. Among them, 60 percent were women and more than one-third lived in rural areas. These loans allowed them to increase their control over resources and pursue the goals of their enterprises and households. A high proportion of these credit clients (72 percent) were accessing both the deposit and credit services of the institutions in the group, thereby strengthening the relationships that are being developed. At the same time, 56 percent of the total clientele were clients with only deposits, while only 12 percent were clients with only loans (table 5-1).

The depth of outreach of the institutions in the group is also impressive. These institutions have consistently reached their target clienteles, as suggested by the average loan outstanding of US$1,250 and a loan disbursement of US$1,295. A small loan size generally is, however, an imperfect indicator of client poverty. In recognition of this inadequacy, the BBVAMF has been approximating the levels of household incomes by carefully measuring the surpluses generated by their enterprises. Although again this is a partial measure of incomes, it has been a reasonably good proxy in the case of households where most incomes are earned from self-employment in their own enterprises. The net returns from these enterprises are the main source of both loan repayments and any welfare impacts of access to finance on the household.

The use of this proxy has made a classification of client households possible, according to their position below the *extreme poverty* line as well as below the *poverty* line, as defined by the corresponding authorities in the countries of operation of the institutions in the group. Further, the BBVAMF has constructed a *vulnerability* line, defined as three times the poverty line in each country (figure 5-1).[23] The poverty and vulnerability status of credit clients is approximated from detailed information from the loan evaluation process. The BBVAMF is currently exploring cost-effective ways of estimating such status for clients with only deposits. Given these definitions,

FIGURE 5-1.   BBVAMF: Shares of Credit Clients in Extreme Poverty, Poverty, and Vulnerability, for New and for All Clients, December 2018 (percent)

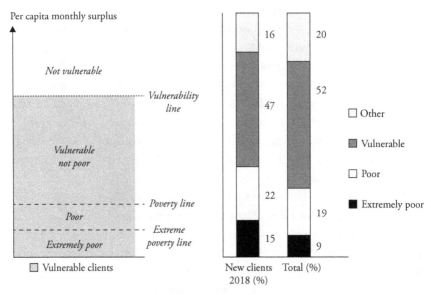

9 percent of the total number of credit clients where extremely poor, as of the end of 2018, while 15 percent of the new credit clients reached in that year were extremely poor. The higher proportion of extremely poor among the new clients than among the total reflects both the BBVAMF Group's sustained commitment to reaching this population segment and the gradual exit from extreme poverty of old clients that were added to the group's portfolios in earlier years. As of the same date, 28 percent of the total number of clients with outstanding loan balances were poor (and because 9 percent were extremely poor, 19 percent of the total were poor but not extremely poor). In turn, among new clients, 37 percent were poor (while 22 percent were poor but not extremely poor). Again, the incidence of poverty among new clients was higher than among the whole clientele. Finally, 80 percent of the number of clients with loan balances were below the vulnerability line (while 52 percent were vulnerable but not poor); among new clients, 84 percent were below the vulnerability line (while 47 percent were vulnerable but not poor).

Over the years, the share of vulnerable clients has been between 80 and 90 percent of the number of new borrowers added to the portfolio. This has been largely true for each institution in the group. For the new credit clients reached during 2018, this share ranged from 75 percent (in the case of Financiera Confianza, which operates in an extremely competitive, saturated microfinance market in Peru) to 95 percent (in the case of Fondo Esperanza in Chile). This is a simple but critical indicator that the BBVAMF Group's institutions continue to focus on their target population and that there has been no mission drift after eleven years of operations.[24] This has been the case even when the larger entities became prudentially regulated and even if all were engaged in—constrained—profit maximization (two features that some microfinance industry observers have associated with mission drift). As the relationships with their clients have grown longer, some proportion of these clients have exited the poverty or vulnerability status that characterized them when they first became clients. Their continued presence in the portfolio of the institutions reflects the strength of the client relationship, not mission drift. The absence of mission drift has, in general, reflected a well-defined mission, the oversight of a board of directors (*patronato*) and a director general vigilant in this respect, and the fact that the BBVAMF is a patient investor.

A key question is what happens to those levels of poverty and vulnerability over the life of the relationship of the clients with the institution. Indeed, *measurement* of key indicators about those circumstances has been a fundamental concern for the BBVAMF. Following their evolution has been a central component of the efforts to know the clients better (a key dimension of knowledge management) and of the concerns about staying on target with the mission. Further, the expensive development of measurement tools in order to learn key lessons about this segment of the population has denoted the willingness of the BBVAMF to create semi-public goods available to the entities in the group and the industry at large.

A formidable effort has been made to create longitudinal panel data for the universe of clients of the institutions in the group. Collecting data about the universe of clients has reflected a willingness to learn about each individual client in the portfolio. Among other results, these data have made it possible to track the poverty and vulnerability status of the clients over time. By 2018, in the case of borrowers who were below their country's poverty line when they were first reached by these institutions, and who had continued in their relationship with the institution for at least five years, 67 percent were already above this critical threshold, while 22 percent of borrowers who were initially not poor had fallen below the poverty line.[25] This represented a net gain of 45 percent among the institutions' borrowers in the battle to rise above poverty.

As shown in figure 5-2, some proportion of poor clients (38 percent) exit poverty even after the first year of the relationship and because 23 percent fall in poverty, there is a 15 percent net alleviation of poverty. By the second year, 52 percent have exited poverty, for a net alleviation of poverty for 34 percent of the total. The proportion of those having exited poverty continues to increase (although at a declining rate) as they

FIGURE 5-2.   BBVAMF: Clients Exiting Poverty, Falling into Poverty, and Net Poverty Alleviation, by Number of Years in the Relationship, 2013 to 2018 (percent)

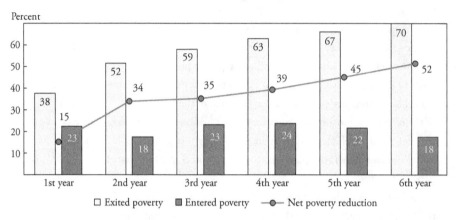

continue to be engaged in the client relationship. The same pattern is true for the net alleviation of poverty. Overcoming poverty takes time and is facilitated by the development of long-term client relationships. Interestingly, the proportion of those who fall into poverty remains fairly constant over time, possibly reflecting the impact of adverse shocks.

The BBVAMF does not claim, however, that the institutions in the group have pulled these clients out of poverty. Rather, by taking advantage of their own productive opportunities (which seem to have been correctly identified while using the foundation's lending technologies), with their own skills and efforts—and as the circumstances of their environment have allowed—they have pulled themselves out of poverty. At the same time, it is true that the institutions in the group have provided their clients with valuable financial services, which have served as powerful tools for success in their endeavors and in the pursuit of their own particular dreams.

This exceptional dataset has made it possible to record the evolution over time of key indicators for each household. Three examples of these indicators are useful here. Figure 5-3 shows the evolution of the monthly sales of the clients' enterprises as their relationship matures. As an average for all the cohorts that received their initial loan in any year between 2013 and 2018 (loan 1 in the figure), their monthly sales amounted to US$1,207. Similarly, average sales at the time a second loan was negotiated had grown to US$1,294 per month, and so on. Consistently increasing over time, at a compounded annual rate of growth of 16.8 percent, by the time of negotiation of the sixth loan, average monthly sales had grown to US$2,071. That is, on average, after

FIGURE 5-3. BBVAMF: Client Sales by Stage of Borrowing
(Number of Loans Received), 2013–18

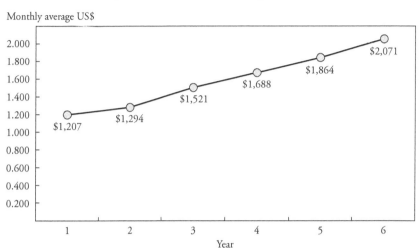

six loans the borrower's enterprise sales had reached 1.7 times their initial level. This is an indicator of the growth of their businesses as their relationships with the institution evolves. Moreover, since the difference between the initial and the currrent value of sales at a particular date grows as the number of loans increases, the total potential gain becomes larger, the longer the client remains in the relationship.

Figure 5-4 shows the evolution of the value of the enterprise assets as the relationship matures. As an average for all the cohorts that received their initial loan in any year between 2013 and 2018 (loan 1 in the figure), the value of their assets amounted to US$5,706. Thus annual sales represented 2.5 times the value of these assets. By the time a second loan was negotiated, enterprise assets had grown to US$6,379, and so on. Consistently increasing over time, at a compounded annual rate of growth of 22.9 percent, by the time of negotiation of the sixth loan, the average value of the borrower's assets had grown to US$13,459. That is, on average, after six loans, the borrower's enterprise assets had grown to 2.4 times their initial level, reflecting a sustained process of wealth accumulation. In turn, by this time, annual sales represented only 1.8 times the value of these assets, suggesting some diminishing returns to enterprise growth.

Likewise, figure 5-5 shows the evolution of the monthly enterprise surplus (earnings minus costs). Again, as an average for all the cohorts that received their initial loan in any year between 2013 and 2018 (loan 1 in the figure), the monthly enterprise surplus amounted to US$397. Annualized, these surpluses were equivalent to

FIGURE 5-4.   BBVAMF: Client Assets by Stage of Borrowing
(Number of Loans Received), 2013–18

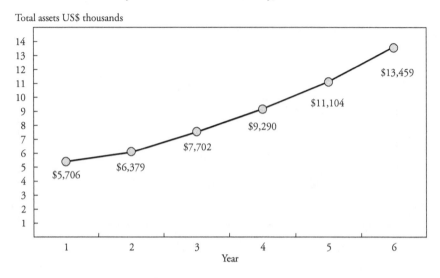

Total assets US$ thousands

FIGURE 5-5.   BBVAMF: Enterprise Surplus of Clients, by Stage of Borrowing
(Number of Loans Received), 2013–18

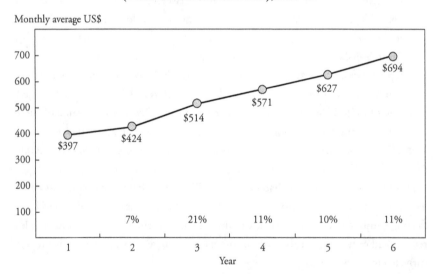

Monthly average US$

FIGURE 5-6.   BBVAMF: Average Relative Income of Clients, with Respect to the Poverty line (= 1), by Stage of Borrowing (Number of Loans Received), 2013–18

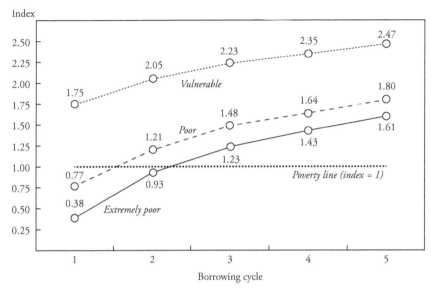

83.5 percent of the value of the firm's assets, suggesting a high marginal rate of return on assets. By the time a second loan was negotiated, this surplus had grown to US$424, and so on. Consistently increasing over time, at a compounded annual rate of growth of 16 percent, by the time of negotiation of the sixth loan the average value of the firm's surplus had grown to US$694. That is, on average, after six loans, the borrower's enterprise surpluses had reached 1.7 times their initial level, reflecting a sustained process of net income growth. As with the other two indicators, the average gap between the initial and the current surpluses increases monotonically as the relationship matures. By the sixth loan, the annual surplus was equivalent to 50.6 percent of the borrower's enterprise assets, suggesting again diminishing returns to growth of the firm.

The foundation has also recorded the evolution of the monthly per capita surplus from the household enterprise for each cohort of clients that initiated their relationship in a particular year. This is the one indicator that is more closely related to the household's poverty status. In order to appreciate the depth of poverty, the foundation has defined an index of 1 when this per capita surplus is equal to the level of the poverty line (figure 5-6). On average, when they get their first loan, this index is -0.38 for borrowers in extreme poverty. That is, they earn per capita surpluses equivalent to just over one-third of the poverty line. It takes them, however, three to four cycles of borrowing to be, on average, above the poverty line. For them, the index reaches 1.61 by their sixth cycle.

In turn, when they get their first loan, this index is 0.77 for borrowers in poverty but not in extreme poverty. It takes this group one to two cycles of borrowing to be, on average, above the poverty line. For them, the index reaches 1.80 by their sixth cycle. Finally, when they get their first loan, the index for vulnerable but not poor borrowers is 1.75, and it reaches 2.47 by their sixth cycle. It is important to emphasize that these are average results and that the outcomes for individual borrowers vary; some clients experience even larger gains and get them sooner, others experience smaller gains and get them later, and others experience losses (fall into or fall back into poverty).

These results hint, nevertheless, at the potential existence of a substantial poverty-alleviation process among the clients of the institutions in the BBVAMF Group. For at least a couple of reasons, however, the foundation does not claim any *attribution* for these impacts. On the one hand, any poverty alleviation outcomes are the result of the choices and actions of the four types of actors in the transactions chain, including and most importantly the clients themselves. These choices and actions (and the financial transactions that result from them) build on the collective knowledge that the different actors possess and reflect the multiple and heterogeneous features and attributes of the clients. These choices and actions also respond to and are influenced by the evolution of the diverse environments where the institutions operate, subject to multiple and diverse (either favorable or adverse) shocks.

Thus the poverty-alleviation results are the joint outcome of a complex web of circumstances, among which the financial services provided by the institutions in the group are just one—quite likely a significant—component. Moreover, for the pool of borrowers, these average results depend on the quality of the credit decisions, given by the nature of the lending technology used and by the capabilities of the human resources (loan officers) in charge of implementing it. The BBVAMF's own "productive finance" technology requires the screening of loan applicants by identifying a productive opportunity with a high probability of generating these results. The correct implementation of the approach, aided by substantial attention to the characteristics and performance of the loan officers, seems to have contributed to these outcomes. In general, in those cases when a profitable productive opportunity is not available, the borrowers cannot improve their lot, and frequently they are actually impoverished by credit. The "responsible finance" technology of the BBVAMF seeks to avoid this outcome.

On the other hand, the results for each cohort of clients who are still using these financial services by a particular date reflect different degrees of attrition. For a number of reasons, some clients do not sustain the relationship: maybe some obtain exceptionally good returns from their opportunities and graduate to other financial intermediaries; maybe others suffer adverse shocks and seek informal sources of financial services to recover their creditworthiness; some might drop out for demographic reasons (such as old age). In some cases, moreover, mistakes in the screening process followed by default lead to the denial of further access to credit.

The poverty-alleviation impacts that have been actually observed are for those clients that have sustained the relationship over time. As indicated, household business sales, assets, and per capita surpluses grow larger as time goes by. The potentially beneficial impacts are then being obtained by those particular clients whose relationships have been sustained over time, and these impacts have grown bigger as the relationships have matured. The BBVAMF's role has been to accompany them during this evolution. Its greatest challenge has been to preserve these relationships.

Some important lessons may be derived from these results:

- First, desired impacts (particularly in the case of poverty alleviation) do take time and patience. Interventions must have a long horizon and must make credible promises that long-term relationships will be rewarded with better terms and conditions as the relationship evolves. Ignoring these factors might have been a weakness of some impact evaluations.

- Second, the achievement of poverty-alleviation impacts through the supply of financial services requires the development of long-term relationships with clients. It is only through the sustained evolution of these relationships that significant outcomes have been obtained. The limited potential to alleviate poverty through financial inclusion exercises that do not create relationships is a weakness shown by some interventions.

- Third, to build long-term relationships, the financial institution must be sustainable—that is, it must be able to promise the delivery of a stream of valuable services over time—and it must project its own sustainability in a credible manner.

- Fourth, potential impacts depend crucially on the quality of the credit decisions, which in turn reflect the appropriateness of the lending technology to the features and circumstances of the target population and the capabilities of the loan officers who implement the technology. This matters given the information and incentive imperfections present in financial markets.

In summary, through an intricate combination of philanthropic interventions and constrained profit-seeking operations, the BBVAMF Group has been immersed in the creation of long-term relationships with a multitude of vulnerable household-firms, which possess attractive productive opportunities. The whole process is anchored in the sustainability of all of the actors along the chain of transactions.

Finally, reducing the exclusion of the poor and the vulnerable from institutional financial markets and improving the contributions of finance to poverty alleviation are formidable tasks. The BBVAMF does not expect to accomplish these things alone. In recognition of the magnitude of the challenge, numerous actors must be involved. Thus, in addition to expanding the supply of financial services for vulnerable populations, the BBVAMF also hopes to influence the development of the microfinance sector through the delivery of a number of public goods.

Among these, the BBVAMF has privileged: (1) the development and dissemination of knowledge about appropriate corporate governance structures and practices, including workshops for hundreds of board members in several Latin American countries; (2) specialized human capital formation through alliances with universities and other training programs; (3) a policy dialogue with prudential regulators and other authorities in order to complement good internal governance practices with optimal external governance norms; and (4) pioneering in the development of measurement tools that capture in a systemic fashion the evolution of the multifaceted livelihoods of its clients. In these endeavors the BBVAMF expects to be where it can be most useful and, in particular, where the actors along the chain can learn the most. These desired outcomes cannot be accomplished in isolation. Success will only emerge from a virtuous and efficient combination of diversity and cooperation in the management of varied sources of knowledge.

Notes

1. Angus Deaton, *The Great Escape: Health, Wealth, and the Origins of Inequality* (Princeton University Press, 2013).

2. Sebastião Mendonça Ferreira, "Inteligencia y aprendizaje en el negocio de las microfinanzas," keynote speech at the VII Cumbre Internacional de Asesores de Microfinanzas, Guayaquil, Ecuador, July 4, 2013.

3. These barriers include several dimensions of distance, imperfect information, incompatible incentives, unenforceable contracts, and covariant outcomes. See Claudio Gonzalez-Vega, "Deepening Rural Financial Markets: Macroeconomic, Policy and Political Decisions," paper presented at the conference "Paving the Way Forward for Rural Finance," Washington, United States Agency for International Development and World Council of Credit Unions, 2003.

4. See, among others, William Keeton, *Equilibrium Credit Rationing* (New York: Garland, 1979); Joseph E. Stiglitz and Andrew Weiss, "Credit Rationing in Markets with Imperfect Information," *American Economic Review* 72 (December (1981): 912–27; Timothy Besley, "How Do Market Failures Justify Interventions in Rural Credit Markets?" *World Bank Research Observer* 9, no. 1 (1994): 27–48.

5. Claudio Gonzalez-Vega, "Innovation in the Design of Formal Financial Services for Greater Inclusion," paper presented at The Mastercard Foundation Symposium on Financial Inclusion, Turin, Italy, July 2013.

6. Mendonça Ferreira, "Inteligencia y aprendizaje en el negocio de las microfinanzas."

7. Alexia Latortue, "Keeping Clients at the Center: An Art and a Science," *Consultive Group to Assist the Poor* (blog), October 14, 2011 (https://www.cgap.org/blog/keeping-clients -center-art-and-science).

8. Ricardo Hausmann, interview in *Progreso* 5 (December 2015), quarterly digital newsletter of the BBVA Microfinance Foundation (http://www.fundacionmicrofinanzasbbva .org/revistaprogreso/en/ricardo-hausmann/).

9. Four out of seven members of the board of trustees (chaired since 2019 by Anna Escobedo Cabral) are women. Parity has been achieved in almost all key governing bodies within the group.

10. In 2008 two Women's World Banks (Bogota and Medellin) were merged and a controlling position was acquired by BBVAMF to create Bancamía in Colombia, while three Peruvian nonbank institutions (*cajas rurales*) were merged into Caja Nuestra Gente. In Chile a controlling position was acquired in Fondo Esperanza in 2009, while another Chilean institution, Emprende Microfinanzas, was created in 2011, from another acquisition. Microserfin, in Panama, was acquired in 2010. In that year, Caja Nuestra Gente was merged with Financiera Confianza in Peru, and the latter's charter and name were kept for the new institution. Finally, in 2012, the BBVAMF acquired a controlling position in Adopem, which was subsequently transformed into a bank, in the Dominican Republic.

11. Worldwide, prominent microfinance institutions in this league included, around 2017, MiBanco in Peru (with a portfolio of US$2.8 billion), Bharat Financial Inclusion in India (US$2.1 billion), Grameen Bank and BRAC in Bangladesh (with a portfolio of US$1.7 billion each), Gentera (Compartamos) in Mexico and Banco Sol and Banco FIE, both in Bolivia (each with a portfolio of US$1.6 billion), and Banco PRODEM in Bolivia (US$1.2 billion).

12. María López Escorial, "Los bancos no se deciden por las microfinanzas," *Radiografía CE,* Compromiso Empresarial, October 10, 2015.

13. Asli Demirgüç-Kunt and others, *The Global Findex Database: Measuring Financial Inclusion and the Fintech Revolution* (Washington: World Bank, 2018).

14. Homi Kharas, Kristopher Hamel, and Martin Hofer, "Rethinking Global Poverty Reduction in 2019," *Future Development* (blog), Brookings, December 13, 2018.

15. BBVAMF, a common Code of Corporate Governance (Código de Gobierno Corporativo), to be applied to the whole group, after the adjustments required by the local legislation in each country, was approved by the board of trustees in December 2015.

16. Two of these institutions have been upgraded and chartered to become commercial banks, Bancamía in Colombia, and Banco Adopem in the Dominican Republic. Although Financiera Confianza, in Peru, qualifies for a bank charter, for the time being it has been

chartered as a financial company (*financiera*). These three financial intermediaries represent the bulk of the group's clientele and assets. In the case of Microserfin in Panama, and Fondo Esperanza and Emprende Microfinanzas, both in Chile, which are not yet regulated entities, the intention is to eventually upgrade them into some class of regulated financial intermediary.

17. Claudio Gonzalez-Vega, "Profundización financiera rural: Políticas públicas, tecnologías de microfinanzas y organizaciones robustas," *Microfinanzas y Banca Social* 1, no. 1 (January 2012): 7–52. See also Liliana Rojas-Suarez and Lucia Pacheco, "An Index of Regulatory Practices for Financial Inclusion in Latin America: Enablers, Promoters, and Preventers," Working Paper 468 (Washington: Center for Global Development, 2017).

18. Marguerite S. Robinson, *The Microfinance Revolution: Sustainable Finance for the Poor* (Washington and New York: World Bank and Open Society Institute, 2001). On the evolution of the client relationships, see Rodolfo Quiros, Claudio Gonzalez-Vega, and Pedro Fardella, "Do Clients Still Matter? Contrasts and Evolution" (San José, Costa Rica: Calmeadow, 2019).

19. All data are reported here as of December 2018, unless otherwise noted. These data and additional information can be retrieved from Fundación BBVA MicroFinanzas (http://mfbbva.org/en/), and in particular from the Foundation's Social Performance Report issued every year. All data are in U.S. dollars.

20. Isai Guizar, Claudio Gonzalez-Vega, and Mario Miranda, "Uneven Influence of Credit and Savings Deposits on the Dynamics of Technology Decisions and Poverty Traps," Fourth European Research Conference on Microfinance, University of Geneva, June 1–3, 2015.

21. In February 2018, Bancamía began operating its first virtual branch.

22. A large proportion of the clients are simultaneously borrowers and depositors. The *net* figure does not double-count those that are both.

23. For 2018, for the five countries and the urban and rural areas in each, the extreme poverty lines ranged from US$31 to US$71 in monthly per capita income; the poverty lines ranged from US$52 to US$174 in monthly per capita income, and the vulnerability lines ranged from US$156 to US$425 in monthly per capita income, depending on the country, and the values differed for urban and rural areas. These thresholds are roughly equivalent to US$1.0 to US$2.4 per day, US$1.7 to US$5.8 per day, and US$5.2 to US$14.2 per day, depending on the country and the area. The lowest figures correspond to Colombia-rural and the highest to Panama-urban. All others are in between.

24. Beatriz Armendáriz and Ariane Szafarz, "On Mission Drift in Microfinance Institutions," in *The Handbook of Microfinance,* ed. Beatriz Armendáriz and Marc Labie (London: World Scientific, 2011), pp. 341–66.

25. Clients who were no longer financed because they had defaulted are not considered in these data.

SIX

Refocusing on Customer Value

Meaningful Inclusion through Positive Partnerships

GERHARD COETZEE

Financial inclusion, narrowly defined as access to formal financial services, is riding on a wave of success. In 2018 the number of financially excluded was at 1.7 billion people, just over half the number of excluded people just a decade earlier—down from 2 billion in 2014 and 3 billion in 2006. The trend is consistent, but it is slowing down: 721 million accounts were opened between 2011 and 2014, but only 515 million from 2014 to 2017.[1]

In 2006 the solutions proposed to expand access were to scale up quality financial services to serve large numbers of people (scale), reach more impoverished and more remote people (depth), and lower costs to both clients and financial services providers (cost).[2] The battle cry was to make financial services for the poor part of every country's mainstream financial system. The advent of digital financial services and more intelligent mobile devices pushed all three of these objectives simultaneously. Digital services through agents cost less than reaching clients through a branch-based system. Wireless mobile systems and mobile services reached deeper into developing economies, especially into rural areas. Thus more poor people were reached at a lower cost.

The Story of Access and Use

When we define financial inclusion as access to and use of financial services by poor people, the emerging picture looks entirely different. As financial inclusion efforts grew around the globe, 1.2 billion accounts were opened between 2011 and 2017.[3] Of this number, approximately 150 million were mobile accounts, two-thirds of which are used less than once every three months.[4] About 20 percent of bank accounts are dormant—not used at all. Most of the remainder are "mailbox accounts," whose customers immediately withdraw all cash upon receipt of wages or social benefits, making it difficult for financial services providers to generate revenue, as no transactions are taking place and no balances are left in accounts.

There are two sides to any problem. Let us start with the customers and consider why customers may not open an account or use financial services. Research in several countries on customer behavior and what disempowers customers found the following:

- Accounts or services are not relevant to their needs.

- Their expectations are not met.

- They see no added value in having an account, besides getting paid or receiving money.

- Costs of formal financial services are too high.

- They lack the confidence to engage with financial services providers.

- They do not trust financial institutions and do not feel valued or respected.[5]

Lack of use translates into a lack of revenue for the financial services provider. A high-level analysis shows that, at current usage rates, providers will find it difficult to recoup the estimated US$20 billion cost to open these accounts.[6] Low usage confronts many providers with some core business questions: What can we do to encourage customers to leave money in their accounts and use digital payment mechanisms? How can we retain customers? How can we provide customers with a comprehensive suite of products and services? How do we expand customer portfolios? When asked, financial services providers identified some even more fundamental problems:

- Many customer segments are too difficult to reach, especially the rural excluded.

- High costs and low revenue are due to low uptake and little or no use.

- No understanding of customer needs, motivations, and behaviors.

- No capacity to design and deliver customer-focused solutions.

- Inability to create value for customers, which leads to a lack of value for providers.

- Failure to identify and build scalable business models.[7]

These points raise three distinct challenges. One, many financial services providers do not have a deep enough understanding of their customers to design valuable products and services for those customers. Two, many providers do not have the internal capacity to do this research, or to design solutions. Not mentioned by the financial services providers but evident when interacting with them, is that they the need to shift to more customer-focused approaches. The third challenge is thus providing access to and use of responsible financial services by poor people that adds value to their lives and protects them from exploitation and predatory behavior. This requires reviewing approaches and asking different questions when considering business models. What do customers need to improve their lives, to build resilience, to empower them to capture opportunities? What are good outcomes for poor customers? Central to these questions is the reality of livelihoods and economic inclusion. Financial services must return to its original role of leveraging and supporting economic opportunity. It needs to focus on catalyzing customers' resilience in the face of shocks—a daily reality of the poor and excluded.

Ironically, the challenge of providing value and meaningful services for poor people points us back to microfinance institutions (MFIs), which traditionally focus on micro- and small entrepreneurs. While many MFIs have been caught in a time warp, doggedly focused on a conventional credit-focused approach, the broader world of financial inclusion turned its attention to digital financial services (DFS) and understanding how to make technology work for financial services providers, and more recently, in some instances for poor customers.

After nearly a decade of trying to make DFS work for all, the question is raised again, financial services for what? This is an important question because it turns the focus back onto the poor customer. We know that if we want to intensify use of services, the services must make sense for customers; or stated differently, the services must have value. Building access and encouraging use are inextricably linked to creating value for poor customers. If poor customers value and use the services, that translates to value for firms. All firms, inclusive of MFIs, should focus on business models that are customer-centric and create a chain of value that begins with the customer.

How can financial services providers create value for customers—and for themselves? The next section provides evidence and guidance on customer-centric models. Later sections argue that MFIs can play a significant role as full partners in the quest for value.

Ensuring Value for Customers and Financial Services Providers

The customer-centric business model provides evidence and guidance. It illustrates what it will take for financial services providers—whether MFI, bank, mobile network operator, technology platform, fintech, or partnerships between these typologies—to move to meaningful inclusion.[8]

No or Low Use and Deterioration in Value Fuels the Search for Better Models

Figuring out how to acquire and retain customers and expand their use of products are core challenges faced by financial services providers serving low-income people. Customers will walk away from accounts if the accounts do not serve their needs. Customers are far better informed in today's connected world, where social media can amplify negative customer experiences and erode customer trust far more quickly than any good comment or "like." Better-informed customers also demand value from their providers. In this new world, competition comes from many new entrants to the financial inclusion market. They range from massive platforms (Google, WhatsApp, Facebook) to mobile network operators (Orange Telecom, Safaricom/Vodafone, Airtel), new banks, and fintechs. Quite often competition is also driven by partnerships between these new players. Conventional players—for example, MFIs, cooperative networks, and group approaches—often find it difficult to compete with the new dispensation. As more and more providers adopt more sustainable models for business growth, they focus on understanding customer needs to help them build better models.

The Business Opportunity in Customer Centricity

Research has established a strong link between customer satisfaction and business performance. Ranjay Gulati of the Harvard Business School demonstrated that organizations that focus on customer solutions rather than products delivered shareholder returns of 150 percent between 2001 and 2007, outperforming the Standard & Poor's 500 (S&P) index, which returned 14 percent over the same period.[9] Notably, these "outside-in" companies thrived even during the massive fallout in financial services markets in the period 2007–08. These companies experienced sales growth of 143 percent, in comparison with 53 percent for S&P firms.

Sunil Gupta and Valarie Zeithaml show that a 1 percent increase in customer satisfaction results in a 2.37 percent higher return on investment (ROI), while a 1 percent decrease in customer satisfaction brings a 5.08 percent decrease in ROI.[10]

What is a customer-centric business model?

A customer-centric business model operates in an ecosystem of customers, employees, suppliers, shareholders, and the communities an organization serves. In this ecosystem, customers are at the center of corporate strategy, decision making, organizational design, and operations.

—Doug Leather, author of *The Customer-Centric Blueprint,* 2013

Pioneer Microinsurance in the Philippines sees the value in delivering positive customer experience by having the right processes in place, hiring the right people, getting feedback from customers, and retooling business processes based on insights and metrics. From 2015 to 2017, Pioneer Microinsurance expanded its portfolio with CARD customers from 600,000 to 1.6 million enrollments, and renewal rates doubled.[11]

Agent networks help financial institutions establish and maintain services in poor countries to spread financial inclusion throughout the world. For service providers, agents offer a lower-cost channel beyond the branch structure for acquiring and serving customers who live in remote places. For customers, they provide a convenient way to make financial transactions, such as arranging a loan or regularly receiving remittances, without having to travel far. Agents also provide a way into the financial system for customers who need help because they are illiterate, are unfamiliar with the technology, or lack the confidence to access services on their own. AMK, a Cambodian MFI, improved and expanded its agent network after it completed in-depth research on what drives agents to provide a great customer experience. AMK realized that the agent is also a customer segment and that improving the agent's experience with AMK helped agents function more efficiently, deliver a better customer experience, and create business value for both the agents and AMK. This was especially important at a time when a new interest cap made branch infrastructure too expensive to maintain and agents had to fill the gap left by branches.[12]

Mobile money services in Haiti were initially set in motion to facilitate distribution of grant payments to victims of the 2010 earthquake. A promising change in mobile money uptake and activity is now evident in Haiti after lackluster results between 2010 and 2015. Digicel, the most prominent mobile money service in Haiti, proved that a customer-centric business model can effect change. It shows that a granular understanding of what customers need, how they are empowered to use products, and how providers organize for delivery are essential elements of a successful model that adds value for both the customer and the financial services provider. Digicel increased the number of active mobile customers from 40,000 in 2015 to 807,000 in 2017.[13]

Keys to a customer-focused approach include:

* a granular understanding of customers

* financial solutions designed specifically for customer needs

* an organizational setup that delivers through a customer-centric business model

The Shift to a Customer-Centric Business Model

Most financial institutions today are still product focused. However, push-and-pull factors are forcing change. On the push side, customers are walking away; they are better informed and driven by the power of social networks and social media. Competition is heating up in many markets— and from diverse sources in the fintech and startup arenas. On the pull side, savvy providers are finding that more focus on customers, better customer experience, and delivering value to customers bring results.

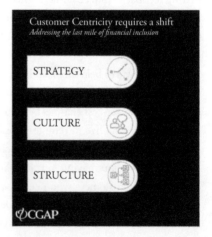

Customer Centricity requires a shift
Addressing the last mile of financial inclusion

STRATEGY

CULTURE

STRUCTURE

CGAP

The move to a customer-centric business model is not simple, and the process is not swift. It requires emphasizing a portfolio of customers rather than a portfolio of products, with growth based on meeting customer needs and creating long-term customer value. The shift begins with leaders who emphasize the strategy and lead by example to build a customer-centric culture, one that rewards employees for solving customer problems and deepening long-term relationships.

A shift in strategy and a culture change are followed by a change in structure: from employees who operate in product silos to business units linked across functions by teams or task forces that serve customers at different points in the customer journey. These diverse groups allow organizations to rally various functions around customer needs and segments.

What to Consider When Facing Acquisition Challenges?

Building business opportunities in markets where customers have limited knowledge of formal financial services is hard work. The number of customers who actively use financial products is usually small, so acquiring new customers can bring significant benefit to the bottom line. The following elements must be considered when working to acquire new customers:

- *New markets.* Providers often look to serve new markets because existing markets are saturated—or they seek new business opportunities. It is first essential to get to know which segments of the market to enter and then tailor offerings to better ensure success.

- *Awareness.* If customers have never heard of a product or service and the value proposition is not immediately apparent, they need time to understand its worth. Alternatively, customers may see the value but feel intimidated by a brand or by formal financial services in general. To overcome these hurdles, customer-centric organizations can develop a more welcoming environment for new customers. They need to factor in the time and effort required to empower customers to understand and use their products and services.

- *Enrollment.* If the value proposition is not clear, customers are unlikely to sign up. When thinking through the customer journey, customer-centric organizations should consider every type of cost and value, including the social and psychological costs to customers who use their products and services. Hidden costs may be associated with poor customer service or with the stresses involved in carving out the time to gather documents required for enrollment. On the positive side, customers who form a strong bond with an agent or experience excellent customer service may perceive more value than expected.

What to Consider When Facing Retention Challenges?

Retention requires anticipating and responding to changing customer needs. For low-income people, life events such as marriage or business expansion often result in significant changes in finances. Customers also can be poached by competitors who offer better incentives and customer experi-

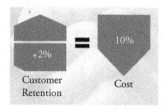

ence. The following elements should be considered when working to retain existing customers.

- *Remove technical barriers.* Customer-centric providers need to find ways to remove technical barriers to onboarding customers and support account usage. For example, they could consider incentives to encourage the first-time use of a newly opened account.

- *Anticipate and respond to customers' needs.* Customers may not understand product value or may not have a sense of loyalty to the provider. Retention requires anticipating and responding to customers' changing needs through constant dialogue.

- *Inspire trust and loyalty.* Low-income customers look for the same things every customer wants: choice, respect, voice, and control. By incorporating these factors into the customer experience, providers can earn their customers' trust, and customers will build confidence in financial services. Customers who trust and use the products will feel empowered and develop loyalty, as well as produce value for both themselves and the organizations.

What to Consider When Facing Expansion Challenges?

Existing customers are critical for growing the bottom line. They drive as much as 50 to 80 percent of revenue, making expansion strategies more cost-effective than acquiring new customers. Providers typically increase customer value through cross-selling, adding to portfolios, or up-selling existing products and services. Consider the following ways to expand customer offerings.

- *Uptake.* If customers do not understand the full range of products or services available, they will listen to outside advice and find other providers to meet their needs. To discourage this, customer-centric organizations must become familiar with the nuances of their customers' financial lives as well as their aspirations and decision-making processes. This knowledge will lead to greater insight and better solutions.

- *Value.* Expanding customer relationships requires more than just the right mix of products and services. Relationships are based on strong foundations of trust nurtured through many forms of feedback and engagement.

What Does It Take to Implement a Customer-Centric Approach?

Finding solutions begins with a granular understanding of customers, their life challenges, money management practices, and context. These insights lead to new design criteria, new concepts, and prototyping. However, few financial services providers have the knowledge and skills to implement the solutions, even though they may have the resources. Some get to the stage of concept, prototyping, and selection of final designs but then face obstacles inside and outside the organization that thwart successful implementation. Organizing for delivery, empowering employees, and managing change efforts are the keys to following through on newly identified customer solutions.

Learn from Customers

This is where customer-centric organizations begin. Developing a solid understanding of customers' lives, motivations, and aspirations is the first step toward improving customer experience—and increasing value for customers and organizations. Learning from customers is the starting point for designing more effective products and services.

Although every member of a customer-centric organization is responsible for thinking about customer needs and experiences, the research team regularly draws

insights from customer information. Ideas can come from existing interactions between customers and tellers or agents, or from specific studies.

A combined qualitative and quantitative research approach is most useful for
understanding customer behavior. An efficient research plan first taps into existing
internal knowledge, then dives into the unknown. If data already exist, focusing on
knowledge gaps may generate more relevant findings. Many organizations already
possess internal data that have the potential to provide significant insights; however,
these data are used only for annual reports. Data analysis follows the data collection
process and is usually of three types:

- **Descriptive** analysis provides a summary of the profile of numerous customers at a specific moment in time.

- **Predictive** analysis helps draw insights that may not be directly observable in
  the data.

- **Prescriptive** analysis recommends actions and indicates likely outcomes.

Interesting patterns and outliers found in analysis can point to behavioral insights.
Organizations may need to hire a data scientist to perform analyses or outsource this
function.

To uncover new opportunities, it is essential to have a solid understanding of target markets. A segmentation exercise looks at a market base and helps organizations
figure out which products or strategies fit specific customer segments. Details about
subsegments further enhance product development, service delivery, and customer
satisfaction.

Design Solutions
Once they have developed insights into customers, organizations are ready to design
for better adoption and use. The customer-centric design is about learning directly
from customers in their own environment, then quickly working with them to develop and refine concepts. This ensures that customer needs and expectations inform
design decisions and, in turn, improves the likelihood of adoption and success. Once
gaps in customer experience are identified, organizations must close them. The process challenges organizations to understand, create, evolve, and test possible solutions,
then repeat the cycle as many times as needed.

It takes time and resources to design and deliver solutions that result in positive
experiences and empowered customers. Interactions with customers must change, and

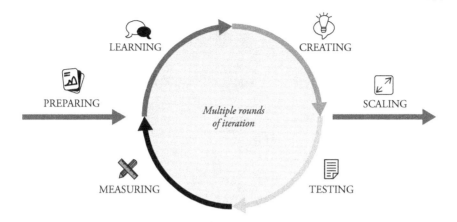

employees must be guided to adopt a customer-empowerment mindset. The shift in attitude starts with simple steps that are not costly or time-consuming. It is an evolution—not a sudden transformation.

Organize for Delivery

Customer-centric organizations structure themselves around customers and their changing needs. The five pillars that support customer-centricity are leadership and culture; focusing operations; people, tools, and insights; customer experience; and value.

Customer-centric organizations create value for several different stakeholders (customers, employees, and shareholders) by targeting change across the organization. It takes time to catalyze change, embed new processes, and shift mindsets toward new behaviors. The pace matches organizational readiness; it does not happen overnight, and every organization creates its own change journey.

Committed leaders must first embrace customer-centricity, then drive change campaigns that rationally and emotionally appeal to employees. An essential part of the change journey is institutionalizing best practices in innovation management systems. This means investing in new business processes and building sustainable learning systems, along with sourcing, developing, and aligning human resources. It is critical to create systems that measure progress and performance, then link them to key performance indicators.

Performance measures also change to include efficiencies, customer-led value drivers, profitability, and social returns. To ensure that customers receive value at an ecosystem level, organizations identify effective new partners to help deliver on customer goals and objectives.

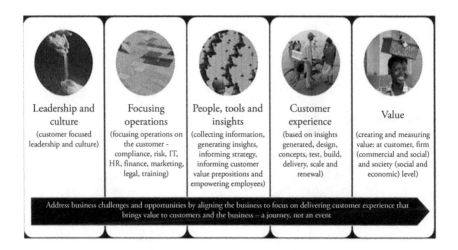

Leadership and culture	Focusing operations	People, tools and insights	Customer experience	Value
(customer focused leadership and culture)	(focusing operations on the customer - compliance, risk, IT, HR, finance, marketing, legal, training)	(collecting information, generating insights, informing strategy, informing customer value prepositions and empowering employees)	(based on insights generated, design, concepts, test, build, delivery, scale and renewal)	(creating and measuring value: at customer, firm (commercial and social) and society (social and economic) level)

Address business challenges and opportunities by aligning the business to focus on delivering customer experience that brings value to customers and the business – a journey, not an event

Developing cross-functional teams that focus on customers enables each employee to understand his or her role in servicing customers. To ensure that new, integrated ways of working are implemented well, organizations build trust and provide teams with internal support that also builds trust within groups.

The journey is most successful when organizations enlist enablers and nurture a culture that supports customer-centric behaviors and systems. They can use digital technology to promote and accelerate the change journey. Language is also critical; leadership teams that tell stories demonstrate the power of change while bringing the effects of a new strategic direction to life. Offering incentives for and rewarding the right behaviors also codifies and embeds those new behaviors.

The Value of a Customer-Centric Business Model

Adopting a customer-centric model enables organizations to support sustainable growth objectives linked to crucial value drivers: customer acquisition, retention, and use of services. The customer-centric approach empowers employees to resolve issues and become more involved in creating value and benefiting from it. The model supports the ability to create more streamlined customer experiences that reduce costs for customers while generating value.

Customer-centric organizations also build customer loyalty. As a result, they see an increase in customer retention and are more successful at acquiring new customers through brand awareness and word of mouth. They are resilient and find it less daunting to face competition or hazardous market conditions.

A customer-centric model leads to value for customers, value for organizations, and value to society, as evidenced in the performance of outside-in organizations. In a study of purpose-driven companies, Richard Ellsworth compares customer-driven companies with shareholder-driven companies.[14] He found that companies that put the customer at the center outperform the shareholder-focused companies on shareholder returns (36 percent to 17 percent over the same period!).

In the final analysis, customers must perceive value. When customers value the ability of financial services providers to solve real-life challenges and resolve the pain, the organization succeeds. In a world where low-income customers make little use of financial services, providing value is the missing piece of the puzzle to growing the business. Organizations that create customer value see stronger revenue growth, improved profits, *and* sustainable growth.

The Tough Part of the Financial Inclusion Journey Lies Ahead

The final frontier of access to financial services is not merely geography. Access is growing continuously, but the speed of growth is slowing down. In the past financial services providers have solved access problems by lowering costs, applying technology to serve more areas, and serving more people, thus building more efficient outreach. The challenges of exclusion of deep rural, illiterate, and innumerate citizens, of women and youth, and of intersections of these categories have always been present, but they are now in even sharper focus as the last frontier of inclusion. And technology developed over the past decade holds promise for meeting the challenges of including these segments head on.

Nearly a billion people are illiterate and innumerate. Almost 60 percent of smallholder families are not linked to markets, and therefore they are largely economically excluded. Economic exclusion where the poor fight for sustainable livelihoods is the next frontier.

Inasmuch as technology is the answer, it can also be a threat. Technology has a broad reach and can be efficient, but persistent factors such as high cost, lack of universal coverage, people's inability to use it, norms that deny access (especially for women), product irrelevance, distrust, and several intersections of these mean that exclusion continues. Thus the digital divide is both a driver and a result of the new exclusion.

The speed and ease of digital access may entice customers, but it can push them back into destitution and poverty. There are many examples of negative results from using digital financial services. In Tanzania, digital credit uptake exploded in the 2010s. Research using transaction data for 20 million loans showed that borrowers defaulted on roughly 20 percent of the loans in the sample and were late repaying 40 percent of the loans. The researchers found that repeat borrowers were at risk of falling into debt traps.[15] Kenya paints a similar picture.

Once again, the question is whether there is a fair and consistent approach to value creation for the people and for firms. It is not clear whether providers of digital credit services are more focused on delivering customer value or value for themselves. What is clear is that if the challenges of digital credit are not addressed, it will be difficult for customers and financial services providers to achieve sustainable and positive outcomes over the medium to long term.

Where Do MFIs Go from Here?

Some argue that the rise and exponential growth of digital credit could have a negative impact on MFIs and their sustainability. Kenya and Tanzania have the longest track record with digital credit in sub-Saharan Africa. In Kenya the partnership between Safaricom (M-Pesa) and the Commercial Bank of Africa launched its M-Shwari product as early as 2013.[16] However, M-Shwari is just one of several events that influenced MFIs in Kenya. Others include an interest rate cap and more expensive loans from banks. The situation in Kenya illustrates the new world MFIs face, which includes many new players and rules that change often as regulators try to expand their reach to include these new players. The new world brings new opportunities and threats for MFIs.

At the same time, investors have invested billions of dollars in MFIs. The international MFI customer portfolio is still growing: from US$114 billion at the end of 2017, it increased 8.6 percent from 2015 to 2016, another 9.4 percent from 2016 to 2017, and again by 15.6 percent by the end of 2017.[17] Most of the growth is driven by MFIs from East and South Asia, but all regions had positive growth between 2016 and 2017. According to MIX, MFIs reported having 139 million clients in 2017. Although the loan portfolio has been growing, customer growth has slowed, year on year, from 2015 to 2017. This implies that loans per customer are larger and could lead to fewer poor customers, which would further exclude the marginalized poor. MFI growth in Africa lags the rest of the world and was indeed negative in 2015–16.

A marked change in the delivery channels MFIs use is also notable. More than 60 percent of MFIs have added digital delivery channels to their channel offering, and at least 40 percent of these early movers developed and implemented mobile money channels; 20 percent were testing mobile money channels at the end of 2017. These changes imply that more than 588 MFIs have embarked on the digital journey, and many of these are large organizations with millions of clients. Also, 62 percent of the borrowers of these institutions lived in rural areas at the end of 2016.[18] The digital approach implies a lower cost per customer, lower cost-to-income ratios, and more sustainable MFIs. MFIs are indeed on a new journey.

MFIs can bring a new perspective to the current financial inclusion challenge. Very few of the new movers (fintechs, mobile network operations [MNOs], platforms, banks), if any, focus on the poor.[19] Most MFIs understand the poor; and their business models, which are integral to their social mission, are based on serving the poor. MFIs can play an essential role in helping partners understand poor people and their needs; they can help partners to design and build products, channels, and distribution systems that poor people will use.

MFIs can shed light on how to support livelihoods for the poor. Most MFIs provide financial services to microbusiness owners and increasingly to small-business owners. With most of their clients in rural areas, they also serve smallholder families. MFIs understand that excluded poor need more than payment services: they need savings, credit, and insurance services to build resilience; they need opportunities to build their livelihoods.

Moreover, MFIs' rural presence can inform and enhance the distribution systems of MNOs, banks, and the many large firms that supply goods and services in rural areas. Two opportunities stand out:

- Person-to-merchant payments in sub-Saharan Africa and Asia markets, where they are lacking. It is estimated that 37 percent of person-to-merchant payments worldwide are digital, while in sub-Saharan Africa it is 14 percent and in Asia 16 percent. The financially underserved are expected to spend more than US$5 trillion per year, suggesting that there is a vast potential for expanding person-to-merchant payments.[20] The assistance provided by MFIs for building this infrastructure can be the basis of mutually beneficial partnerships between MFIs and large firms, platforms, MNOs, and banks.

- The number of large agribusinesses working on distribution solutions in rural areas is increasing.[21] These firms are finding ways to use their agricultural input distribution systems to provide or facilitate financial services to their clients. MFIs can partner with these firms to leverage the relationships MFIs already have with their clients in rural areas as a way of solving the last-mile challenge together.

It follows that partnerships between MFIs and newcomers to the market can benefit poor customers and drive inclusion by lowering costs and scaling reach. Partnerships will be a vital element in financial inclusion going forward. In fact, most of the successful deployments of digital financial services were built on partnerships.

Suggestions for the Road Ahead

The following ideas can help all financial services providers, especially MFIs, advance toward meaningful financial inclusion. The aim is to enhance access, develop products and services that customers will use, protect customers, and create value for customers, providers, and in the final analysis, society.

- *Focus on understanding poor customers and what they value,* starting with their economic and social realities and molding financial services to their needs and what would create value for them. Efforts should focus on financial services that support micro- and small enterprises and smallholder farmers and that primarily include women and young entrepreneurs. MFIs can play an important role by partnering with entities that can bring scale and lower costs.

- *Ensure that customer value translates into firm value.* Or stated differently, ensure that the value generated for the customer translates into lifetime customer value for the firm. This discipline is often overlooked by purely socially driven firms and often results in sustainability problems.

- *Shift to a customer-centric model.* All strategic and business decisions start with the customer, which means making decisions with the customers' best interests in mind. Organizations should learn from customers, design solutions that customers will find relevant, and organize internally and externally to deliver those solutions. This is a long journey, and putting the customer at the center will keep the organization focused on its goal.[22] This journey will empower customers by giving them a choice, allowing them to have a voice, and building their confidence and trust in the financial services.

- *Engage with partners that bring relevant experience and functionality—a value proposition that complements your own and that features poor customers.* Engagement may take the form of a partnership among a platform, fintechs, and MFIs, where the MFI contributes its customer understanding and service experience and the other partners bring digital product solutions and platforms that facilitate distribution.

- *Provide digital services and contribute to building the digital infrastructure.* Think about how the organization can improve the overall digital infrastructure in a digital ecosystem. Building a "critical mass for digital payments" will help tip the scale toward customer acceptance and use of digital channels.[23]

- *Counter the digital divide.* Ensure that customer protection is a foundational focus, and design products, services, and infrastructure with positive customer outcomes in mind. Take extra care to include those who are often excluded: women (because of social norms), youth, rural areas, micro- and small enterprises, smallholder families, and the illiterate and innumerate. Digital solutions should help these marginalized groups, not aggravate their situation.

- *Support and work closely with regulators and policymakers.* A good relationship with regulators is essential to creating understanding and space to improve value-driven services. Focus on customer outcomes and jointly decide how financial services providers could measure and report those outcomes.

Notes

1. Asli Demirgüç-Kunt and others, *The Global Findex Database 2017: Measuring Financial Inclusion and the Fintech Revolution* (Washington: World Bank, 2018); Brigit Helms, *Access for All—Building Inclusive Economic Systems* (Washington: World Bank, 2018).

2. Ibid.

3. Demirgüç-Kunt and others, *The Global Findex Database 2017.*

4. Global System for Mobile Communications (GSMA), *State of the Industry Report on Mobile Money. Decade Edition: 2006–2016* (London: GSMA, 2016).

5. Juan Carlos Izaguirre, Michelle Kaffenberger, and Rafe Mazer, "It's Time to Slow Digital Credit's Growth in East Africa" (CGAP blog), 2018; Demirgüç-Kunt and others, *The Global Findex Database 2017.*

6. Author's calculations using information from Global Findex; Susy Cheston and others, *The Business of Financial Inclusion: Insights from Banks in Emerging Markets* (Washington: Center for Financial Inclusion and the International Institute for Finance, 2016); and James Manyika and others, *How Digital Finance Could Boost Growth in Emerging Economies* (San Francisco: McKinsey Global Institute, 2016).

7. Izaguirre, Kaffenberger, and Mazer, "It's Time to Slow Digital Credit's Growth in East Africa."

8. This section draws from Gerhard Coetzee, "CGAP Customer-Centric Guide—Executive Summary" (http://customersguide.cgap.org/).

9. Ranjay Gulati, *Reorganize for Resilience: Putting Customers at the Center of Your Business* (Boston: Harvard Business Press, 2010).

10. Sunil Gupta and Valarie Zeithaml, "Customer Metrics and Their Impact on Financial Performance," *Marketing Science* 25, no. 6 (2006): 718–39.

11. CARD is a large MFI in the Philippines that works in partnership with Pioneer to provide microinsurance services to their clients. See Antonique Koning and Myra Valenzuela, "Pioneer Microinsurance: Building a Business around Positive Customer Experience Pays Off," CGAP Case Study, 2018 (http://customersguide.cgap.org/why-go-customer-centric/casestudies).

12. Jayshree Venkatesan, "Treating Agents as Customers at AMK, a Cambodian Microfinance Institution," CGAP Case Study, 2018 (http://customersguide.cgap.org/why-go-customer-centric/casestudies).

13. Lisa Stahl and Gerhard Coetzee, "Focusing on Value for Customers Is Good Business—Digicel (MonCash), Haiti," CGAP Case Study, 2017 (http://customersguide.cgap.org/why-go-customer-centric/casestudies).

14. Richard R. Ellsworth, *Leading with Purpose: The New Corporate Realities* (Stanford, Calif.: Stanford Business Books, 2002).

15. Juan Carlos Izaguirre and Rafe Mazer, "How Regulators Can Foster More Responsible Digital Credit" (CGAP blog), 2018.

16. Tamara Cook and Claudia McKay, "How M-Shwari Works: The Story So Far." Access to Finance Forum Series (Washington: CGAP, 2015).

17. "Key Figures of Financial Inclusion," *Microfinance Barometer 2018*, 9th ed. (Paris: Convergences, 2018), p. 2.

18. Ibid.

19. Greta Bull, "Great Expectations: Fintech and the Poor," CEO Essay (CGAP blog), 2019.

20. Dan Salazar, "Reaching the Digital Economy's Last Mile" (MasterCard Center for Financial Inclusion blog) (www.mastercardcenter.org/insights/digital-economy-last-mile).

21. CGAP, "Financial Innovation for Smallholder Families: Lessons from CGAP's Partnerships with Providers," 2018 (www.cgap.org/research/slide-deck/financial-innovation-smallholder-families-lessons-cgaps-partnerships-providers).

22. Guidance on starting and continuing the journey is available at http://customersguide.cgap.org.

23. Salazar, "Reaching the Digital Economy's Last Mile."

SEVEN

Understanding the Impact of Microcredit

TIMOTHY N. OGDEN

The story of *modern* microcredit began in 1980 with the Ford Foundation's creation of a loan guarantee fund for Grameen Bank. (I emphasize "modern" here since the basic concepts of microcredit—the creditworthiness of poor borrowers, the value of access to credit, the use of joint liability in place of collateral—can be traced to at least the 1600s, and possibly the ancient world.) While there is plenty to debate about the details of the history of modern microcredit, it was the loan guarantee that allowed Grameen to significantly scale up, vaulted it to global recognition, set the precedent for "social investment" as the key financing mechanism for microcredit, and perhaps most important, gave legitimacy to the idea that lending could be good for impoverished households. Nearly forty years on, it is easy to underestimate the radical shift from lending to poor households as the province of slavers and loan sharks—the worst of the worst—to the province of do-gooders and heroes.

The foundation of that shift, of course, was the idea that microcredit was a path out of poverty for borrowers. Though not wholly uncontested, the narrative of microcredit as effective antipoverty tool was the generally accepted story, and not without reason. Observation and anecdote certainly played a role, but research did as well. There was sound theoretical reason to believe that extending access to credit would provide substantial benefits. And early academic research seemed to show that substantial numbers of Grameen borrowers escaped poverty.

But dissonant voices began to be heard. Additional research that attempted to control for obvious problems in assessing the impact of microcredit—who took loans chief among them—and found positive effects of borrowing was not forthcoming. Questions about the reliability of the findings from the original research surfaced. As microcredit scaled up, it increasingly failed to pass the eyeball test: villages and regions were not being transformed; most microenterprises were not in sectors that could plausibly generate the kind of returns to capital necessary for widespread poverty impact; indeed, most microenterprises were obviously not growing.

By 2012 the results of rigorous evaluations of microcredit in a variety of contexts began coming in. Six of these evaluations were published together in 2015 in the *American Economic Journal: Applied Economics*. All pointed to a single conclusion: the average microcredit borrower saw very modest gains from access to credit.[1] The findings were consistent, whether in urban India, rural Mongolia, (relatively) wealthy Bosnia, poor Ethiopia, or among women in Mexico or men in Morocco.

Before these evaluations, questions about the future of microcredit typically focused on operational and investment climate issues: Was there adequate management capacity among microfinance institutions (MFIs)? Would capital investment in microcredit continue to grow at the same pace? How would a crisis in a particular country affect the investment climate and regulatory authorities? How did nonprofit and for-profit status affect scale and who was served? Who should properly receive the bulk of profits from MFI operations?

Once the orthodoxy of microcredit as poverty-alleviation strategy was convincingly pierced by independent research, the future of microfinance looked decidedly cloudier. Questions became less about details and growth rates, and more existential. Could the microfinance sector survive if it could not be justified as a tool for alleviating poverty? Should it survive? Should social investors continue to put money into microcredit, and if so, under what conditions?

Answering those questions requires delving into the impact evaluations and understanding their findings beyond the headlines. But it also requires understanding the stream of research that has come after, which is just as important, though far less known.

Microcredit Impact Evaluations

While it is increasingly common to read phrases such as "the research shows" and to hear appeals for evidence of impact, far too often they reflect a naive understanding of research and evidence. Research on complex topics like poverty is almost never going to yield simple and unequivocal answers. Drawing conclusions from research requires understanding individual studies that do not produce a simple binary answer.

Before the publication of the randomized controlled trial (RCT) evaluations of expanding access to microcredit in 2015, the most well known academic study of the impact of microfinance was published in 1998 by Mark Pitt and Shahid Khandker using data from Bangladesh.[2] This work was heavy on statistics, attempting to compare the outcomes of borrowers with just under a half-acre of land to people from the same or similar villages who were ineligible for loans because they owned more than a half-acre of land. The Pitt and Khandker work suggested that there were big differences in outcomes between these groups and that borrowers were able to increase income and consumption. Extrapolating from those results yielded a widely publicized estimate of the percentage of borrowers who could escape poverty as a result of having access to credit.

Shortly after that paper was published, however, other researchers delved into the data and raised questions. After nearly fifteen years of back and forth over the statistics involved, two things became clear: (1) although there was technically a rule that borrowers with more than a half-acre of land were ineligible to borrow, field staff did not follow this rule and many borrowers were better off than originally thought, making it difficult to make meaningful comparisons between borrowers and nonborrowers; (2) the gains seen in the data were the result of a handful of households that did much, much better than the average borrower; if those very successful borrowers were not included, there was no apparent gain from borrowing.[3] The latter, it turns out, would be a recurring pattern in microcredit impact evaluations.

In hindsight, it is clear that the Pitt and Khandker study could not answer the question, Does microcredit work? Until the recent RCTs, then, the reality was that there was little reliable evidence about the impact of microcredit. But just like the Pitt and Khandker work, the results of the recent impact evaluations deserve scrutiny.

There have been more than six randomized evaluations of microcredit, but the six RCTs that were published together in 2015 have attracted the vast majority of the attention. Although the studies examined different microcredit products in different contexts, the results were broadly consistent: the average impact of microcredit is modest, with borrowers reaping little to no statistically or economically significant gains in consumption, business profits, or other key measures. Some of the studies did find increases in consumption or business revenues, but those gains were too small to plausibly suggest that microcredit could have the transformative effects its proponents had hoped for.

The six RCTs were widely viewed as overturning earlier research on the impact of microcredit, and were considered by many to be the "final word" on microcredit as an antipoverty intervention. Neither of those perspectives is accurate.

Delving Deeper

Any impact evaluation is going to present the average effect of an intervention. Averages are undeniably important for informing policy analysis—but any average can also obscure important information about variation. In the case of microcredit, the modest average impact could hide that some borrowers are deeply harmed or that some borrowers gain a great deal, or both.

There was, in fact, important variation in the outcomes for borrowers in the six RCTs. In fact, the findings of the six RCTs, rather than refuting the Pitt and Khandker data, were quite consistent with the reanalysis of the data. A closer look at the results reveals that although the average impact of borrowing was modest—even undetectable—some borrowers benefited substantially. It is also critical to note that there is little sign of borrowers being significantly harmed.

Randomized Control Trials

Some commentators emphasize that a limitation of what can be learned from the six randomized controlled trials is that they were done in contexts where MFIs had already been operating for some time, and the evaluation tested the impact of expanded access to credit, not the introduction of microcredit where it was unknown. Although this is strictly true, it bears further discussion. Financial Diaries studies, like *Portfolios of the Poor*,[4] have made it clear that informal credit is far more prevalent and significant in the financial lives of poor households than had been appreciated. In that sense, even the first arrival of microcredit in a particular place can be thought of as an intervention to expand access to credit. Second, since microcredit has expanded so rapidly over the past forty years, the current relevant question in most contexts where MFIs and investors would actually consider expanding is, in fact, What is the impact of expanding access to microcredit?, not What is the impact of introducing microcredit?

An accurate conclusion from these studies then is: if you expand microcredit access to additional borrowers without any alterations to the product or client selection, you should expect that the average impact will be modest, that a small group of borrowers may substantially benefit, and that there is little danger of harm (provided, of course, that there is not rampant oversupply of credit, as has been seen in some countries).

Beyond the Final Word

Anyone who thought the six RCTs were the final word on microcredit does not know much about how researchers think. Rather than producing a final answer to questions about microcredit's impact, the studies produced even more questions. Are the borrowers who do very well with microcredit just lucky, or is there something different about them? Given that a number of studies—using grants, rather than loans—had found that microenterprises can generate high returns to capital, why is the average impact of microcredit so modest?[5] If the returns to borrowing for the average borrower are so small, why do people take loans at all? Are the low returns to borrowing a factor of the way the loan is structured?

Indeed, many researchers had been working on these questions before the impact evaluations were published. The impact studies served to encourage that work, and to launch additional studies to answer these questions that now had more urgency.

Characteristics of Successful Borrowers

The easiest way to determine why a small number of borrowers gain substantially from increased access to microcredit is to look at the participants in the studies. The researchers involved in the microcredit evaluation in India did just that. They found that the successful borrowers were those they term "gung-ho entrepreneurs"— borrowers who had already started businesses before gaining additional access to microcredit through the program. In contrast, the success of borrowers who were induced to start a business by being given access to microcredit is indistinguishable from that of nonborrowers.[6] Put another way, the data suggest that what was wrong about the original narrative on microcredit was not that microcredit-fueled enterprises could grow substantially and boost incomes, but that large numbers of poor households wanted to or were capable of starting a high-growth small enterprise.

Other research provides additional insight. Earlier studies had established that often men and women had very different rates of return to capital: men in Sri Lanka and Ghana who received business grants generated high returns, while women did not. Reanalysis of the data from those experiments and further work found important differences that were not immediately apparent. Most women borrowers are in households where there is also a male-operated business. In these households the woman's business is usually a secondary source of income. When researchers disaggregated the women participants, they found that when the women were the sole or primary earner for the family, their returns to capital were equal to men's returns.[7] It seems that the same pattern of differential returns observed in the India microcredit study is repeated within households. Some businesses are intended to grow and some are not; those where growth is desired tend to do much better than those that are a "necessary evil."

Additional research in Ghana and Uganda provides further evidence for this pattern—and some important nuance. In Ghana, in one of the locations of the original research that found differential returns between men and women, women who had high returns to capital were those who had higher profits before the grants arrived.[8] The gung-ho entrepreneurs surface again. But these women face an uphill battle even when they are gung-ho entrepreneurs. Because of social norms, women in many cultures are limited to operating only certain types of businesses, and there can be more competition in those business types (either because of norms, or because the women are restricted to operating low-skill businesses like fruit selling or food preparation). For instance, in Ghana, women seamstresses' businesses are consistently less profitable than those of male tailors, primarily because there are many more seamstresses than there are tailors, and customers will only purchase from someone of the same sex.[9] Other studies of microcredit in Uganda found that women who were better able to segregate and protect their own funds from family members had higher returns to borrowing than those who faced heavy demands to share funds with their families.[10]

Overall, the picture from these studies is remarkably consistent with what we know about small businesses in wealthier countries. Most of these businesses are only marginally profitable (especially if you take into account the value of the owners' time), fail to grow significantly, and shut down at a high rate. Only a small number of small-business owners aspire to grow their firms, and only a small number of business owners have the requisite skills and access to capital to achieve their growth goals. Since microcredit was designed to not distinguish between borrowers but to expand access broadly, it should not be surprising that the average borrower does not operate a profitable and growing microenterprise.

Modest Returns

The insight that most poor households are not frustrated entrepreneurs (as the microcredit mythos originally suggested) goes a long way toward explaining why the average returns to borrowing are so modest. But there are additional, interrelated factors. In two of the six microcredit impact RCTs, researchers conducted follow-up studies to better understand why impact was so modest. In Morocco at least some of the microcredit borrowers invested in livestock and increased the hours they spent working on their farms, with positive results. But at the same time, because they were working more on their own farms, they reduced their participation in the labor market and therefore saw no net increase in income.[11] In India some of the same researchers who conducted the impact evaluation took advantage of the microfinance crisis in Andhra Pradesh to look at the impact of microcredit in a different way. Rather than measuring the impact of gaining access to credit, the researchers measured the impact of losing access to credit as a result of the crisis, which caused lending across India to decline dramatically. Using additional data, they were able to measure something that the impact evaluations could not: the impact of microcredit on wages for nonborrowers. They found that in areas which saw the largest decline in access to credit, many microenterprises shut down, the people operating them entered the casual labor market, and wages fell, leading to lower consumption.[12] The strong indication is that microcredit expansion allowed people to switch from casual labor to operating a microenterprise. Those microenterprises may not have grown, and many have not been very profitable, but they reduced the supply of casual labor, which pushed up wages for nonborrowers (what is known in economics as a general equilibrium effect). This is a particularly striking insight because it suggests that measures of returns from borrowing will systematically underestimate the effects of borrowing, at least in areas where there are casual labor markets, because nonborrowers benefit as well through higher wage rates.

Since those findings, additional research has continued to find general equilibrium effects in labor and commodity markets from microcredit or similar interventions. One program designed to benefit the "ultra-poor" found no effect of the program precisely because (for other reasons) casual wage labor rates in the region of the study increased during the program and so participants' income gains were matched by gains of nonparticipants engaged in day labor (and led some participants to drop out of the program).[13] A massive study of India's guaranteed employment program for rural households found again that measures of impact were highly sensitive to measuring the general equilibrium effects on labor markets.[14] An evaluation of a microcredit lending program in Kenya specifically to finance the purchase of grain storage tools found that the majority of the benefits from the program accrued to nonparticipants. In this case, participants were able to avoid selling their crops immediately after harvest, which raised prices at harvest (since there was less supply) and lowered them later in the year (when participants sold their stored grain), so even those who did not participate benefited from higher income or higher consumption. In fact, by one calculation, nonparticipants captured more than 60 percent of the gains from the program.[15]

The bottom line is that many microenterprises are not only not intended to grow, but are also direct substitutes for casual labor income. Borrowers may take loans and start microenterprises because they perceive that a microenterprise is an alternative to wage labor, without expecting or desiring to generate large returns from the loan. Or they may repurpose the loan, investing it in a different business within the family. At the same time, the gains they do see may be hidden by the general equilibrium effects on wages. The average effects of microcredit are still likely modest, but they may be larger, and the presence of microcredit in a community may provide more benefits than impact estimates capture.

Contract Structures

Questions about how microcredit loans are structured, and the impact of that structure on returns to borrowing, predate the impact evaluations. While the weekly repayment schedule of the standard microcredit loan was highlighted as a key ingredient in the formula, many failed to appreciate that the first payment was due a week after the loan was disbursed. With a moment's reflection, it is clear that such a structure strongly discourages risk taking on the part of borrowers. Any investment of the funds borrowed must produce returns quickly and consistently. About the only investment possible that meets that criterion is purchasing inventory or raw materials that require little processing—in other words, investments that by nature are very likely to produce low returns. Indeed, in one of the few instances where researchers have been able to trace exactly what borrowers do with borrowed funds (an extremely difficult task because money is fungible), they find that most of loan proceeds are used to purchase inventory.[16] When the immediate payment requirement is relaxed, borrower behavior can change. Back in 2013, researchers documented that Indian borrowers who took loans with an eight-week grace period before loan repayment began invested in their businesses and had higher profits;[17] further research supports this result.[18]

The finding from the impact evaluation RCTs that some borrowers had high returns reinvigorated the stream of research on contract structure. If some borrowers have high returns, an obvious question is whether it is possible to structure the product to specifically target those borrowers. If that were easy, of course, borrowing would look very different the world over. It is the inability to tell who will generate high returns and who will default that drives the cost (and availability) of credit. It turns out, however, that there are some promising ways to target microcredit. In one experiment, researchers asked middlemen to identify the most productive farmers, who could use credit to expand their production. The middlemen's predictions were mostly correct, and borrowers they selected did see higher returns from borrowing.[19] In another experiment, researchers surveyed members of the community to find out who they thought the best entrepreneurs were. Again the community was largely correct, and the people they selected did have high returns. (It is worth noting that when respondents knew their responses would dictate who would have access to credit, they chose their own relatives and average borrower returns dropped sharply.)[20]

These experiments illustrate not only that there may be creative ways to effectively target lending to borrowers with the potential to generate higher than average returns, but how poorly structured the basic microcredit product is if the goal was investment in growing businesses. The group lending model, whether it includes group liability or not, is all about determining who will repay, not who will have high returns. The difference between these two categories seems clear to community members, and the high repayment rates and low average returns are a powerful testament to that.

The fact that many borrowers see negligible gains from borrowing raises other product structure questions. Anyone who has visited more than a handful of microenterprises has seen that there are likely many ways that these businesses can improve profitability or productivity. Detailed research on small-business management practices has found that, as in much larger companies, a small set of specific behaviors are highly predictive of productivity and profitability.[21] In other words, management matters—and most microenterprises are not well managed. This is hardly surprising. Neither is it an indictment of microenterprise owners. Management is a skill that is not easy to learn just from experience, and there are few opportunities to learn it in developing countries, even for people much higher up the income scale than those operating microenterprises.

Could it be possible to offer microcredit along with training that could improve practices in a way that boosts the average returns? Evidence on this question is tantalizing but decidedly mixed. Multiple experiments in Kenya and Tanzania have found that small tweaks in business practices can produce significant gains: better management of physical inventory for small traders, better management of liquidity for retailers and mobile money agents, negotiating with suppliers rather than accepting the first price.[22] At the same time, most impact evaluations of business training programs find little or no impact.[23] And the experiments that have been conducted generally find that one-off training does not work—participants stop engaging in the better practices unless they receive ongoing encouragement or reminders. A 2017 experiment in Burkina Faso suggests a different approach than skills training. In that experiment, researchers provided self-efficacy training to one group of microenterprise owners and standard business training to another group. The group that received the business training did not see gains, but the self-efficacy group saw significant increases in revenues and profits.[24]

Drawing Conclusions

What can we then conclude from the impact evaluations of microcredit and the stream of research that has come after?

First and foremost, we can conclude that we do not yet have all the answers. Practitioners, investors, policymakers, and researchers should be prepared to be surprised by new research in the coming years. That being said, there is an emerging story that makes sense of much of the research and is well enough supported to guide future action.

It is likely that the majority of people who have access to microcredit are not frustrated entrepreneurs, as much of the early rhetoric around microcredit implied, but frustrated employees. As a consequence, the average impact of microcredit provision that does not attempt to select between borrowers is likely to be modest. The impact in areas where there are opportunities for wage labor, though, may spread well beyond borrowers by lowering labor supply and increasing wages.

Furthermore, absent reckless behavior by lenders (and it is important to note that there are increasing signs of reckless and predatory behavior in digital credit being offered by nonmicrofinance institutions), there is little reason to be concerned about harming people by making credit available. It is worth noting that, before the microcredit revolution, conventional wisdom was skewed toward "debt is bad for the poor." A finding that you could massively expand poor households' access to credit and not harm them would have been surprising and counterintuitive. The modest average results from impact evaluations are disappointing only insofar as expectations changed radically from prior beliefs. Large-scale escape from poverty is not a reasonable goal and never was.

There was plenty of magical thinking around microcredit for many years. The emerging story is what most social investors would have believed absent that magical thinking: most microenterprise opportunities available to poor households do not generate large profits; given other constraints, running a business successfully is difficult and requires skills and effort; entrepreneurial talent and drive is unevenly distributed in any population; if your primary client selection criterion is likelihood of repayment, your loan portfolio is unlikely to be made up of borrowers with the most entrepreneurial talent; a person with little entrepreneurial talent or drive is unlikely to rapidly grow their business. Given that expectation, microcredit's primary achievement is building out a platform to offer credit to more than 100 million people formerly thought to be beyond the reach of formal financial services.

The bottom line is that microcredit is a compelling product platform to build on. It can be highly beneficial to a minority of borrowers and is likely to be modestly beneficial to others, especially in contexts where wage labor is an option or there is little access to financial services.

The Other Side of the Calculation: Understanding Microcredit Subsidy

Choices in social investment are not one-sided, of course. Investors have to consider both the effectiveness of an intervention and its cost-effectiveness. Just as with microcredit's impact on poverty, there have been a great deal of unsupported claims about the cost of delivering microcredit.

The claims that microcredit does not require subsidy, that it can be profitable and self-sustaining, and that it can deliver market-rate returns on investment with no trade-offs are too numerous to count. They are also difficult to challenge or refute given that there are so many different microfinance institutions with diverse structures (not just for-profit and nonprofit, but also those that have relationships with commercial banks, larger charities, and others), a variety of business models, and different global scope.

Still researchers have done painstaking work to help document and understand the role of subsidy in microcredit delivery, and thus shed light on the cost-effectiveness of microfinance. This work has uncovered significant differences, for instance, in the types of clients served by for-profit and nonprofit microfinance agencies. Nonprofits tend to serve poorer customers and a higher proportion of women than their for-profit counterparts. Nonetheless, for-profits in total serve more poor customers and more female customers because of their larger scale.[25]

Reviewing data from 1,335 microfinance institutions, the researchers calculated the accounting profit (revenues less operating costs), the economic profit (revenues less operating costs less cost of capital at market rate), and the amount of subsidy being used. They found that while two-thirds of institutions generated accounting profit, as few as 18 percent generated an economic profit, which would make them truly self-sustaining.[26] If social investors withdrew from the market, requiring microfinance institutions to self-fund through market-rate capital, less than one-fifth would be able to do so without cutting outreach or raising rates.

Instead, most of the institutions were receiving a subsidy from social investors—*virtually all of it in the form of below-market-rate debt or equity.* The subsidy, however, was quite small relative to customers served. The median institution used a subsidy of US$26 per borrower.[27] To put that figure in context, it costs roughly US$2 per child to provide deworming medicine; GiveDirectly makes unconditional cash grants of US$1,000 per household per year. The US$26 per borrower figure, though modest, is somewhat inflated by the very high subsidies from some institutions. The amount of subsidy falls off quickly below the median.

The need for subsidy is a factor of the fixed costs of making loans. The median operating cost for loans is 14 percent of the loan amount. Nonprofits have done better at reducing operating costs, despite, or perhaps because of, the fact that they make smaller loans. As a consequence, for-profit institutions rely more heavily on subsidy than nonprofit ones.

Subsidies are also long-lasting. Despite the rhetoric of microfinance institutions moving quickly to sustainability, the majority of the subsidy—just over three-quarters—was flowing to institutions more than ten years old.

The pervasiveness, but small size per borrower, of subsidies bolsters the case for investing in microcredit. With relatively low costs, even modest benefits from microcredit can yield impressive cost-benefit ratios. But serving poor customers is costly, and there are likely limits to how much operating costs can be cut—particularly if the base product offering changes (as evidence suggests that it should). The drive to cut operating costs to reach self-sustainability goes hand-in-hand with the cookie-cutter approach to microcredit products and client recruitment and selection that has dominated the industry—and plays a role in the modest measured impact.

The other important point to understand about microcredit subsidy is the likely behavior of institutions if subsidies fade out in response to perceptions of disappointing impact. Since subsidies essentially offset high fixed operating costs, loss of subsidy will force institutions to choose between raising costs for borrowers and shifting to serve wealthier customers with larger loans.

Continuing to invest in microfinance can maintain the status quo—and the potentially high cost-effectiveness ratios justify the status quo. But there also is substantial potential for social investors to increase impact by building on the low-cost platform that the microcredit industry has built out.

Notes

1. A. Banerjee, D. Karlan, and J. Zinman, "Six Randomized Evaluations of Microcredit: Introduction and Further Steps," *American Economic Journal: Applied Economics* 7, no. 1 (2015): 1–21, doi: 10.1257/app.2014028.

2. M. Pitt and S. Khandker, "The Impact of Group-Based Credit Programs on Poor Households in Bangladesh," *Journal of Political Economy* 106, no. 5 (1998): 958–96, doi: 10.1086/250037.

3. J. Morduch and D. Roodman, "The Impact of Microcredit on the Poor in Bangladesh: Revisiting the Evidence," *Journal of Development Studies* 50, no. 4 (2014): 583–604, doi: 10.1080/00220388.2013.858122.

4. D. Collins and others, *Portfolios of the Poor: How the World's Poor Live on $2 a Day* (Princeton University Press, 2010).

5. S. de Mel, D. McKenzie, and C. Woodruff, "Returns to Capital in Microenterprises: Evidence from a Field Experiment," *Quarterly Journal of Economics* 123, no. 4 (2008): 1329–72.

6. E. Breza and C. Kinnan, "Measuring the Equilibrium Impacts of Credit: Evidence from the Indian Microfinance Crisis," Working Paper 24329 (Cambridge, Mass.: National Bureau of Economic Research, 2018) (www.nber.org/papers/w24329).

7. A. Bernhardt and others, "Household Matters: Revisiting the Returns to Capital among Female Micro-entrepreneurs," Working Paper 23358 (Cambridge, Mass.: National Bureau of Economic Research, 2017) (www.nber.org/papers/w23358).

8. M. Fafchamps and others, "Microenterprise Growth and the Flypaper Effect: Evidence from a Randomized Experiment in Ghana," *Journal of Development Economics* 106 (2014): 211–26, doi: 10.1016/j.jdeveco.2013.09.010.

9. M. Hardy and G. Kagy, "It's Getting Crowded in Here: Experimental Evidence of Demand Constraints in the Gender Profit Gap," Working Paper (December 2018) (www.dropbox .com/s/kdz1or4r0404k9w/ITS_GETTING_CROWDED_HARDY_KAGY.pdf?dl=0).

10. E. Riley, "Hiding Loans in the Household Using Mobile Money: Experimental Evidence on Microenterprise Investment in Uganda," Working Paper (2018) (https://emmaalriley .files.wordpress.com/2018/12/hiding-loans-household-5.pdf); N. Fiala, "Returns to Microcredit, Cash Grants, and Training for Male and Female Microentrepreneurs in Uganda," *World Development* 105 (2017): 189–200.

11. B. Crépon and others, "Estimating the Impact of Microcredit on Those Who Take It Up: Evidence from a Randomized Experiment in Morocco," *American Economic Journal: Applied Economics* 7 no. 1 (2015): 123–50, doi: 10.127/app.20130535.

12. A. Banerjee and others, "Do Credit Constraints Limit Entrepreneurship? Heterogeneity in the Returns to Microfinance," Working Paper 17-104 (Evanston, Ill.: Buffett Institute Global Poverty Research Lab, 2018) (https://papers.ssrn.com/sol3/papers.cfm?abstract_id =3126359).

13. J. Bauchet, J. Morduch, and S. Ravi, "Failure vs. Displacement: Why an Innovative Anti-Poverty Program Showed No Net Impact in South India," *Journal of Development Economics* 116 (2015): 1–16, doi: 10.1016/j.jdeveco.2015.03.005.

14. K. Muralidharan, P. Niehaus, and S. Sukhtankar, "General Equilibrium Effects of (Improving) Public Employment Programs: Experimental Evidence from India," Working Paper 23838 (Cambridge, Mass.: National Bureau of Economic Research, January 2018) (www.nber.org/papers/w23838).

15. M. Burke, L. Bergquist, and E. Miguel, "Sell Low and Buy High: Arbitrage and Local Price Effects in Kenyan Markets," Working Paper 24476 (Cambridge, Mass.: National Bureau of Economic Research, 2018) (www.nber.org/papers/w24476).

16. D. Karlan and J. Zinman, "Follow the Money Not the Cash: Comparing Methods for Identifying Consumption and Investment Responses to a Liquidity Shock," *Journal of Development Economics* 121 (2016): 11–23, doi: 10.1016/j.jdeveco.2015.10.009.

17. E. Field and others, "Does the Classic Microfinance Model Discourage Entrepreneurship among the Poor? Experimental Evidence from India," *American Economic Review* 103, no. 6 (2013): 2196–226.

18. P. Agarwal and G. Barboni, "Knowing What's Good for You: Can a Repayment Flexibility Option in Microfinance Contracts Improve Repayment Rates and Business Outcomes?" Working Paper (2081) (www.giorgiabarboni.com/home/Research_files/Barboni_JMP.pdf).

19. P. Maitra and others, "Financing Smallholder Agriculture: An Experiment with Agent-Intermediated Microloans in India," *Journal of Development Economics* 127 (2017): 306–37, doi: 10.1016/j.jdeveco.2017.03.001.

20. R. Hussam, N. Rigol, and B. Roth, "Targeting High Ability Entrepreneurs Using Community Information: Mechanism Design in the Field," Working Paper (https://economics.mit.edu/files/14591).

21. D. McKenzie and C. Woodruff, "Business Practices in Small Firms in Developing Countries," *Management Science* 63, no. 9 (2016): 2967–81, doi: 10.1287/mnsc.2016.2492.

22. L. Beaman, J. Magruder, and J. Robinson, "Minding Small Change among Small Firms in Kenya," *Journal of Development Economics* 108 (2014): 69–86.

23. D. McKenzie and C. Woodruff, "What Are We Learning from Business Training and Entrepreneurship Evaluations around the Developing World?" Policy Research Working Paper 6202 (Washington: World Bank, 2012).

24. F. Campos and others, "Teaching Personal Initiative Beats Traditional Training in Boosting Small Business in West Africa," *Science* 357, no. 6357 (2017): 1287–90, doi: 10.1126/science.aan5329.

25. R. Cull, A. Demirgüç-Kunt, and J. Morduch, "The Microfinance Business Model: Enduring Subsidy and Modest Profit," Policy Research Working Paper 7786 (Washington: World Bank, 2016) (http://documents.worldbank.org/curated/en/404501470669620154/The-microfinance-business-model-enduring-subsidy-and-modest-profit).

26. Ibid.

27. Ibid.

Section III

THE CHALLENGE OF TECHNOLOGY
AND NEW PRODUCT INNOVATION
AND DEVELOPMENT

Photo by Kameron Kincade on Unsplash

EIGHT

Microfinance in the Age of Digital Finance

MOMINA AIJAZUDDIN AND MATTHEW BROWN

By making financial services such as savings, loans, remittances, payments, and in-surance accessible to the unbanked and underserved, microfinance is a vital tool for people at the base of the pyramid to manage their financial lives.

Financial services enable low-income people to transfer and receive funds, invest in enterprises to enhance productivity, smooth consumption, and build resilience against shocks such as illness and weather-related events. Moreover, microfinance is an important tool when it comes to empowering women and fostering equitable de-velopment and inclusive economic growth. As a sector, microfinance has pioneered numerous innovations that are now essential elements of inclusive financial systems. To stay relevant, microfinance must further innovate, better serve existing clients, and be at the forefront of developing the next generation of financial service solutions for the 1.7 billion who remain financially excluded in the world today.[1]

From its early stages in subsidized microenterprise lending, microfinance has evolved over the last twenty-plus years into financial inclusion—that is, individuals and businesses have access to useful and affordable financial products and services that meet their needs—transactions, payments, savings, credit, and insurance—delivered in a responsible and sustainable way. Technological innovations, partnerships, and new and improved business operating models are ensuring that an ever-greater number of households and businesses enjoy permanent access to high-quality, afford-able, and convenient financial services. As microfinance continues to evolve, it will need to avoid past pitfalls, adapt to evolving technology and more competitive land-scapes, and continue to play to its strengths by keeping its focus on the customer.

The International Finance Corporation (IFC) is the World Bank Group's main investor in financial inclusion and one of the largest investors in the sector globally. Over twenty years, IFC has made more than 600 microfinance investments totaling some US$5.2 billion and has undertaken 290 advisory projects in ninety-five countries. Among its most important achievements, IFC's microfinance engagements have played key roles in establishing commercial microfinance institutions (MFIs) with the potential to scale, deposit-taking MFIs under appropriate regulatory frameworks that allow MFIs to engage in full financial intermediation, greenfield MFIs in many fragile and conflict-affected situtations and IDA countries[2] such as Afghanistan, the Democratic Republic of Congo, and Liberia, and an asset class of specialized microfinance funds that became a nucleus for the emerging impact investing industry.

Over its twenty-year history of investing in microfinance, IFC has helped create commercial and sustainable microfinance markets with a demonstrated ability to deliver profitability with impact.[3] Although not all projects achieved their desired outcomes, it is worth noting that the financial and outreach performance of IFC investees has been significantly better when they transition into providing a broad range of financial services (deposits; micro, small, and medium-sized enterprise [MSME] loans; and others) and attract local private investors. Significant examples include numerous nongovernmental organization (NGO) MFI transformations; Acleda Bank's successful transition from NGO to Cambodia's largest commercial bank, and expansion regionally; and Bandhan's acquisition of a universal bank license and recent IPO in India. IFC has also contributed at the sector level as a founder and lead implementing partner of the Global Partnership for Financial Inclusion and a co-founder of the sectorwide Responsible Finance Forum; it also co-led the development of Guidelines for Responsible Investing in Digital Financial Services.[4]

In 2007, IFC expanded its microfinance portfolio to include engagements in digital financial services (DFS), initially with a focus on payments, agent banking, and data analytics, and more recently on digital banking and digital transformation. In 2012, IFC launched a joint initiative with the Mastercard Foundation to expand microfinance and advance DFS in sub-Saharan Africa.[5] Through fourteen African financial services providers, including banks, MFIs, and mobile network operators (MNOs), the partnership resulted in 7.2 million new DFS users on the continent (a 250 percent increase from the baseline), 45,000 new banking agents, and US$300 million in monthly transactions. Overall, through these investment and advisory projects, IFC estimates reaching 100 million adults through DFS.

Despite Progress, Large Gaps in Financial Inclusion Remain

The World Bank Group's Universal Financial Access by 2020 initiative (UFA 2020) emphasizes the importance of financial access as a step toward broader financial inclusion. UFA 2020 envisions that adults worldwide—women and men alike—will have access to a transaction account or an electronic instrument to store money, send payments, and receive deposits as a basic building block to manage their financial lives. To reap the full development potential of microfinance, there is a need to move beyond financial access to financial inclusion. This implies that customers have access to and use a range of quality financial services that are delivered in a responsible and sustainable way.

Global Findex 2017 highlights the great progress that has been made in expanding financial access. The number of people worldwide with an account grew by 515 million between 2014 and 2017. Sixty-nine percent of the world's adults have an account; up from 62 percent in 2014. However, 1.7 billion adults globally remain without an account, and the share of adults that have a basic transaction account in low- or middle-income economies is 63 percent, and among adults belonging to the poorest 40 percent just 54 percent. Some lower-middle-income countries such as India and Mongolia have markedly high account ownership rates of 80 percent and 93 percent, respectively, signifying environments with limited barriers to access. In Kenya, where 73 percent of adults have mobile money accounts, the number of adult accountholders jumped from 42 percent in 2011 to 82 percent in 2017, highlighting the role technology can have in enabling financial access.

Globally, the growth in account ownership from 2014 to 2017 has been fueled by financial institution accounts. The notable exception is sub-Saharan Africa, where 21 percent of adults have a mobile money account; globally, the figure is only 4.4 percent. Despite this progress, 1.5 billion adults in developing countries remain without an account, and individual access varies widely across regions and countries. The unbanked are largely concentrated in Asia and sub-Saharan Africa regions and are disproportionately poor and female. Beyond access, use of accounts varies dramatically across regions and remains an issue. In the South Asia region, about 31 percent of accounts were dormant—meaning they were unused for more than a year.

There remain significant gaps in access to financing as well. Global Findex notes that the number of adults borrowing from a financial institution or using a credit card remained flat at under 25 percent between 2014 and 2017. The World Bank estimates that there are 365–445 MSMEs in emerging markets, the majority micro and informal, and 70 percent lack adequate financing to thrive and grow. IFC estimates that there is a US$5.2 trillion financing gap for formal MSMEs and a US$2.9 trillion gap for informal MSMEs in developing countries. The total MSME financing gap for women is estimated at US$1.7 trillion. The financing gap for formal micro-enterprises is US$719 billion, with the largest gaps in East Asia and the Pacific and sub-Saharan Africa.[6]

Agriculture remains among the most neglected sectors for financing despite its significant contribution to gross domestic product (GDP) in many developing countries. An estimated 1 percent of bank lending in Africa is allocated to the agriculture sector despite contributing almost 18 percent of GDP across sub-Saharan Africa.[7] Recent estimates say the demand for smallholder financing exceeds US$200 billion for approximately 270 million smallholder farmers in Latin America, sub-Saharan Africa, and South and Southeast Asia.[8] In addition to lacking access to working capital, smallholder farmers and other agri-value chain actors lack financial products—savings, insurance, and payments—appropriately tailored to their needs in terms of design, accessibility, and affordability.[9]

Country context also matters, and hence greater collaboration among a variety of actors is necessary to foster an enabling environment for financial inclusion and scale. As a positive sign, since 2010 more than fifty-five countries have made commitments to financial inclusion, and more than thirty are developing a national strategy. However, seventy-six governments have introduced interest rate caps to shield consumers from higher interest rates that may also restrict the supply of credit, particularly to the unbanked and underserved.[10] In many countries, progress is required to strengthen the information environment, promote unique IDs, educate and protect consumers, and encourage innovation through regulation. The lack of appropriate and proportional regulation could remain a constraint in many markets moving forward.

These issues and gaps highlight the many challenges confronting MFIs. In addition to external factors, traditional microfinance models have faced two main challenges—cost and efficiency, and limited impact—that point to shortcomings of their business models. Outreach among MFIs has been mainly to clients in urban areas who are engaged in specific economic activities that can cover the cost of borrowing. Nevertheless, a large number of unbanked still exist—Findex data show that there are pockets of large underserved—rural, agriculture and women. It is vital to learn and listen to clients. Often-cited reasons for not taking up financial services are that they are too expensive, too far away, and not useful. Challenges for microfinance in the twenty-first century will be to develop cheaper, faster, and demand-driven services for such clients—including in smaller markets (not India and China) and to bring down costs of delivery. Many of the leading microfinance networks and retail MFIs are reformulating their strategies as a result, particularly in Asia and Africa.

The Changing Landscape–a Digital World

Internet and mobile technologies have the power to transform the financial services sector and dramatically reduce the cost of serving poor households, who transact in small amounts. Internet users now exceed 4 billion globally, and unique mobile users exceed 5 billion with a penetration rate of 67 percent. A total of 1 billion new mobile subscribers have been added in the four years since 2013. Over the past ten years, with the growth of internet and mobile connectivity, DFS—especially digital payments— have taken off. The GSMA reports that there are over 200 implementations of mobile banking in markets across Africa, the Asia Pacific, and Latin America and the Caribbean with many more being planned.[11]

Furthermore, according to the GSMA 2018 State of the Industry Report, the mobile money industry is now processing US$1.3 billion a day; there are 272 mobile money deployments in ninety countries and 866 million registered accounts worldwide.[12] Mobile money has evolved into the leading payment platform for the digital economy in many emerging markets. The most successful providers are integrated with a wide range of third parties, including banks, billers, merchants, and organizations for bulk disbursements. Many of these implementations are led by MNOs, who seek to reduce their airtime distribution costs and customer churn.

Combined with internet and mobile technology, advances in technological innovation hold promise for solving some of the key challenges to achieving full financial inclusion.[13] Artificial intelligence, automation, big data, distributed ledger technology, and machine learning are just a few examples of technology trends that are accelerating the pace of innovation in financial services. New entrants including MNOs such as Telenor and Orange, payment service providers, merchant aggregators, retailers, fintech companies, neobanks, and superplatforms are leveraging these technologies and altering the competitive landscape for financial services.

The potential benefits of DFS to people, business, and governments, however, remain largely untapped. It is estimated that widespread use of digital finance has the potential to boost the annual GDP of emerging economies by US$3.7 trillion by 2025, with one-third coming from additional investment in the MSME sector and two-thirds from the increased productivity of larger businesses and government.[14] There is therefore plenty of room for further innovation by a range of financial services providers, supported by enabling regulatory environments, to take up the challenge of developing new business models, partnerships, and products that can take the financial services industry to the next level and close the remaining gaps to financial access and inclusion.

Digital technologies are also changing the demand side of the financial services equation. Digital affects the way people communicate and interact, get access to and share information, as well as buy and sell goods and services, and as a result, digital technologies are influencing customer preferences and expectations. As microfinance clients become more digitally savvy, they take advantage of these tools to improve aspects of their daily lives. As their preferences and expectations change, MFIs are challenged to become more demand-driven and deliver customer-centric products and services that are more accessible, affordable, flexible, intuitive, and convenient.

This "digital disruption" is changing the economics of financial service delivery to benefit the underserved and unbanked in fundamental ways and forcing traditional MFIs to adapt. In markets ranging from Mozambique to Pakistan to Peru, MFIs have begun embracing the digital wave and have begun demonstrating the ability to increase scale and reach previously un(der)served populations with more convenient products and services. Despite this, the pace of innovation and greater competition continue to pose opportunities and threats for MFIs. Strategic, technology, and competitive risks faced by MFIs are greater than ever (and often overlap), placing ever greater pressure on MFI boards and CEOs to devise innovative solutions and strategies to fulfill their missions and remain relevant and competitive in their markets.

This new reality also presents tremendous opportunities for innovation by MFIs to reduce costs, improve efficiency and productivity, dramatically increase outreach among underserved and unbanked populations, and improve customer engagement and retention. The key challenge is determining the appropriate strategy given each MFI's ambition and goals, business model and customer segments, internal capacity and resources, potential technology partners and vendors, and the local operating environment, including relevant political, economic, social, legal, and regulatory issues—not an easy task for the uninitiated in this new digital world.

Microfinance's Digital Future

Some trailblazing organizations with cultures open to innovation have been fast to benefit from the opportunities DFS bring. Some of the largest microfinance network organizations, including Baobab (formerly Microcred) and ACCION, have begun

BOX 8-1.   Agent Banking at Baobab Madagascar

Baobab is a digital finance group of companies serving low-income individuals and micro and small enterprises in nine African countries and China.

Madagascar, with an annual GDP per capita of US$401, is one of the poorest countries in the world. An unstable political climate further exacerbates conditions for small-business owners, and only 18 percent of adults have access to formal financial services. In 2015, the Madagascar subsidiary of Baobab launched an agent banking network to expand credit and deposit services to new, and especially rural, customers. Using a shared platform and biometric technology for identification, agents began processing cash-in, cash-out transactions via electronic wallets.

By the end of 2017, close to half of Baobab Madagascar's 53,000 active customers had used agents, and digital transactions made up 43 percent of the total volume of cash transactions. Madagascar now has 304 agents, almost ten times the country's thirty-seven branches. Digital uptake has been further promoted through Baobab's launch of "Taka" nano-loans, which can only be processed by agents. Taka loans operate outside of a traditional loan schedule, instead giving customers incentives—such as the opportunity to renew a loan or take out a larger loan—for repayment within fifteen or thirty days.

This case study is further elaborated in Christian Rodriguez and others, *A New Banking Model for Africa: Lessons on Digitization from Four Years of Operations* (Washington: IFC-Mastercard Foundation Partnership for Financial Inclusion, 2019).

looking beyond traditional microfinance and leveraging the power of new technologies such as mobile and agent banking to make financial services more affordable and accessible (box 8-1).[15] Likewise, many progressive banks and MFIs have begun to understand the potential of DFS to improve their businesses, usually focusing on agent services to extend reach and mobile access to improve customer convenience. To date, the most common digital services provided by MFIs are payments (person-to-person: P2P; business-to-person: B2P; government-to-person: G2P) and other over-the-counter transactions by agents, followed by mobile access to savings accounts to increase deposits and in limited cases digital loan products. To keep pace with increasing competition and rapidly evolving technology and innovation, MFIs will need to continue to adapt their business models to ensure their long-term sustainability and competitiveness.

There are still numerous questions about the final outcomes. Will high-tech win over high-touch? Will technology enable DFS to reach the last mile, or will some populations remain structurally excluded? The endgame is far from clear, but the vision for the future of microfinance is less so—ideally, it will be a frictionless ecosystem of diverse financial services providers where accessing quality financial services by the underserved and unbanked is as easy as getting water from a flowing tap. Where will MFIs fit in? Although MFIs cannot control the environments they find themselves, they do need to make choices about how they will face the future, taking into consideration their mission and vision, their strengths and weaknesses, and the opportunities and threats they face in their markets. Based on current experience, we offer eight issues to consider as MFIs look to the future.

There Is a Business Case for Digital Financial Services

From 2014 to 2018, IFC and the Mastercard Foundation conducted a four-year longitudinal study looking at nine MFIs in sub-Saharan Africa as they implemented digital financial services, mainly agent banking and mobile banking solutions. The study found emerging evidence that there is a business case for DFS. For example, transactions through agent networks cost 25 percent less to provide than branch teller transactions, and the opportunity to source deposits from a broader market can have a positive impact on cost of funds. Other research shows that the ability for clients to repay loans anytime, anywhere has improved portfolio quality by as much as 10 percent.

However, the study also found that expectations for the adoption and use of DFS and the potential for direct and indirect income, as well as expense and cost-efficiency gains, need to be carefully calibrated with reality. In many instances, DFS expectations are higher than what reality can deliver, including account activity rates, agent transaction volumes, fee income, and direct agent commissions. MFIs need to develop business models tailored to their specific market conditions and unique capabilities. MFIs' expectations and experiences may differ greatly, depending on their different market contexts. Each MFI launching DFS needs, therefore, to chart its own unique path to self-sustainability, which may require innovative solutions and the layering and cross-selling of products and services to be viable. For these reasons, a well developed business case is key.

Microfinance Strategies Need to Reflect New Digital Realities

The evolving technological and competitive landscapes for microfinance require MFIs to take a renewed look at their strategies. As a starting point, an MFI seeking to develop a digital strategy must identify the broad goal or combination of goals it wants to accomplish. In other words, at the outset of the decision to embark on a digital journey the first question to be answered is Why?. In general, the answer to that question will be among the following:

- to significantly reduce the MFI's costs;

- to enhance customer experience, thereby deepening and broadening its relationship with customers;

- to expand market share, either to gain first-mover advantage in a market or to increase profitability; and

- to defend against new market entrants.

The goals of a digital strategy are also informed by the MFI's mission and vision and desired financial and social outcomes. For instance, if an MFI's vision is serving farmers and micro and small enterprises with a focus on women, this same focus should be reflected in the digital strategy and be made clear in the drivers of a digital transformation process. In other words, the MFI should state whether it is embarking on this journey because of increased competitive pressure (a defensive strategy) or because it is seeking to expand its client base. An MFI may also choose to refine or expand its mission and vision as part of the digital strategy by including serving customers in rural areas—by piloting digital agriculture apps, for instance.

There is no one path or best approach to a successful digital strategy, but there are key issues that an MFI must consider. For example, an MFI must first clearly understand and define what it wants to accomplish and how the market and environment as well as internal factors can facilitate or hinder implementation. There must be a clear business case and understanding of how the business model may need to shift. The MFI must consider its resource needs and understand the key enablers, such as information technology (IT) infrastructure, data and analytics, partnerships, and the "digital" culture. Finally, an MFI must understand the key elements that will drive effective change within the institution and make it possible to implement and accomplish its goals.

Uncertainty Demands Strong Risk Management Frameworks to Achieve Objectives

Technology and innovative business models provide many opportunities for MFIs, but also come with new risks. To fill a gap in existing industry publications on risks associated with DFS, IFC published a handbook on DFS and risk management as a practitioner's guide to identifying, assessing, and mitigating risk specific to DFS.[16] The handbook is based on interviews with practitioners, vendors, and industry stakeholders and on in-depth risk assessments undertaken in sub-Saharan Africa. During the research, IFC learned that there are very few institutions, including both banks and MFIs, with any kind of risk framework for DFS. It concluded that there is a strong need for financial services providers across the industry to strengthen their risk management practices if they are to achieve their business objectives.

Through this research initiative, it also became apparent that, although risks can be described in various categories, they are often strongly related. Technology, strategic, and agent management risks can all lead to reputational risk, and fraud can lead to even bigger financial losses from reputational damage than from the fraud itself. The research also identified the most effective strategies for managing risk—for example, using call centers to track, monitor, and predict eventualities; using strong reconciliation and settlement processes to reduce potential losses; and taking partnerships seriously to ensure that partners are held accountable. A key lesson learned, however, was the overarching importance of strategic risk, the risk that the strategy fails to meet its objectives owing to deployment of inappropriate services, poor technology, customer behavior not aligning with initial model, or unanticipated market developments. As the industry will continue to face new and evolving risks, it is critical that MFIs implement appropriate risk management frameworks to mitigate the "effect of uncertainty on objectives."[17]

Good Governance Remains Critical, and IT Governance Equally So

The Microfinance/Financial Inclusion Banana Skins surveys consistently find governance to be among the top risks facing MFIs.[18] Failure to enact good corporate governance practices has resulted in an inability to achieve the mission and purpose of the MFI, underperformance, and in extreme cases closure of the MFI. In this sense, a basic reason to focus on improving corporate governance is to ensure that the MFI has appropriate structures and processes in place to direct and control it effectively and ensure its long-term viability. Organizations with good governance practices perform better than those with inadequate ones—a reality supported by IFC's global experience and documented in case studies of IFC microfinance investees, including in Jordan and Cambodia.[19]

Despite this, MFIs do not always give governance the priority it deserves and may introduce governance reforms only at a superficial level, to meet legal or regulatory requirements, for example. In so doing, they not only expose themselves to risk but also miss out on valuable opportunities to introduce internal structures and processes that would enable them to build confidence with investors and improve their reputation with stakeholders, increase operational efficiency by establishing a framework to manage risks, and reduce vulnerability to crises with quicker and more effective responses.

Given the expanding role of technology in the delivery of financial services, it is extremely important that MFIs take concrete steps to improve not only their overall governance but IT governance as well. Technological missteps can lead to unintended strategic, reputational, and financial consequences for MFIs and ultimately failure to achieve the MFI's mission and vision. MFIs that align their IT to support their business strategy will be better positioned for sustained success. As technology and innovation continue to evolve, MFIs need to be able to adapt and enhance their existing systems and make significant investments in infrastructure, systems, software, and applications. Related risks such as data privacy concerns and cybersecurity threats further emphasize the need for sound and effective IT governance.

As a first step in improving IT governance, board members need to dedicate time and resources to understanding IT activities and the associated IT-related business risks. Certain responsibilities may be delegated to an IT steering committee, but high-level oversight is critical. Ultimately, IT governance needs to ensure that technology generates business value for the institution and that the risks posed by using it are appropriately managed. The key challenge for MFIs will be attracting appropriate talent at both board and management levels with the required IT expertise and skills to achieve this goal.

Data Is a Key Tool for Innovation and Growth

Through customer acquisition and transaction management, MFIs have built a wealth of data on customer behavior over time. As the use of internet and mobile technologies by MFI clients increases, an even larger digital footprint will open opportunities for MFIs to know their customers at a granular level and use this knowledge to offer high-quality services and improve client satisfaction and retention. At the same time, the analytical capacity of computing is rapidly advancing while the cost of data storage is falling. A data-driven MFI has the potential to act based on evidence, rather than on anecdotal observation or in reaction to what competitors are doing in the market. Data analytics, including techniques such as predictive modeling, can be used to better understand the profile of customers in order to improve customer service and develop new products.[20]

Despite being well-positioned to take advantage of data and analytics, many MFIs have yet to implement a systematic, data-driven approach in their operations and organizations. Common barriers to the application of data insights for product development include a lack of understanding, scarcity of skills, and inability to convert data and insights into practical business decisions. Data can now be used for a specific purpose, such as credit scoring, but can also be employed more generally to increase operational efficiency and drive greater value for customers by developing market insights. A recent example of this is the collaboration between Ant Financial, Alibaba's financial services arm, and the China Foundation for Poverty Alleviation (CFPA), China's largest MFI, which is allowing credit scoring of its client base to differentiate between high-risk and low-risk repeat clients (box 8-2). They are working together to compile information on over 1,000 variables, such as market

---

BOX 8-2.   Ant Financial Providing Inclusive Digital Financial Services

Access to finance is a major challenge for MSMEs in China; 70 percent of MSMEs and 70 percent of women entrepreneurs have difficulty accessing finance. Ant Financial, an affiliate of China's Alibaba Group, officially launched in 2014 and is now the world's largest fintech. The company evolved from Alipay, the world's largest third-party payments platform. Powered by mobile internet, big data, and cloud computing technology, Ant Financial is committed to using technology to provide inclusive financial services. Its 3-1-0 model—which makes it possible for borrowers to apply for a loan in three minutes and get approved in one second with zero human interaction—has reduced transaction costs and the speed of loan processing for MSMEs.

In 2016, Ant Financial become a shareholder of CFPA, China's largest MFI. The partnership allowed CFPA to utilize Ant Financial's risk management, big data, and cloud computing technologies to expand credit scoring of clients and provide products better tailored to their needs.

purchasing patterns, climate, and agricultural data. The treasure trove of data will theoretically allow the MFI to make more informed decisions about prospective clients as well as offer tailored products built on the back of existing provincial-level supply chains.

As microfinance markets mature, it will be increasingly important not just to gain a competitive edge, but also to ensure that the services and products developed for clients meet their needs. For instance, for rural areas the emphasis would need to include financial literacy, access to markets, consideration of economies of scale, and logistics. The major challenge for the sector will be how to leverage the utility of data while ensuring people's privacy, especially when people do not realize how their data are being used.

Partnerships Are Key for Scale

Partnerships may be critical to the future of microfinance for expanding financial inclusion. MFIs can pursue different forms of partnerships, but generally speaking a partnership will have only three key objectives: expand the MFI's product offerings, extend reach, and provide access to data. To expand the product offerings, an MFI may pursue a partnership with a specialized service provider or fintech that offers a product not offered by the MFI (for example, crop insurance). By partnering with agent network managers or providers of mobile financial services, MFIs can expand their reach without expanding their costly branch infrastructure. Furthermore, partnerships with data-rich companies (such as fast-moving consumer goods companies), in addition to providing greater access to data, can help MFIs significantly increase their assets by leveraging data to establish creditworthiness, develop market insights, and improve operational management.

In some of the most challenging microfinance markets, MNOs present partnership opportunities for MFIs. MNOs can help MFIs provide their services more cost efficiently. For example, Musoni, a Kenyan MFI, has reduced the time required to complete a loan application by 80 percent; in addition, clients can repay loans anytime, anywhere, which has improved the MFI's portfolio quality by as much as 10 percent. By partnering with a specialized agent network manager, Caja Sullana in Peru managed to reduce the monthly operating cost of an outlet from US$5,000 to US$500. The cost for the in-house agent network is 38 percent of the cost of a branch (in comparison, the cost for an outsourced network is 65 percent of the cost of a branch). Its transaction costs were reduced by 50 percent overall, and transaction volume increased by 40 percent.[21]

Teaming up with fintechs and technology providers can help financial institutions roll out new offerings to customers in a relatively short time. Such partnerships can be made "above the line" by making them public and highlighting the cooperation between the players; they can also be done "below the line" by simply adopting an existing technology and outsourcing the partner's offerings. Application programming interfaces (APIs) will simplify how these partnerships are implemented.

Partnerships are not necessarily pain- or risk-free. Alignment of interests, negotiating power, revenue sharing, and customer ownership are just a few of many issues that MFIs will have to carefully navigate with potential partners. MFIs will need to carefully weigh the costs and benefits of partnering against going it alone. However, for smaller MFIs partnerships may be the least cost-prohibitive approach to remaining competitive and increasing scale, as well as offer the best means for improving the quality of their services to customers.

Delivering a Better Customer Experience

Financial institutions have been implementing digital solutions for decades. These usually encompass cost-reduction functions such as process automation and online replication of existing functionalities. But now there is an urgent need to become customer-centric by aligning with customer needs and goals and investing in digital, agile, and efficient processes that create mutual trust.

Key questions an MFI should answer when developing a customer's journey:

- How can data best be used to increase personalization of the customer experience? This includes establishing what is known about a customer from past and current behavior.

- How can a customer be better served not only in terms of experience, but also speed? This includes reducing delays and wait times in branches.

- How can convenience be improved so a customer can transact anytime and anywhere? This involves adopting a multichannel or omnichannel approach offering 24/7 access.

- How can the user-interface design be optimized to ensure a smooth and seamless customer experience?

▪ What are customer pain points, and how can they best be addressed? This involves ensuring that customers can gain access to and use financial services with ease.

▪ How can we move from descriptive and diagnostic analytics to predictive and prescriptive analytics to anticipate and deliver new product offerings that meet client needs?

Advances in technology and innovation have vastly increased the opportunities to improve the customer experience. Achieving the prospect of 24/7 financial services (anytime, anywhere) has huge implications for customers and the MFIs' value proposition. Rather than abolishing branches and tellers, MFIs should consider adopting a multichannel or omnichannel approach as a first step. An omnichannel offers more than just multiple ways for customers to transact. It is a seamless and consistent interaction between customers and their financial institution across multiple channels. Whereas a multichannel approach is focused on transactions, an omnichannel approach focuses on the customer experience: making interactions between the institution and the customer as easy as possible. The goal is an improved, tailored transaction experience that should lead to greater use of a particular service and channel. Ultimately, the customer experience may be the key differentiator for MFIs in a crowded marketplace where customers will choose experience over loyalty to any institution.

Culture–the Human Element

A final issue for MFIs to consider as they look to the future is the issue of culture. As the saying goes, "culture eats strategy for breakfast."[22] Many efforts to implement change despite having a well-thought-out strategy, business case and plan fail because of inadequate attention to the human element. Innovation and change require an environment that gives staff confidence to test new ideas and devise new solutions without fear of failure. As MFIs begin implementing strategies that reflect the new digital realities, they must also change old ways of thinking and doing and, essentially, change culture.

Experience to date with DFS deployments by MFIs suggests that stakeholder involvement, skills development and training, and internal communication are critical to achieve this kind of environment. Existing staff may otherwise feel threatened by and create resistance to change (box 8-3). For example, branch staff may fear branch

BOX 8-3.   Change Management at LAPO Microfinance Bank

LAPO Microfinance Bank is the largest national microfinance bank in Nigeria offering financial services mainly via a group lending methodology. In 2017, LAPO piloted an agent network recruiting agents only from its very engaged customer base and became the first MFI to put in place an agent network in Nigeria.

Because of the small scale of the pilot (fifty agents), the MFI did not consider it necessary to communicate to all employees the benefits of having an agent network, which is a fundamental aspect of promoting change and internal buy-in. The lack of communication contributed to field staff viewing the new channel as a threat, resulting in a lack of support for critical activities such as facilitating customer acquisition and deposit mobilization.

To rectify its mistake, LAPO realized it needed to develop a change management strategy to address field staff resistance to the digital channel. The strategy was twofold: introduce both *communication* and *training* activities to keep employees informed of the change process and its impact, to remove obstacles and opposition to change, and to ensure continued productivity throughout the agent rollout process.

This case study is further elaborated in Gisela Davico and Christian Rodriguez, *Field Note 8: Changing Change Management–Adapting Internal and External Culture in Times of Digital Transformation* (Washington: IFC-Mastercard Partnership for Financial Inclusion, 2018).

closures and loss of jobs following the launch of an agent network. It is critical to keep in mind, therefore, that buy-in and involvement from existing branch staff as well as consistent communication and training are equally important to more technical aspects when developing a DFS strategy.

Digital transformations can also result in dramatic changes in the ways MFIs interact with customers. Further lessons from DFS deployments suggest the following should be part of an MFI's change management framework:[23]

- Customer centricity: MFIs must understand the needs and desires of different customer segments to ensure DFS are relevant and accessible to customers and be able to respond to the potential fears and psychological barriers customers might have in the adoption of DFS.

■ Constant feedback and adaptation: When changes are introduced, MFIs must create customer and staff feedback loops and set up mitigating measures to address failure or discontent with change. MFIs should ensure that it has the mechanisms in place to collect, analyze, and respond to any feedback.

■ Addressing emotional aspects of change: The change from high-touch to low-touch interactions with customers tends to produce a range of emotions and negative reactions among customers and staff that need to be appropriately addressed to ensure adequate levels of trust for the full adoption of DFS.

■ Implementing a structured step-by-step approach: The upheaval that a digital transformation brings can clash with the institutional ability to process change. To avoid feelings of exhaustion and uncertainty among staff and customers, MFIs should introduce change incrementally.

Digital transformation, whether of processes, channels, products, or the entire institution, requires a significant culture change if it is to succeed. It is a unique opportunity, however, for MFIs to adapt their business models and operations and ultimately fulfill the organization's vision and mission.

Conclusion

With more than 1.7 billion people and between 365–445 million MSMEs still without access to basic financial services in much of the developing world, increasing financial access and inclusion remains an enormous challenge. The recurrence of financial crises globally has underscored the importance of sustainable microfinance business models with sound corporate governance, risk management, and responsible financial practices for a more stable, resilient, and inclusive financial services sector to achieve economic growth and development impact.

Advances in technology and the pace of innovation hold promise for addressing many of the key challenges to achieving full financial inclusion. New entrants such as MNOs, payment service providers, and fintechs are altering the competitive landscape for microfinance. These disruptive technologies and new entrants are radically changing the financial services industry. New business models and partnerships are shifting profits within the financial services value chain, forcing traditional microfinance business models to adapt and changing the economics of delivery to benefit the unbanked and underserved. The result is more meaningful and attractive customer experiences (such as lower direct and indirect costs, greater convenience, and instantaneous service delivery) than those offered by more traditional MFI products and services.

These new realities present tremendous opportunities for MFIs to reduce costs, improve efficiency and productivity, increase outreach among underserved and unbanked populations, and upgrade customer relations and retention. To stay relevant, MFIs must remain at the forefront of innovation while staying true to their missions. MFIs were once the disruptors and once again need to push the boundaries of the financial frontier by building on an industry that has demonstrated its ability to be socially responsible, sustainable, and resilient through crisis and slow growth, and to reach the base of the pyramid with impact.

Notes

1. Asli Demirgüç-Kunt and others, *The Global Findex Database 2017: Measuring Financial Inclusion and the Fintech Revolution* (Washington: World Bank Group, 2018).

2. International Development Association (IDA) countries are those with low per capita incomes that lack the financial ability to borrow from the International Bank for Reconstruction and Development.

3. Momina Aijazuddin and others, *Smart Lessons: Small Beginnings for Great Opportunities—Lessons Learned from 20 Years of Microfinance Projects in IFC* (Washington: IFC, 2015).

4. The guidelines can be found on the Responsible Finance Forum website (responsiblefinanceforum.org).

5. Fahima Said Bille and others, *Digital Access: The Future of Financial Inclusion in Africa* (Washington: World Bank Group, 2018).

6. M. Bruhn and others, *MSME Finance Gap: Assessment of the Shortfalls and Opportunities in Financing Micro, Small and Medium Enterprises in Emerging Markets* (Washington: IFC, 2017).

7. World Bank Open Data (data.worldbank.org/indicator/NV.AGR.TOTL.ZS).

8. Laura Goldman and others, *Inflection Point: Unlocking Growth in the Era of Farmer Finance*, Dalberg Global Development Advisors, April 2016.

9. For more on providing digital financial services to smallholder farmers, see IFC–Mastercard Foundation Partnership for Financial Inclusion, *Digital Financial Services for Agriculture Handbook* (Washington: IFC, 2019).

10. Samuel Munzele Maimbo and others, "Interest Rate Caps Around the World: Still Popular, But a Blunt Instrument," Policy Research Working Paper No. WPS 7070 (Washington: World Bank Group, 2014).

11. Francesco Pasti, "State of the Industry Report on Mobile Money 2018" (London: GSMA, 2019).

12. Ibid.

13. Simon Andrews and others, *Reinventing Business through Disruptive Technologies: Sector Trends and Investment Opportunities for Firms in Emerging Markets* (Washington: IFC, 2019).

14. James Manyika and others, *Digital Finance for All: Powering Inclusive Growth in Emerging Economies* (San Francisco: McKinsey Global Institute, September 2016).

15. Read further about Microcred and other examples in IFC–Mastercard Foundation Partnership for Financial Inclusion, *Alternative Delivery Channels and Technology Handbook* (Washington: IFC, 2015).

16. IFC–Mastercard Foundation Partnership for Financial Inclusion, *Digital Financial Services and Risk Management Handbook* (Washington: IFC, 2016).

17. Risk as defined by *ISO 31000:2018 Risk Management—Guidelines* (Geneva: International Organization for Standardization, 2018).

18. Since 2008, the Centre for the Study of Financial Innovation (CSFI) Banana Skins survey of the risks in Microfinance, now Financial Inclusion, have listed governance risk among the top risks facing MFIs. Governance risk is the seventh highest risk in the 2018 survey, up from ninth in 2016.

19. Good examples of successful projects undertaken at financial institutions to improve their corporate governance can be found in *Corporate Governance Success Stories: IFC Advisory Services in the Middle East and North Africa* (Washington: IFC, 2010); *Corporate Governance Case Studies: Cambodia* (Washington: IFC, 2018); and *Corporate Governance Case Studies: Vietnam* (Washington: IFC, 2018).

20. IFC–Mastercard Foundation Partnership for Financial Inclusion, *Data Analytics and Digital Financial Services Handbook* (Washington: IFC, 2017).

21. Diana Lewin and others, *Mobile Financial Services in Microfinance Institutions: Caja Sullana in Peru*, IFC Mobile Money Toolkit (Washington: World Bank Group, 2017).

22. The observation originated with Peter Drucker and was made famous by Mark Fields, president at Ford Motor Company.

23. Adapted from Gisela Davico and Christian Rodriguez, *Field Note 8: Changing Change Management—Adapting Internal and External Culture in Times of Digital Transformation* (Washington: IFC, 2018).

Microfinance and Digital Finance

GRETA BULL

The emergence of digital technology in finance poses an interesting dilemma for microfinance institutions (MFIs). By extending the reach and convenience of payment and credit services, nontraditional providers are beginning to encroach on the space traditionally occupied by MFIs, particularly in Africa. Although MFIs have largely operated in parallel with mobile network operators (MNOs) since M-Pesa burst onto the scene in 2008, we are starting to see signs of strain. Recent reports from Kenya illustrate the emerging dynamic and potential risks for MFIs: microfinance banks currently face a serious threat, ironically, not directly from M-Pesa, but from the entry of banks with low-cost deposits into the consumer lending space.[1] Interest rate caps imposed on traditional credit products have encouraged banks to shift toward short-term, data-driven products delivered over digital channels, where providers have largely been able to circumvent the cap. The result has been dramatic growth in digital credit by banks and signs of competitive pressure on microfinance banks, which have collectively chalked up losses for 2016 to 2019.

So, what's a microfinance institution to do in the digital age? In my view, the worst strategy is to do nothing: to keep running the business the way it has always been run and hope to stay under the radar somehow. This strategy might work in a few very challenging places but is a road to oblivion in most markets, where technology is transforming the face of financial services delivery at a rapid pace.

So, what is a winning strategy in this context? The good news is that there is not just one. Microfinance institutions need to take a long look in the mirror to determine what they are good at, and what they are not so good at. They also need to understand what is happening in the markets around them because the competitive landscapes are evolving rapidly but heterogeneously, particularly in Africa and Asia. They need to understand the technology options available to them and how new technologies can help improve or even transform their businesses. They need to invest in staff who understand technology and data. Finally, they need to make careful choices about how to navigate the road ahead.

What are some of the things that should guide them along the way? Here are the ways I think about technology and new business models in microfinance.

- First and foremost, MFIs should embrace the opportunities technology offers. But in doing so they must have a very clear idea of what they are trying to achieve and from this should flow a clearly articulated business case. I have seen many MFIs invest in technology or agent networks without having the faintest idea why they were doing it, and without building a business plan to support the investment. The main reasons for investing in innovation are usually to acquire new customers, improve the experience for existing customers, lower costs, and mobilize deposits. But many MFIs assume, in a leap of faith, that an investment in technology will transform the business, without first building a plan, costing it out, and testing the assumptions. Without a clear business plan and the right pricing in place, this can be an expensive strategy. For example, I once reviewed a project with a Caja Municipal in Peru that provided a very popular bill payment service to its clients via agents. The clients loved it, but that was the problem. For every bill that was paid, the MFI lost money because it had priced the service incorrectly and did not think about the adjacencies that might contribute to its core business, such as deposit collection. The more popular the service, the more money the MFI lost. I met with another MFI in West Africa that was investing in a technology integration with its core banking for an experimental payment device for agents, without having either any sort of business plan for why it was investing in the new technology, or a view on the role of agents. The reason they were doing this? A member of their board was interested in technology. Neither of these scenarios is a winning tech strategy.

▪ Some of the most common reasons MFIs invest in digital finance are to increase outreach and improve efficiency. Agents can help with both, if the investment is managed well. A publication by the International Finance Corporation (IFC) on its work with nine MFIs in Africa indicates that the cost of managing transactions by an agent is about 25 percent lower than the cost of handling the same transaction in a branch.[2] This is a significant saving, although perhaps not quite as much as has sometimes been claimed. That is because it is expensive to manage agent networks. One data point on this comes from the GSMA, which in its 2017 State of the Industry Report estimated that MNOs pay out 52 percent of total revenues from mobile money operations in agent commissions alone.[3] That does not include the costs of training agents, liquidity management, or branding. For this reason, the focus should be on active agents, not on overall agent numbers. A classic mistake is to try to grab market share by engaging many agents at once. I have seen banks do it, I have seen MNOs do it, and I have also seen microfinance institutions do it. Many big players have failed by making this mistake, and donors have contributed to it by providing incentives to scale up rather than insisting on a sustainable business model. Start small and focus on usage. Also, bear in mind that managing agents opens up whole new avenues of operational risk, which must be managed differently than more traditional microfinance risks.

▪ MFIs need to invest in information technology, but they must do it wisely and with an eye to the future. People often speak as though bricks and mortar are the biggest legacy cost of banking. But a branch can be closed relatively easily. My view is that legacy information technology (IT) systems are a much bigger challenge. It is a lot harder to switch IT systems, as anyone who has been through an IT migration knows. MFI IT systems are cobbled together, do not speak to each other, and often require manual workarounds to produce reports. Investing in good IT systems that connect with each other and have the flexibility to grow with the business is an imperative. Technology is a challenge for MFIs, which have limited staff capacity to filter the value of vendors' offers. Common sense can be a useful guide here, as well as investing in good IT staff and consultants to guide the choices in tech investments. As a rule of thumb, choosing simple, low-cost systems that bake in flexibility for the future is crucial to getting this right. MFIs should not try to tackle cutting-edge tech problems like cracking blockchain for the world. They should look at more established solutions like putting their systems in the cloud, building more flexible connectivity between different information systems through application programming interfaces (APIs), and investing in improved data mining and analytics capabilities.

■ With improved IT systems comes the possibility of making better use of customer data, and this is a practice MFIs really do need to adopt. I am not suggesting that MFIs should get into the business of gathering and algorithmically scoring social media data to look for clues about customer creditworthiness. MFIs can start by making much better use of the data they already have on their clients, as it is potentially highly predictive and can offer important insights into customers. The main challenge? Many MFIs still keep paper records! The data are on a shelf somewhere gathering dust. Someone asked me recently where to begin on this—how to digitize all of those years of customer data. My response is this: start today. Structure data in a way that will be useful, and start gathering it now. If possible, try to digitize some historical data, but that daunting task should not stop MFIs from building better data management structures now. Data pools can be built over time. Putting a structured system in place today should be the priority.

■ Importantly, MFIs must put customers at the center of their business strategy. They must thoroughly understand poor customers and their needs and build products and services around filling those needs. They should think of this not only in terms of *what* services the MFI provides, but also *how* they are provided. One of microfinance's key comparative advantages is that it is not an algorithm. Knowing customers and their needs is a core competency of microfinance, but many institutions do not think about how to turn the deep knowledge that sits with loan officers into business intelligence that is actionable by the institution. Another important strength is a strong commitment to responsible financial practices and a social mission, which also differentiates MFIs from many digital competitors.

■ Finally, as digital financial services evolve, MFIs should think carefully about partnerships and how to leverage the digital finance ecosystem more generally. MFIs are not going to be the systemically important players that MNOs or banks are, but that does not mean they cannot leverage digital infrastructure. MNOs are increasingly shifting away from trying to control the entire digital finance value chain toward a model in which they operate as platforms that carry the services of other providers. MFIs will need the technical skills to integrate effectively into these platforms, as well as the negotiation skills to strike favorable deals with the platform players.

I do not believe the entry of technology into finance is a mortal threat for the microfinance sector. It is an opportunity. But it is an opportunity that needs to be approached with knowledge, humility, and a clear business strategy. MFIs will not be the drivers of a new digital ecosystem, but the transformation of finance will require MFIs to adapt. If done right, technology can help MFIs serve more customers at lower cost. It can help them understand their customers better and build products that meet their needs responsibly. And it can help them grow their customer base. But there are also strategic, operational, reputational, and implementation risks related to new technologies that have to be carefully managed. Transformation is not just about copying current practices over to a digital platform to do more of the same at less cost. It is about thinking deeply about how to muster technology to improve the business by fundamentally redesigning its approach.

Often overlooked in this process is the impact that digital transformation has on the culture and mindset of the institution. I worked with an MFI in the Democratic Republic of Congo to build an agent strategy, and in one of our early conversations it became clear to the leadership that mobilizing deposits through agents would fundamentally change the MFI's relationship with its clients. It would move from having a group relationship with *borrowers* to an individual relationship with *customers*. The changing nature of its relationship with its customers required a revolutionary change in the mindset of its staff. For the MFI, it is still a work in progress, despite some initial success in building the new solution.

Microfinance has a relatively good track record of serving the poor in a socially responsible way. But microfinance must enter the digital age so that it can continue to serve those customers responsibly in the face of new and very different competition. There are many paths that MFIs can take to adapt to this brave new world, but the sooner they face the challenge, the more likely they will survive and even thrive in the digital marketplace.

Notes

1. Dominic Omondi, "Mobile Lenders Drive Microfinance Entities to Early Grave," *Standard Digital*, January 15, 2019 (www.standardmedia.co.ke/article/2001309493/mobile-lenders-drive-microfinance-entities-to-early-grave).

2. Christian Rodriguez and Julia Conrad, "Aligning Expectations: The Business Case for Digital Financial Services," IFC–Mastercard Foundation Working Paper (2018) (https://www.ifc.org/wps/wcm/connect/0cc32369-8c7d-4583-8bca-b9d6ca36f045/IFC%2BMCF

_Aligning+Expectations_The+Business+Case+for+DFS.pdf?MOD=AJPERES&CVID
=mjQxNhC).

3. GSMA, "2017 State of the Industry Report on Mobile Money," 2018 (https://www
.gsma.com/mobilefordevelopment/wp-content/uploads/2018/05/GSMA_2017_State_of_the
_Industry_Report_on_Mobile_Money_Full_Report.pdf).

NINE

Governance in the Digital Age

Responsible Finance for Digital Inclusion

LORY CAMBA OPEM

> Responsible finance involves implementing practices, policies and procedures
> to deliver transparent, inclusive, and customer-centered products and services.
> Managing risks for customers is managing risks for competitive resiliency and
> sustainable, prudent growth.
>
> —Lory Camba Opem, *Corporate Governance for*
> *Financial Inclusion* (IFC Report, 2018)

The financial inclusion industry is at a critical turning point: the 2017 Global Findex results document great progress, with 515 million people gaining access to a bank
or mobile money account between 2014 and 2017. Yet despite gains in access, 1.7 billion adults still have no account, and a financing gap of US$5.2 trillion persists for
formal micro, small, and medium-sized enterprises (MSMEs) and US$2.9 trillion for
informal MSMEs in developing countries.[1] Ambitious global development goals such
as the World Bank Group's targets to provide Universal Financial Access by 2020 to
1 billion of the world's unbanked, and the United Nations' Sustainable Development
Goals (SDGs) by 2030, necessitate a sharper understanding of customers as digital
financial services (DFS) scale up to include last-mile customers in rural, remote, and
traditionally underserved segments.

Trends in digital financial services, such as mobile money account adoption,
continued in 2018, with a 20 percent increase from the previous year, representing
143 million new registered customers (for a global total of 866 million registered

mobile money accounts).[2] Early evidence from mobile and tech market pioneers over the past decade, such as Kenya, also showed that the use of digital financial services has helped lift many out of poverty—particularly poor women. Mobile penetration in Kenya reached millions at unprecedented rates, bringing mobile money access to 194,000 households.[3] New digital financial tools are also being developed in Asian economies such as China, embedded through apps and bots to enhance financial capabilities as an integral offer. E-commerce giants, namely Alibaba and TenCent, have dramatically revolutionized financial inclusion in Asia and other regions, including Africa, through big-data analytics to automate access to credit, insurance, wealth management, and broader innovations in payment services for MSMEs. These trends are paving a path for microfinance institutions (MFIs) that are pivoting their internal operations and future growth toward digital financial services. At the core of each MFI transformation the need remains for strong corporate governance, strategic risk, and responsible finance practices to achieve sustainable growth and responsible digital inclusion. A strong board is critical in ensuring that their institution is indeed able to adapt to the rapid pace of innovations and investments in technology. How to do so remains a challenge, for while a select few have already begun moving toward digitalization, the rapid pace of tech innovation is forcing boards to more quickly shift their traditional mindsets. Here I address what boards should focus on in shaping a strategic path toward digital transformation, and the role of responsible investors as shareholders and strategic partners in driving digital transformations and fintech investments in emerging markets.

Responsible Finance for Digital Inclusion: Why It Matters

Corporate governance researchers and practitioners thus far have focused primarily on the traditional risks that directly affect financial institutions,[4] alongside environmental and social performance management. Although these aspects of governance remain important, greater attention also needs to be paid to providing responsible finance: to protect consumers as users of digital financial services. Trust in digital financial services remains fundamentally important for customer uptake and retention over time, particularly given that financial sector crises in the last decade have weakened public perceptions in both developed and emerging markets, which opened the door for alternative digital financial services (DFS) models.[5] This chapter therefore focuses on the board's role in identifying, monitoring, and mitigating potential consumer risks, as well as investing in responsible digital financial innovation for consumers, who are defined as individual customers and micro- and small-business entrepreneurs. It addresses whether self-regulation can help to manage risks, and ultimately harness the opportunities of inclusive finance for the poor and underserved.

Regulations for digital financial services, consumer protection, data privacy, and security are often fragmented or absent in emerging markets; or they have weak supervisory capacity when such regulations do exist. Weak regulation enables digital finance providers and fintechs to disrupt all sectors beyond finance, with low-cost, more convenient access to credit and potentially other financial services. MFI boards are thus faced with the need to make a more strategic decision in defining their MFI's path to digital transformation and determining how to do so, through one or a combination of the following, by: (1) partnering with agent networks and operators; (2) partnering with merchants; (3) partnering with third-party technology providers; and/or (4) working on their own to reengineer traditional processes and systems across operations. In all instances, strategic planning and capacity building for any type of digital transformation must navigate complex or nascent regulations, local market competition, and institutional capacity requirements to adapt effectively. Added to these challenges is how to prioritize implementation when fundamental governance and risk management systems may still need to be strengthened to address the interdependent risks that are inherent in digital financial services. These include credit, operational, market, consumer data privacy, and security risks—among other risks still unforeseen.

In Kenya, for example, the number of digital lenders has increased in recent years to over fifty lenders active in the market.[6] Proprietary credit-scoring models that rely on underwriting criteria collected from nontraditional customer data—such as social media connections, geolocation, and mobile airtime top-ups—together create a profile of customers. Machine learning and dynamic algorithms that are expected to improve over time can refine credit decision making about improvements to products and services that consumers need. Yet evidence on the benefits to customers is still evolving. Among developing markets with the highest rates of mobile access, Kenya has led the mobile revolution, providing early evidence on positive impacts that could be adapted in other markets.[7] Results are somewhat mixed; over 2.5 million Kenyans who have taken digital credit remain blacklisted by Kenya's credit bureau for failure to repay loans worth less than US$10, without any explanation or recourse.[8] Such unforeseen consumer risks add to the complexity that boards need to consider with greater agility to secure the future success of their institutions. Indeed, today's digital transformation in both developed and developing countries—of equal and increasing importance for the future of financial inclusion—must address the risks digital customers face at the outset.[9]

What Are the Risks in Digital Financial Services?

Customer risks in digital finance are more significant in emerging markets and fragile and conflict-affected countries and in more remote parts of the world. Risks arise at the industry level, and more important, as the Kenyan example illustrates, for consumers as users of digital financial services. These risks include: unfair pricing, push marketing, and nontransparent disclosures; weak financial awareness or capability; over-indebtedness; lack of customer recourse; loss of funds or access due to fraud, data breach, and blacklisting; and system errors due to weak DFS infrastructures; among others.

Paying attention to the following thematic areas will help optimize both the opportunities and risks—for customers, providers, shareholders, and investors—when embarking on scaling digital financial services:

- *Pricing, transparency, and financial well-being are foundational to establishing customer resilience.* Globally, two-thirds of adults are financially illiterate, according to a Standard & Poor's survey of over 150,000 adults (age fifteen and older) in more than 140 economies, who were assessed based on their understanding of four fundamental concepts in financial decision making: (1) interest rates; (2) interest compounding; (3) inflation; and (4) risk diversification.[10] The implications of global financial illiteracy were more widespread for the 3.5 billion adult women, the poor, and less-educated respondents, most from developing economies who lack an understanding of basic financial concepts. Fundamental practices can help to promote greater consumer financial awareness and capability, as well as greater understanding of digital products and financial services, through transparent pricing, clearer product terms and conditions, and effective customer recourse. For example, a 2018 study by the International Finance Corporation (IFC) and the Partnership for Responsible Financial Inclusion has shown that institutions certified by the Smart Campaign had fewer nonperforming loans and greater overall portfolio growth.[11] (The Smart Campaign is a global effort to unite microfinance leaders around the common goal of protecting and better serving clients of the microfinance industry.) While certification contributed to positive performance, responsible digital finance practices need to continually adapt to business operations and evolve accordingly as MFIs implement their digital transformation strategies.

- *Data privacy and data security are fundamental to maintaining customer trust in digital financial services.* Technology innovation has created big-data footprints and data trails that capture the personal lives of customers who are using mobile phones, online payment systems, and social media. Although these models are lowering costs and enabling quick and convenient access to finance, they are also raising consumer data protection questions, specifically about data ownership, data use, more effective consent to protect consumer data privacy, and security.[12] Indeed, where mobile money penetration has increased, smart phone adoption has also increased—to 60 percent in 2018, and is estimated to increase to more than 79 percent by 2025. Emerging markets are similarly expected to follow this trend particularly in Asia, Latin America, the Middle East, and North Africa, where the total number of customers using a smart phone app has more than doubled by 2.6 times annually.[13]

- *Strong customer relationships are critical for the future of financial inclusion.* The rising incidence of data breaches, internal fraud, and system errors also calls attention to the need for more timely customer recourse and user-friendly disclosures for authorized consent. The practicality of achieving the latter through basic feature phones owned predominantly by rural users still requires additional research looking at the use of SMS messaging or at regular behavioral nudges to support clients in making positive financial decisions. Moreover, providers who seek to serve the last mile will likely require technology innovation combined with staff able to reinforce customer needs and strengthen customer relationships, particularly for the structurally underserved.

Key Areas for Board Attention to Scaling Digital Inclusion

Current industry trends call for board members' attention in five key areas, particularly for MFIs that are assessing and developing a digital transformation strategy.[14] Appendix 9-1 (at the end of this chapter) describes a customer assessment tool that board members could use in the context of their market and business models. Selected case examples are illustrated in boxes 9-1, 9-2, and 9-3, which follow below. These areas are aligned with how institutions operationalize responsible finance practices across their operations—namely board governance, policies and procedures, and risk management systems. Boards that can address the following questions will be more likely to govern effectively.

1. *Governance and management roles in digital transformation.* Does the MFI-DFS transformation strategy address consumer risks and include responsible finance practices? Do the code of conduct, policies, procedures, and systems incorporate consumer protection practices and principles? For example, particularly for microfinance institutions that have already achieved or are working toward Smart Certification, how are they implementing client protection principles as

BOX 9-1. Data Analytics for Improved Customer Services in Kenya

Safaricom M-Pesa

When Safaricom in Kenya launched the M-Pesa service in 2007, there were no templates or best practices. With over 2 million customers in its first year, the business exceeded forecasts by 500 percent. The growing demand forced rapid scaling, and required operations managers to proactively anticipate problems in both the technology and business processes because any negative customer experience could immediately erode customer trust. As such, a key performance indicator (KPI), "managing against unanswered calls," was collected and analyzed, which ultimately delivered broader operational benefits. Namely, it accomplished two things: first, it successfully identified bottlenecks, passing key insights back into operations; and second, it uncovered other operational issues, such as the extent to which customers erroneously sent money or forgot their personal identification numbers (PINs).

M-Kopa

M-Kopa in Kenya began as a provider in 2011 of solar-powered home energy systems, principally for lighting, but also for charging small items such as mobile phones and radios. The business, among the earliest forms piloted in Africa, combines machine-to-machine technology, using embedded subscriber identification module (SIM) cards with a DFS micropayment solution. This enables the technology to be monitored and made available only when advance payment is received. Customers buy M-Kopa systems using "credits" earned through the M-Pesa mobile money service. They then pay for the systems using M-Pesa until the balance is paid off and they own the product. This provides an asset-based financing business model, and has expanded into other areas in recent years, such as the provision of home appliances and loans using customer-owned solar units as refinancing collateral. These products are offered to customers who have built an ability-to-pay credit score metric, as determined by their initial system purchase and subsequent repayment. M-Kopa has expanded its business operations in Ghana, Tanzania, and Uganda, and uses customer data proactively to improve operational efficiency by analyzing, among others, customer demographics, customer dependence on a device, and repayment behavior. The data can be analyzed to improve service and operational efficiency, and to develop a better understanding of customer behavior.

Source: International Finance Corporation/Master Card Foundation, *Data Analytics and Financial Services* (Washington: 2017), pp. 70–71, 74–75 (https://www.ifc.org/wps /wcm/connect/369c10de-1703-4497-876f-9cdf0367a4d4/IFC+Data+Analytics+and+Di gital+Financial+Services+Handbook.pdf?MOD=AJPERES&CVID=lRrkzEd).

BOX 9-2. Data Governance

Developing a Data Governance Plan

Data governance can be designed in various ways, depending on the provider, local regulations, and business model, among other factors in a given jurisdiction. Generally it involves issues related to how and when data are used and who has access to it—these are critical to protect consumers' data and build trust in the use of digital financial services. A data governance plan involves developing an interface with broader corporate governance policies, legal requirements, and communications policies. The plan should enable access to customers' data and related personal information, while balancing the need for data privacy and security as part of a provider's ongoing relationship with its customers. The effectiveness of a data governance plan should be driven by the scale of data collected and concurrent risks with such larger datasets containing personal or private consumer information. Given that data also flow across national and international borders, data governance should also assess data transit through policy and regulatory environments, such as from a company in Africa to an outsourced analytics provider in Europe. The plan should include the following elements of data transfer:

- *Encryption.* Sensitive or identifying information should be encrypted, obfuscated, and/or anonymized, as well as maintained through the full data pipeline.
- *Permissions.* Access to datasets should be defined on a granular basis by team roles or by access points (that is, from within corporate firewalls, not from external networks).
- *Security.* Datasets placed into the project's "sandbox" environment should have their own security apparatus or firewall, as well as the ability to authenticate privileged access.
- *Logging.* Access and use should be logged and auditable. It should also be enabled for analysis and reporting.
- *Regulation.* The plan should ensure regulatory requirements are met, and nondisclosure agreements or legal contracts should be in place to cover all project stakeholders. Customer rights and privacy issues must also be considered.

Source: International Finance Corporation/Master Card Foundation, *Data Analytics and Financial Services* (Washington: 2017) (https://www.ifc.org/wps/wcm/connect /369c10de-1703-4497-876f-9cdf0367a4d4/IFC+Data+Analytics+and+Digital+Financial +Services+Handbook.pdf?MOD=AJPERES&CVID=IRrkzEd).

BOX 9-3. Customer Data—Sample Key Performance Indicators

Customer Services: Sample Key Performance Indicators

Customer data	Data description	Examples
Call center records	Issues log: type of issues and time to resolution (may include semi-structured data in reports).	Customer insights; operational and performance management and system improvements.
Customer care feedback data	Number of calls; call type statistics; and issue resolution statistics.	Identify technical performance and product design issues; training and communications needs; and third-party issues (for example, agent, biller).
Agent and merchant feedback data	Number of agent or merchant calls; call type statistics; and issue resolution statistics.	Identify technical performance and product design issues; agent training and communications needs; and client issues.
Communication channel interactions	Volume of website hits; call center volumes; social media inquiries; and live chat requests.	Customer insights; operational and performance management; and system improvements.
Qualitative communication data	Type of inquiries; customer satisfaction; and social media reviews.	Customer insights.
Private branch automatic exchange	Number of call center calls; length of calls; queue wait times; and dropped calls.	Operational and performance management.

Source: International Finance Corporation/Master Card Foundation, *Data Analytics and Financial Services* (Washington: 2017) (https://www.ifc.org/wps/wcm/connect /369c10de-1703-4497-876f-9cdf0367a4d4/IFC+Data+Analytics+and+Digital+Financial +Services+Handbook.pdf?MOD=AJPERES&CVID=1RrkzEd).

part of their digital transformation strategy? Are these monitored and reported by management to the board as part of its overall risk governance processes?

2. *Pricing, transparency, and customer disclosures.* How are DFS products priced relative to potential credit risks, such as customer over-indebtedness, and how are customer data being used to tailor better pricing over time? How are prices and fees communicated through key fact statements or digitally to customers? Are multiple communication channels being used to disclose pricing, terms, and conditions to consumers, including their rights and responsibilities? How are digital platforms being used to support financial health and digital literacy throughout the customer's lifecycle in a way that strengthens positive behavioral decisions?

3. *Customer services management.* Do the board and management produce and analyze reports about customer feedback and complaints? How are customer service reports used to assess customer feedback, and to improve products and services? How are complaints escalated and addressed or resolved, particularly in cases of system errors related to authentication, authorization, accounting, or other digital transaction errors? Box 9-1 highlights two examples in Kenya of effective customer services that have used data-driven analytics.

4. *Data governance, consumer data protection, and data security.* How does the company implement customer data privacy and security standards? What policies and procedures are in place to govern data privacy and security? How are customers informed about the way in which their personal data are collected, used, shared, retained, and secured? How is customer consent implemented to promote improved disclosures? Box 9-2 summarizes selected data privacy laws and key aspects of data governance.

5. *Risk and internal audit processes.* Are consumer protection risks monitored or audited and reported regularly to the board? What are the trends and performance of key risk indicators? For example, these could include the number and type of customer complaints received and time to resolve complaints; product usage feedback; agent or network performance; fraud incidence; and the incidence of customer transactions errors. What areas can be improved to guide operations, policies, and procedures to enhance consumer protection and mitigate potential reputational risks? A more nuanced segmentation and understanding of customers' failure to repay or unexpected repayment behaviors could further inform financial capability needs of customers. For digital financial services providers, this has the potential to strengthen their ability to retain and acquire customers, particularly in more competitive environments. Box 9-3 lists selected key performance indicators (KPIs) the institution may choose to use.[15]

Responsible Investing for Digital Financial Services

The areas covered in the previous section are by no means exhaustive, but represent the fundamental challenges that MFI boards may confront as they consider investment opportunities through digital partnerships or roll out digitally delivered products and services. Evidence and research on customer-centric products and services are still evolving and will provide additional essential tools that MFI boards can use to increase their know-how as they embark on a partnership or growth strategy for responsible digital inclusion.

Investments in digital financial inclusion are expected to increase, with impact investors defining digital financial inclusion as an investment theme to diversify and grow their portfolios. In 2018 nearly US$112 billion was invested in fintechs, almost double the previous year's total.[16] During the same year, international funding and investments for financial inclusion reached a historic high of US$42 billion. Investors are recognizing their collective role in reshaping the investment landscape for investing in responsible digital inclusion. Recognizing both the risks and opportunities in scaling digital financial inclusion globally, IFC and a core group of investors led the development of guidelines for "Responsible Investing in Digital Financial Services."[17] Anchored in the G-20 High-Level Principles for Digital Financial Inclusion, the investor guidelines (appendix 9-2) are designed to build broad investor awareness and catalyze new investments and innovations that protect customers. The guidelines focus on refining traditional investment due diligence with evolving DFS; adapting existing industry actions; and improving solutions as business models and market contexts evolve. Signatories to the guidelines share their actual experiences with investments, investees, and industry networks, and through case studies and tools. The investor guidelines aim to build a community of like-minded and open-minded investors in promoting responsible innovation in digital financial services. Over 120 investors and endorsers have become signatories since the launch of the investor guidelines in June 2018. The investor guidelines concurrently reinforce new impact principles introduced in Bali in October 2018 in five areas: strategy, origination and structuring, portfolio management, exit, and verification.

As one of the leading global investors in microfinance and digital financial services, for more than twenty years, IFC has committed over US$6 billion to 640 investments and 180 advisory projects in ninety-five countries. IFC provides advisory services in DFS to more than fifty projects across the regions, and IFC's fintech team established a diversified portfolio that includes digital financial marketplaces and exchanges, companies that are building online payment and capital markets infrastructures, lending-service providers, and other innovative late-venture and growth-stage firms. As of 2018, IFC had invested nearly US$400 million in nearly fifty fintechs on four continents in over twenty countries. Given its global footprint in financial inclusion and digital financial services, IFC and potential co-investors as partners or shareholders in digital transformation have an ongoing role to drive sustainable impacts through responsible finance for digital inclusion.

The Work of the Board Is Ongoing and Ever Evolving

Technological advances and innovations across all sectors beyond finance—health, education, housing, energy—introduce both new risks and opportunities every day, causing dynamic shifts across markets and sectors. Even strong boards with years of experience as a group need to continuously sharpen their individual skills or adapt them to remain agile to better respond to rapid changes in technology and customer demands. Every strategic and significant technical or operational change an MFI makes requires active board involvement. Every material change in the economic, financial, or legal environment necessitates board engagement. More important, every MFI action involving change requires board participation. The environment in which MFIs and their directors operate is increasingly dynamic, and all board members understand that it is never "business as usual."

Appendix 9-1. Customer Assessment Tool for Board Management

The customer assessment should be conducted across core business functions, focusing on observed customer risks and mitigation measures. The objective is to evaluate customer risks and mitigating measures across institutional operations systems, policies, and procedures in the context of the local market and digital ecosystems. This tool is intended to be a "living" and iterative process that considers innovations in DFS and fintech products and services as they occur.

MARKET ASSESSMENT

Local Market Context, Regulations
- **Market and regulations:** Does a regulatory framework for financial consumer protection exist? If so, which regulatory agency performs this function? Is the market potentially evidencing risks of increasing numbers of NPLs, and consumer over-indebtedness?
- **Industry and self-regulation:** If a regulatory framework is weak or nonexistent, are there any industry or self-regulation, voluntary codes of conduct that are being adhered to by financial service providers?
- **Consumer perspective:** What is the perception of the company in the local market? Has it received any public consumer complaints from local media, consumer activists, NGOs, and/or government regulators?

INSTITUTIONAL ASSESSMENT

Board Governance, Management

- **Role of board and management:** Assess board and management awareness of risks related to consumer protection issues. How are these addressed by management and the Board, given the local/market context?

Customer Acquisition

- **Customer acquisition:** Does the company assess multiple lending, potential over-indebtedness and/or debt/income thresholds? If so, how? What are the key indicators used? If credit bureaus exist, are they used by the company and how?
- **Credit scoring:** If alternative data is used for credit scoring, what type of data is collected from customers? How is customer data used to assess creditworthiness and/or capacity to repay?
- **Responsible pricing and comparators:** How is pricing defined by product (annual percentage rate [APR], effective interest rate [EIR], total cost of loan; flat or declining balance calculation method; or transaction fees)?

Pricing

- **Pricing comparison:** Provide relevant comparators from market competitors by product or transaction services, as relevant.

Transparency Disclosure

- **Transparency:** How is pricing indicated to clients? Does the company publicly disclose pricing by product? How does the company share this information? Through websites, digital/mobile means, receipts, contracts (product agreements, loan contracts, or insurance policies)?
- **Customer assistance:** Does the company provide contact details using multiple channels for customer help prior to closing a transaction/sale? How and what information is communicated?
- **Terms and conditions:** Are terms and conditions for clients articulated in simple, local language? How are they communicated prior to a transaction/sale to inform customers about their rights and responsibilities? How is consumer data privacy communicated? Does it include information about how personal information will be used by the company, how data is collected, and who it will be shared with?
- **Customer consent:** How is informed consent obtained from customers? Describe the process, for example, prior to automatic debit authorizations using digital/biometric devices. Is the client given any documentation and how (that is, from a contract, receipt, or email)?

CUSTOMER SERVICES

Customer Feedback and Complaints Resolution Process

- Do staff receive training about Consumer Protection Standards? Is financial education provided for customers? If so, how often and when?
- Is there a written policy that requires customer complaints to be fully investigated until resolved?
- How are customer complaints handled, such as loss of funds, mistaken, unauthorized or incorrect transactions due to weak connectivity, system errors, fraud, platform instability, or IT security breaches?
- How does the company monitor effectiveness of customer services?

- Does the company analyze customer services/complaints data and provide regular reports to management? What are the key customer issues? How many issues are there? How many days does it typically take to address a customer complaint?
- Are staff training and incentives provided to improve customer services?

IT/SYSTEMS

Data Privacy and Security

- Who has primary responsibility for customer data privacy? Are there dedicated staff (legal experts, data protection officers) and/or board/management committees in place to handle such issues?
- How does the company implement data privacy and security for its products and services across multiple countries/jurisdictions?
- Does the company inform clients about how their private data/information will be used, including sharing their personal data, loan history with the credit bureau and other third-party providers, as relevant?
- Does the company enable customers to opt-in or opt-out of using their personal data for marketing, third party or other purposes? Why, or why not?
- In the event of a customer data breach and related security or fraud issues, when and how are customers informed? Is there a plan in place in the event of a breach, security or fraud?
- What types of customer recourse are provided by the company in the event of data/security breach/fraud?

RISK AND AUDIT SYSTEMS, CONTROLS

- Does internal audit include Consumer Protection Standards?
- How are audits performed to assess consumer protection? When and how often?
- What consumer risk indicators does the company use/monitor?
- What is the company doing to monitor and mitigate potential security issues or detect fraud?
- How are risk/audit reports used? Are reports systematically provided to the board and management for review and policy considerations?

Source: International Finance Corporation, *Corporate Governance for Finance Inclusion* (Washington: 2018), https://responsiblefinanceforum.org/wp-content/uploads/2018/04/IFC-CG-report-3-25-18.pdf.

Appendix 9-2: Investor Guidelines for Responsible Investing in Digital Financial Services

Guideline 1: Promote Responsible Investment in Digital Finance: We embrace digital financial services as a priority to drive development of inclusive financial systems. We will actively support responsible DFS providers to innovate and expand the range of financial services available to underserved groups to help them reduce their vulnerability, build assets, and mitigate their risks for an inclusive digital economy. We as investors commit to make responsible investment choices. We commit to supporting improved board governance and management commitment such that access to finance generates resilient, sustainable and value-added growth towards creating markets and opportunities for broader Sustainable Development Goals.

Guideline 2: Manage Risks Comprehensively with Growth of Digital Inclusion: We acknowledge that investors play a role in ensuring that the risks that emerge from innovation are borne by those that are equipped to absorb them, i.e., not by end customers. Investors will identify and assess risks during their due diligence process and manage these during investment. We encourage our investees to incorporate risks for customers or consumers into their business models and operations for a more comprehensive risk management framework.

Guideline 3: Foster a Proportionate Legal and Regulatory Framework: We support a prudent and proportionate legal and regulatory framework. As responsible investors, we commit to ensure compliance to existing regulations (including, by our investee companies) and to engage productively with policymakers so that the regulatory framework reflects both customer protection concerns and commercial concerns.

Guideline 4: Facilitate Interoperability and Infrastructures for DFS Ecosystems: We recognize the need for an ecosystem of enabling infrastructure for DFS and encourage interoperability, where appropriate, within that ecosystem. We encourage investee companies to take responsibility for the actions of agents, employees, and third-party service providers across the value chain. We will support investees to implement appropriate mechanisms for responsible provision of services along the value chain, and encourage investees that provide infrastructure services to providers of DFS to apply these Guidelines along the chain.

Guideline 5: Establish Customer Identity, Data Privacy and Security Standards: We encourage the development, use and implementation, as relevant to market standards and in accordance with applicable laws and regulations, of customer identity and authentication systems by DFS providers. We promote the responsible use of data and practice of data management, including back-end technology infrastructure and/or other mechanisms to protect the privacy and security of customer data and help strengthen approaches for informed customer consent. We encourage the assessment of risk to both customers and providers in adopting various approaches and technologies.

Guideline 6: Promote Fair and Transparent Pricing: We encourage and support investees to apply fair, risk-based and transparent pricing for all financial products and services, that are affordable to consumers while allowing for investees to be sustainable and provide adequate returns to investors. For savings products, investors encourage and support investees to provide real returns on the deposits of customers.

Guideline 7: Improve Disclosure of Terms and Conditions for Customers: We will promote and support investees to improve disclosure of terms, conditions and pertinent information to customers through transparent and clear communication that is easily accessible. This includes transparency in pricing, appropriate product design and delivery, and key supporting facts that enable customers to make informed decisions.

Guideline 8: Enhance Customer Services for Problem Resolution and Product Innovation: We will encourage and support investees to enhance customer services for feedback, problem or complaint resolution in a timely and responsive manner (including redress mechanisms) to build and sustain customer trust and improve the design and delivery of products and services.

Guideline 9: Prevent Over-indebtedness, Strengthen Digital Literacy and Financial Awareness: We promote and support proactive, ongoing approaches that deliver innovative digital literacy & financial literacy and awareness initiatives for consumer protection, to help prevent over-indebtedness and support financial capability throughout the customer relationship.

Guideline 10: Track Progress to Mitigate Risks and Expand DFS Opportunities: We encourage use of impact measurement industry standards for measuring and reporting lessons on responsible and sustainable performance by DFS providers.

Source: Responsible Finance Forum. The complete investor guidelines can be found, with examples of proposed actions for signatories at https://responsiblefinanceforum.org/investor-guidelines/.

Notes

1. Asli Demirgüç-Kunt and others, *The Global Findex Database: Measuring Financial Inclusion and the Fintech Revolution* (Washington: World Bank Group, 2017).

2. GSM Association (GSMA), *State of the Industry Report on Mobile Money 2018* (February 2019).

3. Suri Tavneet and Jack William, "The Long-Run Poverty and Gender Impacts of Mobile Money," *Science* 354, no. 6317 (2016): 1288–92.

4. Matthew Brown and others, *Corporate Governance for Financial Inclusion—Insights for Boards of Microfinance Institutions: Managing Current Issues, Crisis, and Change* (Washington: IFC, 2018).

5. Matthew Saal, Susan Starnes, and Thomas Rehermann, "Digital Financial Services: Challenges and Opportunities for Emerging Market Banks," IFC Emerging Markets Compass Note 42 (Washington: IFC, 2017).

6. Margarete Biallas, Momina Aijazuddin, and Lory Camba Opem, "The Case for Responsible Investing in Digital Financial Services," IFC Emerging Markets Compass Note 67 (Washington: IFC, April 2019).

7. Tavneet and William, "The Long-Run Poverty and Gender Impacts of Mobile Money." The study showed that, since 2008, access to mobile money services increased the daily per capita consumption levels of 194,0000 (2 percent) of Kenyan households, lifting

them out of extreme poverty (living on less than US$1.25 per day). The study also revealed that female-headed households saw greater increases in consumption than male-headed households. In addition, mobile money services have helped 85,000 women move from farming to business occupations. Similar research in Uganda, Tanzania, and Pakistan is being conducted to determine if the effects are isolated to Kenya or are more systematic across countries.

8. FSD Kenya, "Digital Credit in Kenya: Evidence from Demand-Side Surveys" (http://s3-eu-central-1.amazonaws.com/fsd-circle/wp-content/uploads/2018/10/18162055/Digital-Credit-in-Kenya.pdf); Bloomberg Business Data, "Tech Startups Are Flooding Kenya with Apps Offering High Interest Loans," February 12, 2020 (www.bloomberg.com/news/features/2020-02-12/tech-startups-are-flooding-kenya-with-apps-offering-high-interest-loans).

9. Brown and others, *Corporate Governance for Financial Inclusion*.

10. Standard & Poor's, "Financial Literacy around the World: Insights from S&P Ratings Services," Global Financial Literacy Survey, December 2, 2016 (www.bbvaedufin.com/en/publicacion/financial-literacy-around-the-world-insights-from-the-standard-poors-ratings-services-global-financial-literacy-survey/).

11. IFC-PRFI, "An Emerging Business Case for Consumer Protection" (Washington, December 2018). In addition, IFC's internal client portfolio analyses, representing 70 percent of all client protection principles (CPPs) globally, showed similar trends, based on MIX performance data for fiscal year 2018. CPPs, when implemented strategically with corporate governance and risk management systems, were able to respond to external risks or macro shocks, outperforming MFIs in the same region.

12. Responsible Finance Forum and Global Partnership for Financial Inclusion (GPFI), "Opportunities and Risks in Digital Financial Services: Protecting Consumer Data and Privacy" (Berlin, Germany, 2017) (https://responsiblefinanceforum.org/wp-content/uploads/2017/06/RFFVIII-Opportunities_and_Risks_in_Digital_Financial_Services-Protecting_Consumer_Data_and_Privacy.pdf).

13. GSMA, *State of the Industry Report on Mobile Money*.

14. Brown and others, *Corporate Governance for Financial Inclusion*, p. 61, Annex III: Consumer Risk Assessment for Responsible Digital Finance. See link to Investor Guideline #2 (https://responsiblefinanceforum.org/tools_frameworks/investor-guideline-2-manage-risks-comprehensively-due-diligence-risk-matrix/).

15. Useful additional KPI data, sources, and definitions can be found in the IFC-MCF handbooks: (1) *Digital Financial Services and Risk Management*, Part IV: "Insights and Tools," pp. 93–108 (https://www.ifc.org/wps/wcm/connect/region__ext_content/ifc_external_corporate_site/sub-saharan+africa/resources/handbook-dfs-rm_; and (2) *Data Analytics and Digital Financial Services*, chapter 2.2: "Resources," pp. 136–40 (https://www.ifc.org/wps/wcm/connect/region__ext_content/ifc_external_corporate_site/sub-saharan+africa/resources/dfs-data-analytics).

16. KPMG, "The Pulse of Fintech: Biannual Global Analysis of Investments in Fintech," 2019 (https://home.kpmg/xx/en/home/insights/2019/01/pulse-of-fintech-h2-2018.html).

17. Responsible Finance Forum, "Responsible Investing for Digital Financial Services" (https://responsiblefinanceforum.org/investor-guidelines).

TEN

Product Diversification

Consumer Loans for Education and Housing

ALEX SILVA

Most microfinance institutions (MFIs) have traditionally offered a very limited scope of products to their clients—normally only working capital loans. The loans usually have very rigid rules and rely on a step-up lending methodology, where loan terms and conditions are set to minimize the risk and costs for the MFI rather than reflecting the needs and preferences of the clients.

With the passage of time, MFIs have matured, competition has become more intense, and a more client-centric view of the process is being embraced. As a result, the traditional product mix consisting of a few types of working capital loans is being complemented by a wider range of financial products. Indeed, a client-driven positive approach resulting in a more diverse array of financial services for the low-income population is emerging. The reasons for this include:

- new competition, resulting mainly from the entrance of traditional commercial banks into the microenterprise market

- higher client dropout rates, resulting from inflexibility or inappropriateness of current product offerings

- a more sophisticated clientele with more discriminating preferences

Since the sustainability of MFIs depends on reaching and maintaining adequate portfolio size so as to achieve economies of scale, portfolio growth remains of paramount importance to MFIs. To this end, and realizing that business as usual is probably not going to work for very long, MFIs are working on improving existing products and introducing new products and services. The aim is to both retain existing clients and attract new ones.

This shift in approach is positive; it should be encouraged since it signals that the market for financial services to the low-income population is deepening and there is appetite for new products. Most MFIs, however, are ill-prepared to launch new products. Indeed, the introduction of new products into the market without conducting proper due diligence and internal preparation can lead to deleterious results that threaten the long-term viability of the MFI.

New product development and the complete process of bringing a new product to market bring uncertainties and challenges. A well-thought-out approach is required. Indeed, the complex process of delivering new products to the market typically requires the successful implementation of several activities. For starters, it requires an understanding of customer needs and wants, the competitive environment, and the nature of the market. Once these are known, the process moves on to design and development followed by testing and, eventually, product launch. A good design is developed in consultation with all the units of the organization on every aspect of a new product offering: from publication design to information technology (IT) issues to human resources. Product development should also incorporate risk management and controls and follow regulatory guidelines and rules.

New Products in Microfinance: Case Studies

As MFIs feel pressure to diversify their product offerings, they are considering a range of financial products. But the introduction of a new product is never trouble-free and is especially difficult for organizations that have historically offered only one product: working capital loans in the case of MFIs. Other types of loans (including loans to small and medium-sized enterprises [SMEs], housing loans, educational loans, and fixed asset loans), as well as savings, insurance, money transfers, and payment services, are a few of the products that MFIs frequently think of when considering an expansion of their product offerings.

The next section describes how some MFIs have developed and brought to market specific products that were new to them—specifically, "progressive housing loans" in two different MFIs in two countries and student loans.

New Products in Microfinance–Housing Loans

ENLACE (El Salvador)

Enlace Servicios Financieros, S.A. (ENLANCE) is a profitable, privately owned, un-regulated MFI in El Salvador that evolved from a nonprofit nongovernmental organization (NGO) created by Catholic Relief Services in the 1990s. ENLACE provides credit primarily through village banking. While small in portfolio size (US$23 million), it is nevertheless the largest local operator by number of clients (approximately 75,000) and fifth in El Salvador by size of portfolio. Its portfolio quality is very good (portfolio at risk [PAR] 30 days < 1 percent).

ENLACE became interested in shelter-related products as a reaction to a devastating earthquake that in 2001 affected the housing conditions of more than 80 percent of its clients. Initially, credit loans were offered to individual borrowers, but most of the organization's clients did not qualify because of the relatively strict guarantee requirements. Further, since the organization had little experience with individual lending (especially when operating under duress), arrears for this product quickly became quite high.

Nevertheless, realizing that housing products were in high demand by its clients, the MFI chose to continue offering the loan, but with modifications. Through a trial-and-error process, and with technical assistance from Habitat for Humanity, the MFI now has a product that meets its expectations. The product currently offered, a house improvement loan primarily utilizing the village banking methodology, accounts for approximately 20 percent of the MFI's portfolio. The loan arrears are very low (< 1 percent), and some 10 percent of ENLACE's clients make use of it.

To qualify, a client needs to have been with ENLACE for more than a year and can either have its village bank group provide a guarantee or offer another type of guarantee (such as an individual guarantor). In the case of group guarantees, though every member of the group may not be a recipient of the housing line of credit, the whole group is a guarantor of the loan. ENLACE charges its housing clients a materially lower rate than it charges for its working capital products.

Considering that ENLACE is not yet a regulated entity and the legal framework under which it operates does not have strict rules governing private transactions between willing private parties, the housing product has not been hampered by regulatory issues. Rather, the main obstacles to growth of the product are overleveraged clients and the high levels of violence and insecurity in El Salvador.

Edpyme Edyficar/MiBanco (Peru)

MiBanco is a profitable, privately owned, regulated microfinance bank in Peru that evolved from an NGO created by Care International. The bank is fully owned by a holding company that also controls the largest commercial bank in Peru (Banco de Credito del Peru). MiBanco is the largest local operator in terms of both clients and portfolio size.

In July 2015, Peru launched a national financial inclusion strategy, which strengthens the commitment of the government to promote financial development. This plan, which has concrete goals through 2021, aims to expand financial services in seven areas: payments, savings, loans, insurance, consumer protection, financial education, and services to vulnerable groups. The absence of caps on interest rates for loans, the smooth approval process for nonbank intermediaries, and the development of innovative products puts Peru well ahead of the global average in supporting financial inclusion.

As a result of this favorable enabling environment, innovative products such as financing for housing, water, and sanitation, as well as microinsurance and others, have mushroomed. As an example, MiBanco has implemented an innovative program that aims to reduce the acute shelter deficit by supporting housing solutions for low-income families.

In 2010, in partnership with Habitat for Humanity, the bank developed a housing microfinance program called MiCasa. The bank promotes, originates, and books the corresponding loans, and Habitat offers technical assistance. Its success has been showcased around the world as proof of the feasibility of impact-minded, yet sustainable, housing microfinance products. The program focuses on the low-income population: 66 percent of its clients have incomes of up to twice the local national minimum wage. The majority of the loans are used for small-scale, progressive construction. The program has more than 100,000 active housing microfinance loans with an average loan size of $2,500 (though the maximum loan amount is $15,000).

New Products in Microfinance: Student Loans

Education is widely regarded as a universal right and as a vital instrument in promoting economic growth as well as social integration. It is key in helping individuals, families, and groups to break the poverty cycle—so much so that the United Nations' Sustainable Development Goals mention quality education for all as one key objective. Unfortunately, despite recent advances, there is still much to be done.

Latin America has large gaps in its provision of quality education. The Higher Education Finance Fund (HEFF) was launched in 2011 as a partial response to this need. Conceived as a pilot program funded primarily by development financial institutions, the fund is run by a specialized fund manager (OMTRIX, Inc.) based in Costa Rica. The fund's purpose is to "expand the product mix of microfinance institutions and other healthy financial intermediaries serving low-income populations by providing long-term loans to the portfolio companies at adequate terms so that they can in turn provide student loans to underprivileged youths seeking to fund their higher education." In parallel, a technical assistance facility is also being operated by OMTRIX to transfer higher education lending methods to participating financial institutions and support students with financial planning, counseling during their studies and during their job market orientation, and other related activities.

In designing the fund, the promoters took into consideration that, while Latin American governments usually offer a variety of subsidies, these programs do not have a universal reach and, at best, only cover a limited part of the cost of tertiary education, which has risen dramatically in recent times. Further, only a very limited number of private financing schemes exist, especially for the lower-income population. Accordingly, the conditions were ripe for a financing mechanism that would facilitate access to student loans to the low-income population.

The fund seeks to leverage the network of MFIs in Latin America to demonstrate the feasibility of linking higher education finance with these institutions. MFIs, which normally have low portfolio loss rates and are financially sustainable, have proven to be an excellent vehicle for bringing financial services to the base of the pyramid. Further, they have wide geographic coverage through a network of branches.

HEFF aims to demonstrate that, with the right methods and principles, student lending can be done in a sustainable way by any private for-profit financial intermediary. To this end, and unlike government-sponsored loans available to anyone for any type of studies, HEFF targets students preparing for careers in high demand by the labor market (loans are denied to students who select careers that are not in demand). Also, unlike government-sponsored loans at subsidized rates, MFIs are encouraged to charge market rates to their student clients. Accordingly, the resulting programs should be sustainable and able to be replicated by other financial intermediaries.

The fund offers technical assistance to participating MFIs in the design and launching of the student loan program. This assistance includes job market research, customized product development (piloting and adapting), staff training and support, as well as limited student support (such as financial education and counseling services) (see table 10-1).

TABLE 10-1. HEFF Key Statistics

Year	2012	2013	2014	2015	2016	2017	2018
Disbursements to FIs:							
Projection	$4,500,000	$4,500,000	$4,500,000	$4,500,000	$4,500,000	$5,000,000	$0
Real	$250,000	$5,750,000	$4,750,000	$5,250,000	$6,500,000	$5,000,000	$0
Accum. disbursements:							
Projection	$4,500,000	$9,000,000	$13,500,000	$18,000,000	$22,500,000	$27,500,000	$27,500,000
Real	$250,000	$6,000,000	$10,750,000	$16,000,000	$22,500,000	$27,500,000	$27,500,000
Average student loan:							
Projection	$10,000	$10,000	$10,000	$10,000	$10,000	$10,000	$10,000
Real	$0	$4,494	$3,163	$2,760	$2,902	$2,672	$2,528
Number of students:							
Projection	450	450	450	450	450	450	N/A
Real	0	341	733	1,593	2240	1871	N/A
Accumulated no. students:							
Projection	450	900	1,350	1,800	2,250	2,700	3,150
Real	0	341	1,074	2,667	4,907	6,778	7,122

FIGURE 10-1. Growth in Number of Students by Quarter, 2013–18

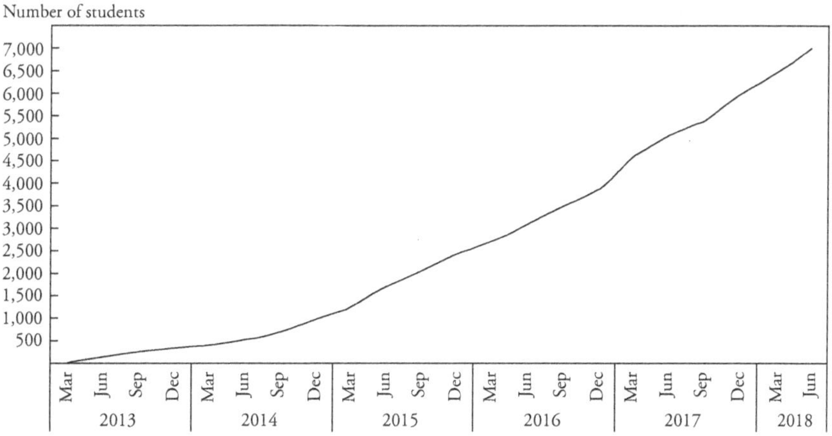

Number of students

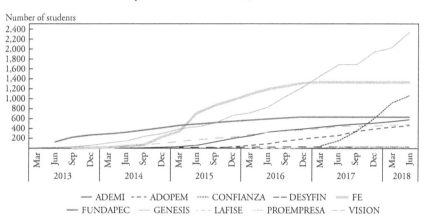

FIGURE 10-2. Growth in Number of Students by Quarter by Financial Institution, 2013–18

Number of students

— ADEMI --- ADOPEM ····· CONFIANZA −− DESYFIN ═══ FE
— FUNDAPEC — GENESIS -- LAFISE ····· PROEMPRESA −− VISION

As of June 30, 2018, over 7,000 young people had benefited from the program. Nearly 70 percent of the loans were under $3,000 and 28 percent were under $1,000 (figures 10-1 and 10-2). The average loan term varied, but the greatest demand was for loans that could be repaid in less than two years. Fifty-eight percent of students were also working when they received their loan.

The fund has achieved and exceeded its programmatic objectives. It has demonstrated that it is possible to provide low-income students access to education financing and support them as they complete their studies and enter the labor force. We also know this can be done in a way that benefits students and financial services providers as well as local businesses, national economies, and governments.

However, getting to this point was not easy. Several adjustments to the initial concept and work plan were needed. Implementing the program demanded much more one-on-one involvement than anticipated and required special adaptations for each MFI's circumstances. Specific lessons learned with respect to product implementation can be summarized as follows:

- *Profitability.* For any new product, implementation requires not only effort and dedication but also patience. Achieving profitability takes time. Reasonable volumes are needed (so as to achieve economies of scale that translate into lower costs); and different products have different margins. Indeed, most new MFI products seem to have much lower returns than the high rates that historically have been possible for working capital microloans.

- *Level of difficulty.* Implementation requires adjustments to operating procedures and systems, even in areas that initially did not seem to be critical parts of the new product development process. For example, risk managers, reacting to the unknown, will intuitively see student loans as very risky and thus be inclined to reject them or impose barriers to product implementation. Also, MFIs' marketing and promotion strategies will need to be adjusted if youthful clients, many new to the institution, do not respond to the traditional media utilized by the MFI (radio, newspapers). New marketing channels will have to be considered (specifically social media and other digital vehicles). Further, the content of the message will also be unfamiliar (messaging needs to go beyond providing details about the product and appeal to the potential client's aspirations). Data processing as well as incentive systems for credit officers will probably also need to be modified to accommodate the new product.

- *Double bottom line.* In addition to the intangible benefits that a product such as student loans can offer an MFI (such as client loyalty, reaching a new demographic group, the possibility of cross-selling products, greater market share), MFIs must recognize the material social impact the product or program can have. Success in product implementation has been strongly correlated with organizational commitment to making the new product a success. In this respect, the organization's recognition of the intangible value associated with a product helps it reach its social objectives and fulfill its institutional mission.

One HEFF donor characterized the big-picture takeaways of introducing a new product such as student loans as follows:[1]

- Begin with the customer needs, preferences, and demands. Country contexts, cultural preferences, risk appetites, employment potential, and local government options will inform customer needs and therefore the demand for student financing products. Deeply understand customers, their networks, and the local market when sizing up product potential.

- Leverage every opportunity to "de-risk" the product offering, as a provider and as an investor, particularly if the financial institution is reaching a new customer segment. De-risking can include job market research, refining creditworthiness by analyzing future cash flows or income-sharing approaches, identifying guarantors (for example, parents), adapting marketing strategies, offering financial education to students, and assigning an institutional product champion. Partnerships with large potential employers and educational institutions can be effective for both marketing and job placement for graduates. All of these measures can help to manage a financial services provider's credit risk.

- Take a long-term, patient view on financial returns as financial services providers and as investors. While social mission, market positioning, or branding strategy often determines which providers or investors offer student financing, there is no question that taking a long-term view of customer value must be considered when "doing the math."

New Products in Microfinance: Conclusions

A compilation of lessons learned and a review of the existing literature on new product implementation point to several important lessons for successful product development. These can be summarized as follows:

Design. The first step in developing a new financial product is to conceptualize it. The concept needs to be well thought through, ensuring that the client's needs are taken into account. It also always helps to look around for "lessons learned" and to subject the initial design to third-party criticism. After conceptualization, the idea needs to be developed into a tangible product. It should be conveyed to all parts of the organization in a form that is simple and easy to understand yet also includes all key components. A good design will also ensure that all key details associated with offering the product are considered. These include everything from developing forms and paperwork to ensuring that all transactions will be accommodated by the IT platform, as well as devising appropriate risk management procedures and controls. Employee training (front office and back office) and supervision are also key. All regulatory aspects and registrations should be in place.

Launch. When a new product is ready to launch, consider testing it in a small or controlled setting and from there expand slowly. Perhaps release it in one or two stages so as to ensure that no design flaws exist; if they appear (as almost always will be the case), the smaller setting should allow for relatively pain-free corrections and modifications. Key aspects to consider:

- Adequate marketing is vital to ensure success. It is important to develop marketing literature that effectively communicates the product's features and to formulate a cohesive media strategy that is appropriate to the target market. New products, especially if they are targeting a new client type, might require different communication strategies than the "proven ones" the organization has used earlier.

- Staff incentives and training will ensure effective product implementation. If the right incentives are not in place, the product will not be promoted and will face an uphill battle to reach volume.

- It should be clear who will "own" the product. Normally, selecting a person to be the product's "champion" is a proven pathway to success.

Client-centricity. Clients' design input and feedback should be sought throughout the process. Their input will ensure that the product is something that the target population actually needs or wants. Too often the microfinance industry has offered to its clients a product that was convenient for the MFIs without much consideration of what would benefit their clients. As options and competition increase, clients have become more discriminating, and MFIs that do not become client-centric will not survive in the long run.

Notes

1. The list paraphrases the HEFF donor's observations, which were conveyed in a private conversation with the author.

ELEVEN

Insurance for Development

How Has It Evolved and Where Is It Going?

CRAIG CHURCHILL AND APARNA DALAL

Insurance has a critical contribution to make to the development agenda. A glance at the United Nations' Sustainable Development Goals (SDGs) suggests that insurance can contribute in some way to the realization of at least ten of the SDGs, especially in the areas of health, food security, climate change adaptation, and decent work.

Yet insurance markets in many developing countries are nascent at best. According to a Swiss Re Sigma report, insurance penetration (the ratio of premiums to GDP) in developed countries is roughly 8 percent, while in most emerging economies it is below 2 percent, sometimes well below. Indeed, there is a causal link between the development of the insurance industry and national economic development.[1] By enabling businesses to operate with less volatility, insurance promotes economic stability. Insurance can be used to manage certain risks faced by creditors more efficiently than other financial instruments, thereby facilitating access to credit and stimulating entrepreneurial effort.

While the problem is an underdeveloped insurance industry in general, more specifically within these countries, large swaths of the population are excluded from insurance, particularly low-income households. This is important because the poor are more vulnerable to risks than others, and yet they are the least able to cope when

213

crises occur. Shocks—such as the illness or death of a breadwinner, the loss of productive assets, and the destruction wrought by disasters—can wipe out a poor family's assets and capacity to earn a basic living in a single stroke. Insurance can make a tangible and crucial difference by allowing policyholders to recover and rebuild after a crisis.

Since 2012, the G-20 has championed financial inclusion, affordable access to financial services for all households. Where the poor have access and know how to use financial services, they can earn more, build assets, and manage risks. But the last point—the ability to manage risks—is often overlooked. The financial inclusion agenda is biased toward productive investments. However, to contribute to sustainable development, these productive investments must be accompanied by a similar emphasis on protection.

The benefits of insurance go beyond financial help in the event of shock. It can:

- *Reduce risk*: Insurance can play a critical role in reducing risk because insurers have a financial incentive to prevent risks from occurring.

- *Stimulate productivity*: The working poor invest more in their livelihoods, and get higher returns, if they are protected by insurance.

- *Aid in asset accumulation*: The working poor can also potentially build savings through a long-term life insurance policy, although in practice these policies that accumulate value do not provide particularly good value for clients. A preferred approach would be to use insurance as an incentive to increase savings balances.

- *Deliver tangible benefits*: Insurance with tangible benefits, such as a hotline for medical advice or health camps that provide vaccinations and mosquito nets, can make a huge difference in the lives of millions.

For the past decade, development partners have made a concerted effort to increase the availability of insurance for low-income households and small enterprises, and in some markets that effort is beginning to make headway. In 2016, sixty of the largest insurers in the world were engaging with the low-income and emerging segments, up from only seven in 2005.[2] But their entry into this market was not philanthropic or because of a sense of corporate social responsibility. Indeed there are profits to be made in serving the working poor, at least for some lines of business.

Some of the progress is due to insurers realizing that there are significant untapped market segments that they can serve, if they want to. Other progress can be attributed to technological developments, with insurers piggybacking on mobile money and digital payment platforms. Government policy is another source of progress; policymakers are turning to insurers to help them achieve public policy priorities, including managing climate change risks, extending health coverage to new population groups, and protecting smallholder farmers.

This chapter reviews eight trends that we are seeing in the sector. Within each trend, we recount the progress made in recent years and project how insurance for development is likely to evolve.

Evolving Definitions

The first trend to consider is what the topic is actually called. The term "microinsurance" emerged in the wake of the microcredit boom around 1999. Indeed the initial thoughts on this topic focused mostly on how microfinance institutions could also offer insurance to their borrowers and savers.

Microinsurance is specially designed for low-income people, with premiums and benefits to match their needs. It is particularly important for those in the informal economy, who tend to be underserved by mainstream commercial and social insurance schemes. Microinsurance provides a critical safety net for households, preventing them from falling into poverty when costly emergencies arise. It helps low-income people avoid problematic risk-coping measures such as putting children to work, eating less food, or selling productive assets.

The inclusive insurance space began to change dramatically when insurers shifted the paradigm. Instead of considering insurance as another financial service for microfinance institutions (MFIs), insurers began to think of MFIs as one of many distribution channels for insurance. That change in perspective made it possible for any organization that had financial transactions with large numbers of low-income clients, and had their trust, to treat them as a potential channel for distributing insurance.

But insurers were not too keen on the term "microinsurance" because it connoted loss-making activities and corporate social responsibility. To make this target market seem more attractive, they began using the term "emerging consumer." This terminology also enabled the insurance industry to realize that the need for insurance goes beyond the micro segment. While the traditional insurance industry has focused on corporations and high-net-worth customers, in developing countries the vast part of the population is not micro and has no access to formal insurance. This segment of emerging customers is growing. One billion people will enter the consuming class (earning more than US$10 a day) by 2025, and, for the first time in history, the number of people in the consuming class will be greater than those struggling to meet their basic needs.[3]

Emerging customers are considered the "missing middle," those earning between US$2 and US$13 per day. This segment had typically been ignored by the insurance industry, but some companies are now paying attention to them. The insurance industry is choosing to focus on the missing middle segment because they have disposable income and assets to protect. In some ways, they have more to lose when a risk event happens, and less access to social protection schemes, than the very poor.

From the perspective of the development community (instead of the insurance industry), "impact insurance" has emerged as a vital contributor to social and economic development. It incorporates the inclusion agenda, but it is also broader, exploring ways in which insurance can further the SDGs. Besides protection for the micro and emerging segments, impact insurance includes coverage for enterprises. An inclusive insurance market boosts the productivity of enterprises of all sizes by enabling entrepreneurs to pursue higher-risk and higher-return opportunities, thereby making a vital contribution to economic growth. Further, insurance can be a powerful tool in helping governments to achieve public policy objectives. The insurance industry can be an indispensable ally in promoting access to vital services, including health care and agricultural services, and in making communities more resilient in dealing with climate change.

Health Insurance

For insurance to attract the interest of the development community, it needs to benefit individuals and households. Research has demonstrated a positive impact of insurance on the lives of the poor and, more broadly, in their communities. Indeed, it is not possible to have meaningful social and economic development without insurance.

The biggest body of evidence highlights the contributions of insurance to better health. For example, insurance reduces out-of-pocket expenditures and increases the utilization of health services. Stefan Dercon and others found a reduction in total medical expenditure for insured patients in Kenya, as well as positive effects on household consumption.[4] In terms of health outcomes, findings from Guinea and Bangladesh show that insurance-enabled access to health services reduces maternal and child mortality.[5] This impact is impressive, however, Sustainable Development Goal 3, universal health coverage, encounters a major obstacle in efforts to extend coverage to workers in the informal economy. A "missing middle" of the population has emerged. Governments often provide health protection to the very poor through subsidies, while workers in the formal sector usually have access to health coverage through compulsory employer-based insurance or social security systems. Those who have neither are left out. Coverage is often lacking for workers in the informal sector and their families because of difficulty identifying and enrolling in them and financing their coverage in an efficient and equitable way.

Moving forward, government health plans looking to close this gap in population coverage will draw valuable lessons from efforts to extend insurance solutions to the working poor, including new ways of communicating to educate and create awareness, with a focus on optimizing the use of digital technology. As illustrated in box 11-1, the application of this expertise to the public health plan in Ghana is starting to show results.

Agriculture and Climate Insurance

The benefits of insurance are also clear when considering agriculture and climate insurance. Smallholders take more risk and invest more in their farms when they know they have protection. In China, Hongbin Cai and coauthors concluded that insurance for sows leads to higher investment.[6] Dean Karlan and coauthors found that insurance leads to higher-risk, higher-return production choices by farmers in Ghana.[7]

This contribution is becoming even more important as the world's exposure to risk increases. The Global Risks 2017 report ranked extreme weather events and natural disasters as top risks in terms of both likelihood and impact.[8] As extreme weather events increase in frequency and intensity, they lead to a loss of income and productive potential. Affected individuals resort to a variety of desperate coping strategies that diminish their ability to deal effectively with the impacts of climate change, both in the present and in the future. Climate change is just one risk that is quickly changing our world; migration, changes in the nature of work, youth unemployment, and economic instability have exacerbated uncertainty. As a result, there is a growing need to explore meaningful options for managing and transferring such risks.

Increasing people's ability to manage, as well as to mitigate climate risk by spreading it among people and across time, can significantly reduce their vulnerability, especially as part of a menu of options to encourage risk-aware behavior. Such interventions could be driven by a range of actors, including insurers and bankers, but it is

BOX 11-1.   Digitizing the Renewals Process for the NHIA in Ghana

The National Health Insurance Authority (NHIA) administers Ghana's national health insurance plan. Each year, the requirement that 11 million members renew their membership at a district office creates a major burden both for members and for the administrators. Further, there is the danger that the healthy will not renew and that those who are sick will (the problem of selective lapsing by the healthy). When the average health of the membership goes down, the average claims cost per member goes up. To ensure that the average health of the membership base does not decline, it is important to make the renewal process as easy as possible and to provide incentives for the healthy to continue their membership. To ensure growth in population coverage, it is likewise important that new members continue to join.

The ILO supported NHIA in its development of a new mobile system that members can use to renew their membership via a USSD menu on their phone. Members can pay their premium through their mobile wallet.

The solution was designed by employing user-centric design thinking and inexpensive prototyping that took the team from ideation to prototype within a week. The prototype product was piloted in two districts; learnings from the pilot were used to refine and significantly expand the scope of the solution. Starting in November 2018, NHIA rolled out the solution nationwide, starting with the digital authentication at all health care provider sites in Ghana.

Source: Authors' own analysis based on the ILO's Impact Insurance Facility's partnership with NHIA.

important that other value chain actors get involved as well. The providers of agricultural inputs and the off-takers have built-in incentives to enhance the resilience of farmers. As a result, bundling agriculture insurance with services like credit and farming inputs makes insurance more tangible, results in better social outcomes, and enables systems to scale more quickly, as illustrated in box 11-2.

Moving forward, climate change represents both an opportunity and a challenge for the insurance industry. It is an opportunity because businesses and households that feel more vulnerable may be more likely to include insurance in their risk management toolkit. On the challenging side, changes in weather patterns and the need

---

BOX 11-2.   Bundling Brings Value to the Agricultural Value Chain

In Zambia, NWK Services, a contract-farming manager, offered weather index insurance to 80,000 cotton farmers to attract more farmers and address problems of farmer loyalty and side-selling. The weather insurance was offered as a voluntary product, along with inputs given on credit. It protected farmers in the event of a severe dry spell or excess rain. In addition, NWK offered free life insurance to farmers who delivered their cotton early and repaid their loans in full. Tens of thousands of farmers got access to life insurance (most were first-time insurance customers), and approximately 7,000 farmers bought the weather index insurance. NWK noticed a positive impact on its business, with increased deliveries and reduced side-selling. In addition, NWK recovered a much greater proportion of the in-kind credit given to insured farmers than it recovered from uninsured farmers. When drought prevented productive harvests, farmers received payouts, and these timely benefits made it easier for them to repay their loans and replant their fields.

Source: Premasis Mukherjee, Manoj Pandey, and Pranav Prashad, "Bundling to Make Agriculture Insurance Work, " Paper 47 (Geneva: International Labor Office, 2017).

---

to diversify risks across geographies require large risk pools that are too much for one insurer to bear. Governments used to deal with these risks in their disaster management programs, but they are increasingly partnering with the private sector to make the cost more predictable. For budgeting purposes, it is easier for governments to set aside regular premium payments than to find surplus funds when an emergency occurs.

The model that is emerging in some regions provides three layers of protection: at the sovereign or national level, at the meso- or portfolio level, and at the microlevel. For example, in the Caribbean, many countries are members of the Caribbean Catastrophic Risk and Insurance Facility (CCRIF), to which they pay insurance premiums. If their countries are hit by a hurricane, the CCRIF immediately pays benefits to kickstart the reconstruction process. Meso-level coverage protects the portfolio of organizations, especially financial services providers, for whom the benefit might be access to a line of credit to keep them liquid and enable them to help put their borrowers back on their feet, in part by refinancing or rescheduling their loans. And at the microlevel one might find business interruption insurance for enterprises and farmers.

Disaster insurance often involves both governments and insurers. Public-private partnerships bring together unusual bedfellows, who may speak different languages and have different motivations. Although the idea of these new business models is compelling, operationalizing them can be challenging. To accelerate the learning curve among policymakers, it is useful for them to learn from each other's experiences. To that end, the International Labour Organization (ILO) is facilitating a peer learning platform that enables members from government agencies—ranging from ministries of agriculture and finance to central banks, planning commissions, and insurance regulators—to share their experiences and learn from each other about how to make agriculture and disaster insurance more accessible and responsive.

One challenge encountered by these partnerships is in the procurement process. Governments need to be objective when awarding contracts, and make sure that they are getting good value for their money. But if the company that "wins" the contract in one year has to compete again next year, and possibly lose the award, then it will not have sufficient incentive to invest in systems and processes needed for the long term. A possible solution to the PPP dilemma that has emerged from these discussions is for insurers to come together and form a risk pool that can be used to achieve public policy objectives, instead of procuring the services of individual companies. This idea is being tested in Kenya and Ghana.

Product Evolution

Over the past decade, insurance providers have made significant progress in their efforts to reach new market segments. A number of schemes have achieved massive scale, primarily by embedding or bundling offerings with other items—such as loans, savings, seeds, and air time—so that consumers are not actually making a purchasing decision about insurance itself.

This approach can be hailed as a success for two reasons. First, millions of low-income households, who never had insurance before, suddenly have access to some degree of protection. Second, and perhaps more important, this approach is envisioned as a market development process, with the intention to demonstrate to new market segments that insurance is beneficial, and to show insurers that these market segments are profitable. It is expected that this knowledge will then lead to a greater demand for and supply of insurance.

However, the jury is still out on whether this approach has indeed been successful. One of the biggest problems is that clients who have access to insurance through this channel do not necessarily know that they have coverage. If, as a result, they do not make a claim, insurance will have no value to them. Another limitation is that embedded insurance has to be extremely inexpensive; otherwise it will make the core purchase—the loan or the seeds—uncompetitive. Consequently, bundled insurance often does not provide useful benefits for consumers.

Despite these limitations, embedded insurance remains the most appropriate entry point for reaching new markets, but concerted effort is required to overcome the limitations. Typically insurers make it known when they do pay claims so that the market sees that they are reliable, but they need to do more. One approach is to ensure that policyholders and beneficiaries know that they are covered, through additional outreach and reminders. Another approach is to invest more in efforts to upsell or cross-sell top-ups to basic insurance to convert customers with embedded insurance to voluntary coverage.

To establish significant uptake of voluntary insurance, insurance products need to provide better value to customers. This can be difficult because the business model for small-ticket insurance requires standardized products. One of the lessons that insurers have learned is that products for their traditional market cannot be easily adapted for low-income clients by taking a couple of zeros off the premium price. Instead, they need to start with a blank sheet and create new products based on the needs and characteristics of this market segment. Awareness about creating and providing client value is growing, but there is scope for improvement. Tools for market research and client value assessment have helped pioneering insurers become more client-centric, and it is hoped that others will follow suit.

The nascent trend toward client-centricity among innovative insurers has illuminated an important reality: it is not possible for consumers to manage all of their risks through insurance. Of course insurers would never have argued otherwise, but if the objective is sustainable development, rather than just selling more insurance policies, then a more integrated approach to risk management is required.

Consequently, we expect financial services providers to start offering integrated solutions that bundle different forms of protection—such as an emergency loan or commitment-savings device—that are unlocked when risk events happen. If these products include an insurance component for high-cost but infrequent events, plus basic prevention measures to reduce households' exposure to risk in the first place, then insurance could be much more valuable to emerging consumers.

Some of these integrated products are being tested, especially those specifically targeting health risks.[9] However, few organizations have developed products that combine savings, credit, and insurance. That is likely to be the next frontier.

The Digital "Revolution"

The conversation has shifted from spreadsheets to blockchain, from paper forms to big data, and from hotlines to chatbots. Advancements in technology, such as mobile phones, data analytics, national identification systems, satellites, and drones, allow providers to reach new clients, automate back-end processes, improve risk identification, and reduce costs. Further, "insurtech" providers are vying to use technology to disrupt the insurance industry. Challenges around privacy and consumer protection remain, as data become more easily accessible and providers move from high-touch to low-touch distribution models.

The expanding world of data is expected to disrupt the insurance sector as insurers gain access to client data from all walks of life. Yet the large volume of client data is only valuable if converted into insights and used in practice, as illustrated in box 11-3.

Technology has long helped insurers better manage and distribute insurance. Now it is changing the nature of the products themselves. With digital solutions, such as telematics and the internet of things, which allow instant individual pricing, real-time data collection, and automatic claims processing, mainstream is introducing new kinds of products, such as usage-based and on-demand insurance.

The insurance industry is bracing itself for these changes, but what do they mean for the development agenda? The experience of other financial services for low-income customers provides clues for how insurance will also likely change. Loan eligibility is already being evaluated based on algorithms that analyze mobile phone usage and social media data. Risk profiling will not be far behind as insurers gain experience in handling alternative data sources. Indeed, these technologies can be game-changers by reducing operational costs through automation, using alternative information about customers for risk assessment and pricing, and utilizing artificial intelligence to enable better servicing. Access to data and new thinking on risk analysis will lead to new insurable events, fuller risk profiles, and the capacity to penetrate underserved markets more efficiently.

Technology is enabling insurers to move from just carrying risks to providing a broader range of services that better prevent, mitigate, and manage risks. By providing risk management advice and relevant value-added services, insurers can provide a more attractive offering to underserved market segments. This promise is yet to be realized, but innovative insurers are using digital technology to build more client-centric products, improve risk identification, and strengthen client servicing and communication. A digital strategy used to be about selecting the right technologies, automating

BOX 11-3.   Using Client Insights: The Experience of Britam in Kenya

Britam, Kenya's microinsurance market leader, has established structures and processes to enable the use and institutionalization of client insights within the organization. Over the years, Britam has established a dedicated associate responsible for market research, contracted a mobile survey firm to conduct periodic mobile surveys on clients' knowledge and reaction to products, and established a Business Intelligence Unit to systematically analyze customer enrollment and claims data.

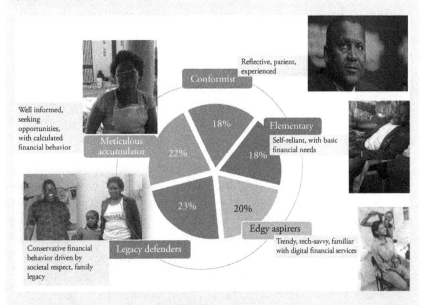

Britam conducted a market segmentation study to inform product design and distribution and organization structure. The study identified five market segments (see figure) with different demographics, behaviors, and attitudes toward financial services, including insurance. Britam used these insights to focus on two segments: "edgy aspirers"–young, urban, tech-savvy customers; and "meticulous accumulators"–older, peri-urban, traditional customers. Both segments have distinct risk management needs and require different outreach approaches. Britam launched a mobile microhealth insurance product in early 2018 to target the "edgy aspirers" and the product has already enrolled more than 90,000 customers. Britam has also partnered with four co-operative organizations (SACCOs) to reach "meticulous accumulators."

Source: Authors' own analysis based on the ILO Impact Insurance Facility's partnership with Britam.

BOX 11-4. How Equity Insurance Agency Is Digitizing Insurance Sales

Equity Insurance Agency (EIA) in Kenya embarked on its digital strategy in 2018. With the overall Equity Group, EIA's parent company, making strides in its digital transformation, EIA needed to resolve how to leverage technology for its insurance business.

One challenge was that most of Equity Group's banking transactions were taking place through alternative banking channels, including banking agents and online platforms, while EIA relied on making sales at Equity Group's branches. Customers were frustrated that they were not able to access insurance through the same platforms they were using for other Equity Group services.

EIA analyzed possible approaches to digitization. Although it planned to digitize all functions eventually, EIA had to figure out where to focus initially—on increasing revenues or reducing costs. Both were important, but the process also had to be manageable, and results needed to be achieved fairly quickly.

EIA decided to focus initially on digitizing sales in order to increase revenues—a key competitive advantage given EIA's role as an insurance broker. The company's digitization strategy has so far been successful. EIA introduced its first mobile-only insurance product in 2018, hospital coverage that offers customers a fixed cash payout per night when they spend three or more nights in any hospital. It is EIA's first product offered completely and exclusively via mobile, and all interactions, including sales, renewals, and claims, are carried out on a smart or feature phone. In the first eight months after its launch, the product reached over 150,000 customers.

Source: Authors' own analysis based on the ILO Impact Insurance Facility's partnership with EIA.

tasks, and gaining efficiency. Today digitization involves fundamentally transforming the way a business works and what it offers (see box 11-4).

It is important to note, however, that technological advancements come with risks themselves, especially as they pertain to data protection and client privacy. Insurers' use of greater information-gathering ability to exclude high-risk persons from their client base is another important concern to keep in mind.

Focus on Client Value, Client-Centricity, and Education

If you ask insurers why low-income people do not buy their products, their initial response usually has something to do with the market's unfamiliarity with insurance. This perception can lead them to suggest that significant investments in consumer education would stimulate demand. In reality, however, the problem is on the supply side; products and processes are not designed for this market segment. Once that problem is solved, there is some justification for investing in client education.

But how do clients get the best bang for their buck? Evidence has led us, and others in the industry, to change our thinking around consumer education—particularly by shifting our focus from classroom learning to "teachable moments." Teachable moments occur when someone receives useful information at the exact time he or she needs it. In the area of personal finance, teachable moments usually occur when someone is making a financial decision or using a financial service. We have found that interactions at relevant moments during the customer journey are more effective than traditional stand-alone classroom interventions.

Each interaction with the client is an opportunity to educate. These opportunities are enhanced by new communication tools, including SMS messages, audio messages, and access to call centers. We no longer have just one way to explain a product or receive information from a client. Technology enables frequent interactions, gradual education, and constant feedback—which are needed and welcome.

Today, much of the education, sales, and enrollment process occurs in person. In the future, the business model will need to evolve from high-touch to low-touch distribution models, from an advice-based approach to self-service, to improve the viability of small-ticket insurance. The timing of that transition, however, is delicate. The market needs to fully understand insurance before they will be willing to adopt low-touch methods, so investments in client understanding are important upfront contributions to developing the market.

Will the move from high-touch to low-touch channels be inclusive, or is there a risk that certain segments will be excluded, such as the elderly, rural populations, and women, who may be less digitally connected? The experience of other industries that have made this change can provide valuable lessons. Insurers need to consider these constraints and provide alternative channels for these population segments. For example, airline travel today can be done through a self-service approach, including buying an e-ticket on your smart phone, but some passengers still prefer a paper ticket and assistance checking in their luggage, so the airlines need to cater to both market segments.

The uptake of voluntary insurance will only succeed if stakeholders focus on clients and their needs. As products and technology evolve, it is important that the new products provide value. To consider the insurance offering from the client's perspective, the ILO has developed the PACE assessment tool, which stands for product, access, cost, and experience. Within each category are a number of subvariables and indicators that insurers can use to compare their products and processes with others, both other insurance products and other means that clients use to manage risks.[10]

One defining characteristic of this market that has proven difficult to change is lack of trust in the insurance industry. Limited presence and low brand recognition, and a shaky history of customer service, have led the insurance industry to be among the least trusted business sectors. It needs to make a concerted effort to change this image through collaboration with other insurers and the regulator. One promising approach is the *responsible insurance* agenda. Responsible insurance provision requires the delivery of appropriate products in an accessible, transparent, fair, responsive, and respectful way to informed consumers who can then use them effectively.[11]

A major dimension of this culture change is transparency. The lack of trust is partially driven by opaque pricing and the dubious claims-handling practices sometimes found in the industry. Business as usual is not going to grow the market. A transition to transparency will enable customers to compare like with like, and give them greater confidence that they know what is and is not covered, so they do not feel like submitting a claim is a lost cause. The emergence of online platforms that enable customers to make product and price comparisons is a welcome development. The transition to transparency will be hard for individual companies to make on their own; national insurance associations need to take the lead on these issues to start the process of refurbishing public opinion.

Regulators will also need to play a greater role in creating trust, but confidence in government institutions is also weak in many countries. Regulators and insurers often have an adversarial relationship. To support market development, the two parties need to team up, each pulling their oars in the same direction, as neither will be successful without the other.

Will we see progress on this front in the coming decade? Certainly it will differ from market to market, but countries that generate the best results will be those where regulators and the industry work together and agree on appropriate mechanisms for protecting consumers that do not discourage insurers from reaching out to new markets. It is important to protect customers, but not to protect them out of the market.

New Players and Business Models

In 2008 the most common distribution channels were microfinance institutions that provided insurers with ready access to an aggregated pool of clients for simple credit life products. More than a decade later, microfinance institutions still play a major role in distribution, but insurers have partnered with a broad range of distribution partners to reach new customers. These include small retailers, supermarkets, co-operatives, money transfer agencies, employers, pawnshops, and of course mobile network operators. Making insurance a priority for these partners can be challenging, as core business requirements take precedence and insurance has to compete with other lines of revenue; but these partners have emerged as powerful conduits for insurance when incentives are properly aligned.

Some countries have created a special regulatory category for microinsurance providers. However, making the business case for exclusively serving low-income households is difficult, and a more effective model seems to be to integrate a microinsurance unit into a larger company because it enables the unit to leverage shared services. While a few specialized microinsurance providers continue to excel and push the boundaries of the industry, insurance for low-income and emerging customers has become mainstream. The possibility to use existing infrastructure, share services with other segments, and cross-subsidize products has created a compelling case for large insurers to enter this segment.

Moving forward, we expect to see a trend away from stand-alone microinsurers and toward dedicated "emerging consumer" teams within insurance companies, especially in companies that embrace a long-term commitment to this market segment and are willing to change their management processes. These dedicated teams have an independent balance sheet, but can use a shared services model to leverage existing systems and resources, thereby making the entry cost more palatable, following the model deployed by successful organizations, such as Britam in Kenya and Pioneer Insurance in the Philippines (see box 11-5).

Traditional insurance company structures will not be relevant in the coming decade. Too bold? Perhaps, but the cost structure is a particular concern for insurers, as they are under threat from technological advancements that are likely to upend their standard business model. Companies that have succeeded in serving the low-income market, however, have learned valuable lessons about creating efficiencies that are relevant for their conventional business as well.

For example, insurers trying to serve new market segments, through alternative distribution points, where the business is based on lower margins per policy and great volumes of policies, will require significant restructuring. To tackle this task, the

BOX 11-5.   Pioneer's Focus on Customers and Claims

Understanding customers and claims has made Pioneer Insurance one of the largest microinsurance providers in the Philippines.

When Pioneer Insurance started offering insurance for low-income households in 2007, it had one distribution partner–CARD MRI. In 2016, after ten years, Pioneer's joint venture with CARD—CARD Pioneer Microinsurance—was working with almost 100 institutional partners and generated US$19 million in premiums.

To establish itself as "the insurer that pays claims," Pioneer took a number of steps. It set up a unit dedicated to the low-income microsegment that had its own underwriting and claims-settling authority. It developed its own guidelines and standards and reengineered operations to respond to the realities of this market segment.

Pioneer realized that it could not do business from behind a desk: it needed to get close to the lives of its clients. The insurer made accommodations for circumstances unique to the low-income market. For instance, for a death that occurred in hospital, insurance companies ordinarily required a death certificate from the hospital before paying the hospital bill. However, because the hospital would not release the death certificate until the bill was paid, the client was left in an impossible chicken-and-egg scenario. Pioneer sends a representative to the hospital to verify each claim and then makes the payment without the certificate.

As Pioneer grows, it is building the organizational, operational, and technological foundations that will allow it to improve claims and services for its first 10 million clients, as well as the next 10 million.

Source: Aparna Dalal, "Case Brief: Pioneer Microinsurance," Impact Insurance Facility, ILO, Case Brief 10 (2017) (http://www.impactinsurance.org/sites/default/files /CaseBrief_june2017_web_version.pdf).

ILO's Impact Insurance Facility has formalized the lessons learned when supporting such transformations. One of the main conclusions is that, to gain trust and meet clients' ever-changing needs, an insurer requires an organizational architecture (comprising human resource management, institutional culture, and organizational structure) that empowers it to listen and respond to clients—a relevant insight for all market segments. Another conclusion is that companies need to be structured to serve customer segments, rather than offer traditional business lines like property, life, and health insurance. Customers want to approach one entry point to support their diverse insurance needs, not different departments for different types of coverage.

Distribution channels such as MFIs, retailers, and utility companies have been in the driver's seat because of their access to customers and sales infrastructure. Some insurers could even lose their role as the primary insurance providers, as other types of organizations, which are more nimble and more responsive to client needs, acquire insurance licenses.

New partnerships with fintech and insuretech firms bring opportunities for insurers to reach customers directly and bundle insurance with an array of other services. But these firms are disruptors and have vastly different cultures and operations than traditional insurers. If they are to work together, insurers will need to think more creatively about the value they bring to the partnerships and how new models can allow them to better reach and service customers. New partnerships are only possible if insurance contributes to the partner's core business or if insurance encourages client behaviors that lead to better production decisions.

The Role of Governments

Governments are increasingly using insurance to achieve public policy objectives, especially those related to universal health coverage, food security, and climate change adaptation. Government-sponsored plans worldwide have partnered with the financial sector to improve efficiency. For instance, workers in the informal sector and their families are often not covered by public health plans because of difficulties identifying and enrolling them, and in financing their coverage in an efficient and equitable way. Government health plans are looking to close this gap in population coverage by using innovative ways of targeting and enrolling excluded populations.

Similarly, there is consensus that any national agricultural development strategy needs to integrate insurance as a risk mitigation tool to make the value chain more resilient. Agriculture production that is primarily for domestic consumption supports food security, whereas export-focused agriculture is an important source of gross national product in many countries. The livelihoods of many rural residents, including smallholder farmers and day laborers, are threatened by climatic volatility, and purely market-based solutions are not usually available. So some governments are looking to crowd in the private sector by providing relevant infrastructure and, in some cases, subsidizing premiums, as in the case of Kenya.

To enable insurance to contribute to the development agenda, there are a number of activities that governments can and should undertake. The starting point is the regulatory environment, which should ensure that insurers are solvent, follow appropriate market conduct practices, and encounter sufficient competition. In many countries the regulations date back many years, before the growing interest in the low-income market began, and certainly before the latest wave of technological developments, so they may not support recent innovations in the sector. For example, regulations need to allow alternative distribution channels without requiring all people working for those channels to be licensed agents. They also need to allow for paperless contracting, without requiring a "wet signature" or a hard copy of the contract. Another regulatory gap may be index insurance, where the payout is based on conditions that exceed a particular threshold, such as rainfall or wind speed, as a proxy for losses instead of actual losses, which is used in the Kenya Livestock Insurance Program, for example.

In addition to developing regulations and subsidizing premiums, governments can encourage or even require insurers to expand their portfolios to unserved markets. A requirement may seem extreme, but that is the expectation of the Indian regulatory authority—that all insurance companies have a percentage of their portfolios in the rural and social sectors or face a fine. A more common approach is for regulators and policymakers to encourage insurers to pursue new opportunities— for example, by creating a regulatory sandbox that allows companies to test new approaches. Mandatory insurance for certain items, such as home loans and automobiles, is another opportunity for the insurance industry to develop new capacities in retail insurance.

Governments can also provide the infrastructure for the effective functioning of insurance markets. The infrastructure might include meteorological information, health care providers, or even national databases such as morbidity and mortality tables. The specifics will vary from country to country, but it is important to note that there are many ways in which governments can help the insurance industry contribute to the development agenda. Doing so will require dialogue between the two.

Conclusion

Insurance is a powerful but underused tool for social and economic development. It should provide tremendous benefits for households, enterprises, and countries. But in many countries the insurance industry is not yet fulfilling its potential. At the microlevel, in a developed insurance market, households and enterprises are more resilient and more willing to make productive investments. At the macrolevel, insurance companies can contribute to infrastructure and capital market developments, especially life insurance companies that can make long-term investments. The industry needs to leverage this potential to make larger contributions and to draw attention to them.

Although progress has been made, there remains an urgent need to accelerate the growth of impact insurance in many countries. Ten years ago, the focus was on working with individual insurance providers and building their capacity. This proved insufficient. A structured market development process that brings together the full range of stakeholders, from regulators to ministries, industry associations, insurers, and distributors, may be more effective in the future.

Notes

1. M. Arena, "Does Insurance Market Promote Economic Growth? A Cross-Country Study for Industrialized and Developing Countries,"*Journal of Risk and Insurance* 75, no. 4 (2008): 921–46.

2. S. Cheston, "Inclusive Insurance: Closing the Protection Gap for Emerging Customers," Center for Financial Inclusion (2018) (https://content.centerforfinancialinclusion.org/wp-content/uploads/sites/2/2018/08/Inclusive-Insurance-Final-2018.06.13.pdf).

3. H. Kharas, "The Unprecedented Expansion of the Global Middle Class: An Update," Global Economy and Development Working Paper 100 (Brookings India, 2017).

4. S. Dercon and others, "The Impact of a Health Insurance Programme: Evidence from a Randomized Controlled Trial in Kenya," Impact Insurance Facility, ILO Research Paper 24 (Geneva, 2012) (http://www.impactinsurance.org/publications/rp24).

5. O. De Bock and D. U. Ontiveros, "Literature Review on the Impact of Microinsurance," Impact Insurance Facility, ILO, Research Paper 35 (Geneva: 2013) (http://www.impactinsurance.org/publications/rp35).

6. H. Cai and others, "Microinsurance, Trust and Economic Development: Evidence from a Randomized Natural Field Experiement," NBER Working Paper (Cambridge, Mass.: National Bureau of Economic Research, 2009).

7. D. Karlan and others, "Agricultural Decisions after Relaxing Credit and Risk Contraints," NBER Working Paper (Cambridge, Mass.: National Bureau of Economic Research, 2012).

8. World Economic Forum, "The Global Risks Report 2017, 12th Edition" (Geneva: 2017).

9. Lisa Morgan and Craig Churchill, "Financial Inclusion and Health: How the Financial Services Industry Is Responding to Health Risks," Impact Insurance Facility, ILO Research Paper 51 (Geneva: 2018) (http://www.impactinsurance.org/publications/mp51).

10. Michal Matul and Eamon Kelley, "How to Conduct a PACE Client Value Assessment: A Technical Guide for Microinsurance Practitioners." Impact Insurance Facility, ILO

(Geneva: 2012) (http://www.microfinancegateway.org/sites/default/files/mfg-en-toolkit-how
-to-conduct-a-pace-client-value-assessment-a-technical-guide-for-microinsurance
-practitioners-jan-2012.pdf).

11. Camyla Fonseca and Craig Churchill, "Providing Insurance Responsibly," Impact Insurance Facility, ILO, Working Paper 52 (Geneva: 2018) (https://www.ilo.org/wcmsp5
/groups/public/---ed_emp/documents/publication/wcms_634983.pdf).

Section IV

A GEOGRAPHIC PERSPECTIVE

Photo by Stefano Alemani on Unsplash

TWELVE

Asia and the Pacific

Tremendous Progress, but Hundreds of Millions Yet to Serve

JENNIFER ISERN

According to the Findex global database, access to formal financial services in developing countries rose to 63 percent of adults in 2017, from a base of 41.8 percent in 2011.[1] Formal providers, as defined by this analysis, include banks, microfinance institutions, mobile money providers, and other regulated financial services providers.

These results are encouraging and reflect significant efforts underway in several countries. Financial inclusion is a means to an end—an enabler for people and small businesses to manage their financial lives by optimizing income and expenses to smooth risk and investments. In doing so, people are able to participate in economic development, reduce poverty levels, and build wealth, all of which contribute to the global sustainable development goals. People without access to formal savings accounts or mobile money accounts rely on cash, which can be unsafe and requires more logistics and often higher costs to make or receive payments, receive income and benefits, and pay bills. Savings accounts and access to short-term loans can also help mitigate financial shocks such as illness or death in the family or loss of wages, as well as help households plan for anticipated large expenses such as school fees and peak business cycles around significant holidays.

235

Six developing countries, of which five are in Asia, have achieved financial access levels above 80 percent: Mongolia, Malaysia, the People's Republic of China (PRC), India, Kenya, and Thailand. Yet access to finance remains uneven across countries and regions, ranging from 71 percent in East Asia and the Pacific to 42 percent in sub-Saharan Africa.

Financial Inclusion in Asia and the Pacific

Over the past decade, Asia and the Pacific has experienced some of the fastest growth levels globally, yet financial inclusion is highly uneven across the region. The Asia and Pacific countries vary greatly in population size, per capita GDP and economic growth prospects, land size and resources, culture, and size and complexity of their financial sectors. Progress toward financial inclusion will reflect these country-specific contexts.

In East Asia, 71 percent of adults hold a formal account, an increase from 55 percent in 2011.[2] As table 12-1 shows, the countries with the highest levels of financial access are Singapore, Mongolia, Malaysia, Thailand, and the PRC. Access is below 35 percent in Cambodia, Vietnam, and the Philippines. Unfortunately, Findex compiles fewer data for Pacific Island countries, where access varies widely from relatively higher levels in Fiji to medium levels in Papua New Guinea (PNG) and lower levels in other countries.

In South Asia, 70 percent of adults hold a formal account, more than double the level of 32 percent in 2011. The highest levels of inclusion are in India, Sri Lanka, and Bangladesh; the lowest level is in Afghanistan. India led tremendous progress in account holding, growing from 35 percent to 80 percent from 2011 to 2017 largely as a result of government campaigns to encourage biometric identification and account openings.

Priority Focus for Inclusion Efforts

In developing countries, a gender gap remains: 9 percent more men than women had access to an account in 2017, the same as in 2011. The gender gap is even higher in Pakistan, Afghanistan, Morocco, the West Bank and Gaza, Jordan, Chad, Algeria, Nigeria, and the Central African Republic. Further, of the 1.7 billion adults without access globally, 56 percent are women.[3]

Adding a gender lens helps improve the picture for access to finance in Asia and the Pacific, with a larger gender gap in South Asia:

- In East Asia and the Pacific, 73 percent of men and 68 percent of women hold an account. The highest gender gap is noted in the PRC (8 percent difference), while the figures for Cambodia, Indonesia, Myanmar, and Vietnam reflect equal access for men and for women.

- In South Asia, 73 percent of men and 64 percent of women hold an account. Yet dramatic differences are seen in Afghanistan (16 percent difference), Bangladesh (29 percent), and Pakistan (28 percent). Of note, India's gender gap decreased significantly, from 20 percent in 2014 to 6 percent in 2017.

Half of the unbanked globally are concentrated in the lower 40 percent of income levels in their countries. Data on access and usage are challenging to disaggregate consistently across rural and urban clients, although data at a country level often flag lower access in rural areas.

Similar patterns exist in Asia, where lower-income households have less access to financial services, especially in East Asia and the Pacific:

- In East Asia and the Pacific, the income gap is 19 percent: 78 percent of adults in the richest 60 percent of households hold accounts, compared with just 59 percent of adults in the poorest 40 percent of households.[4] An income gap is most evident in Cambodia, the PRC, Indonesia, Lao PDR, Myanmar, the Philippines, and Vietnam.

- In South Asia, the income gap is 6 percent, where 72 percent of adults in the richest 60 percent and 66 percent of adults in the poorest 40 percent of households hold accounts. Income gaps are highest in Bangladesh, Nepal, and Pakistan.

Looking globally at results by age group, younger adults aged fifteen to twenty-four have 13 percent less access to formal accounts than adults twenty-five and older. This may change over time, as younger adults increase their use of digital finance options and likely expand their income flows.

Access vs. Usage

Across Asia and the Pacific, some countries are closer to achieving one goal of basic financial access, but many are still far from achieving true financial inclusion. For those with access to formal services with a financial institution, actual use of the services lags behind. Approximately 25 percent of financial institution accounts in developing economies were inactive over the previous year; the

TABLE 12-1. Financial Inclusion: Selected Indicators for the Asia-Pacific Region, 2011–17 (percent)

	Account (age 15+)	Account, male (age 15+)	Account, female (age 15+)	Account, young adults (ages 15–24)	Account, older adults (ages 25+)	Account, rural (age 15+)	Financial institution account (age 15+)	Used the internet to pay bills or to buy something online in the past year (age 15+)	Saved for old age (age 15+)
2011 World	51	55	47	37	54	44	51		
2014 World	62	66	58	47	66	58	61	17	24
2017 World	69	72	65	56	72	66	67	29	21
2011 East Asia & Pacific (excluding high income)	55	58	52	50	56	50	55		
2014 East Asia & Pacific (excluding high income)	69	71	67	61	71	67	69	16	37
2017 East Asia & Pacific (excluding high income)	71	73	68	67	71	69	70	39	23
2011 East Asia & Pacific	60	62	58	54	61	53	60		
2014 East Asia & Pacific	72	74	70	63	74	69	72	19	37
2017 East Asia & Pacific	74	76	71	69	75	71	73	41	26
2011 Hong Kong SAR, PRC	89	88	89	80	91	80	89		
2014 Hong Kong SAR, PRC	96	96	96	89	97	90	96	36	39
2017 Hong Kong SAR, PRC	95	96	95	88	96	94	95	53	37
2011 Singapore	98	98	98	95	99		98		
2014 Singapore	96	97	96	93	97		96	28	50

Debit card ownership (age 15+)	Borrowed from a financial institution (age 15+)	Borrowed from a financial institution or used a credit card (age 15+)	Has a national identity card (age 15+)	Credit card ownership (age 15+)	Deposit in the past year (with a financial institution account, age 15+)	No deposit and no withdrawal from a financial institution account in the past year (age 15+)	Made or received digital payments in the past year (age 15+)	Mobile money account (age 15+)
31	9			15				
41	11	22		18	78	9	41	2
48	11	23		18	69	14	52	4
35	9			7				
43	11	20		13	83	8	39	0
57	11	21	97	16	69	12	58	1
35	9			13				
47	11	23		18	84	7	44	
60	11	26		22	73	11	62	
76	8			58				
70	8	60		64	86	7	81	
83	9	62		65	90	4	85	
29	10			37				
89	14	38		35	86	7	87	6

(continued)

TABLE 12-1.   (continued)

	Account (age 15+)	Account, male (age 15+)	Account, female (age 15+)	Account, young adults (ages 15–24)	Account, older adults (ages 25+)	Account, rural (age 15+)	Financial institution account (age 15+)	Used the internet to pay bills or to buy something online in the past year (age 15+)	Saved for old age (age 15+)
2017 Singapore	98	100	96	98	98	100	98	57	51
2011 PRC	64	68	60	65	63	58	64		
2014 PRC	79	81	76	74	80	77	79	20	39
2017 PRC	80	84	76	87	79	78	80	49	22
2011 Indonesia	20	20	19	13	22	16	20		
2014 Indonesia	36	35	37	35	36	29	36	5	27
2017 Indonesia	49	46	51	47	49	47	48	11	27
2011 Cambodia	4	4	4	5	3	2	4		
2014 Cambodia	22	24	20	26	21	20	13	1	29
2017 Cambodia	22	22	22	20	23	19	18	4	20
2011 Lao PDR	27	27	26	23	28	20	27		
2017 Lao PDR	29	26	32	24	32	22	29	7	27
2014 Myanmar	23	29	17	13	26	21	23	0	16
2017 Myanmar	26	26	26	11	31	25	26	4	13
2011 Mongolia	78	73	82	73	80	77	78		
2014 Mongolia	92	90	93	93	91	91	92	7	8
2017 Mongolia	93	91	95	84	96	94	93	17	9
2011 Malaysia	66	69	63	57	70	52	66		
2014 Malaysia	81	83	78	76	82	74	81	19	54
2017 Malaysia	85	88	82	84	86	81	85	39	42
2011 Philippines	27	19	34	18	30	20	27		
2014 Philippines	31	24	38	19	36	29	28	4	25
2017 Philippines	34	30	39	24	39	27	32	10	26
2011 Thailand	73	73	73	59	75	70	73		
2014 Thailand	78	81	75	71	80	77	78	4	59
2017 Thailand	82	84	80	73	83	81	81	19	45
2011 Vietnam	21	24	19	23	21	17	21		
2014 Vietnam	31	30	32	37	29	26	31	9	23
2017 Vietnam	31	31	30	34	30	25	30	21	18

Debit card ownership (age 15+)	Borrowed from a financial institution (age 15+)	Borrowed from a financial institution or used a credit card (age 15+)	Has a national identity card (age 15+)	Credit card ownership (age 15+)	Deposit in the past year (with a financial institution account, age 15+)	No deposit and no withdrawal from a financial institution account in the past year (age 15+)	Made or received digital payments in the past year (age 15+)	Mobile money account (age 15+)
41	7			8				
48	9	21		16	84	8	44	
67	9	23	99	21	71	12	68	
11	9			0				
26	13	14		2	80	5	22	0
31	17	18	90	2	52	15	35	3
3	19			0				
5	28	28		3	38	5	18	13
7	27	27	89	1	43	5	16	6
6	18			3				
13	9	9	41	1	60	9	13	
2	16	16		0	54	4	4	0
5	19	19	89	0	42	10	8	1
61	25			2				
66	36	36		1	70	11	63	5
76	29	30	96	3	87	8	85	22
23	11			12				
41	20	31		20	73	13	58	3
74	12	23	94	21	69	17	70	11
13	11			3				
20	12	13		3	67	7	20	4
21	10	11		2	76	5	25	5
43	19			5				
55	15	18		6	90	4	33	1
60	15	20	99	10	68	16	62	8
15	16			1				
27	18	20		2	72	6	18	0
27	21	22	94	4	67	6	23	3
7	9			2				

(continued)

TABLE 12-1. (continued)

	Account (age 15+)	Account, male (age 15+)	Account, female (age 15+)	Account, young adults (ages 15–24)	Account, older adults (ages 25+)	Account, rural (age 15+)	Financial institution account (age 15+)	Used the internet to pay bills or to buy something online in the past year (age 15+)	Saved for old age (age 15+
2011 South Asia	32	40	24	24	35	31	32		
2014 South Asia	47	55	38	37	50	46	46	1	9
2017 South Asia	70	75	64	60	73	69	68	5	11
2011 Afghanistan	9	15	3	6	11	6	9		
2014 Afghanistan	10	16	4	7	12	9	10	1	11
2017 Afghanistan	15	23	7	10	18	15	15	1	7
2011 Bangladesh	32	37	26	20	37	30	32		
2014 Bangladesh	31	35	26	21	35	30	29	0	6
2017 Bangladesh	50	65	36	41	54	50	41	4	9
2011 India	35	44	26	27	38	33	35		
2014 India	53	63	43	43	57	52	53	1	10
2017 India	80	83	77	71	83	79	80	4	11
2011 Sri Lanka	69	70	67	69	68	68	69		
2014 Sri Lanka	83	82	83	85	82	83	83	2	14
2017 Sri Lanka	74	74	73	77	73	73	74	6	19
2011 Nepal	25	30	21	24	27	22	25		
2014 Nepal	34	37	31	25	37	31	34	0	9
2017 Nepal	45	50	42	39	48	43	45	2	12
2011 Pakistan	10	17	3	8	11	7	10		
2014 Pakistan	13	21	5	13	13	13	9	2	5
2017 Pakistan	21	35	7	15	25	19	18	8	15

Source: Asli Demirgüç-Kunt and others, *The Global Findex Database 2017: Measuring Financial Inclusion and the Fintech Revolution* (Washington: World Bank, 2018).

Findex data for developing countries in East Asia and the Pacific include: Cambodia; the People's Republic of China; Indonesia; Lao People's Democratic Republic; Malaysia; Mongolia; Myanmar; the Philippines; Thailand; and Vietnam. Pacific Island countries are not currently covered. Several East Asian high-income countries are included; see Findex site for specifics. Findex data for South Asia include: Afghanistan; Bangladesh; Bhutan; India; Nepal; Pakistan; and Sri Lanka. Bhutan and the Maldives are not covered.

Debit card ownership (age 15+)	Borrowed from a financial institution (age 15+)	Borrowed from a financial institution or used a credit card (age 15+)	Has a national identity card (age 15+)	Credit card ownership (age 15+)	Deposit in the past year (with a financial institution account, age 15+)	No deposit and no withdrawal from a financial institution account in the past year (age 15+)	Made or received digital payments in the past year (age 15+)	Mobile money account (age 15+)
92	16	47	95	49	90	4	90	10
18	6	9		3	50	18	17	3
27	7	8	93	3	43	32	28	4
5	7			1				
2	4	4		1			6	0
3	3	4	71	1	66	5	11	1
2	23			1				
5	10	10		0	60	9	7	3
6	9	9	83	0	51	13	34	21
8	8			2				
22	6	9		4	48	22	19	2
33	7	8	97	3	42	39	29	2
10	18			4				
25	18	20		4	52	26	21	0
32	15	17	92	5	52	26	47	2
4	11			1				
7	12	12		0	72	7	9	0
9	13	14		1	55	14	16	
3	2			1				
3	2	2		0			8	6
8	2	3	79	1	56	3	18	7

highest inactivity was in India (39 percent), Sri Lanka (26 percent), Malaysia (17 percent), Thailand (16 percent), Indonesia (15 percent), and Nepal (14 percent).

If people are not using their accounts, is this a sign that the services offered are not yet well adapted to client preferences? For example, accounts may offer only basic short-term loans, rudimentary savings facilities, rigid loan terms, or complex money transfers. Adults holding deposits in a financial institution ranged from 69 percent in East Asia and the Pacific to 43 percent in South Asia. Saving for old age—through long-term savings and pensions—was low (23 percent) in East Asia and the Pacific and even lower (11 percent) in South Asia. The level of adults borrowing from a financial institution or using a credit card is also low: 21 percent in East Asia and the Pacific and just 8 percent in South Asia. In both regions family and friends are the most common source of loans. Making or receiving digital payments is becoming more common across Asia: 58 percent of adults in East Asia and the Pacific and 28 percent in South Asia have at least one digital transaction.

"Too Much" Usage?

With higher levels of financial inclusion, a new concern has been emerging in some countries where competition for clients is intense and access to credit is quick and easy. Concerns are rising about household debt levels globally,[5] since credit bubbles have triggered some of the world's most significant financial sector crises over the ages.[6]

Perceived levels of household debt in Andhra Pradesh in India triggered a massive microfinance crisis in October 2010. This crisis echoed around the world and led to significant reforms across India in policy and regulation, responsible finance measures, market composition, consumer protection efforts, and international and domestic investment in the sector.[7]

Elsewhere in Asia and the Pacific, concerns about over-indebtedness have been rising. Over the past decade, Cambodia has experienced rapid institutional growth, and there is more competition to attract new clients in Phnom Penh and other areas of the country.[8] Learning from the crisis in India, key institutions, investors, policymakers, and the credit bureau in Cambodia are developing lender guidelines and seeking independent verification of institutional behavior and levels of client indebtedness.

In markets across Asia and the Pacific, intense competition for clients can lead to easy credit terms. For example, levels of household over-indebtedness are high in some Pacific Island countries, including Papua New Guinea.[9] Building on a recent country diagnostic, the PNG central bank is working with financial services providers to develop consumer protection guidelines. Likewise, concerns are rising for the Kathmandu valley in Nepal, greater Colombo and the postconflict northern areas of Sri Lanka, Assam in India, Dhaka and secondary cities in Bangladesh, as well as the greater urban areas of Jakarta, Bangkok, Singapore, and Kuala Lumpur.[10] Overheated competition and levels of household and small business debt should be monitored closely across the Asia and Pacific region (and globally).

Hundreds of Millions Still Unbanked

Despite broadly encouraging results, progress is not inevitable. Sixteen countries globally experienced a decline in access to finance between 2014 and 2017.[11] In Asia, over the same period, Sri Lanka experienced a decrease in account holding from 83 to 74 percent of adults, while levels of access remained flat in Cambodia, the People's Republic of China, and Vietnam.

Even after tremendous effort and the resulting greater visibility for financial inclusion, 1.7 billion people globally still lack access to formal services. The majority of the world's excluded adults live in Asia and the Pacific; they are concentrated in six countries: the PRC (224 million people), India (190 million), Pakistan (99 million), Indonesia (92 million), Bangladesh (58 million), and Vietnam (46 million).

Key Actors Expanding Financial Inclusion across Asia and the Pacific

Asia is home to some of the oldest and best-known institutions in the history of financial inclusion—Bank Rakyat Indonesia (BRI), BRAC and the Grameen Bank in Bangladesh, and SEWA in India. Over the past forty years, diverse institutions in the Asia and Pacific region have expanded access to financial services, including microfinance institutions, commercial banks, financial co-operatives, state-owned banks and inclusion programs, rural banks, and digital finance institutions.

Established Financial Services Providers

Across the vast region of Asia and the Pacific, each country offers a unique combination of established institutions that promote access to finance.[12] For more than 120 years, some of the earliest institutions across Asia and the Pacific were created for the purpose of expanding access to finance to both urban and rural low-income people. Today hundreds of institutions across the region have expanded their clientele after developing an understanding of the market opportunity provided by retail banking for households and micro, small, and medium-sized enterprises (MSMEs). This positive development reflects the good work of many dedicated institutions that have demonstrated how to expand useful and meaningful access to clients.

Asian institutions of all types helped spark the global movement for financial inclusion beginning in the 1970s. Well-known pioneers include BRI in Indonesia; BRAC, Grameen Bank, and ASA in Bangladesh; Self-Employed Women's Association (SEWA), BASIX, and dozens others in India; Acleda Bank and Amret in Cambodia; Funding for the Poor Cooperative and Chinese Foundation for Poverty Alleviation in the People's Republic of China; XAC Bank and Khan Bank in Mongolia; Nirdhan in Nepal; Tameer (now Telenor) Microfinance Bank in Pakistan; CARD Bank in the Philippines; Government Savings Bank and BAAC in Thailand; Capital Aid for Employment of the Poor in Vietnam; Bank Rakyat in Malaysia; SANASA in Sri Lanka, and others. Across Asia and the Pacific, two countries merit special mention for fostering the broadest diversity of financial services providers and most significant leaps in financial inclusion—the People's Republic of China and India. The experiences of both countries are covered more extensively in separate chapters of this book.[13]

Microfinance institutions (MFIs) may be purpose-built to provide financial services to low-income people, but they are not alone in pursuing this mission. Depending on the specific financial regulatory framework of each country, MFIs have emerged as nongovernmental organizations (NGOs), associations, nonbanks, specialized and commercial banks, and in other legal forms. The early wave of countries where MFIs launched in the 1970s include Bangladesh, India, Nepal, and the Philippines. During the 1990s and 2000s MFIs achieved significant scale and number in Cambodia, Indonesia, Mongolia, Pakistan, and Sri Lanka. A third wave of MFIs has grown in Afghanistan, Myanmar, Bhutan, Lao PDR, Papua New Guinea, Timor Leste, and Vietnam. Thousands of MFIs offer financial services across rural and urban areas in Asia and the Pacific, with varying levels of success, institutional size, client outreach, and long-term viability. Some of the most successful MFIs have transformed into special-purpose banks and even universal banks.

Several special-purpose banks were created or have evolved into Asian examples of development finance institutions focusing on low-income people and mass retail banking:

- Established in 1895, Bank Rakyat Indonesia is the oldest bank in the country, with hundreds of thousands of village-level access points. BRI went through several name changes, institutional forms, and ownership changes over the past 120 years. It was nationalized in 1945 as the first government-owned bank and undertook a partial public offering of 30 percent of its shares in 2003.

- In Thailand, the Government Savings Bank was established in 1913 and continues to be a leading player in expanding financial services nationwide.

- The State Bank of India, founded in 1806 as the Bank of Calcutta, is one of the largest government-owned banks in the country with a ubiquitous branch network and large outreach, with clients at all income levels. Two government-owned development finance institutions have played fundamental roles in access to finance across the country: the National Bank for Agriculture and Rural Development (NABARD) was launched by the government in 1981 as the focal point for rural credit and development; and the Small Industries Development Bank of India (SIDBI) was created in 1990 to promote lending to and the development of MSMEs.

- In the People's Republic of China, the government established the Agricultural Bank of China in 1951 to specialize in rural lending, and it has evolved over the years to become one of the four largest banks in the country (and the world).

- In Vietnam, the government launched the Vietnam Bank for the Poor in 1995. It was later combined with the Vietnam Bank for Agriculture and Rural Development and transformed into the Vietnam Bank for Social Policies (VBSP) in 2002. As a fully owned government institution, VBSP offers financial services in priority areas for national development.

- In Malaysia, three development finance institutions play a key role: Bank Simpanan Nasional (BSN), Agrobank, and Bank Rakyat. Together, these institutions represent approximately 33 percent of deposit accounts in the country and 23 percent of branch offices.[14]

Financial co-operatives, also known as savings and credit co-operatives or mutuals, provide meaningful financial services to many rural and urban communities across the region. In Asia, some of the first financial co-operatives were launched in India (in the 1890s), Indonesia (late 1890s and again in the 1940s), Sri Lanka (early

1900s), the Philippines (early 1900s), Thailand (1910s and 1940s), and the People's Republic of China (1960s). SANASA in Sri Lanka is often cited as an example of a successful financial co-operative. Starting in the early 1900s, financial co-operatives were created across Sri Lanka, and over time SANASA emerged as the federation of co-operatives, which then transformed into a bank in the 1990s that has flourished across the island. In Vietnam in the 1990s, the People's Credit Funds, a form of financial co-operative, were introduced in rural areas, followed shortly by the Central Credit Fund, which later became the Co-operative Bank of Vietnam. In the People's Republic of China, the rural credit co-operatives (RCCs) and later urban credit co-operatives were launched in the 1960s. The number of RCCs grew massively across the country, reaching 40,000 in the early 2000s, when RCC federations (RCCFs) were created at the provincial level, and more successful RCCFs were transformed into RCC banks. In Thailand, the financial co-operative movement is interwoven with the Bank for Agriculture and Agricultural Co-operatives (BAAC), a government-owned bank launched in the mid-1960s with a focus on rural development.

Rural banks have thrived as another institutional model in some countries of the region. In Indonesia, rural or village banks started in the early 1900s and evolved into the legal form of Bank Perkreditan Rakyat (BPR). Today there are over 1,800 BPRs of varying size, quality, and financial soundness across thousands of Indonesian islands.[15] In the Philippines, the first rural banks were introduced in the 1950s; over 400 are currently active, some of which have become important players in their local areas. In India, rural banks were first created in the 1970s, and over fifty are currently active.

Last and perhaps the largest actors, postal financial services play a critical role for low-income people and a broad range of households globally. Postal financial services may be offered by a postal bank or within a post office network. Services typically include savings accounts, money orders, life insurance, and remittance services. Some also offer provident funds (government-run pension funds), bill payment, checking accounts, mutual funds, foreign exchange services, and other financial services, depending on the country. Notably, postal banks are not usually licensed to offer credit services.

Across Asia and the Pacific, postal financial services are ubiquitous, although their outreach, profitability, and independence from the post office vary. Postal financial services can be found in Afghanistan, Bangladesh, the PRC, India, Indonesia, Japan, Lao People's Democratic Republic (PDR), Malaysia, the Maldives, Myanmar, Nepal, Pakistan, Papua New Guinea, the Philippines, Singapore, the Solomon Islands, Thailand, Timor Leste, Tonga, Tuvalu, and Vietnam.[16] Some of the largest postal banks in Asia are in China, Japan, and India:

■ Although this chapter is about emerging markets in Asia and the Pacific, Japan deserves special mention here, given the size of Japan Post Bank. Japan Post initiated mail service in 1871 and postal savings services in 1875. In 2007, Japan Post created a separate legal entity, the Post Bank. Most communities throughout the country have access to banking services through the network of more than 23,000 post offices and 200-plus bank branch offices.[17] Similar to European governments at the time, the Japanese government decided in 2012 to partially privatize Japan Post Bank, including creating three legal entities—a parent company, a bank, and an insurer. The initial IPO of the three entities in November 2015 was followed by a second share offering in September 2017, although the Finance Ministry retains majority control of all three entities.[18] Japan Post Bank's assets place it among the world's top fifteen largest banks.[19]

■ In the People's Republic of China, the first modern post office was launched in the 1870s and began offering postal savings services thereafter. The post office was reorganized in 1949. It reintroduced postal savings services in 1986, and in 2007 China Post formally created the China Postal Savings Bank. The bank completed a successful partial IPO in September 2016; it was the world's largest IPO in the period 2014–16.[20] Currently the Postal Savings Bank manages an extensive national network of over 45,000 offices for remittances, of which 37,000 offer savings services.[21] An estimated 40 percent of adults (490 million people) hold a savings account with the Postal Savings Bank.[22]

■ After its founding in the early 1800s, India Post began offering postal savings services in 1882 and postal life insurance in 1884.[23] Over the past 140 years, India Post has become one of the oldest and largest banking networks in the country, especially in rural areas. Its deposit base is among the world's largest in terms of volume and number of customers through its network of 155,000 post offices.[24] India Post launched a payments bank in late 2018, one of seven authorized in the country.

New Actors: Digital Finance Institutions

According to the Global Findex Surveys, reasons people cite for not having an account include having too little money, the cost of opening or maintaining an account, distance to a financial institution, lack of necessary documentation, lack of trust in financial services providers, or another family member has an account that they share.[25] But digital finance can make services more convenient for clients in ways that directly address the concerns of many potential clients. For example, clients with a digital account may not even need to visit a physical bank branch location. Applying to open an account is normally easy and fast. Payments can be made in small (micro) transactions tailored to client needs, often at very low cost (or free). Accounts have a low (or no) minimum balance. Finally, clients can open and manage their own personal account through a phone, which frees them from sharing an account with another family member.

For financial services providers, digital finance can fuel economies of scale that reduce costs and enable them to pursue a broader range of clients. Once a digital channel is established, branch outreach no longer drives an institution's growth.[26] Reducing the need for a physical presence lowers costs and operating risks significantly, and consequently, banks and other financial services providers are carefully analyzing the footprint of their branches, automated teller machines (ATMs), and banking agents. Other potential benefits of digital finance include lower costs of conducting customer due diligence; opportunities for electronic "know-your-customer" (KYC) verification; and algorithms to screen potential clients for specific services. Digital platforms can reduce operating costs—perhaps up to 80–90 percent for some financial services, and these efficiencies can be passed to clients through lower- cost services.[27]

Using GSMA data from their most recent state-of-the-industry report of December 2018, mobile financial services continue to grow rapidly. There are over 866 million accounts in ninety countries, and over US$1.3 billion in transactions are processed every day.[28] Across Asia, the share of adults making or receiving digital payments is highest in East Asia and the Pacific and especially in Mongolia (85 percent), Malaysia (70 percent), People's Republic of China (68 percent), and Thailand (62 percent). It is lower, though growing, in South Asia: Bangladesh (34 percent), India (29 percent), and Nepal (47 percent). In the Pacific, although comparable Findex data are not readily available, digital payments and remittances are a lifeline given the distances between islands (even within the same country) and high levels of remittances from Australia, New Zealand, and elsewhere.[29]

Mobile phone ownership and usage have enabled much of the shift to digital finance. Currently 5.1 billion people hold a mobile phone account, representing 67 percent of the world's population. Over the past four years, 1 billion people have joined the ranks of mobile phone subscribers. By 2025, another 710 million people globally are projected to have mobile phone accounts, with half of the growth likely to come from Asia.[30] As with financial accounts, there is a gender gap. Men are approximately 10 percent more likely than women to own a mobile phone and 23 percent more likely to use mobile internet services.[31]

FIGURE 12.1.　Banking on Mobile Phones

Number per 1,000 adults

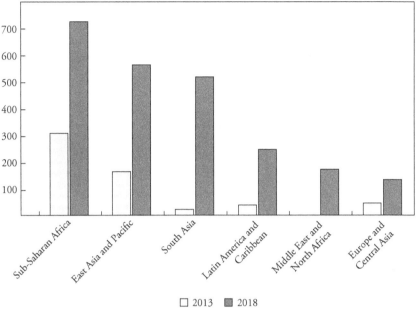

□ 2013　■ 2018

Source: IMF, Financial Access Survey, September 2019.

Global data released in September 2019 from the International Monetary Fund (IMF) support these trends. Figure 12-1 shows the growth in the number of mobile banking accounts across all major regions and especially South Asia, East Asia and the Pacific, and Africa from 2013 to 2018.[32]

Physical availability of branches, ATMs, banking correspondents or agents, and other types of service points all help encourage greater access to and usage of financial services. Availability of ATMs across Asia varies greatly, from just 1.6 ATMs per 100,000 adults in Afghanistan to 22.6 in India, 54.4 in Indonesia, 97.1 in mainland PRC, and 115.2 in Thailand as of September 2019. Unfortunately, reliable comparable data on coverage of banking correspondents or agents and combined coverage of branches of all banks, MFIs, credit unions, and credit co-operatives is spotty globally and in Asia. However, available data on commercial bank branches per 100,000 adults as of September 2019 for Asia suggest a low of 1.5 branches in Papua New Guinea, 8.9 branches in mainland PRC, and a high of 14.5 branches in India.[33]

E-commerce is another factor driving usage of digital payments. Thirty-nine percent of adults in East Asia and the Pacific use the internet to pay bills or make a purchase online. The People's Republic of China leads in East Asia with 49 percent of adults making an internet transaction, compared with just 4 percent in Cambodia and Myanmar. In comparison, only 5 percent of adults in South Asia reported making an internet transaction in 2017, ranging from 8 percent of adults in Pakistan to 1 percent in Afghanistan. E-commerce will only increase across Asia over the coming decade, largely through mobile devices.

Digital Finance and Fintech Institutions

Across Asia and the Pacific, new digital finance actors have emerged over the past decade. Initially focusing on e-wallet solutions, an explosion of fintech firms across the region are expanding the market for payments, remittances, borrowing, insurance, investments, loan comparisons, credit scoring, crowdsourced and other fundraising, and other related services.

The Philippines: While Kenya is often rightly cited for innovation in digital finance, two of the earliest mobile payment providers globally and the first in Asia were Smart Money and GCash launched by the two leading national telecommunications firms (telcos) in the Philippines in the mid-2000s. An early leader in promoting digital finance, the Bangko Sentral ng Pilipinas (BSP) developed good foundations through enabling laws and regulations. Yet despite their early launches, transactions have been largely linked to mobile phone usage (for example account top-ups), with less uptake and usage for digital payments.[34] Smart Money launched PayMaya, a card-based payments option in 2016. In early 2017, GCash partnered with Ant Financial, which infused new growth into the payments market. Global payments platform PayPal is also active in the Philippines. Virtual banks include CIMB Bank of Malaysia and ING Bank of the Netherlands, and a new license was approved for Tonik Digital Bank of Singapore in December 2019.[35] Overall, more than seventy digital finance players are active in payments, remittances, and alternative credit. Digital finance usage remained modest until starting to grow in 2018–19;[36] the BSP is targeting 30 percent of total transactions to be e-payments by the end of 2020. The BSP's creation of QR code standards for payments and a new e-government payment facility in late 2019 should promote greater uptake of digital finance.

Bangladesh: BKash, a subsidiary of BRAC Bank Limited, launched in 2011 and has grown rapidly. BKash's early success attracted others to the market. Eighteen banks offer digital finance, with 76 million active accounts and US$4.17 billion in monthly transactions as of September 2019.[37] Over 950,000 banking correspondents or agents serve clients across the country, and the number of registered clients and the volume and value of transactions have grown rapidly.

Cambodia: Wing in Cambodia launched in 2009 as one of the early digital finance players in East Asia and in 2019 announced a new link with MoneyGram to send and receive remittances through the Wing app or branch offices.[38] More than a dozen other fintech firms have established operations in Cambodia since 2014 offering payments, insurance, invoicing, and alternative financial services.

People's Republic of China: Mobile payments and digital finance have rapidly transformed the financial sector. More than 580 million people made a mobile payment in 2018, an increase of more than 10 percent from 2017.[39] In addition, multiple digital finance platforms operate across the country focusing on different client groups and services, including retail services, supply chain finance, trade finance, and others, and several reportedly use blockchain. Given their dominance and growth in China and now internationally, the financial services efforts of Alibaba and TenCent Holdings are described below. However, a multitude of other digital financial services providers are active across China.

Alibaba started as an e-commerce site in 1999; it later added payment services through Alipay in 2009, which was then spun off as a separate financial services company called Ant Financial in 2014. As of March 2019, Ant Financial provided payment services to an estimated 558 million people across the country.[40] Ant Financial has grown tremendously to include related services through Jiebei, a consumer loan company; Huabei, a virtual credit card company; MY Bank, an online bank; Xiang Hu Bao, a mutual health plan; ZOLOZ, an identity verification service; Sesame Credit (also known as Zhima Credit), a credit rating firm; Yu'E Bao, an investment services company offering money market funds, wealth management, and insurance.[41] The mutual health plan Xiang Hu Bao provides basic medical coverage to over 50 million people, of which 47 percent are migrant workers and 31 percent are from rural areas.[42] After four years of operation, MY Bank had lent over US$290 billion to more than 16 million MSMEs, using online credit scoring to assess potential borrowers in seconds.[43] Over the past five years, Ant Financial began expanding across Asia through joint ventures and investments, including Paytm in India, BKash in Bangladesh, Telenor Microfinance Bank in Pakistan, Elang Mahkota Teknologi (Emtek) in Indonesia, Touch n Go with CIMB Bank in Malaysia, Mynt/GCash in the Philippines, HelloPay with Lazada based in Singapore,[44] Ascend Money in Thailand, and KakaoPay in South Korea. Beyond Asia, Ant Financial has co-invested with Ingenico based in France and active across Europe, Bluecode in Austria, ePassi and Pivo in Finland, Vipps in Norway, Momo in Spain, Pagaqui in Portugal,[45] StoneCo Ltd. in Brazil, and WorldFirst currency exchange in the United Kingdom.

The second fintech behemoth in the PRC, TenCent Holdings Limited created in 1998, launched WeChat in 2011 as an instant messaging platform and gradually expanded to other payment services, including money transfers and e-commerce through WeChat Pay starting in 2013.[46] In 2015, TenCent launched WeBank—an online bank that offers rapid loan decisions using online credit scoring similar to MY Bank. TenCent's vast network includes a range of other companies in the country, including gaming services, e-sports, video and sports streaming, music services, ticket purchases, and other subsidiaries. TenCent is rapidly expanding internationally in e-commerce (with FlipKart in India, for example), gaming services, health care, and multiple other sectors.

Statistics on client outreach are difficult to find; taken together, however, Ant Financial and TenCent represent a massively dominant share (perhaps as much as 94 percent) of the national payments market.[47] Given the ubiquitous nature of digital finance, the People's Bank of China (PBOC), the central bank, has also announced plans to enhance supervision of digital finance and strengthen measures for risk governance of fintechs.[48]

In yet another innovation, the PBOC is reportedly close to introducing a cryptocurrency using blockchain and other technologies.[49] As a step in that direction, in October 2019 the Chinese legislature approved a new law on cryptography, including regulating its use, promoting the development of cryptography, and ensuring information security.[50] Further, the Blockchain-based Service Network was launched in October 2019 as a consortium of the State Information Center, China UnionPay, and China Mobile.[51]

Hong Kong, Special Administrative Region of the People's Republic of China: Hong Kong is a regional banking hub for Asia with a history of innovation in financial services. Residents enjoy access to a plethora of payment cards, broad coverage of ATMs and bank branches, a modern payments system, numerous mobile banking apps, and new fintechs offering retail and wholesale services. In February 2018, the Hong Kong Monetary Authority (HKMA) issued a draft for consultation of the Guidelines on Authorization of Virtual Banks, and the revised guidelines were issued in May 2018.[52] After receiving thirty-three applications, the HKMA approved eight virtual bank licenses between March and May 2019, including a range of consortiums between banks, e-commerce leaders, fintechs, and others.[53] Well-known names in the successful bidding consortiums include Ant Financial, Ping An, Ten-

Cent, Bank of China, Industrial and Commercial Bank of China, Standard Chartered Bank, and Xiaomi. With this policy opening, HKMA set the trend for virtual or digital banks in East Asia. Once the banks become fully operational, their test will be to become profitable, given the constraints and requirements of the virtual bank license. In addition, the HKMA developed the "Faster Payment System" mobile phone application that facilitates free money transfers between bank accounts, with over half the city's population reportedly using this application.[54]

India: Eko and Fino were two of the first banking correspondent networks launched in the late 2000s as third-party agents to help mobilize payments and other services outside bank branches. Others include Paytm, RazorPay, PayUMoney, Instamojo, ItzCash, Novopay, and Citrus. In 2015, the Reserve Bank of India accepted expressions of interest in a new regulatory category of payments bank with a limited operational mandate. With forty-one applicants, the RBI approved provisional licenses for eleven proposed payments banks. Some of the banks did not pursue the licenses, however, and other payments banks were subsequently closed. As of January 2020, six payments banks were operational in India: Airtel, Fino, India Post, Jio, NDSL, and Paytm Payments Bank Limited.[55] Given challenges with the business model and profitability of payments banks, in December 2019 the RBI announced criteria that would allow payments banks to be eligible to convert to small finance banks after five years of operation.[56]

The National Payments Corporation of India (NPCI) was launched in 2009 by the Indian Banks' Association (IBA) and the Reserve Bank of India as an umbrella organization for banks operating retail payments and settlement systems in India. Initially, ten banks invested in NPCI, and the number increased to fifty-six in 2016.[57] The NPCI manages several payments platforms and initiatives, of which the Unified Payment Interface (UPI) is one of the most important as a national enabler of digital finance. UPI was launched publicly in August 2016 as a mobile phone application that gives clients access to their bank accounts and offers several instant payment and banking features. Accounts are protected with two-factor authentication, and each client account has a virtual address, which prevents third-party access to personal account information. UPI enables a range of payment types, including peer to peer, merchant, utility bill, and donations, either in real time or at a future scheduled time. The UPI system is neutral and works with a range of banking applications available from financial services providers in India.[58]

Similarly, fintech innovation is bubbling in India. According to one estimate, there may be over 2,000 fintechs active, triple the number that existed in 2015.[59] Indian fintechs are attracting significant equity from global and domestic investors; several major Indian cities have been listed among the top 100 fintech hub cities globally.[60] Over the past decade dozens of fintechs were initially established as banking correspondents to work with licensed banks and other financial services providers. More recent examples of fintechs include MobiKwick, NeoGrowth, Policy Bazaar, PhonePe, Ziploan, MyLoanCare, Shubh Loans, PayU, Kissht, epayLater, Lending Kart, Faircent, and epiFi. Many of the payment fintechs also offer online and mobile access to loans, often serving as originators for other licensed credit providers.[61] Other fintechs such as ZestMoney, Kaleidofin, Niyo Solutions, Open, Pay Zello, instaDApp, and 0.5Bn FinHealth partner with banks to offer insurance, wealth management, foreign exchange, and other services to households and small businesses.[62] Peer-to-peer lending platforms are emerging as licensed nonbank financial companies (NBFCs), offering a new model for borrowers and investment options for households. One of the older, established platforms is RupeeCircle, and others include LendBox, Lenden Club, OML, India Money Mart, Faircent, and I2I Funding. As of September 2019, several fintechs, including MoneyTap, CredAble and PayMe India, were granted NBFC licenses to offer lending on their own books.[63]

Global players such as Google Pay are also becoming active in India, and Amazon Pay launched in 2019. The messaging platform WhatsApp has developed a beta payments product with about 1 million users, and in August 2019 it applied for RBI approval as a payments service. WhatsApp could rapidly become a significant player, given its 400 million users across India.[64] The RBI allowed WhatsApp to test payment services starting in February 2018 with 1 million users, although full approval was delayed given concerns about their noncompliance with the requirement to host relevant data in India.[65] RBI was subsequently granted approval in early February 2020, and the NPCI has given WhatsApp permission to use its digital platform in a phased manner for up to 10 million users in the first phase.[66]

Indonesia: Telkomsel Cash (T-Cash) is one of the oldest digital money services, as an e-wallet linked with the country's largest mobile phone operator. Dozens of mobile wallets and payment applications have been launched, and multiple banks offer their own applications. In 2015, Go-Jek ride hailing service created the digital wallet GoPay, which has become the most widely used digital wallet in Indonesia; it has plans to expand its payment services.[67] Dana is a more recent e-wallet which has grown quickly in popularity. Go-Jek and GoPay also operate in Vietnam, Thailand, and Singapore. Launched in 2017, the fintech Ovo grew rapidly in number of clients and volume of e-transactions through 2019.[68] The central bank has licensed more than 30 e-wallet services, with the top five being GoPay, Ovo, Dana, LinkAja, and Jenius.[69] In response, many banks are expanding their digital finance operations. As just one example, in February 2019, BRI launched a new mobile app, Pinang, for digital loans, building on its national network of branches and ubiquitous brand name across Indonesia.[70] Multiple fintechs are emerging in Indonesia, such as BantuSaku, which launched in January 2020 in beta version after receiving its license in October 2019,[71] and CredoLab, which received its license in January 2020.[72]

At the national level, Bank Indonesia released its Indonesia payment systems blueprint for 2025 in November 2019,[73] which embraces digital finance, fintechs, and links with existing financial services providers while advocating for consumer protection and continued integrity and stability of the financial sector. Given this policy approach, more digital finance innovations may emerge in Indonesia in the near future.

Malaysia: Several banks offer mobile applications, and regional digital finance players are also becoming active in the country. In early 2018, the mobile network operator Axiata launched the mobile wallet Boost, which has become the most widely used in the country.[74] In late December 2019, Bank Negara Malaysia (BNM) announced plans to issue up to five digital banking licenses by the end of 2020 and shared a draft of the licensing framework for consultation.[75]

Myanmar: Digital finance and financial inclusion are growing, where about a dozen mobile wallets and payments providers operate. The market leader with over 17 million subscribers,[76] Wave Money launched in 2016 in a joint venture with Telenor, FMI, and Yoma Bank. By 2019 it had grown over 240 percent from its 2018 base of 7 million clients; it had conducted US$4.3 billion in transactions and served 89 percent of the country as of the end of 2019. Another well-known service is M-Pitesan, launched by Ooredoo, a national mobile network operator. At a meso-infrastructure level, the Myanmar Payment Union is working with Singapore's Network for Electronic Transfers to promote point-of-sale payments.[77]

Pacific Island countries: Across the Pacific, digital payments have been piloted by several banks; Bank South Pacific shows the most traction and staying power. Headquartered in Papua New Guinea and active in six countries across the Pacific, BSP launched payments about six years ago. Payments and remittances are especially critical for Pacific Island countries, given their interlinkages with other countries in the Pacific and globally. For example, remittances represent 20 percent of GDP in Tonga, 14 percent in the Marshall Islands, and 10 percent in Kiribati (as of 2017).[78]

Pakistan: The mobile network operator Telenor invested 51 percent in Tameer Microfinance Bank in 2008 and renamed it Telenor Microfinance Bank. Telenor eventually acquired 100 percent ownership in March 2016. Starting in 2009, the bank began offering mobile money services under the EasyPaisa brand. Other firms have emerged, especially since 2015, including Habib Bank and Monet, Keenu, Jazz Cash, SimSim, and Inov8 Limited.

Singapore: The government of Singapore designed its Smart Nation Initiative to include a focus on digital payments. Singapore is also the headquarters for many regional banks, financial services providers, and other regional corporations with operations in Asia and the Pacific; there have also been many fintech startups over the past decade. Digital wallets have been popular in Singapore for years; international payment applications such as Apple Pay, Samsung Pay, and Google Pay are widely used. Grab ride hailing service, originally based in Malaysia and now headquartered in Singapore, offers GrabPay as a digital wallet. In December 2019, Grab and Mastercard launched the GrabPay payment card.[79] Grab's ubiquitous presence in several other Southeast Asian countries has allowed GrabPay services to expand beyond Singapore.[80] In 2019, OCBC Bank announced a new payment service, PayNow, in collaboration with the UK-based Rapyd.[81] In May 2019, Singapore- and San Francisco-based online gaming firm Razer announced a partnership with Visa to extend Razer Pay across Southeast Asia.[82]

In a widely anticipated move, in June 2019 the Monetary Authority of Singapore (MAS) announced two newly designed digital bank licenses—a digital full bank (DFB) license and a digital wholesale bank (DWB) license. The DFB would be allowed to take deposits and provide banking services for retail and nonretail customer segments, while the DWB would be allowed to serve nonretail and SME customer segments. Other digital banks are possible under the MAS internet banking framework already in effect. In August 2019, applicants were invited to submit proposals through the end of December 2019, and MAS intends to approve up to two DFB licenses and three DWB licenses by mid-2020.[83] MAS reported that twenty-one groups submitted applications by the deadline.[84] The consortiums of bidders include well-known fintechs, telecommunications, and e-commerce players such as Grab, Singtel, Razer, Ant Financial, Hande Group, EZ-Link, ByteDance, the Singapore Business Federation, and others.[85]

Thailand: Mobile wallet firms have grown over the past five years. The largest are LINE, Mobiamo, and PromptPay, as well as global payment apps such as PayPal. Launched in early 2017, PromptPay was developed jointly by the Bank of Thailand

and the Thai Bankers' Association. In 2019, the United Overseas Bank from Singapore launched TMRW as a mobile-only bank. In December 2019, Siam Commercial Bank announced that its payment service SCB Easy, which already serves more than 10 million clients, would add cross-border payments in conjunction with fintech firm Ripple. Kasikorn Bank rolled out digital banking starting with a payments application and plans to add mobile lending jointly with Line Corporation in 2020.[86]

Vietnam: Despite considerable interest and potential, digital finance usage in Vietnam is still in early stages. When fintech startups began to appear in the early 2010s, BankPlus was one of the first, launched by the mobile network operator Viettel. More than thirty payment providers are licensed, including VinaPay, Vimo, Momo, ZaloPay, ViettelPay, VNPT Pay, and V-FPT.[87] Other regional players such as GrabPay are also active. More than 150 fintechs had launched as of November 2019, and financial transactions using mobile devices grew over 100 percent in volume and over 150 percent in value over the previous year.[88] In 2019, the government signaled its approval for mobile money implementation, which will be led by the ministry of information and communications, the State Bank of Vietnam, and telecommunications companies.[89]

Potential Areas of Concern in Digital Finance

While digital finance offers tremendous opportunities, there are also significant areas of potential concern, including a large digital divide, fraud and abuse, and the impact on financial sector competition and market structure. High current levels and projected future growth in mobile phone ownership may well be an enabler for financial access. About 66 percent of the 1.7 billion unbanked adults already have a mobile phone. However, low-income people, women, older people, and other socioeconomic groups may not have the latest smart phones or regular access to the internet, or they may prefer interacting in person with a bank agent. Those who are illiterate or do not read an official language of the country will also struggle to use the written interface of phone and internet applications. Rural areas often suffer from less mobile phone coverage, lower and more seasonal income, and fewer bank branches, banking agents, and ATMs. What will happen to people without the basic tools that power digital finance? Low-income people, women, older people, and rural households may be left behind in a growing digital divide.

The convenience of digital finance triggers other concerns as well. Quick and easy services make it easier for clients to take risks and borrow,[90] and to overextend themselves financially.[91] Further, reports on fraud through digital finance began shortly after the first deployments over fifteen years ago in countries such as the Democratic Republic of Congo and Kenya.[92] As the number of people using digital finance grows, so do reports of clients losing money through fraud or error.

Kenya serves as a fascinating pilot country for digital finance given its early efforts in the 2000s to create one of the world's most competitive financial services markets. Yet some of Kenya's lessons are sobering. Thirteen percent of the adult population had defaulted on at least one small digital credit loan of less than US$10 as of May 2018, triggering long-term implications for their credit ratings.[93]

Person-to-person lending in the PRC offers another reason for concern. From 2008 through 2015, over 10,000 person-to-person lending operations proliferated across the country, many of which perpetrated fraud and consumer abuse. By introducing new regulations, the People's Bank of China, the central bank, reduced the number of authorized online lenders to 3,500 in 2015 to fewer than 100 in 2017.

When digital finance first emerged globally in the mid-2000s, much of the discussion centered on competition between mobile network operators, fintech firms, and traditional financial services providers such as banks and MFIs. The reality has been more complex, mixing collaboration and competition and many new entrants. New combinations of online services and physical locations are emerging. Market structures are evolving rapidly, and global competition is growing, especially across Asia.

Digital finance follows different paths in different contexts. For example, in the three pioneering countries of Kenya, the PRC, and India, distinct payment models have emerged. In Kenya, mobile network operators dominate the market, and regulations allow them to offer mobile money accounts that are not linked to a bank account. In the People's Republic of China, third-party firms such as Ant Financial and TenPay dominate the market; transactions are enabled within their mobile applications and linked to a bank account. In India, the UPI national payment platform serves as a neutral, independent mobile application that links bank accounts for instant payment and banking features; financial services providers must compete for clients based on other services and fees.

Greater competition and diversity among financial services providers can lead to a more efficient and resilient financial system. However, increased competition also makes it more difficult for banks and other financial services providers to profit in many countries. What about the established institutions—including MFIs, specialized banks, financial co-operatives, rural banks, nonbank financial institutions, postal banks, and others—that historically focused on expanding financial inclusion? Many are partnering with larger banks, mobile money operators, fintech startups, and other actors in order to gain access to broader digital platforms and services. In Pakistan, Pakistan Microfinance Network has announced a venture with Telenor Microfinance Bank to create a digital services platform for its network of MFIs to expand services to clients.[94] Other MFIs are merging and consolidating—with notable and numerous examples in the Philippines and India. MFIs bring decades of history and experience, having earned the trust of their clients and demonstrated their ability to reach low-income clients with financial services. But the reality is that established institutions are also struggling to evolve in several countries. For example, in one of the more dynamic markets globally, MFIs in Kenya are grappling with rising competition from a much broader range of financial services providers.[95] Similar challenges face established institutions in Asia, especially where digital finance is growing rapidly, such as India, Bangladesh, Myanmar, the People's Republic of China, Thailand, and Malaysia.

Institutions struggling for survival may engage in greater risk taking—with new products, greater leverage of their balance sheet, or riskier collaborations than they may have considered in the past. Outsourcing to specialized firms can tap deep experience in small or complex niches, such as leasing, agricultural insurance, housing, or digital marketing that are challenging to master.[96] Examples include outsourcing to manage agent networks, manage payment card processing, maintain ATM networks, secure information databases, and the like. Outsourcing presents its own challenges and regulatory risks. Further, terms of collaboration can shift quickly, as new competitors emerge every month, and former collaborators can even become fierce competitors.

Financial stability may also be affected by the emerging involvement of global technology platforms, concentration of markets, and greater outsourcing and dependencies on third-party firms. Large technology platforms may eventually lead to less competition, if they are able to achieve dominant market position. For example, in the People's Republic of China, Ant Financial and TenPay, the two largest digital finance providers, represent 94 percent of the market.[97]

A Vision for True Financial Inclusion in Asia

In Asia and the Pacific, and globally, the goal of broad financial access is much closer than it was ten years ago. Although 1.7 billion people still lack a formal account, the large gap is narrowing, and governments and the private sector have built some successful models. Yet we are still far from achieving the vision of true financial inclusion.

Financial inclusion means clients are using a relevant range of financial services to manage their household income and expenses to achieve their savings, investment, and risk mitigation goals. The services should be well designed, affordable, convenient, and delivered in a responsible way that ensures client protection. Across Asia and the Pacific, several key steps are emerging as critical to achieving true financial inclusion:

Ensure a Basic Foundation of Unique Identification and Appropriate KYC Regulation

Globally, over 1 billion people have no legal proof of identification.[98] Without such identification, people are denied access to financial services as well as a range of other rights, including the ability to vote, access the labor market, secure government benefits, and receive health care. Identification must be unique, accurate, secure, and free of discrimination. India is a global leader in unique biometric identification, enrolling almost all adults in just seven years and 1.23 billion people (adults and children) as of February 2019.[99] Several other Asian countries have also achieved high levels of identification coverage, including the People's Republic of China, Singapore, Sri Lanka, Malaysia, Thailand, and Mongolia. Other governments across Asia and the Pacific have started national identification campaigns—including Indonesia and the Philippines. These investments in national identification, including e-KYC capabilities, will help lay the foundation for greater financial inclusion and other important services from government agencies and others.

National identification is necessary but not sufficient for financial access. Central banks and governments also need to find the right balance on identification required to open bank accounts and make transactions. The so-called know-your-customer regulations link to global efforts on anti-money-laundering (AML) and combatting the financing of terrorism (CFT), which are important aspects of global security. Well-intentioned policies to strengthen KYC may have the unexpected consequence of creating barriers to financial services. Proportional measures can be tailored to a country's specific context and risks.[100]

Encourage Banks to Offer Basic Accounts

Globally, countries as diverse as South Africa, the UK, India, Malaysia, Australia, and several U.S. states have successfully encouraged banks to offer basic bank accounts. Basic accounts are usually limited in the type of services permitted, such as deposits, withdrawals, and perhaps money transfers or limited life insurance for the account holder. Likewise, basic accounts usually restrict the amount of money that can be held in the account and the value and number of individual transactions each month. As a trade-off for these restrictions, the KYC requirements for basic accounts can be less onerous and include alternative forms of identification.

- In October 2004, South Africa became one of the first emerging markets to launch a national campaign for "Mzansi" basic bank accounts as part of the broader Financial Sector Charter promoting financial inclusion. The percentage of adults with an account increased significantly, from 46 to 63 percent between 2004 and 2008.[101]

- To ensure that all households have access, the government of India launched the Pradhan Mantri Jan Dhan Yojana (PMJDY) campaign in August 2014 to provide first-time bank accounts. Managed by the Ministry of Finance, PMJDY mobilized banks to provide an interest-bearing deposit account with no minimum balance, a debit card, access to digital payments, basic life insurance, a small overdraft facility of approximately US$70, and access to insurance and pension facilities.[102] As of February 2019, PMJDY reported over 340 million new accounts opened, the majority by public sector banks.[103] Further, in every state across the country, 99 to 100 percent of all households hold at least one bank account.[104]

- In Malaysia, the central bank, Bank Negara Malaysia, requires all banks in the country to offer basic savings accounts or basic current (checking) accounts to individuals and small businesses. These accounts allow for six free over-the-counter visits per month, eight free ATM withdrawals, two internet transactions at RM0.5 (approximately US$0.12) each, free deposits of checks and cash through kiosks, free account inquiries and fund transfers within the same banking institution, and free bill payments.[105]

- In Nepal in April 2019, the central bank, Nepal Rastra Bank (NRB), announced plans for a zero-balance account to be available through most financial institutions in the country. As part of the initiative, NRB will simplify paperwork required to open an account for depositors whose transactions do not exceed NR100,000 (approximately US$878) per year.[106]

While basic accounts have been successful in bringing access to more people, usage sometimes trails. For example, six years after the first Mzansi accounts were opened in South Africa, approximately 42 percent of accounts were dormant, although banks were still opening the accounts for new customers.[107] In India, three years after the first PMJDY accounts were opened, 48 percent of adults with an account were not using it.[108] As is discussed in chapter 13 on the Indian experience, account dormancy is declining based on more recent 2019 figures.

Accounts are important but do not ensure use or true financial inclusion. If services are affordable, convenient, secure, and well designed, clients may be more inclined to open accounts and use them. Financial services providers will need to be innovative and agile as they build deeper relationships with their clients.

Build Trust through Quality Services

Since the 1970s, the microfinance movement has elevated the importance of customer convenience—bringing banking agents to household doorsteps, market stalls, and village centers—so clients could easily make a savings deposit or pay their loan installment. This focus on customer service scrambled the prevailing business models, where formerly clients waited in long queues in banking halls, if they even mustered the courage to enter a commercial bank, where they were often not well received or could not meet minimum account requirements.

Earning client trust through reliable quality services is essential. In Asia and the Pacific, many established financial institutions serving low-income clients have succeeded by offering quality services. Digital finance is largely a virtual service, which can exacerbate the challenges of building a client's initial trust. Keeping the client's trust is even more difficult if she faces any service issues and struggles to have them resolved. Troubling reports across the globe include errors sending money to the wrong person; agents overcharging clients; thin coverage of service points, especially in rural areas; service points (agents or ATMs) not functioning or out of cash; and criminal deception and fraud by company insiders, agents, or strangers.[109]

Increasingly, financial services providers are refining the quality of their products and services in an effort to win clients.[110] They need to be creative, combining digital and physical service points, to build strong and deep relationships with their clients. Greater use of technology is inevitable, though it has mixed implications for building trust. The enormous amount of data available about clients and their transactions enable providers to customize their services based on a client's specific profile. Online applications and mobile applications help clients open accounts and apply for services. Automated call centers may enable clients to resolve questions at any time of the day or night. Algorithms fuel rapid online loan approval. Yet these same technologies will affect, and possibly disintermediate, the relationship between a branch officer and client, which may reduce the client's overall satisfaction.

Institutions that focus on the customer experience and building deep client relationships will be more likely to succeed in a competitive market. Making the interaction online or in a branch office convenient is the minimum starting point, and each transaction should be seamless and frictionless. Marketing of services requires transparency in pricing and care to sell services that are appropriate to the client's circumstances. Clients need effective and immediate recourse to raise questions and seek solutions to problems that may arise with their account or specific transaction. To achieve this culture of service, institutions will need to invest in training their staff to support the company's values and ethics of service, and to follow new procedures.

Delivering services in a mindful and responsible manner is easier if it is the norm in the country's financial market. Across Asia and the Pacific, several industry associations have developed codes of conduct for responsible finance, including in Bangladesh, Cambodia, India, Indonesia, Nepal, Papua New Guinea, Sri Lanka, and Vietnam. These laudable efforts will hopefully expand to more countries.

Increase Consumer Protection

Institutional culture for responsible finance and voluntary industry codes of conduct are a useful starting point. However, policy and regulation are necessary to ensure a basic level of consumer protection by all financial services providers. Several countries across Asia and the Pacific have developed consumer protection measures, including requiring transparency of fees and conditions for service, promoting ease of use and availability of service points, establishing toll-free help lines and ombudsmen to help report, track, and resolve complaints, guarding against abusive loan collection and sales practices, and ensuring privacy and protection of client data.

To promote consumer protection, the Responsible Finance Forum and the Smart Campaign, both created in 2009, offer guidelines and case studies for governments, central banks, and financial services providers. Since 2011, the Organization for Economic Cooperation and Development (OECD) has promoted responsible finance and consumer protection at the intergovernmental level. As part of the Smart Campaign, the Fintech Community of Practice finalized standards for digital credit in June 2019.[111]

Ensure the Security of Accounts and Personal Data

Data security is a vital component of consumer protection. Unless accounts and personal data are secure, clients are vulnerable to identity theft and financial losses. The responsibility lies with financial services providers—whether established players or new digital finance institutions—to ensure robust security and systems to minimize the risk of fraud on the accounts and services they offer. At a minimum, people should have access to their own data and a convenient, secure method to correct their information. Further, financial services providers should be required to protect accounts against fraud and ensure data privacy and security, and be penalized severely for data breaches.

Governments are increasingly legislating data privacy laws, and careful enforcement is also necessary. The General Data Protection Regulation adopted by the European Union in May 2018 is a milestone in data protection for consumers that imposes significant penalties if businesses do not comply. Some countries in Asia and the Pacific have started grappling with data privacy, but much more is needed in this emerging and critical area.

Build the Foundation of a Financial Infrastructure

To ensure a well-functioning financial sector, two types of basic financial infrastructure are increasingly vital: interoperable payment networks and credit reporting systems. Several central banks in Asia and the Pacific have established national payment strategies, although few have built interoperable payment networks. Interoperable means that payments can be made regardless of institutional type—across the broad range of financial services providers and mobile money providers; by various types of users, including consumers, businesses, and government agencies; and across markets, both nationally and internationally.

The European Union's Revised Payment System Directive is a good model of an interoperable approach that could be adapted to specific country contexts in Asia and the Pacific. India's Unified Payment Interface is another example as discussed earlier in the section on digital finance.

Credit reporting systems are equally vital for a country's financial infrastructure. Credit reporting systems include the institutions, laws and regulations, procedures, and technology platforms that enable the gathering and reporting of information, including the credit histories of people and businesses. Credit reporting helps financial institutions and their regulators and supervisors to monitor the safety and soundness of the financial sector and reduce systemic risk. Credit reporting helps both individuals and businesses by establishing people's credit history and reducing risk for loan providers, thereby expanding access to finance.[112]

Credit registries are databases typically managed by the public sector, often the central bank or specialized banking supervisor, to gather and monitor information on loans made to borrowers (both individuals and businesses) by each of the lending institutions in its jurisdiction. Credit bureaus are agencies that gather information on individuals and businesses related to their creditworthiness and then sell this information to lenders and other entities for their internal decisions on extending loans.

In Asia and the Pacific, credit registries and credit bureaus are widely prevalent. Many countries benefit from one, while a few countries have both a registry and a bureau (or multiple bureaus). The following countries have either a registry or a bureau: Afghanistan, Bhutan, Cambodia, People's Republic of China, India, Indonesia, Japan, Korea, Lao PDR, Malaysia, the Maldives, Nepal, Pakistan, Papua New Guinea, the Philippines, Singapore, Sri Lanka, Thailand, Timor Leste, Tonga, Vanuatu, and Vietnam. Data quality and coverage vary greatly across the region. The credit registry in the People's Republic of China has the highest coverage at 98 percent of adults. For credit bureaus, using data as of May 2018, Japan and Korea have achieved 100 percent coverage of adults, followed by Malaysia (86 percent), Singapore (60 percent), Thailand (60 percent), and India (56 percent).[113]

Over the past decade across the region, several credit bureaus and registries have been working to incorporate data from MFIs and other financial services providers beyond the core commercial banks in their countries. Likewise, some central banks and credit bureaus are starting to expand their sources of data to include alternative data such as payments to utilities, tax authorities, landlords, mobile phone providers, and stores that offer goods and services on credit. The use of alternative data could help low-income clients establish stronger credit history by expanding data coverage to include these more common types of transactions made by a broader range of the population. Finally, given regional transactions and businesses across Asia and the Pacific, establishing standards and laws for regional credit reporting systems will be increasingly important.

Consumer protection measures discussed earlier should also include credit registries and credit bureaus. Individuals and businesses should be able to request their own credit report, verify the data, and if necessary, dispute and correct their data. Registries and bureaus should ensure timely responses to requests for this information from individuals and businesses and also protect the data to prevent fraud and identity theft.

Encourage Transactions

Incentives for households, governments, and businesses to use accounts for transactions, rather than cash and checks, will help encourage transactions and usage of formal accounts through established financial services providers and new digital players. As e-commerce expands across Asia and the Pacific, digital payments will likely rise in parallel—as has been seen in the People's Republic of China with Alibaba and its affiliates. Likewise, person-to-person payments, which were the initial impetus for the Kenyan digital finance market, WeChat in the People's Republic of China, and the UPI interface in India, can fuel significant growth in transactions. Finally, government-to-person (G2P) payments can help encourage the use of accounts. G2P payments include cash transfers (wages, pensions, and unemployment assistance), subsidy transfers (for example, for food, fuel, and fertilizers), and benefit transfers (for example, child welfare programs, education grants, and health programs).[114] Digitizing G2P payments can be challenging,[115] but where feasible, G2P payments can massively increase the volume and number of transactions through accounts.

Transactions through accounts are usually more convenient and beneficial for consumers, businesses, governments, and financial services providers. However, governments, businesses, and financial services providers need to move at a pace that is acceptable to consumers. Backlash movements have sparked in countries where consumers feel pressured to forsake cash and make transactions only through accounts or digital platforms. In Uruguay, consumers responded with frustration to rapid changes in digital transactions,[116] and similar concerns have been voiced in the United States,[117] the United Kingdom,[118] India,[119] the Philippines,[120] and elsewhere. Until the digital divide is bridged, with broad financial inclusion across income levels, ethnicity, geography, and gender, cash transactions will be necessary to avoid excluding vast numbers of people from the formal economy. Indeed, for this very reason, some jurisdictions are already requiring shops and service providers to continue accepting cash.[121]

Encourage a Competitive and Inclusive Financial Sector

Banks and MFIs are sometimes considered slow movers, especially in comparison with agile new fintech players. As noted earlier, digital finance is triggering significant changes to the structure of financial markets. Collaboration, outsourcing, and joint ventures are expanding, and the emergence of specialized third-party firms adds complexity to the financial sector. Financial regulators and supervisors have a vital role in encouraging fair competition, proportionate and risk-based regulation, effective supervision, and consumer protection. These measures should be adopted by all financial services providers regardless of their institutional type.

Digital finance and other modern financial operations enable more rapid change across the financial sector. Surprises can shift the market situation overnight. For example, India's demonetization in November 2016 led to market confusion by removing approximately 86 percent of all currency from circulation, placing limits on withdrawals from accounts, and leading to considerable economic disruption for households and small businesses.[122] Shifts in KYC rules have triggered change and confusion in many countries—sometimes halting access to accounts or enabling more people to open accounts by allowing electronic verification of identity or a broader range of identification papers. In January 2019, the People's Bank of China revised regulations on deposit of customer funds by third-party payment operators, which must now be held at the PBOC.[123] The balance of customer funds held by third-party firms reached US$183 billion in November 2018. This regulatory change will remove the interest earned on these funds that payment providers such as Ant Financial and TenPay had been receiving, thereby reducing their overall profitability. Given the potential for rapid, significant changes and increasingly inter-connected financial systems, greater caution and international cooperation are needed by regulators and policymakers to mitigate negative impacts of change on market structure and operations.

New licensing options for digital finance providers and other fintechs are emerging to encourage more competition and innovation. Banking regulators in Hong Kong, Taiwan, Malaysia, and Singapore are issuing virtual banking licenses,[124] which will open opportunities for the larger players such as Ant Financial/Alipay, TenCent, LINE, Rakuten, Telenor, and other internet and telecom firms and banks to operate at a new level. Hong Kong made the first move, approving eight virtual bank licenses starting in April 2019. In July 2019, Taiwan followed with three virtual bank licenses but no plans to expand the list.[125] The Monetary Authority of Singapore announced plans to issue up to five virtual banking licenses.[126] If the virtual banks are limited in their operations—for example, by restrictions on lending and deposit taking—their business model may struggle to turn a profit and expand. In India, a similar experience with narrow payments banks over the past four years has yielded meaningful lessons but exposed obstacles to their operational viability. In response, the RBI has announced that payments banks may be eligible to transform into small finance banks that are able to lend and offer other services, albeit not full banking services.

Increasingly, governments and central banks are promoting an inclusive financial sector. In Asia and the Pacific, multiple countries have promoted financial inclusion through campaigns, national strategies, and policies, including Bangladesh, Bhutan, Cambodia, the People's Republic of China, Fiji, India, Indonesia, Malaysia, Mongolia, Nepal, Pakistan, Papua New Guinea, the Philippines, Singapore, Sri Lanka, Thailand, and Vietnam. The Global Microscope survey provides an independent assessment of government and policy support for financial inclusion, stability, and integrity. It reports that, among the top twenty-five performing countries, India and the Philippines are tied for fourth globally, followed by Indonesia (seventh), China (thirteenth), Thailand (sixteenth), and Pakistan (twenty-first).[127]

In Conclusion: A Choice

The speed of change in financial services markets is accelerating across the globe. The more complex and dynamic financial ecosystem presents both a challenge and an opportunity. Financial services are offered by an ever-expanding network of firms outsourcing to third-party firms for key aspects of the transaction chain. The ecosystem includes financial services providers, mobile network operators, networks of banking agents, technology platforms, policymakers, regulators and supervisors, financial inclusion advocates, consumer goods retail stores, employers who pay salaries into bank accounts, buyers and sellers across agriculture value chains, schools, utility companies, government agencies making payments, and investors.

The new market realities make it a challenge to coordinate any strategic effort among such a diverse group of institutions. Yet the diversity of actors also presents an opportunity to identify strategic leaders who understand the true market potential of offering financial services that people want to use, in a secure, convenient, affordable, transparent, and responsible approach.

In this flurry of disruption, can we maintain a focus on the more vulnerable—women, low-income people, and rural populations—where advocates for financial inclusion started in the 1970s?

We face a choice. Will financial services be customer focused and responsible in the delivery of services that improve household well-being across genders, geographic locations, and income levels? Or will people face a tsunami of over-indebtedness and massive data fraud powered by soulless algorithms? Careful, responsible product design and market conduct can help ensure that people are not left behind, or even worse, harmed by reckless financial services. Hopefully we, as financial inclusion advocates, can contribute to a positive global impact and improve people's lives with meaningful, high-quality financial services.

Notes

This chapter was completed in January 2020, and market changes after that date are not included in the analysis.

1. Unless noted, all figures for financial inclusion in this chapter are based on the most recent Global Findex data for 2017, published in April 2018, and relate to the data for developing countries, as defined by Findex. Adults are defined as people over fifteen

years of age. Asli Demirgüç-Kunt and others, *The Global Findex Database 2017: Measuring Financial Inclusion and the Fintech Revolution* (Washington: World Bank, 2018).

2. These data exclude high-income countries in East Asia and the Pacific, although when they are included, the level of account holding only increases to 74 percent (as of 2017).

3. Elisabeth Rhyne and Sonja Kelly, "Financial Inclusion Hype vs. Reality: Deconstructing the 2017 Findex Results" (Washington: Center for Financial Inclusion, Accion, May 2018).

4. The income gap is measured by subtracting 59 percent (the percentage of adults in the poorest 40 percent of households holding accounts) from 78 percent (the percentage of adults in the richest 60 percent of households holding accounts).

5. Nico Valckx, "Rising Household Debt: What It Means for Growth and Stability" (Washington: International Monetary Fund, October 3, 2017).

6. Ira Lieberman, *In Good Times Prepare for Crisis* (Brookings Institution Press, 2018).

7. See, for example, Jennifer Isern, "Financial Inclusion in India—A Himalayan Feat," chap. 13 in this volume.

8. See, for example, Maryann Bylander and others, "Over-indebtedness and Microcredit in Cambodia: Moving beyond Borrower-centric Frames," *Development Policy Review* (10.1111/dpr.12399). Also see Philip Heijmans, "Cambodia Has a Big Problem with Small Loans," Bloomberg, October 1, 2018.

9. Gian Luciano Boeddu and Rosamund Grady, "Papua New Guinea Financial Consumer Protection Diagnostic" (Washington: International Finance Corporation, 2018).

10. See, for example, Sabine Spohn, "Over-indebtedness: The Flip Side of Financial Inclusion" (blog), Asian Development Bank, March 2, 2018. See also Quinn Lisbon, "Household Debt Rising across Southeast Asia," Asia News Network, October 11, 2018.

11. Rhyne and Kelly, "Financial Inclusion Hype vs. Reality: Deconstructing the 2017 Findex Results."

12. Entire books have been written about financial inclusion markets in individual countries, so any attempt to summarize all established players across the Asia and Pacific region would be inadequate. This section aims to provide a broad overview of institutions and trends.

13. Isern, "Financial Inclusion in India"; see also Enjiang Cheng, "Inclusive Financial Development in China," chap. 14 in this volume.

14. Jose de Luna Martinez and Sergio Campillo-Diaz, "Financial Inclusion in Malaysia: Distilling Lessons for Other Countries" (Kuala Lumpur: World Bank Group, 2017).

15. Badan Kredit Desa (BKDs) are another type of rural financial institution in Indonesia.

16. Nils Clotteau and Bsrat Measho, "Global Panorama of Postal Financial Inclusion," in *Postal Savings: Reaching Everyone in Asia*, ed. Naoyuki Yoshino, José Ansón, and Matthias Helbl (Manila: Asian Development Bank, 2018).

17. Japan Post Bank, "History" (https://www.japanpost.jp/en/corporate/changes/).

18. Tomohiro Ebuchi, "Japan Post Privatization Heads to Finale with Up to $12bn Share Sale," *Nikkei Asian Review*, April 10, 2019.

19. FXXSI, "Top Twenty Largest Banks in the World by Assets," December 20, 2019 (https://fxssi.com/top-20-largest-world-banks-in-current-year).

20. "Postal Savings Bank of China IPO Raises $7.4 Billion after Pricing at Low End," Reuters, September 20, 2016.

21. China Post, "China Postal Savings" (http://english.chinapost.com.cn/).

22. Clotteau and Measho, "Global Panorama of Postal Financial Inclusion."

23. Shweta Punj, "India Post: In Letter and Spirit," *India Today*, August 11, 2017.

24. India Post, "Financial Services" (https://www.indiapost.gov.in/Financial/Pages /Content/Financial.aspx).

25. Demirgüç-Kunt and others, *The Global Findex Database 2017*.

26. McKinsey and Company, "Rewriting the Rules: Succeeding in the New Retail Banking Landscape" (February 2019).

27. McKinsey Global Institute, "Digital Finance for All: Powering Inclusive Growth in Emerging Economies" (September 2016).

28. GSMA Intelligence, *2018 State of the Industry Report on Mobile Money* (February 25, 2019) (https://www.gsma.com/mobilefordevelopment/resources/2018-state-of-the-industry -report-on-mobile-money/).

29. Of concern for access to finance in the Pacific Island countries over the past five years, several international banks across the Pacific are closing or selling branches or reducing their correspondent bank networks given concerns about perceived anti-money-laundering risks and thin operating margins. Although this trend can be seen across several countries globally, it is especially troubling for the Pacific given the importance of correspondent bank networks for money transfers, which are vital for households and businesses in the islands. For more, see Pierre-Laurent Chatain and others, "The Decline in Access to Correspondent Banking Services in Emerging Markets: Trends, Impacts, and Solutions—Lessons Learned from Eight Country Case Studies," *FCI Insight* (Washington: World Bank Group, 2018).

30. Jan Stryjak and Mayuran Sivakumaran, "The Mobile Economy 2019" (London: GSMA Intelligence, February 25, 2019).

31. GSMA Intelligence, "The Mobile Gender Gap Report 2019" (London: February 20, 2019).

32. International Monetary Fund, "Financial Access Survey" (Washington, September 30, 2019).

33. Ibid.

34. Katrina Domingo, "Why Filipinos Find It Hard to Trust Cashless Payments," *ABS-CBN News*, April 20, 2019.

35. Lawrence Agcaolili, "Singapore-based Virtual Lender Cleared to Operate in Philippine—BSP," *PhilStar*, December 31, 2019.

36. Mayvelin Caraballo, "E-Payment Transactions in PH Now at 30%—BSP," *Manila Times*, November 20, 2019. This article quotes the BSP that e-payments were estimated at just 1 percent of total transactions in 2013 and remained flat until 2018–19.

37. "Mobile Banking Subscribers Now Over 7.0 Crore," *The New Nation*, October 31, 2109. See also Bangladesh Bank, Dhaka "Mobile Financial Services (MFS) Comparative Summary Statement of January 2019 and February 2019."

38. "MoneyGram and Wing to Launch a New Mobile Wallet Service in Cambodia," PR NewsWire Asia, November 14, 2019.

39. "Mobile Payment User Numbers Surge in China," *Mobile World Live*, March 8, 2019.

40. Stella Yifang Xie, "More Than a Third of China Is Now Invested in One Giant Mutual Fund," *Wall Street Journal*, March 27, 2019.

41. See Ant Financial website at antfin.com, as well as independent company profiles for Pitchbook (pitchbook.com) and Craft (craft.co). Of note, Alibaba also maintains other subsidiaries across the economic sector.

42. "China's Ant Financial Amasses 50 Million Users, Mostly Low-Income, in New Health Plan," Euronews, April 12, 2019.

43. "Jack Ma's $290 Billion Loan Machine Is Changing Chinese Banking," Bloomberg News, July 27, 2019. See also "China's Mobile Banks Offer 1-Second Loan Decisions in Farmland," *Nikkei Asian Review*, August 9, 2019.

44. The Lazada e-commerce site is also active across Indonesia, Malaysia, the Philippines, Singapore, Thailand, and Vietnam, extending the regional reach for Alipay Singapore (formerly HelloPay).

45. Zen Soo, "Alipay and Six European Digital Wallets Join Hands to Increase Adoption of Mobile Payments with QR Code," *South China Morning Post*, June 10, 2019.

46. TenCent is the holding company for a broad set of subsidiaries, similar to Alibaba. TenPay, which operates WeChat Pay, is similar to Ant Financial in approach and recent expansion.

47. Financial Stability Board, "Market Developments and Potential Financial Stability Implications" (Basel, Switzerland, February 14, 2019). For more recent analysis from an investor's perspective, see also Adam Seessel, "Soaring or Sinking with a Super App," *Fortune*, August 2019.

48. "China to Enhance Regulatory System for Fintech Development," *Regulation Asia*, January 9, 2020.

49. "China Is Issuing Its Own Cryptocurrency Answer to Facebook's Libra," *Fintech News*, August 12, 2019. See also Aaron Klein, "Is China's New Payment System the Future?" (Brookings Institution, June 2019).

50. "China Focus: China Adopts Law on Cryptography," Xinhua Net, October 26, 2019.

51. Zoran Spirkovski, "China's Blockchain-based Service Network (BSN) and Why It's Extremely Relevant," *CryptoNews*, January 3, 2020.

52. Hong Kong Monetary Authority, "Banking Ordinance: Authorization of Virtual Banks" (February and May 2018).

53. Hong Kong Monetary Authority, "Granting of Virtual Banking Licences" (March 27 and May 9, 2019). See also "8 Virtual Banks Approved for Hong Kong," *China Business Law Journal* (June 11, 2019). The licenses were awarded to: Ant SME Services owned by Ant Financial; Livi VB backed by Bank of China (Hong Kong), JD Digits, and Jardines; Ping An OneConnect; Infinium from the consortium of TenCent, the Industrial and Commercial Bank of China, Hong Kong Exchanges and Clearing, Hillhouse Capital, and others; SC Digital Solutions from the consortium of Standard Chartered, PCCW, HKT, and Ctrip; Insight Fintech backed by Xiaomi and AMTD Group; WeLab, a Hong Kong fintech company; and ZhongAn Virtual Finance.

54. "Hong Kong Hits Major Fintech Milestone as Half the City's Population Signs Up for HKMA's Faster Payment System," *South China Morning Post*, January 13, 2020.

55. See website of the Reserve Bank of India for a list of Indian banks at www.india.gov.in/list-banks-reserve-bank-india.

56. Reserve Bank of India, "Guidelines for 'On Tap' Licensing of Small Finance Banks in the Private Sector" (Mumbai, December 5, 2019). "Payments Banks May Be Allowed To Convert Into Small Finance Banks," Hindu Businessline.com, September 13, 2019.

57. National Payments Corporation of India (NPCI), "Background" (https://www.npci.org.in).

58. NPCI, "UPI Product Overview" (https://www.npci.org.in/).

59. "Fintech Startups Paving Way for a Financially Smart India," *Economic Times*, March 28, 2109.

60. "India Emerging as Fintech Hub: Findexable Report," *Moneycontrol News*, December 11, 2019.

61. "Fintech Startups Paving Way." See also Srikanth, "Top 5 Financing Platforms for MSMEs & SMEs in INDIA," *TechieExpert*, October 16, 2019.

62. Adait Palepu, "India's Neo-Banks: What's So 'Neo' About Them?," Bloomberg Quint, December 4, 2019.

63. Pratik Bhakta, "Fintech Startups Look for Total Makeover with Lending Licence," *Economic Times*, September 6, 2019.

64. Rishi Ranjan Kala, "WhatsApp Seeks RBI Approval for Payments Service," *Financial Express*, August 30, 2019.

65. Aarzoo Mittal, "WhatsApp Payments Service Isn't Compliant for Launch: RBI to SC," Entrackr.com, November 8, 2019.

66. "WhatsApp Pay Set for Phased Roll Out in India; Granted NPCI Permission," *Business Standard*, February 7, 2020.

67. "Go-Pay Sets Out to 'Strengthen' Its Digital Wallet Presence in Cash-Reliant Indonesia," CNBC, March 21, 2019. See also "Gojek Ranks among Top 20 in Fortune's List of Companies," *Antara News*, August 28, 2019.

68. "OVO Becomes Indonesia's Fifth Unicorn Startup, Rudiantara Says," *Jakarta Post*, October 8, 2019.

69. "Indonesia's e-wallet players draw users with discounts, cashbacks; Firms fight for bigger piece of multibillion-dollar market as digital payments surge in cash-reliant country," *The Straits Times*, January 28, 2020.

70. "Bank BRI's Pinang Goes Head-to-Head with P2P Lenders in Southeast Asia," PR Newswire, January 1, 2020.

71. "BantuSaku: Innovative Online Lending Platform You Can Rely On," PR Newswire Asia, January 8, 2020.

72. "OJK Officially Recognizes CredoLab as First Credit-Scoring Fintech Firm," *The Jakarta Post*, January 15, 2020.

73. Bank Indonesia, "Indonesia Payment Systems Blueprint for 2025" (Jakarta, November 28, 2019).

74. "Dominating Malaysia's Digital Payment Landscape," The Tech Collective, November 27, 2018 (techcollectivesea.com).

75. Bank Negara Malaysia, "Exposure Draft on Licensing Framework for Digital Banks" (Kuala Lumpur, December 27, 2019).

76. "2019 Wave Money Highlights," Wave Money, January 9, 2020 (https://www.wavemoney.com.mm/).

77. "P2P Money Transfers Take Off in Underbanked Myanmar," *Asian Banking and Finance*, August 27, 2019.

78. World Bank, "Remittances Dataset." On remittances and migration globally, see also the website of Knomad at knomad.org.

79. "Grab Introduces Mastercard-branded Numberless Card in Singapore," MarketLine NewsWire, December 6, 2019.

80. "Moving beyond Ride-hailing, Southeast Asia's Grab Is Rolling Out Financial Services," CNBC, March 19, 2019. See also Nidhi Singh, "Grab Now Enters Southeast Asia's SME Lending and Micro-Insurance Space," Entrepreneur, March 19, 2019; "Grab and Gojek," *The Economist*, May 2, 2019.

81. Samantha Hurst, "Create Instant Mobile Payments through PayNow in Singapore," *CrowdFund Insider*, April 15, 2019.

82. "Razer and Visa Announce Partnership to Transform Payments in Southeast Asia," Business Wire, June 23, 2019.

83. Monetary Authority of Singapore, "Digital Bank Licence," December 31, 2019.

84. Chanyaporn Chanjaroen, "Singapore Sees 'Strong Interest' in Digital Bank Licenses," Bloomberg, January 6, 2020.

85. Manesh Samtani, "At Least Nine Applicants for Singapore Digital Bank Licences," *Regulation Asia*, January 6, 2020. See also "Here Are the Contenders to Singapore's Digital Banking Race," *Fintech News Singapore*, January 6, 2020. As of this writing, only nine consortiums of the twenty-one that bid have been publicly acknowledged. These include: Grab and Singtel; Razer Youth Bank led by Razer Fintech (subsidiary of the e-sports firm) with Sheng Siong Holdings, FWD, LinkSure Global, Insignia Venture Partners, and Carro; Ant Financial; iFast with Yillion Group and Hande Group (launched by the former chairman of WeBank in China); Beyond with V3 Group, EZ-Link (contactless payments card), Far East Organization, Sumitomo Insurance Co. Ltd., Heliconia Capital Management, and the Singapore Business Federation; ByteDance (owners of TikTok video sharing app); Funding Societies; Sheng Ye Capital with Advance AI and Philip Capital; and Treasury Consulting Pte Ltd.

86. Rajarshi Mitra, "Thailand's Oldest Bank Launches Ripple-Powered Cross-Border Payments App," *FX Street*, January 20, 2020; "Digital Drive Gains Momentum," *Bangkok Post*, January 8, 2020.

87. "Overview of Vietnam's Major E-Wallet and Mobile Payment Players," *Fintech News*, August 6, 2019.

88. "Vietnam: Billion-Dollar Fintech Market Awaits Sandbox for Breakthrough," *Voice of Vietnam*, November 11, 2019.

89. Ministry of Information and Communications of the Socialist Republic of Vietnam, "Telecom Firms Ready for Mobile Money Service," April 22, 2019.

90. "Not So Fast: New Forms of Lending Bring Old Problems," *The Economist*, November 17, 2018.

91. Center for the Study of Financial Innovation, *Finance for All: Wedded to Fintech, for Better or Worse* (New York and London, 2018).

92. Lara Gilman and Michael Joyce, "Managing the Risk of Fraud in Mobile Money" (London: GSMA, 2012). See also Joseck Mudiri, "Fraud in Mobile Financial Services" (Nairobi and New Delhi: MicroSave Consulting, November 26, 2012).

93. Graham Wright, "The Digital Transformation: Four Opportunities and Three Threats for Traditional Financial Institutions" (Nairobi and New Delhi: MicroSave Consulting, November 18, 2018).

94. Ammara Khan, "PMN & TMB Inked to Digitize Pakistan's Microfinance Industry," *Technology Times*, April 24, 2019.

95. Ecofin Agency, "Kenya: Microfinance Institutions' 2018 Losses Rose by 447% YoY to –935 Mln Kenyan Shillings," March 5, 2019 (https://www.ecofinagency.com/).

96. Charles Wendel, "Independents: Banking on the Non-Bank." (Equipment Leasing and Finance Foundation, February 8, 2019) (https://www.store.leasefoundation.org/cvweb /Portals/ELFA-LEASE/Documents/Products/Independents2019.pdf).

97. Financial Stability Board, "Market Developments and Potential Financial Stability Implications" (Basel, Switzerland, February 24, 2019).

98. Identification 4 Development, "ID4D Annual Report 2018" (Washington: World Bank, 2018). Of the 1 billion people without legal identification, 47 percent are children and young adults whose births were not registered.

99. Unique Identification Authority of India (UIDAI), Government of India, Aadhaar Dashboard (2019) (https://uidai.gov.in/aadhaar_dashboard/asa_transactions.php?asacode =0000001400).

100. For early analysis of this issue, see Jennifer Isern and others, "AML/CFT Regulation: Implications for Financial Service Providers that Serve Low-Income People," *Focus Note* 29 (Washington: CGAP, World Bank, July 2005). Many other authors have analyzed this issue over the ensuing years.

101. FinMark Trust and Bankable Frontier Associates, "The Mzansi Bank Account Initiative in South Africa" (2009) (http://www.finmark.org.za/wp-content/uploads/2016/02/Rep _MsanziBankAccInitiativeSA_2009.pdf).

102. Pradhan Mantri Jan-Dhan Yojana (PMJDY) (National Mission for Financial Inclusion), Government of India, "Program Overview and Basic Statistics" (2019) (www.pmjdy .gov.in/scheme).

103. Ibid.

104. PMJDY, "State-wise Statistics." Note that these figures are more recent than the latest Findex information that is based on 2017 surveys and published in 2018.

105. Bank Negara Malaysia, "Your Guide on Basic Savings and Current Accounts" (Kuala Lumpur) (https://www.bnm.gov.my/index.php?rp=guidelines_on_basic_banking_serv).

106. Rajesh Khanal, "Central Bank Makes It Easier to Open Accounts," *Kathmandu Post*, April 11, 2019.

107. Maarten Mittner, "Banks Back Dormant Mzansi" (Johannesburg: Fin24) (www .fin24.com/Money/Money-Clinic/Banks-back-dormant-Mzansi-20100613).

108. *Global Findex Data 2018* (Washington: World Bank). Inactivity is defined as no deposit or withdrawal to the account in the previous twelve months.

109. Graham Wright, "In Our Digital Financial Service We Trust?" (Nairobi and New Delhi: MicroSave Consulting, June 24, 2015).

110. McKinsey and Company, "Rewriting the Rules: Succeeding in the New Retail Banking Landscape" (New York and London: February 2019).

111. Alex Taylor and Wayne Hennessy-Barrett, "Partnering with Providers to Set DFS Standards for Client Protection" (Washington: Center for Financial Inclusion, Accion, January 15, 2019); Smart Campaign, "Consumer Protection Standards for Digital Credit," June 2019 (http://smartcampaign.org/about/smart-microfinance-and-the-client-protection-principles /digital-credit-standards).

112. World Bank, "Credit Reporting" (Washington, October 10, 2015).

113. World Bank, "Doing Business Database: Getting Credit Indicators" (Washington). Data as of April 2019.

114. Jennifer Isern and others, "Government to Person Health Payments in Bihar, India: Diagnostic and Recommendations" (New Delhi: International Finance Corporation, June 2011).

115. Jennifer Isern, Anita Sharma, and Georgina Marina, "Transforming Health through E-Payments in India," Finance in Focus Series of the Finance and Markets Department (Washington: World Bank, August 2017).

116. Elizabeth Rhyne, "Financial Inclusion Backlash in Uruguay" (Washington: Center for Financial Inclusion, Accion, April 24, 2019).

117. Rebecca Bellan, "As More Cities Ban Cashless Businesses, New York Wants to Follow," City Lab, March 6, 2019 (www.citylab.com/equity/2019/03/cashless-cash-free-ban -bill-new-york-retail-discrimination/584203/).

118. Anna Tims, "The Rise of Cashless Britain: The Poor Suffer as Banks and ATMs Are Closed," *The Guardian*, October 1, 2018.

119. Pragya Srivastava, "Cashless India Is Not Happening; Here's Why," *Financial Express*, November 16, 2018.

120. Katrina Domingo, "Why Filipinos Find It Hard to Trust Cashless Payments," ABS-CBN News, April 20, 2019.

121. Bellan, "As More Cities Ban Cashless Businesses."

122. Isern, "Financial Inclusion in India."

123. "PBOC Reins in Funds of Payment Platforms," January 16, 2019.

124. See, for example, DigFin Group, "Asia's Virtual Banks Need to Redefine MVP" (Hong Kong, August 26, 2019).

125. "Taiwan Joins Asia Digital Banking Push with Three New Online Licenses," Reuters, July 30, 2019.

126. "7 Things You Need to Know about Singapore's Digital Banking Licenses," *Fintech News Singapore*, July 2, 2019.

127. Economist Intelligence Unit (EIU), "Global Microscope 2018: The Enabling Environment for Financial Inclusion" (New York, 2018) (https://www.eiu.com/public/topical _report.aspx?campaignid=Microscope2018).

THIRTEEN

Financial Inclusion in India—A Himalayan Feat

JENNIFER ISERN

Financial inclusion in India is a captivating tale with a long history of money lenders and more recent players including co-operatives, postal finance, self-help groups, microfinance institutions, payment providers, fintech players, and banks of many sizes, scope, and capacity. The world watched in horror as the microfinance crisis exploded in Andhra Pradesh in October 2010. Since that crisis, financial inclusion efforts intensified, like a phoenix rising from the ashes. Extraordinary efforts include an ambitious national financial inclusion campaign promoted by the government, prudent regulation and supervision by the central bank, leading innovations in payment systems, and tremendous dynamism across many new types of financial services providers. As a result, hundreds of millions of people across India have been brought into the formal financial sector in the past decade. India is truly a global role model for the potential of financial inclusion efforts across both public and private sectors.

History of Financial Inclusion Efforts in India

History often helps to explain the present. India is home to some of the oldest cultures in the world with over 5,000 years of history. Formal and informal savings and credit systems are deeply intertwined in society. Ancient texts of the Vedas dating back to 2000 BC reference lending and usury, and letters of credit and bills of exchange for business lending are cited in historical accounts from the Mauryan kingdom of 300 BC and medieval period of the Mughal era.[1] More recently, Rabindranath Tagore's beloved short story "Kabuliwala" written in 1892 offers a timeless and poignant perspective on the life of a merchant and money lender far from his home in Kabul, as he interacts with his clients and the broader community in Kolkata.

Early History

Focusing on just the past several hundred years, access to finance in India (and globally) followed some similar paths. In local economies, farmers, households, and small businesses typically relied on family, money lenders, larger merchants, gold dealers, and landowners for short-term credit. Savings was largely through investments in land, livestock, gold, jewelry, and other in-kind options.

The first formal banks to be established included the Bank of Hindustan and Bank of Bombay in 1770 and the Bank of Bengal in 1784.[2] The 1800s witnessed a growth in new types of banks, including joint stock banks, presidency banks, exchange banks, and foreign banks. Calcutta (present-day Kolkata) emerged as the banking and political capital during the colonial period, although over time the banking capital shifted to Bombay (present-day Mumbai).

In these early days, limited credit was available, especially in rural areas, and informal lenders were largely free to set interest rates, seize collateral, and enforce other loan terms with impunity. One account notes an early but small-scale colonial program dating to the 1860s that provided loans to subsistence farmers to help reduce dependence on money lenders.[3]

In the 1890s, the first savings and credit co-operatives were launched in India, building on the successful German Raiffeisen model that was also being adapted in other countries globally. The Indian Co-operative Credit Societies Act was passed in 1904.[4] Government led, these early co-operative efforts were neither savings based nor community led and were largely seen as channels for government credit to the agricultural sector.[5] Over time, the co-operative movement in India has evolved significantly, and key current results are discussed later in comparison with other types of financial services providers. In the early 1900s as part of the Swadeshi movement, linked to Indian nationalism and the independence movement, Indian businessmen and community leaders started a number of new banks.

Established by a parliamentary act in 1934, the Reserve Bank of India (RBI) began operations in 1935 with a focus on managing currency and public accounts.[6] Before the RBI's existence, some of these functions were managed by the Imperial Bank of India. The 1948 Banking Regulation Act clarified the RBI's role as a central bank, established its authority to regulate and supervise banks, and laid the foundation of the modern financial sector. The Indian banking sector expanded after World War II and independence in 1947, although the quality of the banks and their portfolios was uneven, and much of the lending was limited to trade credit.

Early Government Programs

The 1951 All India Rural Credit Survey commissioned by the RBI concluded that formal, institutional sources, including financial co-operatives, accounted for only 7 percent of rural credit and that co-operatives were an "utter failure" in rural credit but played an important role in agricultural credit.[7] Given pressures to increase food production and linked to the input-intensive agricultural practices of the Green Revolution in the 1960s, agricultural credit became a national policy priority. The Imperial Bank of India, which later became the State Bank of India (SBI), was directed by the Indian government to expand branches in rural areas and offer agricultural credit.[8] In parallel in the 1950s, the RBI created a division for rural credit and launched a program of wholesale lending to banks to expand agricultural loans.

In a momentous event for India, in 1969 the top fourteen commercial banks were nationalized overnight through an act of Parliament under the leadership of Prime Minister Indira Gandhi.[9] These fourteen banks represented 85 percent of banking assets nationwide, and another six commercial banks were nationalized in 1980. Nationalization set the trajectory of the financial sector for decades, and its impact can still be felt today.

In the 1970–90 period, the Indian government launched a series of efforts to promote financial services, especially in rural areas given that they were home to over 70 percent of the population. The Regional Rural Bank (RRB) Act of 1975 enabled the launch of the first six RRBs in selected states; ownership is shared by the central government, the relevant state government, and a sponsoring commercial bank.[10] This RRB license was one of the first "light" bank licenses to be designed in India. Based on performance and portfolio quality, the number of RRBs in operation has decreased since the first RRBs were established in the period from the 1970s to the 1990s. While regulated by the RBI, the National Bank for Agriculture and Rural Development (NABARD) supervises the network of RRBs across India, which included fifty-three RRBs as of August 2019.

Starting in the 1970s, government policy for all banks expanded lending targets for rural areas. Forty percent of lending was to be channeled to priority sectors such as agriculture and small-scale industry at lower interest rates—and these targets continue today. In addition, banks were required to increase the number of branches in rural and less-served locations of the country. The government also launched other programs to promote rural economic development at the state and national levels—for example, the Integrated Rural Development Program.

During this period, with the best of intentions, the government focused on lending volume, paying less attention to whether loans were repaid, impact on bank portfolio quality, and socioeconomic impact of the lending. Given ongoing concerns about rural lending, plus growing demonstrations by farmers and reports of suicide by some borrowers, in 1990 the government implemented the nationwide Agricultural Debt Relief Scheme of INR100 billion (approximately US$1.4 billion).[11] Later in 2008, a second national debt relief program—the Agricultural Debt Waiver and Debt Relief Scheme (ADWDRS)—was implemented. Although the program ran for several years, already in 2008–09 the scale of the program was massive; the ADWDRS eventually covered 43 million farmers and cost INR716 billion (US$10.1 billion).[12] Loans issued through public sector banks, regional rural banks, scheduled commercial banks, and financial co-operatives were eligible for this program. Farm loan (and other loan) waivers were also used by several state governments during that period and up to the present day, often preceding elections or after natural disasters such as cyclones or droughts. These farm waivers from 2008 to 2017 were estimated at INR890 billion (US$12.5 billion).[13] Several agricultural specialists, bankers, opposition members, and others raised concerns about the program, including negative effects on the banking sector and future availability of agricultural credit. Further, critics noted that the likely beneficiaries of the program would be larger landholders with access to formal loans rather than subsistence farmers who relied on informal money lenders and merchants.[14]

In 1992 and 1998, new rounds of financial sector reforms were launched, linked to the government's broader policies to liberalize the Indian economy. During the 1990s, new private sector and foreign-owned banks were licensed, reserve requirements in banks were reduced, and the RBI's ability to regulate and supervise the various categories of banks was reinforced.[15] In addition, interest rates were deregulated, and some targets for directed lending to priority sectors such as agriculture were recommended to be reduced.[16] These reforms helped inject more competition into the financial services market with new banks and greater focus on bank financial performance, including portfolio quality. However, during this time credit to small borrowers as a share of total bank credit declined from 18.3 percent in 1994 to 5.3 percent in 2002 to 1.3 percent in 2010. Likewise, the number of small-borrower accounts at formal financial institutions dropped from 55 million in 1994 to 1.9 million in 2010.[17]

The decline in the number of small borrowers coincided with the rise of other financial inclusion programs during the same period.

Government Institutions Supporting Financial Inclusion

Several government institutions have played a significant role for many decades in promoting access to finance in India including India Post, NABARD, and SIDBI.

India Post Financial Services

India Post is one of the world's largest postal networks. Launched during the colonial period, India Post delivered millions of letters annually by the 1860s through its network of approximately 900 post offices. An act of Parliament in 1873 approved the Post Office Savings Bank (POSB), which India Post established throughout the country in 1882; it began offering postal life insurance shortly thereafter, in 1884.[18]

Over the past 140 years, the POSB has emerged as one of the largest banking networks in the country, especially in rural areas. The core services historically offered by India Post included basic savings accounts, money orders, and life insurance. Over the decades, these services grew to include a range of savings accounts, remittance services, provident funds, mutual funds, and foreign exchange services offered through a network of 155,000 post offices.[19] A study in 2008 of India Post and its financial services estimated that the POSB managed 162 million accounts and annual deposits of INR1.6 trillion (US$22.5 billion). At such a size, the POSB would have been double the size of all other banks in the country combined.[20] After considerable internal analysis and national policy debates, India Post launched a payments bank in late 2018 (discussed later in the chapter).

NABARD

In 1981, a parliamentary act established the National Bank for Agriculture and Rural Development (NABARD) as a focal agency for development credit in rural areas. NABARD is a central pillar of the government's efforts to promote rural development nationwide. With numerous well-known programs over the decades, NABARD has played a key role in promoting the self-help group model and broader microfinance efforts across India since the 1980s. In 1998, NABARD launched the Kisan credit card program, essentially a line of credit for agricultural inputs for qualifying farmers. Administered by commercial banks, co-operatives, and regional rural banks, the Kisan credit card program simplified agricultural lending for both borrowers and lenders, and continues to this day as a major credit delivery mechanism.[21] Throughout the chapter, NABARD's activities will be discussed further.

SIDBI

In 1990, the Small Industries Development Bank of India (SIDBI) was established by parliamentary act to promote lending and development of micro, small, and medium-sized enterprises (MSMEs). SIDBI played a critical role in promoting microfinance institutions and the broader financial inclusion ecosystem in India, and this will be discussed throughout the chapter.

Indian Flavors of Microfinance: SHGs and MFIs

In line with other efforts globally to promote access to finance to low-income people and micro, small, and medium-sized businesses, several nongovernmental associations (NGOs) and associations were launched in the 1970s–90s across India. Group-based lending was already practiced in many areas—for example, the *sheetu* and *chit* systems in Tamil Nadu and Andhra Pradesh and the *bhisi* system in Mumbai. Building on these approaches, early entrants to promote financial inclusion included the Self-Employed Women's Association (SEWA) in Gujarat in 1974, Mysore Resettlement and Development Agency (MYRADA) microfinance operations in Karnataka in 1985, and Professional Assistance for Development Action (PRADAN) microfinance operations in Rajasthan in 1987. These early efforts laid the foundation for two dominant approaches for financial inclusion in India—self-help groups (SHGs) and microfinance institutions (MFIs). Chit funds remain an important source of financing across the country, and they made new headlines with a November 2019 amendment to the 1982 Chit Funds Act that clarifies legal chit fund operations.[22]

Self-Help Groups

Starting in the mid-1980s, MYRADA, PRADAN, and later many others experimented with having small groups of people (twenty plus), especially women, pool their savings and make loans within the group; these became known as self-help groups (SHGs). Since the 1970s, similar efforts were underway in neighboring Bangladesh (by Grameen Bank and BRAC, for example) and several countries in Latin America and Africa, often under labels such as village banking and similar variants. In early pilot programs from 1987 to 1992, NABARD played a key role in helping promote and then scaling up the SHG program nationwide in the decades that ensued under the SHG Bank Linkage Program supported by GTZ (now GIZ, the German Agency for International Cooperation), the International Fund for Agricultural

Development (IFAD), the Asian Development Bank (ADB), and the World Bank, among others.[23]

The SHG program initially grew most rapidly in three states in southern India—Andhra Pradesh, Tamil Nadu, and Karnataka—and over time the program grew nationwide into one of the largest financial inclusion programs in the world. A broad range of NGOs, banks, microfinance institutions, specialized development institutions, and state governments linked with NABARD to promote SHGs across the country. Banks and other financial services providers were allowed to classify their loans to SHGs against the priority sector lending target of 40 percent of their total loan portfolio. The national government included support to SHGs, through policy and budget support, in the national annual plan starting in 2000.

Many scholars have analyzed the SHG program over the years, and most conclude that the program generates significant social and economic benefits to participants, especially women and low-income people, through empowerment, leadership opportunities, awareness raising on development issues, expanded household savings, and greater access to credit in rural areas.[24] Concerns about the program were related to potential political influence through SHG groups, subsidized interest rates between banks and the SHGs, the cost of creating and sustaining SHGs and their support structures to keep the program viable, and uneven quality both of bank portfolios for their loans to SHGs and for the internal loan portfolio among SHG members.[25]

As of March 2010, just before the microfinance crisis, NABARD reported more than 6.9 million SHGs, of which more than 5.3 million were women-only groups. NABARD estimated that 97 million families across the country were reached through an SHG. Approximately 4.8 million SHGs had loans outstanding at that date. Over the years, a range of banks began to lend to SHGs, and these loans could also be included toward meeting a bank's priority sector lending targets. As of March 2010, loans outstanding to SHGs were estimated at INR230.4 trillion (US$3.25 billion) from commercial banks, regional rural banks, co-operative banks, microfinance institutions, and others. The average outstanding loan per member was INR4,128 (US$56).[26]

Microfinance Institutions

In parallel to the rise of NABARD's SHG program, microfinance institutions grew to become a second dominant model for financial inclusion in India. The first of the modern-era MFIs, SEWA, launched the Mahila Co-operative Bank in 1974 in Gujarat.[27] Some of the key pioneer MFIs are listed in table 13-1. MFIs took many forms, based on the legal options available such as NGOs, societies, trusts, associations, local

TABLE 13-1. Significant MFIs Launched in India, 1974–2011

Institution	Launch date	Founding state[a]
SEWA Mahila Co-operative Bank Ltd.	1974 as co-operative bank	Gujarat
SHARE Microfin Ltd.	1989 as a not-for-profit; later transformed into an NBFC[b]	Andhra Pradesh[c]
Satin Creditcare Network Ltd.	1990 as a not-for-profit; later transformed into an NBFC	New Delhi, National Capital Region
North East Small Finance Bank Ltd.	1990 as RGVN Society;[d] transformed into an NBFC in 2010; started operations as small finance bank in 2017	Assam
ESAF Small Finance Bank Ltd.[e]	1992 as an NGO; 2008 as an NBFC; started operations as small finance bank in 2017	Kerala
AU Small Finance Bank Ltd.	1996 as an NBFC; started operations as a small finance bank in 2017	Rajasthan
Bhartiya Samruddhi Finance Ltd. (BASIX)	1996 as an NBFC, part of the BASIX group	Andhra Pradesh
CashPor	1996 as not-for-profit	Uttar Pradesh
IndusInd Financial Inclusion Ltd.	1997 as SKS Society;[f] 2005 as NBFC, renamed Bharat Financial Inclusion Ltd. in 2016; merged with IndusInd Bank in 2019 and renamed IndusInd Financial Inclusion Ltd.	Andhra Pradesh
Spandana Sphoorty Financial Ltd.	1998 as a society; later became an NBFC	Andhra Pradesh
Jana Small Finance Bank Ltd.	1999 launched as Sanghamitra Urban Program (SUP); became Janalakshmi in 2006; became an NBFC in 2008; became a small finance bank in 2017; received scheduled bank status in 2019	Karnataka
Krishna Bhima Samruddhi Local Area Bank Ltd. (Samruddhi Bank)	Incorporated in 1999; started operations in 2001, as part of the BASIX group	Andhra Pradesh
Capital Small Finance Bank Ltd.	2000 as local area bank; started operations as a small finance bank in 2016	Punjab
Bandhan Bank Ltd.	2001 launched as not-for-profit; later purchased an NBFC license; received bank license in 2014	West Bengal

TABLE 13-1.   (continued)

Institution	Launch date	Founding state[a]
Belstar Investment and Finance Pvt. Ltd.	2003 launched as NGO Hand in Hand; acquired Belstar NBFC in 2008; acquired by Muthoot Finance Ltd. in 2016	Tamil Nadu
Adhikar Microfinance Pvt. Ltd.	2004 as a society; later as an NBFC	Odisha
Ujjivan Small Finance Bank Ltd.	2005 as NBFC; started operations with a small bank license in 2017	Karnataka
Arohan Financial Services Ltd.	2006 as an NBFC	West Bengal
Sonata Finance Pvt. Ltd.	2006 as an NBFC	Uttar Pradesh
Swadhaar Finserve Pvt. Ltd.	2006 as FinAccess not-for-profit; 2008 as Swadhaar as an NBFC	Mumbai urban focus, within Maharashtra
Equitas Small Finance Bank Ltd.	2007 as an NBFC; started operations with a small bank license in 2016	Tamil Nadu
Saija Finance Pvt. Ltd.	2007 as a society; later as an NBFC	Bihar
Suryoday Small Finance Bank Ltd.	2009 as an NBFC; started operations with a small bank license in 2017	Maharashtra
Utkarsh Small Finance Bank Ltd.	2009 as an NBFC; started operations with a small bank license in 2017	Uttar Pradesh
Annapurna Finance Pvt. Ltd.	2007; acquired NBFC license from another business and renamed in 2010	Uttar Pradesh
Fusion Microfinance Pvt. Ltd.	2010 as an NBFC	New Delhi, National Capital Region
IFMR Rural Channels and Services Pvt. Ltd.[g]	2011 as an NBFC	Tamil Nadu

Source: Compiled by author from company profiles and the RBI website.

a. Most MFIs subsequently expanded to other states.

b. NBFC = Non Banking Financial Company.

c. Andhra Pradesh was divided into two states in 2014; the new state is Telangana, with Hyderabad as its capital. Consequently, many of the MFIs listed above that started in Andhra Pradesh now also operate, and in many cases have their head offices in, Telangana.

d. RGVN Society = Rashtriya Grameen Vikas Nidhi Society.

e. ESAF = Evangelical Social Action Forum.

f. SKS Society = Swaya Krishi Sangam Society.

g. IFMR = Institute for Financial Management and Research.

area banks, co-operative banks, and nonbank financial companies (NBFCs) until other legal options became available after 2011.

As noted earlier, the early pioneers of the SHG model and the MFI model in India were SEWA Mahila Co-operative Bank Ltd. (1974), MYRADA (founded in 1968 as a project and expanded in the mid-1980s with SHGs), and PRADAN (1983). From table 13-1, surprisingly, the bulk of key MFIs emerged later in India than in many other countries. One of the oldest and most important MFIs globally is Bank Rakyat Indonesia (1895). Examples of other early MFIs around the world include the Bangladesh Rural Advancement Committee (BRAC) (founded in 1972 as an NGO) and the Grameen Bank (founded in 1976 as a project), both in Bangladesh; Réseau des Caisses Populaires du Burkina (RCPB) in Burkina Faso (1972); MiBanco in Peru (initially Grupo ACP in 1982); Banco Sol in Bolivia (initially a foundation in 1986); CVECA Pays Dogon in Mali (1986); Sidian Bank in Kenya (initially the lending NGO K-Rep in 1989); Mata Masu Dubara (MMD) in Niger (1990); and Women and Associations for Gain both Economic and Social (WAGES) in Togo (1992).

Many of the early MFIs in India started with an SHG approach to group lending, and over time approaches across the industry evolved to include smaller groups, especially joint liability groups of five to twenty (and more) women, while other MFIs piloted individual lending and other types of financial services such as basic remittances and life, crop, and health insurance. MFIs operating as NGOs or NBFCs were not allowed to mobilize deposits under RBI policy at the time.

Supporting Institutions

Many MFIs emerged during this period, often with the support of incubator and support organizations, and the most significant ones are described briefly here.

- Over several decades, SIDBI provided training, funding, and policy advocacy to support financial inclusion and the emergence of MFIs, other incubator institutions, consulting firms, rating agencies, training institutes, payment companies, and other institutions that built out the ecosystem for financial inclusion in India. SIDBI received support from UK Aid (formerly DFID), the World Bank, ADB, the U.S. Agency for International Development (USAID), GIZ, and other multilateral and bilateral funding institutions.

- NABARD may be best known for its SHG program, the Kisan credit card, and many other initiatives to promote financial inclusion in India. NABARD also supported organizations that became MFIs. NABARD received support from IFAD, the World Bank, ADB, USAID, GIZ, and other multilateral and bilateral funding institutions.

■ CARE India promoted rural development and started microfinance activities in 1989 through projects such as savings and loan association promotion in Andhra Pradesh, Odisha, and Uttar Pradesh; CREDIT 1 and 2 in Bihar, Odisha, and Madhya Pradesh; and CASHe. The CASHe project operated from 1999 to 2006 in Andhra Pradesh, West Bengal, Odisha, and Madhya Pradesh to help incubate new MFIs and advocate for enabling policy reforms. CARE's CASHe project also launched ACCESS Development Services in the mid-2000s and later ACCESS ASSIST, which continue to be leading players in the financial inclusion sector today.

■ Friends of Women's World Banking (FWWB) launched in 1981 with links to SEWA, and incubated many early-stage MFIs that later grew to national prominence. FWWB provided a broad range of technical assistance and wholesale lending to more than 300 small and nascent MFIs throughout the country. FWWB launched Ananya as an NBFC to expand its lending to MFIs in 2009. FWWB/Ananya also advocated at senior levels of the government and RBI for national policies on financial inclusion and through Sa-Dhan and other networks for financial inclusion. FWWB/Ananya continues to play a key role today.

■ EDA Rural, founded in 1983, was one of the first firms to provide research, management, and training programs for development agencies, with a focus on financial inclusion, livelihoods, and agricultural value chains. In 1998, EDA Rural established M-Cril, the first rating agency for MFIs in the country. In 2016 the two entities merged as M-Cril, which continues to work across India, Asia, and globally.

■ Grameen Foundation began operating in 1998 in India with a focus on providing technical assistance and funding to new MFIs; advocating for health, agriculture, and social issues; and promoting national initiatives for financial inclusion.

■ Andhra Pradesh Mahila Abhivruddhi Society (APMAS) received its registration in 2001. It supports women's SHGs, SHG federations, farmer-producer organizations, and other community-based organizations. Originally operating primarily in Andhra Pradesh, over the years APMAS expanded operations to Telangana (after the bifurcation of Andhra Pradesh), Bihar, Rajasthan, Uttar Pradesh, Madhya Pradesh, and Maharashtra.

- Aavishkaar, launched in 2002, has become a global player in impact investing across Asia and Africa. Aavishkaar helped establish, advise, and fund many new MFIs, technology firms, and inclusive businesses in agriculture and other sectors that helped to promote a sustainable ecosystem. In 2007, Aavishkaar created Intellecashe together with CashPor, a well-known MFI based in Uttar Pradesh, to incubate new MFIs in unserved areas of the country. Intellecap is the advisory arm of the Aavishkaar group.

- MicroSave, now MSC, is a global financial inclusion consulting firm operating since 1998 that began operating in India in 2006. MSC advises, trains, and provides policy advocacy for a wide range of financial services providers, technology firms, donors, policymakers, and others across India (and globally).

- IFMR Trust, founded in 2008, piloted new financial services and technologies, conducted research across a broad spectrum of financial inclusion, and advocated policy reforms; it is now called Dvara Trust. IFMR also launched IFMR Capital, which has since become Northern Arc Capital.

Table 13-1 shows where MFIs first operated. Coverage was scattered across the country, although a higher number of MFIs were based in Hyderabad, Andhra Pradesh. In practice, as MFIs began to expand, many opened branches in southern states and especially in Andhra Pradesh, where approximately forty MFIs were active in 2010. The 2010 ACCESS Development Services state-of-the-sector report raised concern about saturation and the potential for over-indebtedness, noting that the number of microfinance loans greatly exceeded the number of low-income households in Andhra Pradesh, Tamil Nadu, Karnataka, West Bengal, and Odisha. The same report estimated that there were 1.5 loans for every household in Andhra Pradesh, and 9.6 microfinance loan accounts for every poor household in the state; it questioned whether there was any space left for MFIs to expand in either Andhra Pradesh or Tamil Nadu.[28] In addition to MFIs, SHGs were especially widespread in Andhra Pradesh and promoted by a range of institutions, including the state government through the SERP Velugu program.

Given the burgeoning sector, other players emerged to build the ecosystem in the mid- to late 2000s. Sa-Dhan launched in 1999 as the first national association of community development finance institutions for all types of institutions promoting financial inclusion. Later in 2009, the Microfinance Institutions Network (MFIN) was created as the association for the subset of MFIs operating as NBFCs. Both Sa-Dhan and MFIN have played critical roles in training, reporting on trends, policy advocacy, and shaping the sector.

At the meso-level of the financial sector, rating agencies specialized in microfinance operations emerged. They included EDA Rural (which later became M-Cril), ICRA, CRISIL, CARE Ratings, and others. ACCESS launched its first state-of-the-sector report on microfinance in 2006. Fino and Eko launched operations in the mid-2000s as technology companies working with MFIs and other financial services providers to facilitate payments and money transfers. Discussions started on how to incorporate MFI clients in credit bureaus. Initial efforts began to promote responsible finance and social performance monitoring. Training programs flourished, as MFIs grew rapidly and needed to train their growing numbers of new staff. Both SIDBI and NABARD, in addition to multilateral and bilateral funders, provided significant advice and funding to many of these emerging players across the ecosystem of financial inclusion.

In the public sector, the RBI launched the first campaign for "no-frills" accounts through banks, and the national financial switch came online in 2004–05. In 2006 the government approved the Micro, Small and Medium Enterprises Development (MSMED) Act, setting definitions for these types of enterprises—which was then linked to priority sector lending targets. Under the 2007 National Payments and Settlement Systems Act, the National Payments Corporation of India (NPCI) began operations in 2008 as a joint initiative of the RBI and the Indian Banks' Association (IBA). The critical role of the NPCI is discussed later in the section on payments.

The Microfinance Crisis

During the late 2000s, MFIs felt under pressure to achieve growth targets that they had agreed on with lenders and investors and also to continue growing to attract new funding. The largest five MFIs as of March 2009 (SKS, Spandana, SHARE, Bandhan, and AML) recorded an aggressive annual growth of 50–60 percent in number of clients between 2009 and 2010.[29] Both Indian and foreign investors began to actively court MFIs for funding as the sector started to heat up, becoming one of the most active, if not *the* most active, microfinance sectors in the world.

Early Seeds of the Crisis

In 2010, self-help groups represented 37 percent of the total estimated number of accounts, followed by 28 percent of accounts held by commercial banks (including RRBs)
and 18.6 percent of accounts held by primary agricultural co-operatives (PACs). Clients of microfinance institutions represented just 16.5 percent of estimated microfinance accounts nationwide as of March 2010.[30] Both SHG and MFI programs grew
rapidly between 2008 and 2010, although increases were also notable for commercial
banks, including RRBs. The average loan size was higher for MFI loans (INR6,060,
or US$85) than for SHG loans (INR4,570, or US$64), according to data from
March 2009.[31] Table 13-2 summarizes the number of accounts by type of financial
services provider active in financial inclusion in India from 2008 to 2010.

SIDBI especially, but also NABARD, FWWB, and some multilateral and bilateral donors, provided important initial grant and debt funding for MFIs. For several
years, commercial banks had been lending to SHGs through the bank-linkage program led by NABARD with cofunding from multilateral and bilateral donors. Eventually commercial banks began lending to MFIs, as these could be included in their
priority sector lending targets starting in 2000. In the mid-2000s, several MFIs that
started as not-for-profit entities began transforming into nonbank finance companies, which enabled them to attract equity and larger amounts of debt from banks
and investors to grow their operations.

TABLE 13-2.   Estimate of Microfinance Credit Clients in India
across the Range of Financial Services Providers 2008–10

Millions of accounts

Agency	March 2008	March 2009	March 2010
Commercial banks (including RRBs) small loan accounts[a]	41.00	39.2	45.2
PACs borrowers[b] (small, vulnerable)	28.5	28.7	30.0
SHGs—members[c]	47.1	54.0	59.6
MFIs—clients[d]	14.1	22.6	26.7
Total	130.7	143.9	161.5

Source: N. Srinivasan, Microfinance India: The State of the Sector Report 2011 (New Delhi: Sage/
ACCESS Development Services, 2011).

a. RRBs = regional rural bank.
b. PACs = primary agricultural co-operatives.
c. SHGs = self-help groups.
d. MFIs = microfinance institutions.

TABLE 13-3.   Lending to MFIs in India, March 2010

	Lending volume	
Lender	Indian rupees	U.S. dollars
Small Industries Development Bank of India (SIDBI)	38.1 billion	536.5 million
Public sector banks, other than SIDBI	47.4 billion	667.4 million
Private sector banks	41.1 billion	579.5 million
Foreign banks	19.9 billion	280.9 million
Friends of Women's World Banking (FWWB)	3.6 billion	50.7 million
Regional rural banks (RRBs)	520 million	7.3 million
Others	210 million	3.0 million
Total	150.85 billion	2.125 billion

Source: N. Srinivasan, *Microfinance India: The State of the Sector Report 2010* (New Delhi: Sage/ACCESS Development Services, 2010).

TABLE 13-4.   Investors in MFIs in India, 2007–10

National investors	International investors
Lok Capital	International Finance Corporation (IFC)
Aavishkaar Goodwell	Sequoia Capital
India Microfinance Development Co.	Incofin
Bajaj Allianz Life Insurance	Microvest Capital Funds
SIDBI	Temasek Holdings
Catamaran Venture Fund	Blue Orchard Private Equity
Bellwether MF Fund Pvt. Ltd.	ACCION Gateway Funds
Dia Vikas Capital	MicroVentures SpA
SVB India Capital	DWM Investment Ltd., NMI Frontier Fund, Tree Line Asia Master Fund
Matrix Partners	Unitus Equity Fund, Elevar Equity Advisors, Microvest, CLSA Capital, Triodos Bank

Source: N. Srinivasan, *Microfinance India: The State of the Sector Report 2010* (New Delhi: Sage/ACCESS Development Services, 2010).

Table 13-3 summarizes lending volume to MFIs as of March 2010. SIDBI, the single largest lender, represented 25 percent of all lending to MFIs. Lending by SIDBI and other public sector banks combined totaled 56 percent of lending, with private sector banks at 27 percent and foreign banks at 13 percent.

In the mid-2000s, several global investors began operations in India, and a range of Indian investors emerged that were active in the microfinance sector, as profiled in table 13-4.

TABLE 13-5.   Equity Investments in Indian MFIs, 2007–10

Financial year	U.S. dollars (million)	No. of deals
2007–08	52	3
2008–09	178	11
2009–10	209	29

Source: N. Srinivasan, *Microfinance India: The State of the Sector Report 2010* (New Delhi: Sage/ ACCESS Development Services, 2010).

Table 13-5 summarizes the growth in equity investments to MFIs in India from 2007 to 2010. Investments grew 400 percent in annual volume and 1,000 percent in number of annual deals from 2007 to 2010. Indian MFIs at the time reported highly efficient operating expense ratios, high staff productivity levels, and healthy loan portfolio quality indicators,[32] especially in comparison with global averages from the MIX market. The cost per borrower for a sample of sixty-six MFIs, including many of the most representative nationally, analyzed by M-Cril in 2009–10, was only INR536 (approximately US$11.90 at the time, now US$7.55). These figures were very low in comparison with the global median at the time for MFIs from the MIX of US$139 and even the Asian MFI median of US$27.[33] Interest rates, and corresponding yields on portfolio, were lower than global averages. While return on equity averaged 14 percent, fairly modest in comparison with global averages, large MFIs in India were being valued at six (and more) times book value, at a time when the average MFI valuation globally was approximately twice book value.[34] These figures suggest that investors were chasing the high growth rates of Indian MFIs or that there was too much capital chasing too few deals. High valuations led to further pressure for MFIs to grow quickly and generate profits, to compensate investors, and so the spiral continued.

During this rapid growth in the microfinance sector, warning lights started to flash. In 2006, in the Krishna district of Andhra Pradesh, the state government closed some MFI branches after raising concerns about perceived high interest rates, loan collection practices, and competition among the various types of financial services providers across MFIs and SHG promoters. The Reserve Bank of India and other actors helped to mediate the crisis between leaders at the state level and in the Krishna district together with MFI leaders, who agreed to make changes in their operating practices. In 2009, in the Kolar district (and later elsewhere in the state) of Karnataka, community leaders issued warnings to MFIs about perceived concerns, and loan repayments plummeted for a period.[35] These red flags spurred the larger NBFC-MFIs to launch MFIN as their industry asso-

TABLE 13-6.   Client Outreach: Borrowers with Outstanding Accounts
from SHGs and MFIs, 2006–11

Millions of borrowers

Segment	2006–07	2007–08	2008–09	2009–10	2010–11	Growth percentage 2010–11
Banks and SHGs[a]	38.0	47.1	54.0	59.6	62.5	4.9
MFIs[b]	10.0	14.1	22.6	26.7	31.4	17.6
Total	48.0	61.2	76.6	86.3	93.9	8.8
Adjusted for overlap	44.9	56.0	70.0	71.0	76.7	8.0

Source: N. Srinivasan, *Microfinance India: The State of the Sector Report 2011* (New Delhi: Sage/ACCESS Development Services, 2011).
a. SHGs = self-help groups.
b. MFIs = microfinance institutions.

ciation to help advocate for reasonable market practices and policy reforms, as well as more focused discussions on incorporating microfinance clients into the existing credit bureaus.

The SHG model and the MFI model developed parallel but complementary approaches over the years, and many MFIs also lent to SHGs. However, during these years of peak growth, proponents of the two models began to clash, with perceived greater competition for clients. As seen in table 13-6, the number of clients/borrowers grew for both SHGs and MFIs from 2006 to 2011.[36] From 2010 to 2011, growth was estimated at almost 5 percent for SHGs and over 17 percent for MFIs nationally. The overlap of clients between SHG programs and MFIs was widely acknowledged and estimated at 17.2 million people (or accounts) as of March 2011, as noted in table 13-6. MFI portfolios plus loans by banks to SHGs together represented 1.5 percent of total national bank credit, and the outstanding microfinance loans of MFIs and SHGs totaled 4.3 percent of priority sector loans outstanding as of March 2011.

The Andhra Pradesh state government supported the SERP Velugu self-help group promotion program, which achieved impressive results, and the state had the highest outreach of self-help groups. The SERP Velugu SHG program also benefited from funding from the World Bank and other multilateral funders. As of March 2010, SHGs were estimated to serve 17.1 million members in Andhra Pradesh, representing almost 27 percent of SHG members nationwide. At the time, MFIs served 6.2 million clients in the state, or approximately 20 percent of all MFI clients nationwide.[37] Concerns grew about multiple organizations lending to the same clients, and some families who borrowed from several lenders were no longer able to meet their loan repayment schedules. Reports of suicide by borrowers began to appear, especially in Andhra Pradesh, which increased pressure on lenders to moderate their operating practices.

In the middle of an already tense environment, SKS became the first MFI to launch an initial public offering of equity in August 2010, raising US$358 million and valuing the company at US$1.6 billion. The shares were more than thirteen times oversubscribed, with a 6:1 market-to-book value.[38] Since its founding, SKS had pursued an aggressive growth model, promoting for-profit microfinance and rapid growth as a means to serve more people. At the time of the IPO, SKS was the largest MFI in the country, with 5.8 million clients. The success of the SKS IPO generated considerable global discussion about MFI staff and investors profiting excessively from their clients, who are often from marginalized and low-income groups. At the time, at least another six Indian MFIs were in discussions for their own IPOs, although these cooled rapidly after October 2010.

The Crisis Erupts in 2010

Not surprisingly, this charged environment, with rapid growth, reports of distressed borrowers, and the high-profile SKS IPO, led to a political backlash. On October 16, 2010, the Andhra Pradesh state government promulgated an ordinance with immediate effect titled "An Ordinance to protect the women Self-Help Groups from exploitation by the Micro Finance Institutions in the State of Andhra Pradesh"; the name was shortened to "Andhra Pradesh MFI Ordinance of 2010."[39] With its very title, the state government clearly meant to punish MFIs, and many analysts at the time noted the perceived competition between the state-run SERP Velugu program and leading MFIs in Andhra Pradesh.[40] Further, the manager of the SERP Velugu program publicly blamed MFIs for the suicides of borrowers in the state.[41] The ordinance was then passed as a state government act in December 2010.

The Andhra Pradesh government issued the MFI ordinance "in the larger public interest and to protect the poor from exploitation," noting that "MFIs are giving loans to SHGs at very high or usurious rates of interest and are using inhuman coercive methods for recovery of the loans. This has even resulted in suicides by many rural poor who have obtained loans from such individuals or entities."[42] In practice, the ordinance completely shut down normal MFI operations across the state. Key provisions of the ordinance included:

- MFIs were required to register in each district of Andhra Pradesh where they operated, noting their interest rate and fees, due diligence for analyzing credit applications, system for loan recovery, and list of staff conducting operations in the district.

- MFIs were not allowed to make new loans or recover existing loan payments until they registered in each district.

- Members of SHGs could only belong to one SHG.

- MFIs were no longer allowed to seek or hold any loan collateral or other security from clients.

- MFIs were required to post their interest rates in visible notices in their lobbies.

- MFIs were no longer allowed to lend to SHGs or their members, unless they presented to the district authorities a written consent from the bank already lending to the SHG.

- Any loan repayments by clients were to be made in the office of the Gram Panchayat—the village self-governance council. MFI staff and third-party agents could no longer approach clients in any other location for regular interactions, especially for loan collections.

- MFIs were required to provide the district authorities with a monthly list of all borrowers.

- The district authorities were given power to search and seize documents and to summon MFI staff or other relevant people during an inquiry into MFI practices.

- To settle any loan disputes between SHGs and MFIs, fast-track courts were to be established throughout the state.

- Any MFI staff or third-party agent found to be coercing or intimidating clients or failing to register with district authorities could be imprisoned for up to three years or required to pay a fine of up to INR100,000 (US$1,409), or both.

- Any MFI staff or third-party agent found to be contravening the ordinance could be imprisoned for up to six months or required to pay a fine of INR10,000 (US$140), or both.

- Government officers and others acting under the ordinance were given protection as public servants under the Indian penal code.[43]

The ordinance effectively stopped all MFI lending and loan recovery in Andhra Pradesh, and MFI staff were afraid to circulate. In addition to the ordinance, some district- and state-level political leaders encouraged borrowers not to repay their loans to MFIs.[44] The combined effect of these actions triggered a statewide default crisis for MFIs and other financial services providers. Repayments dropped from reported 99 percent levels before the ordinance to less than 20 percent as of January 2011.[45] Given the confusion and rising defaults, banks and investors immediately stopped lending and investing in MFIs in Andhra Pradesh and also throughout the country. The ensuing crisis became the largest microfinance crisis in the world—and remains so today. Over 9.2 million loans worth INR72 trillion (US$1.014 billion) became overdue, and 90 percent remained unpaid for years (if they were ever recovered).[46]

The crisis ignited debate across India on microfinance, SHGs, and broader issues related to financial inclusion. Many researchers, industry specialists, policymakers, and MFI and SHG practitioners tried to analyze the crisis in an effort to understand it, resolve it, and prevent anything like it from happening again. MFIN, the newly formed association of nonbank financial company MFIs, requested an independent judiciary inquiry to investigate the allegations against MFIs in Andhra Pradesh.[47]

The concerns about over-indebtedness and the role of MFIs and SHGs were central to the crisis and next steps for the industry. In 2009, before the crisis, the Center for Microfinance at IFMR Research had conducted a household survey of 1,920 rural households in Andhra Pradesh to understand their access and usage of financial services.[48] The survey was designed to be representative of the entire rural population across the state and across all socioeconomic levels. It focused on household borrowing and saving behavior with a range of financial services providers, including SHGs, MFIs, and banks, as well as informal sources such as money lenders, friends, family, and others. The study by the Center for Microfinance included findings that questioned the roots of the crisis:

- An estimated 93 percent of rural households in Andhra Pradesh had some type of debt outstanding. The sources of outstanding loans for these households were

MFIs (11 percent of households); commercial banks, including RRBs (37 percent); SHGs (53 percent). However, a surprising 82 percent of households had a loan outstanding from informal sources such as friends, family, money lenders, and landlords. The median amount of outstanding loans ranged from approximately US$778 for informal loans to US$444 for commercial banks, to US$181 for MFIs, and US$102 for SHGs.

- Households indeed borrowed from multiple sources; 84 percent of households had at least two outstanding loans. Yet the sources included banks, MFIs, SHGs, and especially informal sources. Only 7 percent of households had loans outstanding from both SHGs and MFIs, which was considerably less than critics had claimed.[49]

Other researchers came to similar conclusions about the relative dominance of informal credit in both client reach and lending volume among rural households in Andhra Pradesh, including a second survey by the Center for Microfinance at IFMR Research and separate qualitative research by MicroSave, both in 2011.[50] Likewise, a study by the Indian National Council for Applied Economic Research (NCAER) found that informal sources were the main source of indebtedness for households, and with much higher loan amounts than from MFIs or SHGs.[51] The NCAER study included Andhra Pradesh and four other states: West Bengal, Tamil Nadu, Uttar Pradesh, and Rajasthan. A later study in 2013 by researchers at the Indira Gandhi Institute of Development Research (IGIDR) indicated that household consumption in Andhra Pradesh fell by 19 percent after the ordinance was passed; the greatest reduction in spending was on food and education, and there was evidence of greater volatility in overall household consumption.[52] The IGIDR study found that the microfinance crisis directly affected households that were borrowing from MFIs, but that the crisis also reduced all households' access to finance and household spending.

Rebuilding after the Crisis

The microfinance crisis that erupted in October 2010 shook the country (and the world) far beyond the state of Andhra Pradesh. The crisis caused financial services providers, policymakers, industry actors, clients, and funders to reassess the best ways to increase access to finance in India. The postcrisis period starting in late 2010 catalyzed significant innovation across India: there emerged more focus on client rights and privacy; new types of financial services providers; and a national campaign for bank accounts underpinned by unique biometric identification, interoperable payments, growth in mobile phone access, and critical financial infrastructure. Financial inclusion more than doubled in India from 2011 (35.2 percent) to 2017 (79.9 percent) for people over fifteen years of age holding an account with a financial services provider (that is, a financial institution or mobile phone account, using most recent data available from Findex).[53] These truly impressive results are a culmination of many public and private sector efforts.

The Microfinance Code of Conduct

The unprecedented scale of the 2010 crisis rallied the microfinance sector to take action itself to improve its operating practices and differentiate the irresponsible MFIs from those that treated clients fairly. Both Sa-Dhan and MFIN, the two microfinance industry associations, had already developed acceptable practices for member MFIs, although these unfortunately did not prevent some of the excesses of the late 2000s. Even before the crisis, in early 2010, some industry players had organized workshops and provided technical assistance on establishing responsible finance approaches.[54] Then, after the crisis erupted in October 2010, these efforts became more accepted by a broader range of MFIs that recognized the need to take action. In late 2010, a group of industry players, including Sa-Dhan, MFIN, ACCESS, SIDBI, multilateral and bilateral funders, and other supporters, began meeting to develop an all-India common code of conduct for MFIs.[55] Building on earlier efforts from Sa-Dhan and MFIN, the working group also benefited from global perspective from the Responsible Finance Forum, the Smart Campaign, Cerise, and others. The final Code of Conduct was jointly approved by the Sa-Dhan and MFIN membership in December 2011 at the Microfinance India Summit. The Code of Conduct for MFIs included a value statement focused on integrity, quality, appropriateness, transparency, and fair dealings with clients. The code provided detailed principles for MFI operations in the following areas: integrity and ethical behavior; transparency of financial and operating conditions; client protection on fair practices, including avoiding over-indebtedness, appropriate interaction and collection practices, and privacy of client information; governance of the MFI; staff recruitment; client education; data sharing with RBI-approved credit bureaus; dedicated client feedback and grievance redressal mechanisms.[56]

The code also included client protection guidelines and institutional conduct guidelines. These practices were in sync with RBI requirements, including the Guidance for Fair Practices for NBFCs. SIDBI, MFIN, Sa-Dhan, and others funded dozens of MFI assessments, organized workshops to raise awareness, and trained assessors on the Code of Conduct, to help MFIs improve their operations and ensure compliance. In addition, many banks and other lenders, as well as investors in MFIs, began to require a Code of Conduct assessment as part of their due diligence of the MFI. To help implement the new code, MFIN launched an ombudsman effort, establishing a toll-free phone line for clients to report anonymously concerns in MFI operations and also submit claims for redressal.

To further strengthen the sector, the RBI issued norms for self-regulatory organizations in November 2013; and MFIN, the organization of MFIs legally recognized as NBFCs, received self-regulatory organization (SRO) status in June 2014. The RBI later accorded SRO status to Sa-Dhan, as the association for the broader group of all MFIs (including the NBFC legal category and other categories) in 2015.

In December 2015 and again in September 2019, MFIN and Sa-Dhan presented revised codes of conduct, building on the experience of the previous four years, changes in regulation, the introduction of small finance banks and new universal banks, and the RBI's earlier approval of both MFIN and Sa-Dhan as self-regulatory organizations. The revised 2015 code included a new supplementary document, "MFI Commitment to Customers," intended to be given to MFI clients at the time their loan was disbursed. The revised 2019 code further expanded provisions on risk management, staff training, and client education.[57]

In addition, in September 2019, MFIN, Sa-Dhan, and the Finance Industry Development Council (FIDC) jointly issued the Code for Responsible Lending, which extends many of the provisions of earlier codes of conduct to a broader group of financial services providers.[58] This is an important step given the new types of players entering the market over the previous five years. The earlier codes and RBI regulations focused only on NBFC-MFIs (monitored by MFIN) and MFIs (monitored by Sa-Dhan), prohibiting them from becoming the third lender to any single client, in an attempt to reduce over-indebtedness. Further, total loans were to be limited to INR100,000 (US$1,409) per client. However these provisions did not apply to small finance banks, universal banks, other types of NBFCs, and other lenders. As the self-regulatory body for all registered NBFCs, FIDC's involvement in the Code for Responsible Lending is a significant step forward to include a larger group of lenders. Several universal banks and small finance banks have also agreed to the new code. The Code for Responsible Lending focuses on fair interactions with clients, suitability of financial products, avoiding overlending, transparency and education, privacy of client information, and grievance redressal.[59]

Appropriate Regulation: The RBI's Role

In the aftermath of the crisis, the RBI encouraged banks and development finance institutions to renew their lending to MFIs and agreed to restructure existing bank loans to MFIs given the broad liquidity crisis across the sector. In addition, the RBI quickly launched the Malegam Commission, which in January 2011 recommended the following: creation of a separate category of nonbank finance companies (NBFCs) for MFIs; adoption of responsible practices for MFIs, including transparency in pricing and fair loan recovery methods; continuation of priority sector benefits for bank lending to MFI-NBFCs; and specific recommendations on interest rates, interest margins, maximum loan amounts for MFIs, and loan loss provisioning requirements.

The RBI broadly accepted the Malegam Commission recommendations in May 2011 through a monetary policy statement. In June 2011, the first draft of the Microfinance Institutions (Development and Regulation) Bill was introduced in Parliament. After significant discussion and several drafts, a revised version of the bill was submitted to the Lok Sabha, the upper house of Parliament, in February 2014. Unfortunately, the bill languished in Parliament and was never passed. Thankfully the RBI was able to address the legal and regulatory issues exposed by the 2010 crisis through other means.

To help the sector continue rebuilding, the RBI issued directions to create a new category of NBFC specialized for non-deposit-taking MFIs in December 2011. This sweeping and comprehensive regulation for NBFC-MFIs introduced several major changes:

- Minimum capital requirements or "net owned funds" of INR50 million (US$704,500), or INR20 million (US$281,800) for NBFC-MFIs in the northern regions of the country, with milestones to be met by 2012 and 2014 for existing MFIs to convert to NBFC status and meet these requirements. (The requirements have subsequently been adjusted for large, medium-sized, and smaller NBFC-MFIs.)

- Requirement that an NBFC-MFI hold at least 85 percent of net assets (for assets originated after January 2012) in the form of loans that fit the new definition of "qualifying assets":

  ○ loan disbursed by an NBFC-MFI to a borrower with a rural household annual income not exceeding INR100,000 (US$1,409) or urban and semi-urban household income not exceeding INR160,000 (US$2,254). In October 2019, these limits were increased to INR125,000 (US$1,761) for rural households and INR200,000 (US$2,818) for urban and semi-urban households[60]

- ◦ loan amount does not exceed INR60,000 (US$845) in the first loan cycle and INR100,000 (US$1,409) in subsequent cycles. The total indebtedness of the borrower does not exceed INR100,000 (US$1,409), minus any education or medical expenses paid by the loan. In October 2019, the loan limit was increased to INR125,000 (US$1,761)[61]

- ◦ loans must be extended without collateral requirements

- ◦ loan tenure of at least twenty-four months for loans over INR30,000 (US$423) and no prepayment penalty

- ◦ loan to be repaid in weekly, fortnightly, or monthly installments at the choice of the borrower

- ▪ More stringent requirements for capital adequacy limits and calculation, revised asset classification approach, and new loan loss provisioning norms

- ▪ Greater transparency in interest rates, with an interest rate cap of 26 percent per year calculated on a declining balance basis, a 12 percent margin cap, and a 1 percent processing fee cap. In addition, no penalty could be assessed for late loan payments from clients. The loan terms were to be provided to clients in clear language noting all pricing and loan conditions. In addition, the effective interest rate must be posted in the customer lobby of each of the MFI's offices and on its website. (After a short period, the RBI adjusted some elements of the NBFC-MFI directions, such as reducing the margin cap from 12 to 10 percent for large MFIs and introducing new calculations for adhering to the interest rate and margin caps.)

- ▪ Borrowers could belong to only one joint liability group, and a maximum of two NBFC-MFIs could lend to a borrower

- ▪ Requirement for NBFC-MFIs to establish a code of conduct, including non-coercive loan recovery practices, and build on the existing Fair Practices Code issued by the RBI in 2006 for NBFCs

- Requirement for NBFC-MFIs to comply with broader corporate governance regulations for NBFCs

- Confirmation of NBFC-MFI status qualifying for priority sector lending

The RBI went further in September 2013 by setting up the Mor Committee on Comprehensive Financial Services for Small Businesses and Low-Income Households, with a broad representation of members from the public and private sectors. The committee report in January 2014 marked a shift in the discussion about how to pursue meaningful financial inclusion in India; it made the following key recommendations:[62]

- Universal electronic bank account access for all Indians over eighteen years of age

- Access to service points for payment and deposit services within a fifteen-minute walk

- Universal access for low-income households and small businesses to a formally regulated lender offering a range of suitable and affordable credit, deposit, and investment products, as well as a suite of insurance products

- Customer right to suitable financial services and legal redress in the case of gross negligence by a financial services provider, which signaled a new approach in the global discussion on responsible finance

- Recommendation for public policy to pursue principles of stability, transparency, neutrality, and responsibility. Any approach to financial inclusion should maintain overall stability of the financial system. Financial services providers should provide transparent balance sheets and frequent reporting. Market and regulatory treatment of financial services providers should be neutral and not based on their institutional character, but on the role they perform in the market. Financial services providers should be responsible for offering suitable services that are welfare enhancing

- Recommendation for RBI to develop licenses for differentiated institutions such as payments banks, wholesale consumer banks, and wholesale investment banks[63]

Credit Reporting

Lack of data on client indebtedness contributed to the excessive growth in lending by MFIs, and this was flagged even before the crisis. Recognizing this problem, key MFIs began discussing how to incorporate microfinance clients in the credit bureaus in the mid-2000s. Starting in mid-2009, the Microfinance Institutions Network and the International Finance Corporation (IFC) jointly conducted the initial feasibility study, built market awareness, developed a common data format, helped MFIs sync their data with credit bureaus, and advised credit bureaus on linking with MFIs. By May 2011, Equifax and HighMark had launched services to MFIs, and within four months, thirty-five MFIs had already submitted 55 million loan account records, indicating their significant interest in the value of credit reporting.

The credit bureaus in India have evolved quickly, building on RBI regulation, their own expertise, and a sector hungry for this information. In July 2014, the RBI issued notifications (strengthened in January 2015) requiring all credit institutions (and largely aimed at NBFC-MFIs) to join one of the licensed credit bureaus, submit data to at least one credit bureau, and seek a credit enquiry on each client to ensure they would not be offering a third loan to any client.[64] It is noteworthy that these requirements do not mandate that they report data for individual SHG clients to the credit bureaus, although this has been in discussion for at least six years.[65] When the RBI issued these notifications, four credit bureaus had been licensed by the RBI and were rapidly expanding their operations: CIBIL, the oldest credit bureau in India, which later joined with TransUnion; Experian; HighMark, which later joined with CRIF; and Equifax. Later RBI notifications required credit institutions to provide historical data on clients,[66] thereby leveling the playing field among the four bureaus. To promote consumer awareness and protection, beginning in 2016 the RBI required each bureau to provide one free credit report per year to clients of credit institutions, so they could verify their own information and take steps to correct errors.[67]

Credit bureau coverage of households and businesses in India has grown tremendously since 2014. Extensive coverage and use of credit reporting has helped reduce over-indebtedness, helped credit institutions manage risk, and contributed to greater stability of the overall financial sector. The World Bank Group's Doing Business database tracks coverage through an indicator on "getting credit." Doing Business data for 2019 suggest that 478.6 million people, 17 million firms, and 55.9 percent of the adult population are covered by the existing credit bureaus in India.[68] Overall, the "getting credit" score for India improved to the rank of twenty-two globally as of 2019, and this score is largely based on laws, regulations, and national coverage for credit bureaus.

TABLE 13-7.   Coverage of India's Credit Bureaus, as of July 2018

TransUnion CIBIL	*CRIF HighMark*
Launched 2004	Launched 2010
3,500+ subscribers	4,000+ subscribers
1 billion + credit records	1.2 billion + credit records
Experian	*Equifax*[a]
Launched 2010	Launched 2010
4,600+ subscribers	Global coverage: 820 million consumers
720 million + credit records	

Source: Pallavi Nahata, "Will RBI's Public Credit Registry Disrupt India's Successful Credit Bureaus?," Bloomberg Quint, July 12, 2018.

a. India-specific data not available from Equifax.

As noted in table 13-7, the coverage of the four licensed credit bureaus is significant. CRIF HighMark reports the largest number of credit records among the four bureaus, perhaps in part because of their dominance in serving MFIs with large numbers of clients. CRIF HighMark's database includes over 1.2 billion credit records, which it estimates can be attributed to 390–400 million individuals.[69] TransUnion CIBIL reports over 1 billion credit records, partly reflecting the advantage they gained as the sole bureau for several years in the 2000s.

Although the coverage of bureaus is impressive, given the size of the Indian market, more work is needed to ensure comprehensive data quality. For example, as noted earlier, lenders to SHGs are not yet required to report to credit bureaus. In addition, clients may not have accurate information, especially if they take loans from multiple lenders such as banks, NBFCs, co-operatives, and regional rural banks that have different levels of capacity and accuracy when reporting to the bureaus. In case studies across the country, analysts have noted that the records for some clients are inaccurate;[70] accuracy is especially critical given the RBI limit on total borrowing per client of INR125,000. As fintechs grow their lending operations, their loans should also be tracked through the credit bureaus. Finally, given the importance and pervasiveness of credit bureau data, clients should be more informed about their rights to view and correct their data.

In November 2017, the RBI convened the Deosthalee High-Level Committee on Credit Reporting; its report, published in June 2018, calls for a unified public credit registry to be housed initially at the RBI, which would supplement the various private credit registries.[71] The public registry would serve as the single point of mandatory reporting for all loans across the financial sector, to enable the regulator to track material events across institutional loan portfolios.[72] The Deosthalee report recommended that the public registry not provide services currently offered by private reg-istries, such as credit scores. The concept of a public bureau is moving forward, as the RBI seeks a technical firm to manage the platform.

Long discussed among specialists and already done in many other countries, the RBI is also considering expanding credit bureau data to include alternative data such as payments to utilities and mobile phone companies and transactions covered by the Indian Goods and Services Tax Network.[73] The use of alternative data could help low-income clients establish stronger credit history by expanding data coverage to include these more common types of transactions made by a broader range of the population.

Government of India Initiatives

Since 2009, the government of India has gradually developed an unprecedented na-tional campaign for unique identification, bank accounts, interoperable payment plat-forms, and digitization of government payments. The components of this campaign were built separately—and under two different national government administrations—and then linked to make the combination of services even more useful. The campaign became known as JAM—Jan-Dhan (bank account campaign), Aadhaar (unique identification), and mobile connectivity (linking payments to mobile phones). No other government on the planet has attempted such an ambitious campaign in such a short period of time. The government of India's efforts have contributed to a tre-mendous increase in financial inclusion and digital payments across the country.

Unique Identification: Aadhaar

In 2009, the government of India launched an ambitious campaign to offer a unique identity number to every resident of India. Discussed for years as a way to unify mul-tiple identity numbers used for subsets of the population (for example, voting card, ration card, income tax account, and driver's license numbers), the Department of Information Technology proposed a new biometric approach in 2006. The Unique Identification Authority of India (UIDAI) was created in 2009 to manage the new identity program. The first biometric UIDs using fingerprints and iris scans known as "Aadhaar numbers" were issued in September 2010.[74] The enrollment campaign ramped up progressively thereafter. Within the first year, 100 million people had en-rolled, 99 percent of Indian adults were enrolled by 2017, and 1.23 billion people were enrolled as of February 2019.[75] E-payment campaigns and demonetization in 2016 may have encouraged people to enroll in Aadhaar for access to electronic payments. Regardless, the UIDAI campaign is the largest such identification program and biometric database in the world. National coverage was effectively achieved in nine years. Given the sheer number of people involved, in the second largest country in the world, this is an impressive accomplishment.

Rapid growth of the UIDAI campaign and its broad coverage sparked controversies and opportunities. Concerns about incorrect enrollments began emerging in 2011, and as the campaign expanded, the incidence of inaccurate data was closely monitored by UIDAI and activists, although this seems to have become less of an issue now that the program is mature.[76] Advocates have also raised concerns about data privacy and security. One reported data breach occurred in January 2018 when a journalist claimed to have paid INR500 (US$7) and received access to the entire UIDAI database.[77] Although the UIDAI has denied this account, there have been other claims of data leaks through third-party applications and unsecure websites.[78] For such a sensitive database affecting almost the entire population, data privacy and security deserve close scrutiny by advocates and careful management by UIDAI.

The Indian social welfare system includes hundreds of entitlements and subsidies, including cooking gas subsidies, prenatal care benefits, education grants, and fertilizer subsidies to a wide range of low-income people, vulnerable groups, farmers, students, and others. Starting in 2011, pilots began to emerge that would link these benefits to the UID, to track identity more accurately and reduce fraud and error.[79] Government-to-person payments are discussed further later in the chapter.

Financial services providers and mobile network operators saw an opportunity for the UID to strengthen information on their clients, to help fulfill regulated know-your-customer (KYC) requirements, and they soon began requiring clients to furnish their UID for account opening and maintenance. Globally, KYC requirements have been challenging for financial services providers working with low-income, rural, and vulnerable groups who sometimes are unable to produce birth certificates, utility bills, passports, rental contracts, and other common methods of identification.[80] KYC issues were particularly acute in India given a fractured identification system across several ministries and agencies, fraud and errors with paper-based documents, and disparate approaches by states and the central government. Given its national scope and rigorous biometric approach, the UID was welcomed as a useful KYC solution by financial inclusion advocates, banks, regulators, and government agencies.

However, legal challenges have complicated use of the UID. The Supreme Court ruled in September 2013 that people could not be refused public benefits or services if they lacked a UID; the Supreme Court further ruled that the UID could not be made mandatory. The Parliament passed the Aadhaar Act in March 2016 to provide a legal foundation for the unique ID and for the UIDAI as a statutory authority.

Again in September 2018, the Supreme Court ruled that the UID was constitutional, including the requirement that it be used for income tax filing and government benefits such as subsidies and welfare programs, although children cannot be excluded from services for lack of a UID. However, the court determined that the UID could not be compulsory for KYC requirements by private sector entities such as financial services providers, telecommunications (telco) companies, and schools.[81] Further, the court urged the government to develop more protections for privacy and security of consumer data, and a data protection measure is now being considered.[82] In partial response, the Parliament amended the UIDAI Act in January 2019, promulgated in February 2019, to allow people to voluntarily provide their UID for KYC requirements with banks and telco providers, although a client who does not provide a UID cannot be refused service.[83] As of August 2019, a further amendment to the anti-money-laundering statutes allows for digital KYC to open a bank account with a voter ID or driver's license, if a UID is not available, which is similar to the norms for opening a mobile phone account.[84]

National Campaign for Bank Accounts: Pradhan Mantri Jan Dhan Yojana

The government of India launched the Pradhan Mantri Jan Dhan Yojana (PMJDY) campaign in August 2014 to ensure that all households have access to bank accounts. Managed by the Ministry of Finance, PMJDY mobilized banks to provide an interest-bearing deposit account with no minimum balance, a RuPay debit card, access to digital payments, basic life insurance, a small overdraft facility of approximately US$70, and access to insurance and pension facilities.[85] Within the first six months, PMJDY reported 136.8 million new accounts had been opened. In 2018, the PMJDY program expanded the account package, including higher overdraft of INR10,000 (US$140) and accident insurance benefits. As of January 2020, PMJDY reported over 378 million new accounts opened, the majority with public sector banks.[86] Further, 99 to 100 percent of all households hold at least one bank account in every state across the country.[87]

Analysis of the PMJDY program has been largely positive, although concerns about duplication and dormancy have persisted. Some of these new, multibenefit accounts were likely opened by households that already had a bank account. However, estimates vary on the magnitude of these duplicate accounts—from a minor percentage to 33 percent or even 79 percent of new accounts.[88] Banks were initially reluctant to engage in the program, but given the strong signals from the government, they obliged. Yet the high dormancy of new accounts raised concerns in the early years of the program. On top of the expense of account opening, dormant accounts are costly for banks to maintain and can drain their enthusiasm for financial inclusion.

Dormancy may have been fueled by a number of factors, including clients slowly becoming familiar with their new accounts, duplicate accounts per household, and fictitious or incomplete client information used by banks to open accounts in order to meet their targets. Estimates for account dormancy ranged from 63 percent (March 2015) to 28 percent (August 2016) from independent studies.[89] Some banks—especially public sector banks—reportedly added as little as a single rupee to potentially millions of dormant accounts in order to reduce the number that they needed to report as dormant.[90] Demonetization on November 8, 2016, may have also helped increase usage of all bank accounts, including PMJDY accounts. For example, total deposits in PMJDY accounts more than doubled to approximately US$12.8 billion in the forty-five days following demonetization.[91] The dormancy issue seems to be abating; reports on PMJDY as of September 2019 suggest that there are 48.8 million zero-balance accounts (13 percent of total accounts), and 66 million accounts dormant over the previous year (17.8 percent of total accounts).[92] Further, the average deposit balance in PMJDY accounts rose from INR1,000 (US$14) in March 2015 to INR2,853 (US$40) in October 2019.[93]

Interoperable Payments Platform

The RBI established the Board for Payment and Settlement Systems in 2005 and promoted the Payment and Settlement Systems Act of 2007. Following from this framework, the National Payments Corporation of India was launched in 2009 by the Indian Banks' Association and the RBI as an umbrella organization for operating retail payments and settlement systems in India. Initially ten banks invested in NPCI, and the number increased to fifty-six banks in 2016.[94]

The NPCI manages several payment platforms and initiatives:

- Immediate Payment Service (IMPS) launched publicly in November 2010 to provide instant 24/7 interbank electronic funds transfer, building on the existing NEFT and RTGS systems available for fund transfer during normal banking hours. IMPS can be used on mobile phones, the internet, at ATMs, in text messages (SMS and USSD), and at bank branches.[95]

- RuPay launched in 2012 as a domestic debit card scheme offering an open-loop, multilateral system to connect all Indian banks and financial institutions in India with electronic payments.[96] Clients can request a RuPay debit card linked to their PMJDY accounts. There were 298 million RuPay cards issued and linked to the 378 million PMJDY accounts opened as of January 2020.[97]

▪ Unified Payment Interface (UPI) launched publicly in August 2016 as a mobile phone application that allows access to a client's different bank accounts and offers several instant payment and banking features. Security is high, with two-factor authentication and a virtual address for the client's bank account—which prevents access to personal account information by unauthorized users and does not require clients to reenter information while using the application. UPI enables a range of payments, including peer to peer, merchant, utility bill, donations, and others, either in real time or at a future scheduled time. The UPI system works with a range of banking applications available from financial services providers in India on both Apple and android platforms.[98]

▪ Bharat Interface for Money (BHIM) is a bank and payment application also launched in 2016 that works on the UPI system using a mobile phone number, the virtual address from UPI, an account number, or even a quick response (QR) scan. Clients can send and request money, pay merchants, check UPI transactions and account balances linked to the application, and block payments or users from interacting with the client's own account. BHIM is available in twelve major languages spoken in India.[99] In 2017, BHIM added an Aadhaar or unique identity feature that allows clients to pay using their biometrics (such as a fingerprint) as authenticator, instead of a signature or security code.

These useful and groundbreaking NPCI services are enabling a true leap forward for access to digital payments across India. Use of these services is surging across the country in response to the well-designed products, as well as a deliberate focus on keeping the services affordable (and free for some products). As of September 2019, the number of payment cards in India reflects continued growth with 52.6 million credit cards and 835.6 million debit cards outstanding.[100] Credit and debit card transactions exceeded 1.39 billion valued at over US$46.3 trillion in September 2019, with debit cards enabling 87 percent of transactions.[101] For the month of December 2019, NPCI reported 2.5 billion financial transactions over all of their payment networks valued at US$191.4 trillion.[102] Of these transactions, the UPI platform (including BHIM) enabled 1.3 billion transactions (52 percent of all NPCI transactions) valued at US$28.4 trillion (15 percent of all value of NPCI transactions) for December 2019.[103]

Thus, according to December 2019 data, monthly card payments were about equal in transaction number and about 1.6 times higher in value than monthly mobile payments.[104] However, payments on the UPI platform grew dramatically, from 915 million payments valued at INR1.1 trillion (US$15.4 billion) for the year ending March

2018 to 8.6 billion transactions valued at INR14.87 trillion (US$208.4 billion) for the nine months from April to December 2019.[105] These numbers reflect a ninefold growth in volume and thirteenfold growth in the value of transactions over the period.

Over the past five years the RBI and NPCI have introduced multiple revisions and improvements to the overall payment infrastructure, available products, and pricing to encourage greater usage of digital finance. For example, the RBI will enable global payments through UPI, and NPCI already demonstrated this payment mechanism in Singapore in November 2019.[106] In addition, the RBI announced that, beginning in January 2020, banks would not be allowed to charge fees for online NEFT payments from savings accounts.[107]

Further fueling mobile payments, mobile phone penetration continues to grow across India. As of October 2019 TRAI, the telecommunications regulator, reported the existence of 1.183 billion mobile phone accounts, 981.2 million of which were active.[108] However, the overall mobile teledensity of 89.6 percent reflects a density of 156.8 percent in urban areas and 57.9 percent in rural areas.[109] Prices in India for mobile phone service are among the lowest in the world, which has helped fuel mobile usage across a wide range of socioeconomic groups in both urban and rural areas.[110] Clearly, the UPI platform and other NPCI services are already encouraging impressive uptake in digital payments, building on growing mobile phone usage across India.

At least three additional factors have helped promote the use of payment services over the past decade: an expanding network of ATMs and bank agents, the government's transition from cash and checks to digital payments, and demonetization.

Expanding Service Points: ATMs and Banking Correspondents

As people start to use digital payments, they still need to be able to exchange cash in and out of the system. This cash in/cash out challenge requires service points connected to the digital payment network with sufficient cash liquidity to service clients, at least until more clients prefer digital payments over use of cash.[111] Given the cost of opening bank branches, more cost-effective and nimble solutions are necessary to expand physical service points.

The RBI recognized this challenge early, encouraging banks to install ATMs and allowing third-party or white-label ATMs starting in 2011. The number of ATMs grew by double digits for several years but declined slightly in 2019, to 232,000 ATMs as of November 2019.[112] In the past four years, so-called micro-ATMs have emerged. As modified point-of-sale (POS) devices located at retailers and business correspondents, the micro-ATM is connected through the payment system to bank accounts so clients can deposit and withdraw cash from their accounts using a debit card. More limited functions are available at micro-ATMs than at regular ATMs, including a limit of INR10,000 (US$140) on withdrawals. In November 2019, when the RBI began reporting, over 235,000 micro-ATMs were in service.[113] The number of standard POS devices is also growing across India, with RBI reporting over 4.88 million as of November 2019, a 39 percent increase from November 2018.[114] The actual number of POS devices across the country is larger, as this figure includes only POS devices linked to banks, not those managed by fintechs. Five banks account for 76 percent of the POS devices, led by Ratnakar Bank with 27 percent of the POS devices.[115]

The RBI also developed guidelines for agent banking in 2006 and for progressively expanding the eligibility criteria to serve as an agent. In India, business correspondents (BCs, also known as banking agents and other terms in other countries) have emerged as a useful way to expand the network of service points, although managing this channel brings its own challenges—both for the BC network and for financial services providers that outsource client relations through BCs.[116]

In the past ten years, several BC networks have emerged to help banks expand their physical network across the expanse of India. Eko and Fino were two of the first BC networks launched in the late 2000s; others included Paytm, RazorPay, IFMR Rural Channels and Services, Oxigen Services, Instamojo, ItzCash, A Little World, the Drishtee Foundation, Samvriddhi Trust, Novopay, Ekgaon, and ZeroMass. BC networks in India have learned key lessons on business viability and agent management, including how to attract and screen potential agents, how to remunerate agents through financial and other incentives, and how to retain their best agents. Successful BC networks developed scalable models for BC operations, including agent training, client training, cash management, and fraud management.

As a way to combine the old and the new in financial inclusion, MFIs and SHGs have also been serving as BCs for payment providers and banks across India for several years. MFIs and SHGs know their customers and already have agents and branch offices in rural and semi-urban areas where banks are less present. However, serving as a BC can detract from the MFI's or SHG's core operations and raise new issues, including managing cash liquidity, serving a larger clientele without the deep relationships established through microfinance groups, ensuring the agent's safety, and avoiding hollowing out their own operations and client relationships in favor of relationships with their partner banks. In the author's discussions with MFIs and SHG networks over the years, few say that they have pursued BC operations as a core operational strategy. However, for some MFIs or SHG networks, serving as a BC could be a reasonable strategy if the gains outweigh the additional risk.

Given their growing presence and proximity to clients, BCs have helped increase clients' comfort with and use of digital payments. However, BCs can also add to client angst by refusing to provide cash, preferring to focus on their core business (such as gas stations or grocery stores, for agents based in those locations), defrauding clients, being closed during key hours, or providing substandard customer service. Over 20 percent of BCs have also been subjected to fraud and abuse by clients and business partners.[117] The BC sector's development and professionalization is supported through the Business Correspondent Federation of India (BCFI), the industry association of both corporate and agent business correspondents active since 2014. With over forty-five member companies, the BCFI offers training, certification, and BC registry; standards of customer service; a code of conduct; a grievance redressal mechanism; and technology platforms for the BC industry.[118]

The BC model in India has not developed as exponentially (per capita) as in other countries such as Kenya or Tanzania, where BCs are ubiquitous and vital to the provision of financial services in those countries. The BCFI currently estimates that there are more than 787,000 agent BCs across the country.[119] India's trajectory for BCs and other service points will be different given the confluence of financial inclusion efforts by both public and private sector agents.

Government-to-Person (G2P) Payments

The government of India made a strategic decision to convert to digital payments, a move that has produced efficiency, cost savings, and transparency for government services and benefits. Yet perhaps its largest impact has been to drive greater use of digital payments by hundreds of millions of people and businesses receiving or paying government transfers.

Government payments include a wide range of transfers to and from other governments (state, local, international), to and from businesses (procurement for services and goods, taxes, fees, licenses), and to and from people (taxes; social welfare payments; public sector staff, such as military, government bureaucrats, and public school teachers; salaries; benefits; and pensions). As a gateway to financial inclusion, government-to-person payments can bring people into the formal financial sector by giving them a bank account where they can receive social welfare payments. For low-income and vulnerable people, government-to-person payments may be a lifeline of income, and perhaps their largest single financial transaction in a month.

In India, government-to-person payments include cash transfers (wages, pensions, and unemployment assistance), subsidy transfers (for food, kerosene, and fertilizers), and benefit transfers (welfare programs, including the well-known National Rural Livelihood Mission and the Mahatma Gandhi National Rural Employment Guarantee Act). One study from 2012–13 estimated that annual G2P payments in India exceeded $236 billion at the time—approximately 55 percent was in cash transfers, 33 percent in subsidy transfers, and 12 percent in benefit transfers.[120]

Gradually, pilots to digitize G2P payments began to emerge, although the challenges were immense.[121] At the time, most records at government offices were entirely paper based, fragmented across multiple registries, and managed by multiple layers of staff and outsourced workers at multiple locations. Not surprisingly, errors in these records were inevitable, through human error and sometimes by design in cases of fraud. Digitizing the actual records of the benefit programs and people eligible to receive government payments was an onerous undertaking. Thereafter, convincing banks (even public sector banks) to open accounts for the beneficiaries of government payments was extremely difficult, especially before the UID and PMJDY programs enabled hundreds of millions of identification and bank accounts. One example is the IFC pilot program with the State Health Society in Bihar for digitizing health benefits and records, linking with the Public Finance Management System, and enabling G2P payments across this large state of more than 100 million people.[122] Even in the early years of the pilot programs, the G2P payment pilots struggled to help beneficiaries enroll, receive their UID numbers in the mail, open bank accounts linked to their UID, actually receive their government benefits according to program rules, and then withdraw the cash from their accounts, often at bank branches or through business correspondents several kilometers from their homes.[123]

To facilitate government payments, the Ministry of Finance, through the Office of Controller General of Accounts, developed and launched the Central Plan Schemes Monitoring System in 2009. The online platform was conceived as a financial tracking and reporting system on the flow of funds from the central government to state and local governments for a range of government funding, including subsidy and benefit transfers. The platform was renamed the Public Finance Management System (PFMS) and expanded in 2013 to include government-to-person payments. As part of the government's broader Digital India initiative, the Ministry of Finance continues to improve the PFMS platform with new functionality, including real-time links to core banking systems of most banks in the country, allowing PFMS to be used for almost any government payment to people and vendors across the country.[124]

To give even more impetus to this strategic transformation, in 2013 the government created a specialized unit to coordinate direct benefit transfers (DBTs), the DBT Mission, originally in the Planning Commission and shifted in 2015 to the high-level Cabinet Secretariat.[125] As of December 2019, the DBT Mission reported 429 cash and in-kind government benefit G2P programs using their platform. For the cash DBT programs, the eight-month expenditure for April to December 2019 of INR1.1 trillion (US$15.3 billion) indicates that the program's annual results may match the 2018–19 fiscal year expenditure of INR2.1 trillion (US$30.16 billion) for 440 government programs.[126] Channeling digital payments for such a large number of programs and beneficiaries is a master stroke by the government of India to accelerate financial inclusion while greatly increasing the efficiency, transparency, and effectiveness of government benefit programs.

The government of India is also considering universal basic income (UBI) to replace some of the existing benefit programs. The hundreds of current benefit programs are mostly conditional, meaning they are limited to specific people based on socioeconomic conditions, specific geographies, triggered by certain actions such as buying fertilizer, receiving prenatal care at approved clinics, or enrolling in university, or tied to specific expenditures such as approved food purchases. UBI as a concept could be unconditional, provided to a broader range of citizens, and used for any purchase, according to the analysis laid out by the Ministry of Finance in January 2017.[127]

Demonetization

On November 8, 2016, the Indian prime minister made a surprise evening announcement that all 500 and 1,000 rupee notes (US$7 and US$14, respectively) would no longer be legal tender as of midnight that day. At the time, these two currency bills represented a staggering 86 percent of all currency notes in circulation.[128] In promoting demonetization, the prime minister cited concerns about cash used for terrorism, and to avoid taxes, as well as the prevalence of counterfeit currency. People were told they could exchange their currency in bank accounts and receive the new 500 and 2,000 rupee notes (US$7 and US$28, respectively) for fifty days until December 30, 2016, although this currency exchange was then curtailed in late November 2016. In addition, daily limits on currency exchanges per person and cash withdrawals from banks and ATMs were imposed. The sheer logistics of such a transition, given the size of the country and population, were overwhelming.

Not surprisingly, the shortage of cash affected everyone—perhaps proof that cash is still king in India. The informal sector is almost fully cash based and used by the vast majority of the low- and middle-income Indian population for their livelihoods and many household purchases. Almost every household had people queuing in long lines at banks to exchange their currency. Researchers, industry associations, and even the RBI and others have studied the economic and social effects, including lower agricultural production (given the lack of cash to buy inputs), lower agricultural prices (given the lack of cash to buy produce), loss of jobs in manufacturing and other sectors, and loss of sales, production, and wages for MSMEs that provide most households with their regular supply of food and commodities.[129]

However the cash crisis propelled the use of digital payments, at least in the short term. The use of payment cards and digital wallets rose during this period and remained high even after the liquidity crunch eased. One study published almost two years after demonetization suggests that overall debit card use increased 84 percent, clients added 82 percent more funds to digital wallets, and people increased peer-to-peer payments by 745 percent and e-shopping by 405 percent.[130] As of June 2019, cash in circulation grew to INR212 trillion (approximately US$3 trillion), or over 24 percent more than in October 2016, just before demonetization.[131] Yet the trend in payments continues to grow, especially in urban areas. According to the RBI, payments volume and value grew at 54.3 percent and 14.2 percent, respectively, in 2018–19, and this builds on increases of 44.6 percent and 11.9 percent, respectively, in 2017–18.[132] A notable difference in India's trajectory is that payments and broader use of digital finance are growing most rapidly through use of mobile devices, while usage of debit and credit cards at POS terminals is declining, relatively. In mid-2019 both the RBI and the government announced additional measures to encourage businesses to accept payments and consumers to use payment options.[133] As the economy develops and service providers continue to add features, digital payments will likely continue to grow significantly across India.

MUDRA Bank: Pradhan Mantri MUDRA Yojana

In April 2015, a new entrant emerged in the financial services sector: Pradhan Mantri MUDRA Yojana (PMMY), also known as the MUDRA Bank.[134] Not actually a licensed bank, MUDRA is the Micro Units Development and Refinance Agency, a government fund to increase lending to micro, small, and medium-sized enterprises across the country. The loans are granted through banks, NBFC-MFIs, regional rural banks, co-operative banks, and other financial services providers in three categories of lending up to INR1 million (US$14,090).

According to MUDRA's March 2018 annual report, the program worked with 200 institutions, including 93 banks, 72 MFIs, 32 NBFCs, and 6 small finance banks. More than 48 million loans were granted in the fiscal year April 2017 to March 2018, with disbursements of INR2.46 trillion (US$34.6 billion), of which 40 percent was in loans to women and 33 percent to vulnerable socioeconomic groups.[135] In addition,

MUDRA launched a credit card scheme, similar to the Kisan card offered by NAB-ARD described earlier. In the 2017–18 fiscal year, 152,000 card accounts were opened (over 850,000 cumulative card accounts since 2015), and INR14.3 billion (US$201.5 million) in loans was disbursed. The program grew in the 2018–19 fiscal year, when MUDRA reported approving more than 59.8 million loans with a value of INR3.2 trillion (US$45.3 billion) from April 2018 to March 2019. Operations continue at a robust pace; provisional data for the eight months of activity in fiscal year 2019–20 through December 2019 indicate approval of 35.5 million loans with a value of INR1.79 trillion (US$25.2 billion).[136]

Concerns are rising about the portfolio quality of the program. RBI issued cautions in January and November 2019 and said nonperforming MUDRA loans had risen from INR110 trillion (US$1.55 billion) in January 2019 to INR164.8 trillion (US$2.31 billion) in November 2019 across their partner banks.[137] Given these portfolio concerns, the Ministry of Finance is reported to have asked public sector banks participating in the program to review eligibility criteria, geographic reach, and program features.[138] Reporting in the Indian press suggests that portfolio quality remains a concern, as nonperforming MUDRA loans at some public sector banks are estimated to exceed 20 percent of their MUDRA portfolio.[139] The data on nonperforming loans should be clarified and measures taken to remediate the portfolio given the magnitude of the MUDRA program.

Perhaps more important, the broader economic impact of MUDRA, especially for job creation and stabilizing incomes of self-employed people, is not yet known. A draft analysis from the Labour Bureau under the Ministry of Labour and Employment suggests that new job creation is lower than originally anticipated, estimating that 11.2 million additional jobs were created during the initial period of the program from April 2015 to December 2017. An initial cost-benefit calculation suggests that each job created cost INR510,000, and that only 20 percent of borrowers have started new businesses.[140]

New Banks and Other Players Emerge

In 2014, the RBI built on helpful recommendations from its technical committees to add new categories of players to the Indian financial sector: payments banks and small finance banks. Over the past decade, several new fintech companies have emerged, often in partnership with other licensed financial services providers. As mentioned earlier, many started as BCs; they have gradually expanded their operations, and some have recently been granted NBFC licenses.

Payments Banks

Given the large and complex market and need for financial services, a multitiered approach with a range of financial services providers makes sense in India. The Mor Committee report in January 2014 helped to reinforce this approach by recommending the creation of a new category of bank for payments banks. The RBI moved quickly on this, releasing draft guidelines for payments banks in July 2014 and approving the final guidelines in November 2014.[141] Operating guidelines for payments banks were released by the RBI in October 2016.[142]

Payments banks are restricted to providing payment and remittance services, deposits can have a maximum account balance of INR100,000 (US$1,409) per client, and debit/ATM cards must be linked to accounts. In addition, payments banks may serve as the banking correspondent of another bank and distribute simple insurance products on behalf of other insurance companies.[143]

The new banking license generated significant interest, given the potential for payments business in India. In 2015, forty-one firms expressed interest in the payments bank license, and eleven firms were given in-principle conditional approval by the RBI to submit a full proposal.[144] Finally, seven firms with deep experience in telecommunications, banking, information technology, payments, and postal services were granted payments bank licenses (table 13-8). The first to launch, in January 2017, was Airtel Payments Bank, backed by the largest Indian telecommunications provider Bharti Airtel and Kotak Mahindra Bank.[145]

The seven payments banks are an interesting group. Four mobile phone operators linked with commercial banks launched payments banks. They bring advantages such as a large network of physical outlets and agents, a large client base, experience with mobile money, deep financial resources, and good brand recognition. India Post brings its massive network of physical outlets and brand recognition. Fino builds on its long history as a banking correspondent. The oldest institution to apply, India Post

TABLE 13-8.   Payments Banks Granted Licenses as of March 2019

Aditya Birla Idea Payments Bank Limited
Airtel Payments Bank Limited
Fino Payments Bank Limited
India Post Payments Bank Limited
Jio Payments Bank Limited
NDSL Payments Bank Limited
Paytm Payments Bank Limited

Source: Reserve Bank of India, "Banks in India," March 2019.

was also approved for a payments bank license, building on its long history of financial services and massive physical presence across the country.

The RBI designed payments banks to spur competition in the financial sector, and the new banks have certainly raised the hopes of financial inclusion advocates. However, this category of bank has inherent challenges:

- When payments banks were designed, the market for payments was already highly price competitive. Competition has become even more fierce given advances by NPCI across a range of payment services, and especially with UPI.

- While payments banks are allowed to serve as a BC for another bank and sell other firms' insurance policies, the commission income will be modest for the effort involved. Their income is further limited by their inability to lend.

- Deposit accounts cannot exceed INR100,000 (US$1,400), which limits their attractiveness for savers who would normally add to their balances over the long term.

- The investment income of payments banks is limited by the requirement that they maintain 75 percent of their liquidity in treasury bills or government bonds.

Noting the challenges of the initial payments bank model, three of the eleven firms given conditional approval eventually declined to pursue their bids in 2016.[146] Further, two significant players with links to the largest telco firms, Aditya Birla Idea Payments Bank and Vodafone's M-Pesa payment service, announced their plans to close in July 2019.

As anticipated from their initial design, the business model for payments banks is challenging, given the limited revenue options and thin margins. Of the six remaining payments banks, only Paytm recorded a profit for fiscal year 2018–19, while the others incurred losses in 2017–18 and 2018–19.[147] Payments are a small-value and large-volume business, and payments banks need to leverage technology, customer service, links with other providers, and economies of scale to be successful. Recognizing these challenges, in September 2019 the RBI issued draft guidelines to allow payments banks to apply for small finance bank licenses. In December 2019 the RBI announced criteria for "on tap" small finance bank licenses, including eligibility criteria for payments banks to convert to small finance banks after five years of operation.[148] This policy shift may address many of the challenges facing payments banks, and it is a welcome move.

Small Finance Banks

Building on the recommendations of the Malegam Committee in 2011 and subsequent analysis across the microfinance sector, the RBI announced the small finance bank license in 2014. Small finance banks were conceived as providing a graduation path for strong NBFCs to expand their services to include deposits and other financial services. The RBI guidelines for small finance banks are coherent with this objective:[149]

- Banks should focus on deposits and lending to unserved and underserved households, small and marginal farmers, and micro, small, and medium-sized enterprises.

- There is no geographic restriction of operations; however, at least 25 percent of branch offices are to be in unbanked rural centers, as defined by the RBI based on the Indian census.

- At least 75 percent of loans must go to priority sector lending as defined by the RBI (as discussed in earlier sections).

- For 50 percent of the lending portfolio, loans are limited to a maximum of INR2.5 million (US$35,225), which is much higher than the earlier limit of INR100,000 for NBFC-MFIs (US$1,400). With this larger lending authority, small finance banks are able to offer appropriate loans to their long-term clients and also compete more effectively with larger banks to serve small and medium-sized enterprises. Lending to a single individual or firm is capped at 10 percent and 15 percent of capital funds, respectively.

- Banks are required to have capital of INR1 billion (US$14 million), which is much less than the capital requirement of INR5 billion (US$70.45 million) for a private sector universal bank.[150]

- Prudential norms are the same as for existing commercial banks, including cash reserves and statutory liquidity ratios.

A total of seventy-two firms expressed interest in the small finance bank license, and in September 2015 ten firms were given in-principle conditional approval by the RBI to comply with the requirements and receive a full license within eighteen

TABLE 13-9.   Small Finance Banks in Operation

Ujjivan Small Finance Bank	Fincare Small Finance Bank
Equitas Small Finance Bank	ESAF Small Finance Bank
AU Small Finance Bank	Suryoday Small Finance Bank
Capital Small Finance Bank	Utkarsh Small Finance Bank

Source: Reserve Bank of India, "Banks in India," August 2019.

months.[151] All ten were eventually approved for licenses. The current list of small finance banks operating is in table 13-9.

After many years of consideration, the small finance bank license is a real step forward in enabling strong MFIs with a proven track record to graduate and offer a broader range of financial services, especially deposit services. Nonetheless, small finance banks face challenges as they transform from NBFCs and pursue this new path:

- Attracting and managing deposits requires a completely different business model than making loans. Many specialists have written about this over the past twenty years. Some of the key requirements include building client trust, managing liquidity requirements for on-demand deposits, ensuring that clients have ready access to their deposits through branch offices or ATMs or agents, managing more dynamic assets and liabilities, and training staff for the new approach.

- Regulatory requirements and reporting are significantly higher for small finance banks than for NBFCs, and the new banks will understandably be under tight scrutiny by the RBI to ensure that they comply.

- Given the broader scope of operations, the new banks may seek new talent, perhaps attracting candidates from other commercial banks. Given experience with institutional transformations across the globe for several decades, these personnel changes may trigger internal challenges among the new staff and existing staff who have transitioned from the NBFC, who may have been loyal to the firm for years.

- Governance may also need to evolve, given higher capital requirements and the need to attract investors, but also to comply with RBI requirements for an independent board of directors.

- The investment required in this massive institutional transformation will affect the banks' profitability for several years. Investments will include adapting systems, head and branch office changes, developing new products and client groups, new technology platforms, compliance functions, additional reporting to the RBI, staffing changes, adapting staff training, rebranding the NBFC as a small finance bank, additional treasury functions, expanded requirements for annual auditing and reporting, and enhanced risk management.

The firms that converted from NBFCs to small finance banks all bring extensive experience serving microfinance clients over many years, and so far the new small finance banks seem to be performing well.[152] In June 2018 the RBI announced that urban co-operative banks would be eligible to become small finance banks starting in August 2018.[153] Further, in December 2019 the RBI announced criteria for "on-tap" small finance bank licenses, with specific reference to eligible local area banks, urban co-operatives, NBFCs, MFIs, and payments banks.[154] Under this expansion of the small finance bank license, applicants could be reviewed and granted licenses on an ongoing basis, rather than responding to periodic calls for applications from the RBI. This welcome move should enable strong urban co-operatives, NBFCs, MFIs, and payments banks to make a similar successful transition.

The future of small finance banks depends on mastering the deposit business, incorporating new technologies, expanding to other relevant services such as SME or agricultural lending, and attracting long-term clients by offering quality and affordable financial services.

Two Other New Bank Entrants

After a ten-year period, the RBI opened competition for new commercial bank licenses in 2013. Of the original twenty-seven applicants, only two firms were selected in April 2014 for in-principle approval and given eighteen months to comply with the full requirements: IDFC Bank and Bandhan Bank.[155] This outcome surprised the financial services industry, as several applicants with deep corporate links, another well-regarded NBFC-MFI, and a housing finance NBFC were not selected.

IDFC Bank is specialized in infrastructure lending and builds on years of experience. Bandhan converted from an NBFC-MFI to a full bank license, which has even more stringent requirements than the small bank license. Bandhan grew rapidly during the 2000s in eastern India, managed its growth well, and was not heavily affected by the microfinance crisis that erupted in Andhra Pradesh in 2010. The RBI's selection of Bandhan, together with the graduation of ten NBFCs to small finance banks, helped reinforce the morale and image of the stronger MFIs that managed the crisis and demonstrated years of serving low-income clients responsibly.

New Fintechs

Across the globe, new fintech players are entering the financial sector, and many are becoming significant at national and even international levels. Similarly, fintech innovation is bubbling in India; one estimate is that over 2,000 fintechs are active, triple the number in 2015.[156] Indian fintechs are attracting significant equity from global and domestic investors, and several major Indian cities are listed among the top 100 fintech hub cities globally.[157] As noted earlier, dozens of fintechs initially launched as banking correspondents, working with licensed banks and other financial services providers. More recent entrants include MobiKwick, NeoGrowth, Policy Bazaar, PhonePe, Ziploan, MyLoanCare, Shubh Loans, PayU, Kissht, epayLater, Lending Kart, Faircent, and epiFi. Many of the payments fintechs also offer online and mobile access to loans, often serving as originators for other licensed credit providers.[158] Other fintechs such as ZestMoney, Kaleidofin, Niyo Solutions, Open, Pay Zello, instaDApp, and 0.5Bn FinHealth partner with banks to offer insurance, wealth management, foreign exchange, and other services to households and small businesses.[159] Peer-to-peer lending platforms are emerging as licensed NBFCs, offering a new model for borrowers and investment options for households. One of the older, established platforms is RupeeCircle, and others include LendBox, Lenden Club, OML, India Money Mart, Faircent, and I2I Funding. As of September 2019, several fintechs, including MoneyTap, CredAble, and PayMe India, had been granted NBFC licenses to offer lending on their own books.[160]

Global players such as Google Pay are also becoming active in India, and Amazon Pay launched in 2019. The messaging platform WhatsApp has developed a beta payments product with about 1 million users, and in August 2019 it applied for RBI approval as a payments service. WhatsApp could rapidly become a significant player given its 400 million users across India.[161] The RBI allowed WhatsApp to test payment services starting in February 2018, although full approval was delayed given concerns about their noncompliance with the requirement to host relevant data in India.[162] RBI subsequently granted approval in early February 2020, and the NPCI has given WhatsApp permission to use its digital platform in a phased manner for up to 10 million users in the first phase.[163] As seen globally, fintechs and other types of virtual players introduce new competition in the sector, and successful new business models can change dynamics quickly.

Current Status

As described throughout this chapter, India is perhaps the most dynamic country for financial inclusion in the world, and it has achieved tremendous results. Clear gains have been made by the private and public sector dramatically increasing access to finance across India.

From a wider perspective, it should be noted that the Indian economy slowed its long-term growth trajectory in 2017–19. Many factors were at work, including the impact of demonetization, launch of the new goods and services tax, and concerns in the financial sector. Surprisingly, reports from the government's Niti Aayog suggest that poverty levels increased in 2018–19 in twenty-two states and union territories after a decade of progress in reducing poverty from 2005 to 2016.[164]

The Financial Sector

In the financial sector, bank nonperforming assets and provisions against losses increased significantly in 2017, at levels not seen since 1993–94, resulting in banking sector losses for the 2017–18 fiscal year ending March 31, 2018.[165] Public sector banks accounted for approximately 87 percent of nonperforming loans in 2018.[166] For the 2018–19 fiscal year, performance of commercial banks improved across asset quality, capital adequacy, and profitability, although financial sector activity remained low given overall macroeconomic conditions. The government infused significant capital into restructuring public sector banks in late 2019; however, the overhang of nonperforming loans continues, and new concerns emerged from NBFCs and co-operatives.[167]

Table 13-10 summarizes the composition of the Indian banking sector.

The sector experienced two large surprises in 2018, when the Punjab National Bank (PNB) was found to have committed fraud and Infrastructure Leasing and Financial Services defaulted. The PNB fraud was made public in early 2018, when it was revealed that a bank manager had used falsified letters of undertaking and letters of credit to defraud a large client of INR120 billion (US$1.69 billion) over the previous six years.[168]

The debt default by Infrastructure Leasing and Financial Services (IL&FS) of US$13 billion starting in August 2018 again rattled the financial sector; the stock market plunged when the default was made public.[169] IL&FS is a specialized lender for infrastructure and partially government owned. The default triggered concerns across the debt market given the number of Indian development finance institutions, insurance companies, banks, mutual funds, and others holding IL&FS bonds. The

TABLE 13-10.   Type and Number of Banks in India, 2019

Bank category	Number of banks
Public sector banks	18
Private sector banks	22
Foreign banks	47
NBFC-MFIs	95
Regional rural banks (RRBs)	53
Co-operative banks (scheduled and unscheduled)	33
Local area banks	3
Small finance banks	8
Payments banks	6
Financial institutions and development banks	4

Source: Reserve Bank of India, "Banks in India," August 2019. This list does not reflect the ongoing consolidation of public sector banks announced in August 2019 and closures of regional rural banks, nonbank financial companies, and co-operatives from August to December 2019.

ensuing liquidity crunch was especially hard on housing finance companies and NBFCs that borrow from the market to on-lend.

A number of financial sector specialists, including from the government and RBI, have advocated for several years that public sector banks should be reformed. Given the history of nationalization of banks in the 1970s, public sector banks dominate the banking sector. However their dominance is declining.[170] When the RBI licensed the first new private sector banks in 1990, public sector banks managed 90 percent of the banking market. The public sector bank market share declined to 80 percent in 2000 and to 75 percent in 2014. According to RBI reporting in December 2019, as of March 2019 public sector banks managed 64 percent of bank advances.[171] Further, annual growth of bank advances in public sector banks dropped from 73 percent in 2014 to 24 percent in 2019; the results were similar for annual growth of deposits.[172] Over the past ten years, new banks, NBFCs, and fintechs have increased competition and triggered changes across the financial sector.

In April 2017, the RBI announced a revised framework for prompt corrective action for banks (both public and private sector), in which performance triggers would be based on nonperforming assets, capital adequacy ratio, and return on assets.[173] Thereafter, the RBI placed eleven public sector banks under the prompt corrective action framework, requiring closer monitoring and remedial action such as limits on dividends, branch expansion, and other operating limits.[174]

Reflecting these concerns, the Ministry of Finance announced in late August 2019 that ten public sector banks would combine into four banks over the coming months.[175]

This consolidation had been under discussion for years, and if the mergers and re-capitalizations are successful, it will represent an important step forward for finan-cial sector health. The mergers include: Punjab National Bank with Oriental Bank of Commerce and United Bank; Syndicate Bank with Canara Bank; Union Bank of India with Andhra Bank and Corporation Bank; and Indian Bank with Allahabad Bank. The consolidation builds on the September 2018 decision to merge Bank of Baroda, Vijaya Bank, and Dena Bank in April 2019. With this decision, the number of public sector banks declined to twelve from twenty-seven in 2017.

In addition to public sector banks, the RBI is addressing portfolio and perfor-mance issues with NBFCs by canceling registrations of more than 1,850 NBFCs in FY2018–19 through March 2019.[176] The number of cancellations is eight times greater than in the previous fiscal year and reflects the RBI's attention to financial sector health. Other NBFC cancellations continued throughout calendar year 2019, includ-ing twenty in late December 2019.[177]

Dozens of struggling financial co-operatives have also been closed in both urban and rural areas over the past several years. A case attracted headlines in Novem-ber 2019 when the RBI restricted operations and limited withdrawals by depositors at the Punjab and Maharashtra Co-operative Bank (PMC). In addition to other fi-nancial and governance irregularities, PMC reportedly loaned over US$920 million to a now bankrupt housing developer.[178] In December 2019, the RBI announced re-strictions on urban co-operative banks, including lower exposure norms, requirements for large co-operatives to report to the credit registry, and improvements to cyberse-curity systems.[179] In February 2020, the government cabinet approved changes to the banking law that bring regulation and supervision for the 1,540 co-operatives across the country fully within the RBI's mandate. Previously, responsibility for oversight of co-operatives had been shared between the RBI and respective state-level co-operative societies.[180] This policy change removes ambiguity and gives RBI more authority to resolve issues in the co-operative sector.

In its 2017–19 policy changes the RBI focused on lowering the level of nonper-forming assets of financial services providers, reducing new cases of troubled assets, requiring higher loan-loss provisions, and requiring financial services providers to recapitalize where needed.[181] In February 2020, the RBI increased deposit insurance from INR100,000 (US$1,400) to INR500,000 (US$7,000) for deposits in insured banks.[182] Going forward, the RBI plans to revise its supervisory framework and de-velop a prompt corrective action framework for NBFCs to be implemented in 2022.[183] Another key achievement in strengthening the financial system is the Insol-vency and Bankruptcy Code passed by Parliament in 2016 and launched in Novem-ber 2017. This code will help address the overhang of nonperforming assets, stimulate economic growth, and give banks more tools to manage their lending risk. An amendment to the Insolvency and Bankruptcy Code approved in November 2019 includes NBFCs under the coverage of this code, which will help resolve distressed finance companies in an orderly manner.

These reforms will address some of the concerns of low-performing public and private sector banks, the implications of the IL&FS crisis, and related troubles in the NBFC and co-operative sectors. Successfully implementing the public sector bank mergers, reducing the number of nonperforming loans, and other reforms will be critical for overall financial sector stability, competition, financial inclusion, and economic growth for India's future.

Financial Inclusion

India has made tremendous progress on financial inclusion. The number of Indian adults with a bank account more than doubled, increasing from 35 percent in 2011 to 53 percent in 2014 to almost 80 percent in 2017, according to Findex data. Actual levels of financial inclusion were even higher as of January 2020, according to PMJDY accounts and NPCI mobile payment information. India's level of financial inclusion compares favorably with that of other large emerging markets: 80 percent of adults hold a bank account in the People's Republic of China, 70 percent in Brazil, and 69 percent in South Africa. In 2014, men were 20 percent more likely to hold an account than women in India, and the gap shrank to just 6 percent in 2017.[184] According to PMJDY statistics, almost every household in India has a bank account.[185] Still, approximately 190 million Indian adults do not have an account, of which 60 percent are women.[186] Further, according to Findex data for 2017, 48 percent of adults with an account did not use it, which is almost twice the 25 percent average for developing countries and an increase from 42 percent in 2014.[187] According to more recent data from September 2019, an estimated 17.8 percent (66 million) of PMJDY accounts are dormant.

According to comparable microfinance data from March 2019, lending through MFIs, NBFC-MFIs, and banks served 56 million clients with a portfolio of INR1.86 trillion (US$26.3 billion).[188] For the same period, over 10 million SHGs held savings accounts with banks, with deposits of INR233 billion (US$3.3 billion). Of these, about 50 percent or 5 million of the SHGs had an outstanding loan from a bank, totaling INR871 billion (US$12.3 billion).[189] NABARD estimates that these SHGs reach 120 million households across India.

As of this writing in early 2020, data on the microfinance industry show growth of 47.9 percent in the loan portfolio from September 2018 to September 2019, with a total outstanding portfolio exceeding INR2 trillion (US$28.2 billion) across banks, NBFCs, and small finance banks.[190] Of the outstanding portfolio, banks manage 40 percent of loan volume while NBFC-MFIs hold 31 percent, small finance banks hold 17 percent, other NBFCs hold 11 percent, and other MFIs hold 1 percent. The three states with the largest volume of outstanding loans were Tamil Nadu, West Bengal, and Bihar. Concerns about overlending and saturation of markets are growing again. Over 60 percent of the microfinance portfolio is concentrated in just six states, and more alarming, 54 percent of the microfinance portfolio is reported in 100 districts.[191] High levels of indebtedness and protests in Assam that began in late 2019 are a reflection of these concerns.[192] The rapid pace of growth is challenging to manage well, and the financial services providers and their boards and investors should act on lessons of the earlier experience and avoid another crisis.

Future Challenges

Financial inclusion goes well beyond simply access to credit, although typically credit receives much of the attention. Actual financial inclusion involves having access to a range of financial services: loans, deposits, payments, insurance, investments, and pension products. Further, access to financial services is only a first step; the ability to use these services to manage household and business needs is the real goal.

India faces several remaining challenges to achieve full financial inclusion. As part of the solution, the RBI and the Ministry of Finance have coordinated with public and private sector players to develop a new national financial inclusion strategy, which was approved in March 2019 and formally released by the RBI in January 2020. The strategy for 2019–24 highlights a comprehensive approach to making financial services available, accessible, and affordable, including providing universal access, a basic bouquet of services, livelihood and skills development, financial literacy and education, customer protection and grievance redressal, and effective coordination among key players in the financial sector.[193]

Market innovation with proportional regulation will play a key role in addressing the remaining inclusion challenges, especially in such a vibrant and creative economy as India. The following areas merit special attention in the effort to achieve full financial inclusion.

Enable greater usage of accounts. According to Findex data of 2017, 48 percent of adults with an account did not use it, which is almost twice the 25 percent average for developing countries.[194] In September 2019, 17.8 percent of accounts (66 million) were still dormant. Although access to services is increasing, greater usage is now the focus for the future.

Expand geographic coverage, especially in rural areas. Given the highly successful rollout of bank accounts under the PMJDY program since 2015, the focus can shift to usage of financial services. Clients need convenient access to service points such as bank branches, ATMs, and business correspondents. Over time, the need for physical service points may shift as clients become more comfortable making transactions on their phones and reducing their reliance on cash.

Financial services providers are gradually increasing their coverage of the country. However there are areas with thin or nonexistent coverage, including northern and northeastern India.[195] Coverage for financial services is also uneven in urban centers and rural areas. Branch offices are expensive to maintain, especially in rural areas.

On a positive note, access to credit in rural areas expanded to 69 percent, from 56 percent in 2013, according to the 2018 All India Financial Inclusion Survey managed by NABARD.[196] The 2019–24 national financial inclusion strategy includes a focus on access to finance in rural areas.[197] Further, in 2019 both the RBI and the Ministry of Finance established committees on rural services, agriculture, and MSMEs; their recommendations were under review at this writing.

In absolute terms, India benefits from over 120,500 commercial bank branches, although these are concentrated in urban and semi-urban areas. Another 597,155 outlets serve rural areas as of March 2019.[198] The number of ATMs stabilized at 232,000; most are in urban and semi-urban areas, and just 16.5 percent in rural areas.[199] The number of micro-ATMs continues to grow; over 235,000 are available across the country.[200] Mobile phone coverage is 155 percent in urban centers and 59 percent in rural areas.[201]

Given India's vast geographic expanse and large population, these numbers need to be analyzed more carefully on a regional and per capita basis. Globally comparable data from 2017 suggest that, on a per capita basis, the numbers are improving: there were 14.7 commercial bank branches and 22.1 ATMs per 100,000 people in 2017, an increase from 10.5 branches and 8.9 ATMs in 2010. However, the number of ATMs per capita in India is still much lower than in Brazil (106.8 per 100,000) or the People's Republic of China (81.5).[202] The business correspondent model can help expand service points, as described earlier. The growth in transactions via business correspondents increased 41 percent for the year ending March 2019, and the Indian Banks' Association launched a new database of information on BCs in February 2018 that will help clients identify BCs and improve transparency of their operations.[203]

To help retain BCs and continue growing their coverage, the transaction fees paid to banks and BCs must be adequate to cover the actual costs and risks they incur, especially in semi-urban and rural areas. An earlier taskforce had recommended transaction fees of 3.14 percent for distributing direct benefit transfers for G2P payments;[204] however, banks pay BCs 0.5 percent of the transaction amount or INR15 (US$0.21), whichever is lower, for government DBT payments.[205] In comparison, fees for distributing government DBT payments are much higher in Brazil (US$0.84), Colombia (US$6.24), Mexico (US$2.52), and South Africa (US$3.5) according to 2012 data.[206] BCs incur different costs and dedicate varying amounts of time with clients for account opening, accepting deposits, providing withdrawals, and facilitating money transfers. Median monthly revenue for BCs has more than doubled, from US$40 in 2015 to US$93 in 2017, yet monthly operating costs are relatively higher in India at US$62 than in other countries with large BC networks.[207] The viability and outreach of BCs remain concerns, and a comprehensive review of costs for each type of service and fair margin, perhaps graduated based on size of the transaction, would be important to address in order to expand and maintain the viability of service points across India.

Review usage with a gender lens. Usage can be further analyzed looking at discrepancies by gender. A minority of 27.2 percent of women participate in the formal labor force in India, down from 36.8 percent in 2005.[208] Mobile phone usage directly affects mobile payment usage. Just 38 percent of women use mobile phones, in comparison with 71 percent of men, and men are 33 percent more likely than women to own a mobile phone.[209] The digital divide is real: if women do own phones, they are usually feature phones, not smart phones that can access the internet and could enable them to use banking and payment applications.

In financial services, men were 20 percent more likely to hold an account than women in India, although the gap decreased to just 6 percent in 2017.[210] This progress is largely due to the PMJDY program to open bank accounts. In his budget speech of January 2019, the finance minister noted that almost 70 percent of PMJDY accounts are held by women.[211] Women purchased 32 percent of life insurance policies in the 2017–18 fiscal year.[212] This progress is heartening, although more research is needed to verify that women are actually using the accounts. For example, in India and globally, there have been instances of microfinance loans disbursed or accounts opened in the name of a woman, but a man (such as her husband or father) actually controlled the account.

Promote product diversification. Full financial inclusion goes well beyond simple credit, although typically credit receives much of the attention. Financial inclusion involves a range of financial services: loans, deposits, payments, insurance, investments, and pension products. Tremendous potential exists for other financial products that would help households and businesses manage their financial lives.

- Deposit accounts are a critical and foundational financial service for households and businesses. Only 19.6 percent of adults reported saving at a financial institution in 2017, up slightly from 14.4 percent in 2014.[213] By qualifying for a small finance bank license, NBFC-MFIs and now also urban co-operative banks can qualify to offer their clients deposits and a broader range of services. Payments banks may also help increase deposits, although the cap of US$1,400 on these accounts will limit the usage. Across the globe low-income and low-middle-income clients already use multiple means of saving money, both formal and informal, and on an aggregate basis, this represents a massive volume of funds. Increasingly, financial services providers understand this market potential, which can also help mobilize new sources of financing for their operations. There is enormous opportunity to innovate in deposit services using greater personalization to structure deposits, including a range of tenures, number of free deposits and withdrawals per month, minimum balances, interest paid, convenient access through mobile apps, and other features. Other longer-term investment options may also become viable in the medium term for these client groups.

- According to Findex data, 28.7 percent of adults reported sending or receiving a digital payment in 2017, a good increase from 19.3 percent in 2014.[214] Payments banks, the UPI, and other platforms managed by NPCI are helping expand the use of payments and remittances. Payment volume through cards and mobile phones is surging. Nonetheless, greater innovation and outreach could improve their usefulness to clients and businesses.

- Of the millions of microfinance clients in India, a surprising 60 million loan clients are still organized through joint liability groups (JLGs), while 120 million households are reached through self-help groups (SHGs). Since the 1990s, many financial services providers across India have used the standardized JLG model of 5–20+ clients and larger groups of clients for SHGs. Approximately 18 percent of JLG clients also have an individual loan, in addition to their group loan.[215] Individual loans are growing as a percentage of lending, but given RBI regulation, NBFC-MFIs are limited to just 15 percent of their portfolio in individual lending. Nonetheless, NBFC-MFIs still have room to grow to reach this limit. Individual lending for business and household loans represents a growth opportunity in India, and fintechs are already pursing this with success.

In many other countries globally since the 1990s, once individual lending was introduced, it proved highly popular and less cumbersome to microfinance clients, and as a result group lending declined dramatically. Yet individual or retail lending requires a significantly different approach than group lending, and institutions must analyze their markets with more refined client segmentation. Given today's data capabilities, much greater personalization is available to screen clients and tailor services, and indeed, clients in India and globally are enjoying hyperpersonalization in many online and retail transactions. To pursue this market opportunity, institutions will need to adapt their client screening, product design, marketing, staff training and hiring, internal procedures, IT, portfolio management, risk management, and collections practices to ensure careful growth of individual loans.

■ More than 328 million life insurance policies were in effect in 2017, and analysts generously estimate that this corresponds to 25 percent of the population being covered.[216] In addition, the PMJDY accounts offer a life insurance option, although this could be further expanded and promoted.

■ Approximately 12 percent of the labor force contributes to a mandatory or voluntary pension program,[217] and this may be a high estimate. Public pension programs include the Indira Gandhi National Old Age Pension Scheme, focused on low-income people. Other programs for informal sector workers include the National Pension Scheme-Swavalamban, the Atal Pension Yojana announced in 2016, and the new Pradhan Mantri Shram Yogi Mandhan (PMSYM) announced by the government in February 2019. Given the growing population over age sixty, and the incidence of old-age poverty, a comprehensive approach to public pensions should be a priority. Consideration should include eligibility for coverage, adequacy of the benefit payment, sustainability of the program including the need for government transfers, and logistics for payments to reach the intended recipients, including use of bank accounts and access to service points.[218]

In a positive move, the RBI is renewing its focus on insurance and pensions through the new financial inclusion strategy of 2019–2024.[219] As new products are developed, they should be adaptive and inclusive in their design and avoid a supply-led or aggressive target-driven approach. Financial services need to be convenient, appropriately designed, affordable, and delivered in a responsible way. With this focus, financial services providers can increase the likelihood that their target clientele will actually use the services.

Continue innovating in the payments and fintech ecosystem. India has made a significant leap forward in its payments infrastructure, government policy, regulation and supervision, and financial services providers over the past five years. As examples of recent deep thinking in the policy arena, the RBI released two major analyses of retail and digital payments in January and May 2019.[220] In May 2019, the RBI approved the new Payments Vision 2021 to promote positive customer experience with lower cost, higher confidence, and more convenience, together with building an enabling payments ecosystem.[221] Use of digital payments is lower in rural areas, including secondary and tertiary cities and smaller communities, and these are areas for focus. Nationally, key aspects of achieving this vision would include reducing the costs for merchants to accept payments, expanding the number of point-of-sale devices, promoting QR codes to facilitate payments, allowing a broader range of financial services providers to acquire cards, developing offline payment options, tracking fraud cases and facilitating redress by consumers, and reducing the cost to the consumer to use digital payments.

The Ministry of Finance released a new analysis on fintech related issues in September 2019.[222] The policy analysis from both the RBI and the Ministry of Finance suggests a useful evolution in thinking to promote digital payments: it would improve KYC (and e-KYC) requirements and cybersecurity; consider virtual banks; dematerialize financial instruments including land and real estate titles; and incorporate alternative data in credit scoring. Payment and other fintech providers are driving innovation, although this is an area to monitor closely for potential credit bubbles, lack of data privacy and protection, and consumer issues. Already, India's payment system is among the most advanced and innovative globally, and the RBI benchmarks itself against other countries' systems.[223] Both public sector and private sector entities should continue to focus on the appropriate enabling environment for payments, defining the most effective role of NPCI, encouraging greater competition among banks and nonbanks, and ensuring efficient and quality payment services with relevant consumer and data protections.

Consider the most effective role for government policy and programs. The government of India has played an important role in promoting financial inclusion, especially over the past ten years. The Reserve Bank of India is a highly technical central bank that has effectively focused on soundness of the financial sector and financial inclusion over many years.[224] Government policy and programs will need ongoing recalibration to ensure their effectiveness as the financial sector continues to evolve:

- The PMJDY program dramatically expanded access to bank accounts. Usage of bank accounts is growing, although millions of accounts are dormant. G2P programs and related policy measures for direct benefit transfers could help increase use of these accounts and identify which accounts are redundant so they can be closed.

- Concerns about nonperforming loans in the MUDRA program should be analyzed and steps taken to improve portfolio quality and overall program effectiveness.

- Both the agricultural sector and small and medium-sized businesses play a critical role in employment and economic growth across India. Approximately 44 percent of the total labor force work in the agricultural sector.[225] Multiple financial inclusion programs linked to these two sectors are coordinated by India's leading development finance institutions, especially SIDBI and NABARD. The RBI expert committee on MSMEs with its report of June 2019, and the current RBI internal working group on agriculture, will provide useful analysis for improving financial services in these two critical sectors.

- Earlier sections reviewed India's past experience with farm loan waivers, which many states continue to use. For example in 2017, at least four states, Uttar Pradesh, Maharashtra, Punjab, and Karnataka, announced farm loan waivers, with an estimated cost of US$13.6 billion.[226] New loan waivers were predicted in 2019,[227] despite long-standing RBI concerns about farm loan waivers and their impact on credit culture.[228] The agricultural sector, especially smallholder farmers and related SMEs in the agricultural value chain, is key to economic growth for the country. Yet financial services, and especially credit lines, remain challenging for many working in the agricultural sector; it is estimated that 40.9 percent of smallholder and marginal farmers have access to credit.[229] At this writing, an internal working group of the RBI is analyzing options for agricultural credit. The national program to expand crop insurance, the Pradhan Mantri Fasal Bima Yojana (PMFBY), launched in 2016,[230] is a potentially more effective approach to mitigating risks for farmers and encouraging agricultural development. However, concerns by farmer groups about mistakes in the calculation of claims and violations of procedures should be verified and addressed.[231]

▪ Appropriate government and central bank policy could be a game changer in diversifying financial services, including deposits, life insurance, pensions, and other investment products, by providing incentives for financial services providers to expand their usage.

Strengthen efforts to improve consumer protection and data privacy. As more people gain access to bank accounts and use sophisticated digital finance, consumer protection, transparency of service conditions and fees, data privacy, and grievance redressal become increasingly important. From the lessons of the microfinance crisis of 2010, responsible finance through fair treatment of customers is a cornerstone of stability and continued expansion of financial services. In late 2019, growing concentration of lending in six states and 100 districts raises alarms. Reports of over-indebtedness in specific regions and with certain client groups should be investigated carefully to resolve the issues before they escalate into a larger conflict. For example, reports on indebtedness in Assam starting in late 2019 and an MFIN investigation suggest that average indebtedness is twice the national average, and in five districts of Assam average indebtedness is four times the national average.[232] Given the protests and difficult circumstances of clients in Assam at this writing, care will be required to resolve them in a manner that is fair to clients and respects the laws, regulations, and codes of conduct governing financial services providers.

Digital finance requires additional measures for consumer protection given its virtual nature and the burgeoning number of new fintechs offering a broad range of services. At the time of writing, the RBI has just announced two welcome additions to help monitor and regulate the digital payments industry. A new self-regulatory organization will be created by April 2020 for digital payments companies, similar to the role MFIN and Sa-Dhan play for NBFC-MFIs and MFIs, respectively. In addition, the RBI will launch a digital payment index by July 2020 to monitor usage of payments across the country.[233]

As a subset of fintechs, the peer-to-peer lending industry is emerging rapidly in India. At least fifteen peer-to-peer lending companies are registered with the RBI as NBFCs. In December 2019, the RBI approved an increase in the limit per individual investor across all peer-to-peer lending platforms from INR100,000 to INR500,000 (US$1,400 to US$7,045).[234] As seen in other countries, peer-to-peer lending offers new sources of borrowing for households and businesses, in addition to opening new options for investment for those with excess capital. Yet this lending model can also trigger new types of consumer protection issues, both for the borrower and for the lender/investor, as well as challenges to manage nonperforming loans. In the period 2015–20, the People's Republic of China experienced a bubble of peer-to-peer lending involving millions of clients and billions of dollars. Over 6,000 such lending platforms have either closed or defaulted; one estimate puts the losses at over US$30 billion for 2.7 million household investors.[235] Given fraud, pyramid schemes, nonperforming loans, and growing public concern, the People's Bank of China, China's central bank, took a series of measures beginning in 2016 to tighten control of the industry, and some provinces have tried to ban outright peer-to-peer lending firms. In November 2019, the Chinese government announced that most peer-to-peer lenders will be required to resolve their portfolios and close within a year, and only a few well-established firms will be allowed to convert to small loan companies.[236] The Chinese experience is not unique; other countries are looking carefully at their own peer-to-peer lending industries. As this sector emerges in India, proportional regulation and careful monitoring will be vital to consumer protection and financial stability.

As a cornerstone, clients need to be informed about their rights and responsibilities when availing themselves of financial services. Several NGOs, NBFCs, and banks have piloted a range of financial-awareness programs across India over the past decade or more, with varying levels of effectiveness. Through their Consumer Education and Protection Department, the RBI has spearheaded the development of financial-awareness materials and translated them into numerous languages spoken across the country. In 2019, the RBI and SEBI, IRDAI, and PFRDA, the other three leading financial sector supervisory agencies, launched the National Centre for Financial Education (NCFE), which provides materials for client awareness, conducts surveys and exams on level of knowledge on financial services, and organizes educational programs with a range of organizations focusing on clients and staff of financial services providers.[237]

In 1995, the RBI created the Banking Ombudsman program, which allows clients to register complaints and seek redress. The ombudsman covers commercial banks, urban co-operative banks, regional rural banks, small finance banks, and payments banks. Building on that experience, the RBI extended the existing Banking Ombudsman program to NBFCs in February 2018,[238] later adding non-deposit-taking NBFCs and digital transactions.[239]

Consumer complaints about financial services providers submitted to the twenty-one Banking Ombudsman offices managed by the RBI increased in fiscal year 2018–19 to more than 195,900, almost 20 percent more than in the previous year.[240] This builds on an increase from 2017 to 2018 of 25 percent. These two years of significant increases in complaints may have been caused by greater awareness of grievance redressal procedures, more banking clients, greater use of digital channels, or a greater number of incidents of fraud and mismanagement. The top issues flagged by complaints were nonobservance of fair practices; problems with ATMs and debit cards and mobile and electronic banking; failure to meet commitments; problems with credit cards and deposit accounts; and levy of charges without notice. The ombudsman tracks complaints about NBFCs separately; it received over 3,990 during this same period, a sixfold increase from the prior year, when NBFCs were added to the ombudsman coverage. For NBFCs, the complaints centered on nonadherence to fair practices, nonobservance of RBI directions, levy of charges without notice, and lack of transparency in contracts.[241]

Taking the approach a step further, in September 2018 the RBI ombudsman developed guidelines for banks with more than ten outlets to establish internal ombudsman programs. Enforcing these guidelines will be important for increasing the independence of internal ombudsmen to flag and resolve issues related to customer service and for closely monitoring cases raised to the RBI's ombudsmen offices and ensuring appropriate remediation. Given the large number of cases related to lack of fair practices, a verification program on accuracy in marketing, akin to "secret shopping," may also be useful to consider.[242]

Reports on fraud through digital finance are increasing across India,[243] perhaps in line with the rising use of such services. Of the ombudsman complaints described above, mobile and electronic banking, which started to be tracked separately in July 2017, now represent 7.5 percent of grievances. ATM and debit card issues represent more than 18 percent of grievances; the main complaint is that accounts are debited without cash being dispensed by the ATM.[244] In a timely move, the RBI announced a new ombudsman scheme for digital transactions in January 2019.[245]

Given breaches of information across the globe and rising awareness of potential uses of personal information, data privacy is becoming a cornerstone of consumer protection. Many players already seek client data, and this will only increase given the emergence of fintechs, artificial intelligence and greater use of credit scoring, and emerging trends in the financial and e-commerce industries. A new type of data entity is also emerging—account aggregators. In late 2018, the RBI issued the first five in-principle licenses for account aggregators that gather client information to share with financial services providers and other companies.[246] Designing and implementing appropriate regulation for this expanding universe of players who track and manage client data will be critical.

On this front, India is ahead of many countries. The technical committee to the Ministry of Electronics and Information Technology has already drafted a Personal Data Protection Bill. The bill was introduced in the Indian Parliament in December 2019 and was under deliberation at this writing. Reviews of the draft bill are mixed, and analysts have proposed revisions to the final version of the bill.[247] Nonetheless, the initial draft includes important provisions that will improve consumer protection, such as requiring consent for personal data collection, enabling people to correct their data, and allowing the right to be forgotten.

Conclusion

The epic story on financial inclusion in India is not yet complete. In a vibrant economy with such diverse financial services providers, hundreds of millions of people are able to use financial services for their household and business needs. Although full financial inclusion is not yet ensured, India is well placed to remain a global leader. Few other countries in the world offer such an optimal mix: dynamism and innovation by financial services providers, an engaged and enlightened central bank making key investments in financial infrastructure and ensuring financial stability, and large-scale government initiatives on identification and financial inclusion. Achieving a sound and inclusive financial sector will be a truly Himalayan feat. The people of India deserve nothing less.

Notes

This chapter was completed in January 2020, and market changes after that date are not included in the analysis.

1. Reserve Bank of India (RBI), "Evolution of Payment Systems in India," December 12, 1998 (https://rbidocs.rbi.org.in/rdocs/Publications/PDFs/4452.pdf).

2. RBI, "The Advent of Modern Banking in India: 1720 to 1850s" (https://m.rbi.org.in/scripts/ms_banks.aspx).

3. Vijay Mahajan, "Call for an Inclusive Banking Structure for India by 2019, Fifty Years after Bank Nationalization" (New Delhi: UK Aid, 2013).

4. Ibid.

5. Smita Premchander and others, *National Study on Financial Cooperatives in the Context of Financial Inclusion in India* (New Delhi: United Nations Development Program, 2015).

6. RBI, "Brief History" (https://www.rbi.org.in/history/Brief_History.html).

7. RBI, "Report of the Technical Group Set up to Review Legislations on Money Lending, 2006."

8. Mahajan, "Call for an Inclusive Banking Structure."

9. D. N. Ghosh, *No Regrets* (New Delhi: Rupa Publications, 2015).

10. RBI, "Speech by Deepali Pant Joshi, RBI Executive Director, to the Conference of Chairmen of Regional Rural Banks, July 15, 2013, Mangalore.

11. All conversions of Indian rupees (INR) to U.S. dollars (US$) are as of January 10, 2020. "History and Details of Farm Loan Waivers in India," *The Logical, Indian,* June 13, 2017 (https://thelogicalindian.com/story-feed/awareness/farm-loan-waivers).

12. "FM on Whys and Hows of Farm Loan Waiver," *Rediff India Abroad,* May 24, 2008.

13. "Just Loan Waivers Will Not Work," *New Indian Express,* June 19, 2017.

14. N. Srinivasan, "Farm Loan Waiver: Right Choice for Supporting Agriculture?" *CAB Calling,* April–June 2008 (Reserve Bank of India, College of Agricultural Banking).

15. James Hanson, "Indian Banking: Market Liberalization and the Pressures for Institutional and Market Framework Reform," Working Paper 104 (Stanford Center of Global Poverty and Development, August 2001).

16. Sujay Dixit, "Liberalisation of Indian Banking and Regulation," Legal Service India (http://www.legalservicesindia.com/article/1023/Liberalisation-of-Indian-Banking-&-Regulation.html).

17. Mahajan, "Call for an Inclusive Banking Structure."

18. Shweta Punj, "India Post: In Letter and Spirit," *India Today,* August 11, 2017.

19. India Post, "Financial Services" (https://www.indiapost.gov.in/Financial/Pages/Content/Financial.aspx).

20. "India Post—Financial Services" (New Delhi: World Bank, 2008).

21. See "Kisan Credit Card" at www.wishfin.com/kisan-credit-card/.

22. "Transparency in Chit Fund Schemes," Studycafe.in, December 2019.

23. A. Fernandez, "History and Spread of the Self-Help Affinity Group Movement in India: The Role Played by IFAD" (Rome: International Fund for Agricultural Development, 2007).

24. EDA Rural Systems Pvt. Ltd. and APMAS, "Self Help Groups in India: A Study of the Lights and Shades" (CARE, Catholic Relief Services, GIZ, and U.S. Agency for International Development, 2006); Rosenberg and others, "Sustainability of Self-Help Groups in India: Two Analyses," Occasional Paper 12 (Washington: Consultative Group to Assist the Poor [CGAP], World Bank, 2007).

25. Ibid.

26. National Bank for Agriculture and Rural Development (NABARD), "Status of Micro Finance in India 2009–2010" (Mumbai, 2010).

27. SEWA Bank, "History" (https://www.sewabank.com/history.html).

28. N. Srinivasan, *Microfinance India: The State of the Sector Report 2010* (New Delhi: Sage/ACCESS Development Services, 2010).

29. Ibid.

30. N. Srinivasan, *Microfinance India: The State of the Sector Report 2011* (New Delhi: Sage/ACCESS Development Services, 2011).

31. Srinivasan, *Microfinance India: 2010.*

32. Portfolio indicators, and indeed almost all of the indicators during this rapid growth period, may have been distorted by the costs of growth (hiring and training new staff, launch-

ing new branch offices, growing operating costs, and others) and by the rapidly growing loan portfolios.

33. M-Cril, *M-CRIL Microfinance Review* (New Delhi, 2010).

34. Srinivasan, *Microfinance India: 2010.*

35. "Six Microfinance Crises That the Sector Does Not Want to Remember," *Microfinance Focus* (www.microfinancefocus.com/6-microfinance-crises-sector-does-not-want-remember).

36. Srinivasan, *Microfinance India: 2011.*

37. Ibid.

38. Srinivasan, *Microfinance India: 2010.*

39. "Andhra Pradesh MFI Ordinance of 2010" (Hyderabad: Andhra Pradesh State Government, 2010).

40. Vineet Rai, "India's Microfinance Crisis Is an Effort to Monopolize the Poor," *Harvard Business Review*, November 4, 2010; Elizabeth Rhyne, "On Microfinance: Who's to Blame for the Crisis in Andhra Pradesh?" (Washington: Center for Financial Inclusion and Huffington Post, November 2, 2010); Eric Bellman and Arlene Chang, "India's Major Crisis in Microlending," *Wall Street Journal*, October 28, 2010; Justin Oliver, "Who's the Culprit? Accessing Finance in Andhra Pradesh" (blog), CGAP, November 11, 2010; Graham Wright and Manoj Sharma, "The Andhra Pradesh Crisis: Three Dress Rehearsals . . . and then the Full Drama" (Lucknow, Uttar Pradesh, India: MicroSave, December 2010).

41. Rai, "India's Microfinance Crisis."

42. "Andhra Pradesh MFI Ordinance of 2010."

43. Ibid.

44. Mahajan, "Call for an Inclusive Banking Structure."

45. M. A. Ghiyazuddin and Shruti Gupta, "Andhra Pradesh MFI Crisis and Its Impact on Clients" (Centre for Microfinance and MicroSave, 2012).

46. Mahajan, "Call for an Inclusive Banking Structure."

47. "MFIN Demands Independent Judiciary Enquiry for Allegations against MFIs," *Microfinance Focus*, October 20, 2010.

48. Oliver, "Who's the Culprit?"

49. Ibid.

50. Ghiyazuddin and Gupta, "Andhra Pradesh MFI Crisis."

51. Rajesh Shukla, Prabir Kumar Ghosh, and Rachna Sharma, "Assessing the Effectiveness of Small Borrowing in India" (New Delhi: NCAER Centre for Macro Consumer Research, 2011).

52. Renuka Sane and Susan Thomas, "The Real Cost of Credit Constraints: Evidence from Micro-finance," Mumbai Working Papers 2013-013 (Mumbai: Indira Gandhi Institute of Development Research, 2013). Also published as Renuka Sane and Susan Thomas, "The Real Cost of Credit Constraints: Evidence from Micro-finance," *B. E. Journal of Economic Analysis Policy* 16, no. 1 (2016): 151–83.

53. World Bank, *Global Findex Data 2018* (Washington, 2018). This 2018 report is based on 2017 data.

54. For example, the author and her team at IFC incorporated responsible finance and social protection principles in technical assistance agreements and organized workshops on responsible finance starting in early 2010 with a range of MFIs and industry players.

55. The author and her team at IFC plus colleagues at the Michael and Susan Dell Foundation helped facilitate these meetings, as part of the India Responsible Finance Forum, which included support to MFIN and Sa-Dhan as they harmonized their codes of conduct and adapted relevant global lessons.

56. Author's copy of "Code of Conduct for the Microfinance Industry" (New Delhi: MFIN and Sa-Dhan, December 2011).

57. "Code of Conduct for the Microfinance Industry."

58. "MFIN, Sa-Dhan Release Code for Responsible Lending for Micro-Credit Industry," *Times of India*, September 16, 2019.

59. "Code for Responsible Lending in Micro-Credit" (New Delhi: MFIN, Sa-Dhan, and FIDC, September 2019).

60. "RBI Increases Household Income Limits for Borrowers of NBFCs and MFIs," *News On AIR* (All India Radio), November 9, 2019.

61. Ibid.

62. RBI, "Report of the Committee on Comprehensive Financial Services for Small Businesses and Low-Income Households," 2013 (https://rbidocs.rbi.org.in/rdocs/Publication Report/Pdfs/CFS070114RFL.pdf).

63. RBI, "The Non-Banking Financial Company: Micro Finance Institutions," *Directions*, 2011.

64. RBI, "Data Format for Furnishing of Credit Information to Credit Information Companies and other Regulatory Measures," June 27, 2014 (https://www.rbi.org.in/Scripts/NotificationUser.aspx?Id=8968); RBI, "Membership of Credit Information Companies (CICs)," January 15, 2015 (https://www.rbi.org.in/Scripts/NotificationUser.aspx?Id=9485). This requirement was consistent with the NBFC-MFI regulation issued by the RBI in December 2011 interdicting any MFI from becoming a lender to a client that already had two loans from other MFIs. Subsequently, the RBI required credit institutions to seek two credit enquiries, in order to increase the accuracy of credit decisions.

65. Despite considerable advocacy and effort, data on borrowers organized in SHGs are not required to be reported to the credit bureaus. As discussed in the chapter, banks of all types, NBFC-MFIs, MFIs, and others lend to groups of clients organized in SHGs, but the level of information on individual loans within SHGs is uneven at best. Given the millions of SHG clients and outstanding loans, this remains a significant gap in credit bureau data across India.

66. RBI, "Issue of Comprehensive Credit Information Reports," August 2, 2017 (https://www.rbi.org.in/Scripts/NotificationUser.aspx?Id=11077).

67. RBI, "Free Annual Credit Report to Individuals," September 1, 2016 (https://www.rbi.org.in/Scripts/NotificationUser.aspx?Id=10590).

68. World Bank Group, *Doing Business Database* (Washington) (https://www.doingbusiness.org/en/rankings).

69. Email from CRIF HighMark to author, February 27, 2019.

70. K. Nishanth and Deepti George, "Let's Stop Kicking the Can Down the Road: Highlighting Important and Unaddressed Gaps in Microcredit Regulations" (Dvara Research, October 23, 2019) (https://www.dvara.com/blog/2019/10/24/lets-stop-kicking-the-can-down-the-road-highlighting-important-and-unaddressed-gaps-in-microcredit-regulations/).

71. RBI, "Report of the High-Level Task Force on Public Credit Registry for India," April 4, 2018 (https://rbidocs.rbi.org.in/rdocs/PublicationReport/Pdfs/PCRRR09CF7539AC3E48C9B69112AF2A498EFD.PDF).

72. Pallavi Nahata, "Will RBI's Public Credit Registry Disrupt India's Successful Credit Bureaus?" Bloomberg Quint, July 12, 2018. See also "Public Credit Registry: Why Its Implementation Will Be a Milestone in Ending MSME Credit Woes," *Financial Express*, September 8, 2019.

73. Nikhat Hetavkar and Abhijit Lele, "Credit Bureaus May Soon Be Allowed Access to Data from Utility Providers," *Business Standard*, August 22, 2018.

74. "PM, Sonia Launch Aadhaar, the Unique ID Project," Press Trust of India, *Deccan Herald*, September 29, 2010.

75. H. K. Varun, "SC's Aadhaar Verdict: Privacy vs. Identity," *Deccan Herald*, September 20, 2018; Mahendra Singh, "99% of Indians over 18 Now Have Aadhaar Cards," *Times of India*, January 28, 2017; "Aadhaar Dashboard," Unique Identification Authority of India (https://uidai.gov.in/).

76. Varun, "SC's Aadhaar Verdict."

77. Rachna Khaira, "Rs 500, 10 Minutes, and You Have Access to Billion Aadhaar Details," *The Tribune*, January 3, 2018.

78. Tanmay Patange, "Two Sides of the Aadhaar Controversy from This Week," *Indian Express*, July 14, 2018 (updated).

79. Varun, "SC's Aadhaar Verdict."

80. Jennifer Isern and others, "AML/CFT Regulation: Implications for Financial Service Providers That Serve Low-Income People," *Focus Note* 29 (Washington: CGAP, World Bank, July 2005).

81. "What Supreme Court's Aadhaar Verdict Means for You: 10 Points," *Livemint*, September 26, 2018.

82. Vindu Goel, "India's Top Court Limits Sweep of Biometric ID Program," *New York Times*, September 26, 2018.

83. "Lok Sabha Passes Bill to Amend Aadhaar Act," *Economic Times*, January 4, 2019. See also "Cabinet Approves Aadhaar Ordinance to Allow Its Use as ID Proof for Bank Accounts, SIM Connection," *News 18*, February 28, 2019.

84. "eKYC, Digital KYC for Opening Bank Accounts to Make Process Secure," *Livemint*, August 28, 2019.

85. Pradhan Mantri Jan-Dhan Yogana (PMJDY), "Program Overview and Basic Statistics," Government of India (https://www.pmjdy.gov.in/).

86. Ibid.

87. PMJDY, "State-wise Statistics," Government of India (https://www.pmjdy.gov.in/).

88. Graham Wright and Manoj Sharma, "India's Enabling Triangle for Financial Inclusion," MicroSave Consulting, September 26, 2018 (https://www.microsave.net/2018/09/26/indias-enabling-triangle-for-financial-inclusion/); Manuela Gunther, "The Progress of Financial Inclusion in India: Insights from Multiple Waves of Survey Data" (Overseas Development Institute and CAFRAL, 2017) (https://cafral.org.in/sfControl/content/Speech/65201730802PMManuela_Kristin_Günther.pdf).

89. Aishwarya Singh, Lokesh Singh, and Mukesh Sadana, "PMJDY: Improved Financial Inclusion, but Roadblocks Remain" (Washington: CGAP, World Bank, 2015); Sakshi

Chada, "PMJDY: Commendable Growth, yet Low-Hanging Barriers Persist" (Washington, CGAP, World Bank, August 24, 2016).

90. Anuj Srivas, "Jan Dhan Yojana: One Rupee Balance and the Dormancy-Duplication Problem," *The Wire*, September 14, 2017.

91. "Demonetisation: Jan Dhan Account Deposits Double to Rs 87000 Crore," *Livemint*, January 1, 2017.

92. Anand Adhikari, "Jan Dhan Yojana Data Shows Rural Area Residents Using Bank Accounts More Often," *Business Today*, November 20, 2019.

93. Anand Adhikari, "Jan Dhan Yojana: Average Deposit Balance Doubles Despite Rural Distress, Economic Slowdown," *Business Today*, November 6, 2019.

94. National Payments Corporation of India (NPCI), "Background"(https://www.npci .org.in/).

95. NPCI, "IMPS Product Overview" (https://www.npci.org.in/).

96. NPCI, "RuPay Product Overview" (https://www.npci.org.in/).

97. PMJDY, "Program Overview and Basic Statistics."

98. NPCI, "UPI Product Overview" (https://www.npci.org.in/).

99. NPCI, "BHIM Product Overview" (https://www.npci.org.in/).

100. RBI, "Bankwise ATM, POS, and Card Statistics."

101. Ibid.

102. NPCI, "Statistics"(https://www.npci.org.in/).

103. Ibid.

104. Unfortunately card data are not available for December 2019 as of this writing, so this comparison is using September 2019 data for cards and their transactions and December 2019 data for UPI and NPCI transactions.

105. NPCI, "Statistics."

106. "BHIM UPI Goes Global; QR Code-Based Payments Demonstrated at Singapore FinTech Festival," *Business Standard*, November 13, 2019.

107. Already in July 2019, the RBI had waived fees for outward transactions using the RTGS and NEFT systems. This latest change removes the authority of financial services providers to charge clients using savings accounts for these transactions. Nikhil Agarwal, "NEFT, RTGS Transfer Charges to Be Waived for Savings Account, RBI Issues Order," *Livemint*, December 18, 2019.

108. Telecommunications Regulatory Authority of India, 2019, "Highlights of Telecom Subscription Data as on 31st October 2019," December 30, 2019.

109. Ibid.

110. However, because prices are so low and competition by providers is high, the telecommunications industry is struggling, and the industry has witnessed significant consolidation as several providers have exited. The industry and related pricing for mobile services may change in the near term. See, for example, "A Price War Has Undermined India's Big Telecoms Companies," *The Economist*, December 12, 2019.

111. Many researchers have analyzed the tipping point when cash in/cash out points become less critical, so this is not developed further in this section. However, for low-income and vulnerable groups, cash in/cash out points will be important to maintain for the medium to long term in India and globally.

112. Reserve Bank of India, "Payment and Settlement System Statistics," January 11, 2020; and RBI, "Bankwise ATM, POS, and Card Statistics" (https://www.rbi.org.in/scripts/paymentsystems.aspx).

113. RBI, "Payment and Settlement System Statistics."

114. Reserve Bank of India, "Payment and Settlement System Statistics," January 11, 2020; and RBI, "Bankwise ATM, POS, and Card Statistics" (https://www.rbi.org.in/scripts/paymentsystems.aspx).

115. Reserve Bank of India, "Payment and Settlement System Statistics," January 11, 2020; and RBI, "Bankwise ATM, POS, and Card Statistics" (https://www.rbi.org.in/scripts/paymentsystems.aspx). See also "Total Number of POS Machines Grew 39% YoY to 4.88 Million in November 2019," Medianama, February 10, 2020.

116. The BC model in India and several markets across Asia and Africa has been extensively analyzed; two of the best resources for further information are MSC (MicroSave Consulting) and CGAP.

117. Aakash Mehrotra and others, "State of the Agent Network, India 2017" (MicroSave Helix, February 2018) (http://www.microsave.net/wp-content/uploads/2018/12/Agent_Network_Accelerator_Research_Country_Report_India.pdf).

118. Business Correspondent Federation of India, "Programs and Membership" (http://bcfi.org.in/).

119. Anand Shrivastav, BCFI Founder, correspondence with the author, January 11, 2020.

120. Author's unpublished files based on public data.

121. Jennifer Isern and others, "Government to Person Health Payments in Bihar, India, Diagnostic and Recommendations" (New Delhi: International Finance Corporation, June 2011).

122. Jennifer Isern, Anita Sharma, and Georgina Marina, "Transforming Health through E-Payments in India," Finance in Focus Series of the Finance and Markets Department (Washington: World Bank, August 2017).

123. Ibid. For another view of G2P payments in India, see also Paul Breloff and Sarah Rotman, "An Overview of G2P Payment Sector in India" (Washington: CGAP, World Bank, September 2011). See also MicroSave Consulting (MSC) for high-quality analysis of G2P programs in India and globally.

124. Controller General of Accounts, Ministry of Finance, Government of India. "PFMS Description" (https://pfms.nic.in/NewDefaultHome.aspx).

125. DBT Mission, Government of India, "DBT Description" (https://dbtbharat.gov.in/).

126. DBT Mission, Government of India, "MPR FY2018-2019 and MPR FY2019-2020 as of end December 2019" (https://dbtbharat.gov.in/).

127. Ministry of Finance, Government of India, "India Economic Survey 2016–17" (https://www.india.gov.in/content/economic-survey-2016-17). For more analysis, see Saksham Khosla, *India's Universal Basic Income: Bedeviled by the Details?* (Washington: Carnegie Endowment for International Peace, 2018).

128. Prabhash Dutta, "Demonetisation: What India Gained and Lost," *India Today*, August 30, 2018.

129. "Demonetisation Hit Small and Medium-sized Enterprises," *Financial Express*, January 25, 2017. See also Suparna Dutt D'Cunha, "One Year Later: India's Demonetization

Move Proves Too Costly An Experiment," *Forbes*, November 7, 2017; and Gabriel Chodorow-Reich and others, "Cash and the Economy: Evidence from India's Demonetization," Working Paper (Harvard University, December 2018).

130. Sumit Agarwal, "India's Demonetization Drive: A Necessary Jolt Towards A More Digital Economy?," *Forbes*, September 1, 2018.

131. Samrat Sharma, "Two and a Half Years of Demonetisation: Cash Rules, Digital Payments Grow, Credit Cards Drag," *Financial Express*, August 21, 2019.

132. RBI, Annual Report 2019.

133. Anubhutie Singh, Beni Chugh, and Malavika Raghavan, "Digital Payments in India: Reflections from the Union Budget, the RBI's Payments Vision 2021 and the Nilekani Committee Report" (Chennai, India: Dvara Trust, August 20, 2019).

134. "PM Launches Pradhan Mantri MUDRA Yojana," April 8, 2015, website of the Office of the Prime Minster, PMINDIA.

135. Pradhan Mantri MUDRA Yojana (PMMY), MUDRA Annual Report 2017–18 (https://www.mudramitra.in/).

136. Ibid., MUDRA statistics 2018–19 and 2019–20 (https://www.mudramitra.in/).

137. "RBI Cautions Government over NPA Spike in MUDRA Loans," *Economic Times*, January 13, 2019; "RBI Deputy Governor Red-Flags Rising Stress in Mudra Loans," *Times of India*, November 26, 2019.

138. Banikinkar Pattanayak, "NPA Crisis: PSU Banks Likely to Revamp Mudra Scheme," *Financial Express*, September 2, 2019.

139. See, for example, Anand Adhikari, "Mudra Loans Report Card: PNB NPAs at 23%, other banks above 20%," *Business Today*, November 27, 2019. See also Majid Alam, "Bad Loans under Mudra Scheme on a Rise, Reveals RTI," *News18*, December 31, 2019.

140. "Mudra Loan Reality Check: Each Job Costs Rs 5.1 Lakh; Only 20 Percent Borrowers Started New Business," *Financial Express*, September 4, 2019.

141. RBI, "RBI Releases Guidelines for Licensing of Payments Banks," November 27, 2014.

142. RBI, "Operating Guidelines for Payments Banks" (https://www.rbi.org.in/SCRIPTs/NotificationUser.aspx?Id=10635).

143. RBI, "RBI Releases Guidelines."

144. Joel Rebello and Anup Roy, "Reliance, Airtel, Nine Others Get RBI Nod to Open Payments Banks," *Livemint,* August 20, 2015.

145. Amrit Raj and Upasana Jain, "Airtel Payments Bank Launched, with Vow to Shake Up Old Banking System," *Livemint*, January 13, 2017.

146. Pratik Bhakta, "Surrendering of Payments Bank Licences Not a Worry, Says RBI Governor Raghuram Rajan," *Economic Times*, June 8, 2016.

147. Radhika Merwin, "Why Five Out of the 11 Payments Banks Have Shut Shop," *Hindu Business Line*, September 10, 2019.

148. RBI, "Guidelines for 'On Tap' Licensing of Small Finance Banks in the Private Sector," December 5, 2019 (https://rbidocs.rbi.org.in/rdocs/Content/PDFs/SFB130920194F5B25F26CF34E5F83756F304C704236.PDF).

149. RBI, "Guidelines for Licensing of Small Finance Banks in the Private Sector," November 27, 2014 (https://rbidocs.rbi.org.in/rdocs/Content/PDFs/SMFGU271114.pdf).

150. RBI, "Licensing of New Banks in the Private Sector," February 22, 2013 (https://www.rbi.org.in/scripts/BS_PressReleaseDisplay.aspx?prid=28191).

151. RBI, "RBI Grants "In-Principle" Approval to 10 Applicants for Small Finance Banks," September 16, 2015 (https://www.rbi.org.in/scripts/BS_PressReleaseDisplay.aspx?prid=35010).

152. Author discussions with leadership and staff of small finance banks and information shared publicly by small finance banks over the past four years. See also Andreas Nilsson and Nina Freudenberg, "Moving Past Microfinance: How India's Small Finance Banks Aim to Take Financial Inclusion to the Next Level," *Next Billion*, August 29, 2018 (https://nextbillion.net/microfinance-india-small-finance-banks/).

153. RBI, "Statement on Developmental and Regulatory Policies," June 6, 2018.

154. RBI, "Guidelines for 'On Tap' Licensing of Small Finance Banks." The draft guidelines were originally released in mid-September 2019 for public review.

155. RBI, "RBI Decides to Grant 'In-Principle' Approval for Banking Licences," April 2, 2014. Of note: Two applicants later withdrew, reducing the pool to twenty-five applicants.

156. "Fintech Startups Paving Way for a Financially Smart India," *Economic Times*, March 28, 2019.

157. "India Emerging as Fintech Hub: Findexable Report," *Moneycontrol News*, December 11, 2019.

158. "Fintech Startups Paving Way for a Financially Smart India." See also Srikanth, "Top 5 Financing Platforms for MSMEs & SMEs in India," *TechieExpert*, October 16, 2019 (www.techiexpert.com/top-5-financing-platforms-for-msmes-smes-in-india/).

159. Adait Palepu, "India's Neo-Banks: What's So 'Neo' About Them?," Bloomberg Quint, December 4, 2019.

160. Pratik Bhakta, "Fintech Startups Look for Total Makeover with Lending Licence," *Economic Times*, September 6, 2109.

161. Rishi Ranjan Kala, "Whats App Seeks RBI Approval for Payments Service," *Financial Express*, August 30, 2019.

162. Aarzoo Mittal, "WhatsApp Payments Service Isn't Compliant for Launch: RBI to SC," Entrackr.com, November 8, 2019.

163. "WhatsApp Pay Set for Phased Roll Out in India; Granted NPCI Permission." *Business Standard*, February 7, 2020.

164. Prasanna Mohanty, "Budget 2020: Niti Aayog Shocker; Poverty, Hunger and Income Inequality Up in 22 to 25 States and UTs," *Business Today*, January 8, 2020.

165. RBI, "Report on Trend and Progress of Banking in India for the Year Ended June 30, 2018," December 28, 2018 (https://rbidocs.rbi.org.in/rdocs/Publications/PDFs/0RTP2018_FE9E97E7AF7024A4B94321734CD76DD4F.PDF).

166. Tamal Bandyopadhyay, "The Status of Public Sector Banks in India Today," *Livemint*, August 26, 2018.

167. RBI, "Report on Trend and Progress of Banking in India for the Year Ended June 30, 2019," December 24, 2019 (https://rbidocs.rbi.org.in/rdocs/Publications/PDFs/0RTP241219FL760D9F69321B47988DE44D68D9217A7E.PDF).

168. "How PNB Recovered from Biggest Bank Fraud to Top Spot in 'Reform Agenda' in Just 9 Months," *Financial Express*, March 1, 2019.

169. George Matthew and Sandeep Singh, "IL&FS Defaults, NBFC Whiplash: Understanding the Debt Market Crisis," *Indian Express*, September 26, 2018.

170. Tamal Bandyopadhyay, "The Status of Public Sector Banks in India Today," *Livemint*, August 26, 2018.

171. Tamal Bandyopadhyay, "Accept or Not, Bank Privatisation Is On," *Business Standard*, January 12, 2020. See also Reserve Bank of India, "Report on Trend and Progress of Banking in India for the Year Ended June 30, 2019."

172. Ibid.

173. Reserve Bank of India, "Revised Prompt Corrective Action (PCA) Framework for Banks," April 13, 2017.

174. Ira Dugal, "Half of India's Listed Government Banks Now under RBI's Watch," Bloomberg Quint, January 4, 2018.

175. "Govt Banks on Big Bang Mergers as GDP Tanks," *Hindu Businessline*, August 30, 2019.

176. Rahul Satija and Suvashree Ghosh, "Cancelled Registrations of 1,851 NBFCs in the Year Ended March 31," *The Print*, August 22, 2019.

177. RBI, "RBI Cancels Certificate of Registration of Thirteen NBFCs" and "Seven NBFCs Surrender Their Certificate of Registration to RBI," both on December 26, 2019 (https://www.rbi.org.in/scripts/BS_PressReleaseDisplay.aspx?prid=48971; and https://rbidocs.rbi.org.in/rdocs/PressRelease/PDFs/PR1518689E6EEE5627492FA2685B507AB6E6 2F.PDF).

178. "PMC Crisis: This Tiny Bank in Maharashtra Is a Canary in India's Coalmine," *Economic Times*, September 30, 2019.

179. Shayan Ghosh, "After PMC Crisis, Tighter Norms in Place for Urban Cooperative Banks," *The Mint*, December 6, 2109.

180. "RBI Given Power To Regulate Cooperative Banks As Centre Approves Changes To Banking Laws." Scroll.in, February 5, 2020.

181. RBI, Annual Report 2019.

182. RBI, "Deposit Insurance and Credit Guarantee Corporation (DICGC) Increases the Insurance Coverage for Depositors in All Insured Banks to ₹5 lakh," February 4, 2020.

183. Somesh Jha, "RBI Plans PCA Framework, Different Supervisory System for NBFCs by 2022," *Business Standard*, November 11, 2019.

184. World Bank, *Global Findex Data 2018*.

185. PMJDY, "Program Overview and Basic Statistics."

186. World Bank, *Global Findex Data 2018*.

187. Ibid. Inactivity is defined as no deposit or withdrawal to the account in the previous twelve months.

188. Alok Misra and Ajay Tankha, "Inclusive Finance India Report 2019" (New Delhi: Access and Access Assist, December 2019).

189. NABARD, "Status of Microfinance in India 2018–2019" (Mumbai, 2019).

190. MFIN, "MicroMeter Edition 31: September 2019" (New Delhi, August–November 2019). See also "Microfinance Sector Sees 47.85% Growth in Loans," *Hindu Businessline*, November 25, 2019.

191. Misra and Tankha, "Inclusive Finance India Report 2019."

192. Atmadip Ray, "MFIs Stare at Repayment Crisis in Rural Assam," *Economic Times*, November 22, 2019.

193. RBI, "National Strategy for Financial Inclusion," January 10, 2020 (https://rbidocs .rbi.org.in/rdocs/content/pdfs/NSFIREPORT100119.pdf; and https://www.rbi.org.in/scripts /BS_PressReleaseDisplay.aspx?prid=49116).

194. World Bank, *Global Findex Data 2018*. As noted earlier, inactivity is defined as no deposit or withdrawal to the account in the previous twelve months.

195. Mukta Mani, "Financial Inclusion in North India: Status and Insights," *IUP Journal of Bank Management* 18, no. 1 (2019).

196. RBI, "Report on Trend and Progress of Banking in India for the Year Ended June 30, 2018." Note that this survey is based on 2016 data.

197. RBI, Annual Report 2019.

198. RBI, "Report on Trend and Progress of Banking in India for the Year Ended June 30, 2019." Note that the data on branches are limited to scheduled commercial banks only; the number would be higher if the other financial services provider branches were included.

199. RBI, "Payment and Settlement System Statistics." See also RBI, "Report on Trend and Progress of Banking in India for the Year Ended June 30, 2019."

200. RBI, "Payment and Settlement System Statistics."

201. Telephone Regulatory Authority of India, "Highlights of Telecom Subscription Data as of 31st December, 2018," February 28, 2019.

202. *World Development Indicators 2010–2017* (Washington: World Bank).

203. RBI, "Report on Trend and Progress of Banking in India for the Year Ended June 30, 2019."

204. Pawan Bakhshi, Manoj Sharma, and Graham Wright, "What's Undermining India's Financial Inclusion Progress?" (Washington: CGAP, World Bank, June 5, 2015).

205. Ashwin Manikandan, "Business Correspondents' Income Model Based on Commissions Unviable," *Economic Times*, April 11, 2019.

206. MicroSave and Business Correspondent Federation of India (BCFI), "Business Correspondent Channel Cost Assessment," April 2015.

207. Mehrotra and others, "State of the Agent Network, India 2017."

208. Shaikh Zoaib Saleem, "Women Bought 32% of Life Insurance Policies in 2017–18, Shows Irdai Data," *Livemint*, January 23, 2019.

209. Giorgia Barboni and others, "A Tough Call: Understanding Barriers to and Impacts of Women's Mobile Phone Adoption in India" (The Kennedy School at Harvard University, October 2018).

210. World Bank, *Global Findex Data 2018*.

211. PMJDY, "Program Overview and Basic Statistics."

212. Saleem, "Women Bought 32% of Life Insurance Policies in 2017–18."

213. World Bank, *Global Findex Data 2018*.

214. Ibid.

215. CRIF High Mark, "Emerging Trends and Patterns of Retail Lending to Microfinance Customers," presented at the Inclusive Finance India Summit, New Delhi, December 2019.

216. Aparajita Singh, "Are We Protected Enough?" (Chennai, India: Dvara Trust, March 2019).

217. Richard Jackson, "Meeting India's Retirement Challenge," Global Aging Institute. Presentation made at the World Bank office in Washington, January 16, 2019.

218. K. Nishanth, "Old Wine in a New Bottle? An Analysis of the Pradhan Mantri Shram-Yogi Maandhan" (Chennai, India: Dvara Trust, February 5, 2019).

219. Atmadip Ray, "RBI Prepares for Full Financial Inclusion in Hinterland," *Economic Times*, January 22, 2019.

220. RBI, "Policy Paper on Authorisation of New Retail Payment Systems," January 21, 2019. See also RBI, "Report of the High Level Committee on Deepening of Digital Payments," May 17, 2019 (https://rbidocs.rbi.org.in/rdocs/PublicationReport/Pdfs/ANRPS21 012019A8F5D4891BF84849837D7D611B7FFC58.PDF; and https://rbidocs.rbi.org.in/rdocs /PublicationReport/Pdfs/CDDP03062019634B0EEF3F7144C3B65360B280E420AC.PDF).

221. RBI, Annual Report 2019.

222. Department of Economic Affairs, Ministry of Finance, Government of India, "Report of the Steering Committee on Fintech Related Issues," September 2019.

223. RBI, "Report on Benchmarking India's Payment Systems," June 2019.

224. For an excellent review of RBI policy and decision making over the decades, see M. S. Sriram, *Talking Financial Inclusion in Liberalised India* (New Delhi: Access Assist with Routledge India, 2018). See also Raghuram Rajan, *The Third Pillar: How Markets and the State Leave the Community Behind* (New York: Harper Collins, 2019).

225. RBI, Annual Report 2019.

226. Susan Desai, "India's Farm Loan Waiver Crisis," *Pacific Exchange* (blog), Federal Reserve Bank of San Francisco, September 11, 2017.

227. Mayank Bhardwaj and Rajendra Jadhav, "India's Modi Seen Forgiving Farm Loans as He Seeks to Win Back Rural Voters," Reuters, December 11, 2018.

228. RBI, "Edited Transcript of Reserve Bank of India's First Bi-Monthly Post Policy Press Conference," April 7, 2017. See also "Avoid Farm Loan Waivers: RBI's Internal Working Group," *New Kerala*, September 3, 2019.

229. George Matthew, "Financial Exclusion: 40.9 percent of Small and Marginal Farmers Not Covered by Banks," *Indian Express*, September 15, 2019.

230. Ministry of Agriculture, Government of India, PMFBY website, https://pmfby.gov.in/.

231. Poorvi Kulkarni, "Why Farmers across India Are Complaining of Being Cheated by Prime Minister's Crop Insurance Scheme," Scroll.in. February 27, 2019.

232. Atmadip Ray, "MFIs Stare at Repayment Crisis in Rural Assam," *Economic Times*, November 22, 2019.

233. "RBI Proposes Self-Regulatory Body for Digital Payment System," *Economic Times*, February 6, 2020.

234. Pratik Bhakta, "RBI Raises Aggregate Exposure Limit to Rs 50 Lakh on P2P Lending Platforms," *Economic Times*, December 11, 2019.

235. Daniel Ren, "A 71-Year-Old Victim's Tale Reveals Extent of Greed in China's US$30 Billion Peer-to-Peer Lending Fiasco," *South China Morning Post*, December 30, 2019.

236. "P2P: China's Once-Booming Lending Industry Must Close within Two Years, Government Notice Says," *South China Morning Post*, November 28, 2019.

237. RBI, Annual Report 2019. The other supervisory agencies that co-launched the NCFE are Securities and Exchange Board of India (SEBI), Insurance Regulatory and Development

Authority (IRDAI), and Pension Fund Regulatory and Development Authority (PFRDA). See also the website of the National Centre for Financial Education at NCFE.org.in.

238. RBI, "Report on Trend and Progress of Banking in India for the Year Ended June 30, 2018"; RBI, "Report on Trend and Progress of Banking in India for the Year Ended June 30, 2019."

239. RBI, Annual Report 2019.

240. RBI, "Report on Trend and Progress of Banking in India for the Year Ended June 30, 2019"; "Report on Trend and Progress of Banking in India for the Year Ended June 30, 2018."

241. RBI, "Report on Trend and Progress of Banking in India for the Year Ended June 30, 2019."

242. The secret shopping investigation by *Economic Times Wealth* is a good example, and MicroSave Consulting has also conducted similar exercises in India and globally. Narendra Nathan, "Banks Continue Mis-selling Financial Products: Here's What You Must Know to Protect Yourself," *Economic Times Wealth*, November 21, 2018.

243. Saikat Das, "RBI Spots Fraud That Wipes Out a Customer's Bank Balance Via UPI, Alarm Sounded," *Economic Times*, February 17, 2019. See also "Woman Shares Her Banking Details, Loses Rs 10.36 Lakh," *Times of India*, March 1, 2019.

244. RBI, "Report on Trend and Progress of Banking in India for the Year Ended June 30, 2019."

245. RBI, "The Reserve Bank Introduces Ombudsman Scheme for Digital Transactions," January 31, 2019.

246. Srikanth Lakshmanan, "Exclusive: RBI Issues In-Principle Licenses to 5 Account Aggregators," *Medianama*, November 22, 2018.

247. Dvara Trust, "Our Response to the Draft Personal Data Protection Bill, 2018" (Chennai, India, October 10, 2018). See also Bhumika Khatri, "The Personal Data Protection Bill 2018 Does Everything but Protect Personal Data," *Inc42*, July 29, 2018; Brahma Chellaney, "Data Is Wealth. India Must Protect It.," *Hindustan Times*, August 20, 2019.

FOURTEEN

Inclusive Financial Development in China

ENJIANG CHENG

Inclusive finance in this chapter refers to the provision of financial services, including savings, lending, insurance, money transfer, and other financial services at reasonable costs to low-income groups and the poor and to micro and small enterprises (MSEs) in China's urban and rural areas. The policy discussions regarding inclusive finance within China have so far focused on lending services, particularly microlending services to rural households for income generation and to MSEs in rural and peri-urban areas. In many cases, because of small landholding, rural finance overlaps with microfinance in China. Most loans for rural households are microloans. Also, rural areas cover not only the villages but also the county seat and other large townships in a county. Because many microentrepreneurs and small-business owners operating in urban areas come from rural areas and still maintain rural residences, financial services to them can be regarded as part of rural finance. Thus the boundary between urban and rural is blurry because of integrated urban and rural development today.

The development of inclusive finance in China has been shaped mainly by three factors: (1) the state- and subnational-government-dominated financial institutions, especially the urban and rural commercial and co-operative banks; (2) financial policies and regulations, which on the one hand restrict entry of private capital and nongovernmental organizations (NGOs) into inclusive banking institutions, and on the other hand encourage banks to do small and medium-sized enterprise (SME) lending and rural lending; and (3) new financial technologies and their application in inclusive finance in China.

This chapter first provides a snapshot of inclusive finance development in China, including the main indicators and major players and the policy and regulatory landscape. Next it discusses two cases of inclusive finance development in China, the rural microloans by the China Foundation for Poverty Alleviation Microfinance (CFPA MF), a nonbanking financial institution, and microfinance downscaling by selected urban and rural commercial banks. Finally, it documents the rapid development of fintech institutions and their application in financial inclusion efforts in China, as well as the implications for policy.

A Snapshot of Financial Inclusion in China

Since 2015, two documents have served as guidelines for inclusive financial development in China: the "Plan for Promoting Inclusive Finance in China 2016–2020" released by China's State Council in 2014, and "G-20 Documents for Developing Inclusive Finance."[1] The People's Bank of China (PBOC) also developed eight indicators to measure inclusive finance development in China: percentage of the population with an active bank account; percentage of the population using digital payments; percentage of the population purchasing wealth management products (WMPs); the number of active loans to individuals; percentage of the population with a bank loan; percentage of the population with a loan from nonbanking institutions; amount of financial knowledge; and financial behavior.

Following the high rate of economic growth and the process of urbanization and digitization of the economy in China, financial services—especially savings, payments, and remittance services—have become more accessible to the population, including China's rural poor. According to the PBOC, the use of bank accounts and bank cards has become common in China, including in remote rural areas. But according to the Global Findex Database of the World Bank Group, by 2017 around 200 million rural adults in China remained outside the formal financial system. The database confirms, however, that China has achieved a high rate of ownership of bank accounts: the share of adults with a bank account reached 80 percent; in comparison, the world average is 69 percent and 63 percent in developing economies.[2]

Digital payments have also become more popular in China. The Global Findex Database of the World Bank Group indicates that in 2017 digital payment (payments using the internet) reached 49 percent in China (the figures were 29 percent worldwide and 11 percent in developing economies). The share of the population who made purchases and paid bills online was as high as 85 percent in China, in comparison with 53 percent in developing economies. Globally, about 1.1 billion people, or two-thirds of all unbanked adults, have a mobile phone; 82 percent of the unbanked in China had a mobile phone in 2017.[3]

Access to institutional lending in China has not improved to the same extent. About 40 percent of China's adults (35 percent of rural adults) had individual or household loans from financial institutions. Another 22.7 percent of adults borrowed from nonbanking financial institutions and through peer-to-peer institutions (P2Ps) and other internet platforms. Micro- and small-enterprise loans increased slowly in 2017; by the end of 2017, loans outstanding to MSEs from banking institutions reached RMB6.773 trillion, an increase of 10 percent over the previous year. MSE loans constituted 10 percent of total banking loans in China, 0.15 percent less than in the previous year.[4] By the end of 2017, bank loans outstanding to rural households for income-generation purposes totaled RMB4.6 trillion, an increase of 6.5 percent over the previous year and 3.91 percent of total banking loans in China. By the end of 2016, about 92.5 million rural households had loans from banking institutions. According to the PBOC and the China Banking and Insurance Regulation Commission (CBIRC), the poverty loan portfolio reached RMB249.6 billion in 2017: RMB41,100 per poor household, to over 6 million state-designated poor rural households in China, about one-quarter of all the designated poor rural households in China.[5]

Key Players in China's Inclusive Finance Space

China's financial market is highly regulated. Regulated banks have dominated China's financial services, including deposit savings, money transfers, lending, and insurance services. The providers of inclusive financial services in China fall into three categories: (1) regulated financial institutions, mainly deposit-taking banking institutions regulated by the CBIRC;[6] (2) semi-regulated financial institutions, including the lending-only microcredit companies (MCCs), financial guarantee companies, and pawnshops supervised by local government agencies; and (3) nonfinancial institutions providing inclusive financial services, including rural co-operatives engaging in microlending activities and village funds, NGO microfinance institutions (MFIs), and P2P institutions. NGO MFIs and most village funds in China are registered as nonprofit social organizations, while P2Ps and most rural co-operatives are registered as commercial entities. Nonfinancial institutions in China are not regulated by central or local financial regulators and have provided mostly microcredit services in pilot programs.

Of the regulated banks, city commercial banks (CCBs) and rural credit co-operatives (RCCs) have been the major providers of financial services to rural households and MSEs in China. Services provided by the Postal Savings Bank of China, which has led rural savings and remittance services for low-income people, are gradually being replaced by digital finance. China's regulated banks have done well in the provision of deposit, payments, and domestic money transfer services.[7] RCCs in many areas of China have also achieved good outreach in their lending services under guidance from CBIRC. Following several rounds of reform, RCCs in China currently consist of rural commercial banks (RCBs), rural co-operative banks (RCOBs), and rural credit co-operative unions (RCCUs).[8] Each province has a provincial-level RCC federation (RCCF), except for Beijing, Shanghai, Tianjin, Chongqing, and Ningxia, where a provincial-level RCB has been set up. The paid-in equity capital of the RCC system soared from RMB62.5 billion in 2003, when the latest round of the RCC reform was launched, to RMB578.1 billion at the end of 2013 (at current prices), which allowed RCCs to lend an additional RMB6.4 trillion at a leverage of 12.5 times.[9]

Other banks engaging in inclusive financial services include new types of rural financial institutions (RFIs) that entered after 2006 following the financial reforms in 2005–06. By the end of 2016, these new RFIs included 1,519 village and township banks (VTBs), 13 loan companies, and 48 rural fund co-operatives, all of them regulated by CBIRC. One major constraint on the new RFIs was that their scale is too small to achieve long-term financial sustainability while trying to reach rural households and MSEs. By the end of 2015, the ratio of assets of all VTBs to the total assets of banking institutions in China was less than 1 percent whereas the ratio was 7.8 percent for RCBs and 11.7 percent for CCBs. As a result, about 20 percent of VTBs suffered financial losses in 2015.[10] Subsequently, policy discussions and consultations led to more than ten private banks, including three internet banks (e-banks), being licensed by CBIRC in 2014 and 2015 to provide inclusive financial services to MSEs and rural communities and households in China.

The semi-regulated financial institutions in China presented in table 14-1 include MCCs, pawnshops, and leasing companies. It was reported that by March 2018, there were 8,471 registered MCCs in China, with more than 100,000 employees and a loan portfolio of approximately RMB936 billion.[11] Nonfinancial institutions, such as NGO MFIs and the community-based village funds, have been more active in China's poor areas, where it is difficult for the formal banks to penetrate. The pilot village community funds (VCFs) or village development self-help funds were launched by the Poverty Alleviation and Development Office under the State Council (LGOP), with support from the Ministry of Finance (MOF) in 2006. VCFs consist of grants from

TABLE 14-1. Development of Nonbanking Microloan Institutions
in China, 2012 and 2013

	Microcredit companies (MCCs)	*Pawnshops*	*Leasing companies*[a]	*NGO microfinance institutions*
Number[b]	7,839	6,084	540	About 100
Total portfolio (billion RMB)	819.1	70.61	890	
Supervisors	Financial Offices (Bureau)[c]	Ministry of Commerce	Ministry of Commerce	Unclear
Main clients	Micro and small enterprises (MSEs), micro-entrepreneurs, farmers	MSEs, micro-entrepreneurs, individuals	Enterprises	Mainly rural households

Source: Hanhua Corporation, unpublished report, 2014.

a. Refers to financial leasing companies.

b. The number of MCCs in the table is for 2013, and 2012 for all other institutions.

c. In most cases, local government financial offices.

the ministry and contributions from villagers for revolving loans within a village. The grant from the MOF for each village is in the range of RMB150,000–250,000. From 2001 to 2010, the grant funds from the central government for VCFs reached RMB5.415 billion. The rules and decisions for lending for RCFs are supposed to be determined by the villagers themselves.[12] By the end of 2013, there were more than 17,000 VCFs across twenty-seven provinces of China.[13] These village funds were financed by government poverty funds. P2Ps in China, which have been regarded as a type of internet finance, are discussed in detail later in the chapter.

Another important player in China's inclusive finance is the credit bureau system set up by the PBOC. The system started keeping records for institutional entities in 1997 and for individuals in 1999. By 2015, the system had identified 20.68 million enterprises and 864 million individuals in China. Of those 864 million individuals, 361 million had credit records. The commercial banks and the nonbanking financial institutions, such as trust, leasing, asset management companies, and some MCCs, have been connected to the credit bureau system. In 2014, the credit bureau created a connection facility for micro and small financial institutions, which significantly reduced the costs for those institutions to use the credit bureau system.[14]

Donors have acted as a catalyst in China's development of inclusive finance. The United Nations Development Program (UNDP), the United Nations Children's Fund

(UNICEF), and other multilateral and bilateral donors such as the Australian Agency for International Development provided funds and technical assistance (TA) to many rural microfinance pilot programs in China. The World Bank started its microfinance pilot in China as early as 1995 under its Qianba Mountain Poverty Reduction Project; since then the bank's pilot program has been developed into the largest rural MFI in China, CFPA MF. The World Bank and the German Development Bank (KfW) helped to introduce microfinance downscaling to MSEs in China by supporting twelve CCBs and RCBs with IPC lending technology through a project with China Development Bank (CDB). The Consultative Group to Assist the Poor (CGAP) has supported capacity building, translation, and publication of microfinance best practices and materials in China. UNDP, the Asian Development Bank, and CGAP have also supported policy studies for microfinance in China. The German Technical Cooperation Agency (GTZ) was a major backer of the MCC pilot by the PBOC around 2005. Visa China has consistently supported financial education in China by working with CFPA MF and the China Academy of Inclusive Finance at Renmin University.[15]

The Policy and Regulatory Landscape for Financial Inclusion in China

In a country like China, where the financial system is heavily regulated and the formal financial institutions have been dominated by state-owned banks, the national government plays an important role in the formation of an inclusive financial market and in the downscaling of financial services to farmers, other low-income communities, and MSEs. The major motivation for the Chinese government and financial regulators in supporting inclusive finance has been to provide agricultural support and create jobs for urban unemployed and migrant workers following the reform of state-owned commercial banks in the middle 1990s. Microloans and MSE financing have also been related to private sector development in China, as the state-owned banks have lent more to state-owned enterprises and local government financial platforms. However, globally, the measures undertaken by the government in promoting rural and microenterprise financial services have varied from one country to another, and many of them have not been successful. There has also been disagreement over whether the government should use market or administrative means to bring financial services to low-income farmers and micro and small enterprises.

Since the mid-1990s, the Chinese government and financial regulators have made a series of regulatory and policy changes to downscale China's financial services for rural households and MSEs, especially for those in rural and peri-urban areas. The regulations and policies for developing inclusive finance in China in the post-1990s period can be divided into four phases: pilot rural microcredit programs for rural poverty reduction (from mid-1993 to 1996); large-scale microcredit programs implemented by institutional finance supported by subsidized policy loans and agricultural on-lending (1997 to 2004); development of commercial microfinance marked by the entry of microcredit companies and village and township banks (2006 to 2010); and the application of fintech to MSE and consumer lending.[16]

Following the comprehensive financial reforms marked by bank commercialization in the mid-1990s, the state-owned commercial banks in China, including the Agricultural Bank of China (ABC), cut back on their branches in townships and rural areas and moved their lending authorities from county-level branches to the prefectural and even the provincial offices. The efforts by the state-owned commercial banks to control their nonperforming loans and lower operating costs reduced the access of rural households and MSEs to loans and other financial services from institutional finance. The access of rural households and MSEs to loans from rural credit cooperatives was affected as well, with fewer loans from state-owned commercial banks and an increasing number of RCC nonperforming loans. More funds were channeled from rural to urban areas and from small clients to large clients and large projects.

Following complaints from local governments and farmers, the central government agencies, including the Poverty Alleviation Office (LGOP) and the People's Bank of China (PBOC), encouraged the creation of microloan pilot programs by allowing them to use donor funds and government poverty funds. The PBOC issued a few licenses authorizing pilot microloan programs by the Chinese Academy of Social Sciences, UNDP/CICETE (China International Centre for Economic and Technical Exchange), and the China Foundation for Poverty Alleviation in the mid-1990s.[17] The financial regulators in the local areas also took a flexible attitude toward Grameen-model microloan pilots using donor funds in China.[18] Consequently, more than 300 microloan programs using donor funds were developed by the late 1990s and early 2000s.[19] The donor-funded microfinance pilot programs were acknowledged by the Chinese government and followed by financial institutions in China. According to Xiaoshan Du, the turning point occurred in 1996 when China's central government called for the poverty funds to reach out to the villages and households in China's poor areas.[20] The Agricultural Bank of China, which had been responsible for managing subsidized poverty loans, began offering subsidized microloans to poor households. Supported by agricultural on-lending from the PBOC, RCCs began offering microloans to rural households without requiring physical collateral in 1999 and 2000.[21] Following the rural microcredit pilot programs funded by donors, China's banking regulators changed the credit policy, and banking institutions were no longer required to demand physical collateral from rural borrowers for small loans.[22]

The development of rural microfinance pilot programs in China, even those with very limited scale, indicated that poor farmers in China were bankable and that major microfinance mechanisms, such as group guarantees, dynamic incentives, and targeting female borrowers, were applicable in China. The pilot microloan programs also revealed major challenges to inclusive finance development. First, the lending rates charged by many MFIs in China were 6–8 percent, which was lower even than the interest rates charged by RCCs. The annual interest rate for subsidized poverty loans was around 3 percent. Second, most donor-funded microfinance programs (MFPs) were very small in scale (from RMB200,000 to RMB1 million per county), and many were operated by temporary project offices. Most of those MFPs and MFIs were not financially viable and institutionally sustainable given the low rates of interest charged, small scale of operation, and nonprofessional staff operating in a temporary program or office. The microloan programs by RCCs supported by PBOC's on-lending faced a similar challenge since the operating costs for microloans to rural households were apparently higher than those for other loans, and the RCC could not raise interest rates to cover the additional costs and loan losses for microloans without collateral.[23]

More policy and regulatory changes occurred in 2005 and 2006 when the PBOC started to liberalize the lending rates of interest and allowing the entry of microcredit companies in China. In 2005, the PBOC enabled the creation of MCCs to compete with banks for credit provision. The pilot is a big step forward as private capital was allowed to enter the financial industry for lending operations under the rules set up by the PBOC. MCCs are lending-only institutions subject to nonprudential regulation by provincial government agencies. In May 2008, the then China Banking Regulatory Commission (CBRC) and the PBOC jointly issued guidelines for the MCC pilot, which was later replicated throughout China. MCCs are allowed to lend to, and borrow money from, no more than two commercial banks. Financial institutions in the wholesale credit business could also take responsibility for supervising microfinance corporations. These institutions will work with provincial supervision departments to regulate the behavior of MCCs.[24] In 2006, the government through the CBRC established a legal and regulatory framework for three new types of rural financial services providers: village and township banks, village fund co-operatives (VFCs), and loan companies. VTBs are county-level deposit-taking banks subject to CBRC regulation, and they were allowed to engage in full banking operations.[25] However, VTBs can be set up only by an existing commercial bank with at least a 20 percent share in the total equity investment. In March 2007, the Postal Savings Bank of China replaced the China Postal Savings (Postal Savings became a bank in 2007, before 2007, it was a savings service provided associated with China Post and had no lending operations) and immediately started its microlending operations. The Poverty Alleviation and Development Office (PADO) and the Ministry of Finance started their pilot village development funds (VDFs or village funds) in more than 100 villages in six provinces in 2006 and expanded coverage to twenty-seven provinces in 2007.[26]

More important, the government has partially liberalized China's loan interest rates to encourage financial institutions to provide loans to MSEs and rural households. Banks in China can lend to their small and micro enterprise customers at up to four times the base lending rate set by the PBOC. However, when lending to rural households, RCCs can float their lending rates upward up to 2.3 times the base lending rate only to protect the interests of small farmers.

The government has also strengthened its support to China's rural economy and MSEs in urban and peri-urban areas through the provision of fiscal subsidies and agricultural on-lending, tax concessions, and other policy measures, including but not limited to the following:

- Subsidized interest rates for poverty loans: The subsidized lending rates apply mainly to loans to state-designated poor households (a subsidy of 5 percent of the loan portfolio) and agriculture-related enterprises in poor areas (a subsidy of 3 percent of the loan portfolio). The local LGOP has been responsible for selecting target enterprises and households, with the grants provided by the Ministry of Finance and the relevant local governments.[27]

- Subsidies provided to new types of rural financial institutions, from 2008 to March 2014: A subsidy equivalent to 2 percent of the average loan portfolio in the previous year was provided to new types of RFIs meeting the following criteria: the average loan portfolio (the total loan portfolio of an RFI) exceeded the previous year's; the ratio of total loans to total deposits exceeded 50 percent at the end of the previous year;[28] and other regulatory requirements were met.[29] This subsidy supports new types of RFIs under the supervision of the CBRC because they are new and likely have higher operation costs.

- Subsidies for loans to agriculture: In 2009, the Ministry of Finance introduced a direct fiscal subsidy to RFIs linked to growth in agricultural lending. Any county-level RFIs whose average loan portfolio increased by more than 15 percent in the previous year are eligible to receive a fiscal grant, which is equivalent to 2 percent of the increase in the average loan portfolio over 15 percent.[30]

The subsidies apply to all formal financial institutions at the county level (that is, the RFIs supervised by CBRC).

■ Tax concessions to financial institutions: Since 2010, sales tax for interest income from loans smaller than RMB50,000 by formal financial institutions has been exempted (taxed at 5 percent as general interest income). The interest income for RFIs operated at the county level and below, including RCCs, VTBs, loan companies, and rural fund co-operatives, is taxed at 3 percent instead of 5 percent; the profits of rural commercial banks and VTBs are taxed at 15 percent.[31]

■ Agricultural support for on-lending to RFIs.[32]

■ Differential reserve rate requirements (RRRs) for RFIs: Since 2010, the Chinese government has tightened its monetary policies several times by raising RRRs for deposit-taking institutions to curb lending. Currently, the reserve ratio for RCCs and VTBs is 6–7 percentage points lower than that for other deposit-taking institutions in China.

Some of the subsidies, such as tax concessions for the newly created village banks and direct grants for microloans, are expected to increase lending to rural smallholders. Other interventions, such as the lending rate caps applied to rural household lending by RCCs, may have distorted rural financial markets by discouraging RCCs from lending to the household sector.

Inclusive Finance by Nonbanking Financial Institutions in China: The Case of CFPA MF

The NGO microfinance pilot programs in China were initiated in the early and mid-1990s by the Chinese Academy of Social Sciences following the Grameen model of microfinance and funded mainly by donor agencies.[33] In its heyday, China had more than 300 NGO microfinance programs and institutions. By 2005, UNDP had more than thirty-two and UNICEF more than sixty-eight microfinance programs in China's poor areas. Almost all of the pilot programs failed to achieve financial sustainability, however, and today fewer than ten of them remain active.[34] The three largest active MFIs developed from the pilot programs in the 1990s are CFPA Microfinance Management Ltd. (CFPA MF), Dongfanghuimin Micro-Credit Company (DF Microloan Co.), and Chifeng Zhaowuda Women's Sustainable Development Association (Chifeng MFI).[35] CFPA Microfinance is by far the largest MFI transformed from a nonprofit NGO MFI in China. By July 2018, CFPA MF had about 400,000 active clients in 303 counties in twenty provinces, with a loan portfolio of RMB8 trillion; DF Micro-loan Co. had 24,400 active clients with a loan portfolio of RMB500 million. By the end of 2017, Chifeng MFI had 4,816 active clients with a loan portfolio of RMB39.17 million, the smallest of the three.[36]

This section looks at the development process and key factors in the success of CFPA MF in order to draw some lessons for the development of NGO microfinance in China. The policy environment, institutions, and market for inclusive finance in China have implications for inclusive finance in other global south countries as well.

CFPA MF provides microcredit and microinsurance services to vulnerable populations in underdeveloped areas. By the end of 2018, CFPA MF had 313 branches and subsidiaries across twenty-one provinces of China, covering 80,000 villages, and it employed 4,970 staff. The loan portfolio at the end of 2018 was RMB8.9 billion, with 356,989 active clients and an average loan size of RMB29,943. Total loan disbursement in 2018 reached RMB12.9 billion, with 430,855 loans. The portfolio at risk (loan overdue > 30 days) was 1.04 percent.[37] Statistics from CFPA MF show that 89 percent of CFPA Microfinance clients were previously unable to borrow from traditional financial institutions; among these, more than 93 percent were women.[38]

CFPA MF grew out of a pilot microcredit program started in 1996 under a World Bank–funded poverty reduction project in the Qingba mountainous area. Several factors contributed to the success of CFPA MF in China's microfinance market, where most other NGO MFIs failed. The success factors of CFPA MF include, but are not limited to, commercialization of microfinance operations, improvements (or reforms) to the Grameen model of microfinance piloted in China based on China's conditions, policy and fund support from government agencies and banks, and the use of up-to-date MIS (management information system) financial technology.

CFPA started its process of commercialization around 2005, when it had fewer than ten MFPs across China. Before 2005, CFPA adopted a co-operative model working with county-level MFIs. CFPA contributed funding and technical and management services. But because the county MFIs were controlled by the county government, CFPA found it difficult to manage and supervise the programs and to standardize the microcredit products. Loan quality declined in some counties, and the number of nonperforming loans went up. In 2005, CFPA launched a broad reform of its microcredit program. A single line of command was established between CFPA headquarters and the county MFIs (hereafter referred to as "county branches"), thereby giving the program unambiguous property rights and clear responsibilities, and allowing more efficient management. The commercialization process likewise strengthened branch operating rules and regulations, as well as the information technology systems at the head office. In contrast, UNDP/CICETE, which have funded and provided technical support to more than forty MFPs in over thirty counties, failed to create a single chain of command over their county-level programs. As a result, most of the county MFPs in China had little chance to reach operational and financial sustainability because of their small-scale operations and lack of continuous funding and TA support after the UNDP projects ended. The UNICEF microfund schemes in China were even smaller.[39] The largest surviving UNDP MFP today is Chifeng Zhaowuda, which had fewer than 5,000 active clients in July 2017 after almost twenty years of operation; it also received project support from KfW. Likewise, the Chinese Academy of Social Sciences also had limited control over its MFIs in three poor counties of China.

The two major changes in the microfinance model implemented by CFPA MF were the increases in interest rates on loans and the individual and microenterprise loan products introduced. After 2005, by raising interest rates from 10–12 percent to 18–22 percent,[40] CFPA MF was able to pay a decent wage to its loan officials and to link wages to their performance. For example, in Zuoquan County of Shanxi, branch employee salaries more than doubled, from RMB700–800 monthly before 2005 to RMB4,000–5,000 in 2008. The branches, like the other service branches, have also been providing their staff with endowment, medical, unemployment, employment injury, and maternity insurance since 2006. Unlike other NGOs in China, whose county branches or institutions recruit loan officers and other staff, CFPA Microfinance, through its head office, takes a direct hand in recruitment, to ensure good-quality hires. The head office selects and oversees the performance of branch managers.

Following the implementation of the World Bank/KfW microfinance downscaling project in China, CFPA MF quickly introduced individual loan products for MSEs in China's peri-urban areas. The individual loans and microenterprise loans of CFPA MF are based on cash flow analysis, similar to the individual loans disbursed by those city and rural commercial banks in China which adopted the IPC model of microlending.[41]

Following the commercialization process, the county MFPs of CFPA were institutionalized, marked by the creation of the CFPA Microfinance Management Corporation (CFPA MF). With a model for sustainable microfinance operation while targeting China's rural households and SMEs in China's poor counties, CFPA MF quickly attracted equity investments from the International Finance Corporation (IFC) and Sequoia Capital, so CFPA Microfinance became a joint-venture company in January 2011.[42] As CFPA MF continued to grow, Ant Financial joined it as a shareholder in 2016 and immediately became the second largest shareholder after CFPA, followed by TPG in 2018.[43] These important shareholders have helped CFPA MF to improve its governance and management system, attract wholesale funds, and develop new products and services. Since then, Ant Financial has played a crucial role in developing fintech and new financial products for CFPA MF.

The success of CFPA MF can also be attributed to support from the Chinese government agencies and financial institutions. CFPA MF was one of the three MFIs with formal permits from the PBOC to pilot microfinance programs in China.[44] CFPA was able to bring its microfinance operation to many poor counties of China partly with assistance from CFPA and LGOP, as the latter has a network in China's poor areas. In 2006, CFPA obtained the first wholesale loan from the China Development Bank to support its microfinance operations. Since then, CFPA MF has received wholesale loan support from CDB, ABC, Standard Chartered Bank, and other financial institutions in China. In 2011, CFPA MF was connected to the PBOC's credit bureau system, which has helped CFPA MF to improve its loan performance. In 2015, CFPA MF raised funds from China's Shenzhen Stock Exchange through asset securitization. In 2016, CFPA set up its first microcredit company, Hainan Microcredit Company, a lending-only financial institution. Currently, CFPA MF has used this microcredit company as the legal entity to perform its lending-only microfinance operations in all 300 counties.

Some of the success factors for CFPA MF cannot be replicated by other MFIs and RFIs in China, such as its connection with LGOP and the CFPA system in China's poor areas. However, the principle of commercial operations and management, including the application of a market rate of interest, incentives provided to its managers and loan officials, the development of new financial products and services, and the use of up-to-date technology, could easily be adopted by similar institutions in China. The ownership and governance structure of CFPA MF could also be adopted by other rural and microfinance institutions.

Inclusive Finance Programs by Commercial Banks in China

Before MSE lending models were introduced, China's commercial banks had lent mainly to large and medium-sized enterprises, especially state-owned enterprises, because of the higher costs and risks associated with lending to MSEs.[45] A complicated organizational structure, centralized lending decisions, and a lack of proper credit techniques have also been blamed for the failure of the banks to reach out to

MSEs. Of all the efforts by banking institutions to develop inclusive finance in China since 2005 and 2006, microfinance downscaling by CCBs and RCCs has been widely regarded as one of the most effective instruments for reaching MSEs.

The IPC model of MSE lending was introduced into China through a project sponsored by the World Bank and KfW. The China Development Bank was selected as the implementation agency. CDB provided microfinance technical assistance (TA) and wholesale loans to the participating financial institutions (PFIs) to build their capacities for microlending from December 2005 to June 30, 2008.

The microfinance downscaling project consisted of two closely related components: a credit facility for on-lending to eligible PFIs and a technical assistance facility to support the capacity building of the CDB and the PFIs. According to the project completion report commissioned by CDB, after slow progress at the start, the pilot project grew quickly, and the model has since been tested by at least ten CCBs serving urban and peri-urban MSEs with an average loan size of RMB100,000 (range: RMB20,000–500,000) and nonperforming loans below 1 percent of the loan portfolio (usually below 0.5 percent). All reached the breakeven point in twelve to twenty-four months. The project supported MSE lending by twelve Chinese banks (PFIs), including Maanshan Rural Commercial Bank.

The IPC model is centered on evaluating the capacity and willingness of clients to repay loans. The procedure for assessing loan repayment capacity includes field visits by a credit officer to understand the client's production, marketing, and fund flows, and to prepare simplified financial statements for the client in order to harden soft data. During the field visits, the loan officer collects information on the purposes of the loan and on the client's assets and liabilities, income, profit and loss, cash flow, and sources of funds for loan repayment. To evaluate the client's willingness to repay loans, the IPC model uses soft data, such as personal reputation and credit history. For instance, the banks collect nonfinancial information about the client pertaining to honesty, family relations, and reputation, and they then cross-check the information. The microloans are assessed by a credit commission consisting of MSE loan managers and loan officials who are also responsible for loan collection.

The commercial banks in China have made institutional and management changes to apply the IPC model in China's context. First, many banks have set up special branches or departments responsible for piloting MSE lending, as the lending procedures for MSE loans are very different from those for other bank loans in China. Second, the banks have created new systems for recruiting and managing microfinance managers and loan officials.[46] Finally, many of the innovations made in applying the model have been replicated in the overall management and operation of these banks, raising the overall banking efficiency in serving MSEs and rural people.

The project's TA component has been singled out for positive comment by the participating financial institutions. An overwhelming number have expressed the view that the TA component has been much more useful to them than the provision of wholesale loans, as the city and rural commercial banks in China have adequate low-cost funds. According to the PFIs, the two major contributions of the project were (1) the training provided by the consultants, and the selection and management of loan officers, and (2) the systematic approach to MSE lending characterized by cash flow analysis.

The microlending technologies and management systems introduced by the project have been transferred to a growing number of commercial banks and microfinance institutions through the PFIs and consultants, many of whom were trained by IPC. By the end of 2014, it was estimated that more than 100 Chinese banks had chosen to adopt the model. The introduction of the model has had a profound effect on China's banking system and on MSE lending. The following financial and nonfinancial institutions are among those that have hired former project consultants to provide MSE technical support: Changchun Rural Commercial Bank (Jilin Province); Changshu RCB (Jiangsu Province); Chengdu Rural Commercial Bank (Sichuan Province); China Postal Savings Bank; Dongying City Commercial Bank (Shandong Province); Jiaxing Rural Commercial Bank (Zhejiang Province); Jijin Rural Cooperative Bank (Jiangsu Province); Jingjiang Rural Commercial Bank (Jiangsu Province); Jining Bank (Shandong Province); Pingdingshan City Commercial Bank (Henan Province); Suqian Minfeng Rural Cooperative Bank (Jiangsu Province); Wuhan Rural Commercial Bank (Hubei Province); Xinyu Rural Co-operative Bank (Jiangxi Province); and Zhangjiagang Rural Commercial Bank (Jiangsu Province).

In addition to the city and rural commercial banks, many microcredit companies and village and township banks have received similar technical support in microlending, including CFPA MF. Many project consultants hired by IPC to provide project technical assistance have been employed as high-level or mid-level managers in charge of MSE lending operations by the banks. It is expected that more city and rural commercial banks and other MFIs will follow suit as the financial reforms deepen.

At the national level, the project impact can be understood from the following two perspectives. First, the implementation of the project among the twelve PFIs strongly indicates that microloans to urban and semi-rural microentrepreneurs and small enterprises can be provided in a commercially sustainable way. In other words, commercial financial institutions, especially the local banks, can earn a profit, increase local market share, and develop a diversified loan portfolio by providing MSEs with microloans ranging from RMB10,000 to RMB500,000, without subsidies from the government. Likewise, urban and semi-rural microentrepreneurs and small enterprises can benefit from the institutional microloans, which provide them with increased working capital and funds for business expansion. Second, universally accepted lending practices, such as microlending based on cash flow analysis that was introduced in China by IPC, can be applied elsewhere in the country, with some modifications. International cooperation and mutual learning have been important in implementing China's banking and rural finance reforms.

The Evolution of Financial Technologies in China and Their Implications

The Chinese government has encouraged the development of digital finance, including the use of internet finance for financial inclusion. The government has a clear objective to use new technology to bring financial services to the poor in remote areas and to privately owned MSEs that have little access to formal financial services. In 2015, China's State Council issued a plan to develop inclusive digital finance.[47]

In addition to the rapid development of internet and mobile banking for savings, money transfer, and payment services, the most significant developments of fintech for financial inclusion in China are the emergence and fall of peer-to-peer services and the entry of three internet banks (e-banks) between 2014 and 2016. Both have important implications for financial inclusion and economic and social development in and beyond China. This section discusses the P2P development and e-banks in some detail.

The Emergence and Fall of P2P in China

Peer-to-peer service providers (P2Ps) in China have registered as consultant companies specializing in matching small depositors (small investors in the P2P industry) and borrowers (fund users in the P2P industry) on and off the internet; they are not financial institutions and are prohibited from providing deposit, savings, lending, and insurance services.[48] According to regulations by CBIRC and other ministries in China, P2Ps can collect and assimilate information about microloan applicants, do creditworthiness analyses, and provide intermediary services for borrowers and lenders. P2Ps are not allowed to raise funds for lending, to bear credit risks, or to set up fund pools to compensate for loan losses. As consultant companies engaging in information collection and analysis, and in matching fund users with small investors, P2Ps are not regulated or supervised by financial regulators in China.

According to research by the Inclusive Financial Institute at Renmin University, the development of P2Ps in China can be divided into three phases: the startup phase from 2007 to 2011 by which time there were about sixty P2Ps (about twenty were active) with roughly 10,000 small investors; the rapid growth phase from 2012 to 2014; and the adjustment phase since 2015. By 2017 and 2018, panic withdrawals and bank runs had occurred in a large number of P2Ps in China, and millions of small investors lost their money, which gave rise to street demonstrations and social anxiety.

A statistical report by P2P Services indicates that by July 2018 there were 1,465 operational P2Ps in China, with an aggregate loan portfolio of RMB956.1 billion.[49] By then the number of P2Ps was half what it had been at their peak (3,476 P2Ps). Moreover, the top fifty P2Ps were located mainly in Beijing, Shanghai, Zhejiang, and Guangdong provinces. Another report in Ifeng News shows that from June 1 to July 12, 2018, there were bank runs on 108 P2Ps, about 2.6 per day. In most cases, the owners of P2Ps were absent when the bank runs occurred and P2Ps delayed payments to investors (de facto depositors).

The Entry of China's E-banks and the Implications for Financial Inclusion

The regulatory decision to allow the entry of e-banks in China had three objectives: to provide small loans to MSEs and farmers to clear the bottleneck for MSE growth at a time of economic slowdown and transformation; to encourage technological innovations in China by applying them to financial industries; and to test the entry of private banks in China. The three e-banks, all owned and controlled by private capital (large private enterprise groups), began operations between 2014 and 2016. Basic information about the three e-banks is presented in table 14-2 and information about their loan products is presented in table 14-3. It is important to note that the initiators of the e-banks are mainly large internet service providers in China: MY Bank is controlled by Alibaba; WeBank is controlled by TenCent; XW Bank was permitted because it is located in China's western region (Sichuan Province).

As table 14-3 shows, the loan products of e-banks were typical microloans for consumption and MSE loans in size and loan conditions, with no requirements for physical collateral or guarantees. Both WeBank and MY Bank link the lending rates of interest to the creditworthiness of loan applicants using a risk rating. MY Bank has provided microloans mainly to microentrepreneurs and farmers using transactions data collected by the internet shopping sites of Alibaba. MY Bank's clients have focused on the service industries, including restaurant and beverage services, education,

TABLE 14-2.   Statistics for Digital Banks in China

	WeBank (2017)	MY Bank (2017)	XW Bank (July 2018)
Year of entry	2014	2014	June 2018
Year became operational	2015	June 2015	Dec-18
Major shareholder and initiator	TenCent	Ant Financial	New Hope Group
Total assets (RMB billion)	81.7	78.17	16.3
Operating revenues (million RMB)	6,748	4,275	
Net profits (million RMB)	1,448	404	144
Nonperforming loans (%)	0.64	1.23	
Total deposits (billion RMB)	5.3	25.1	
Funds from other sources (billion RMB)	46.7	38.14	
Loans outstanding (billion RMB)	47.7		
Cumulative loans disbursed (billion RMB)	870		90
Cumulative number of borrowers		5,170,000	
Cumulative number of loans	12,000,000		
Average loan size (RMB)	72,500	28,000	3,300
Total loan disbursement (RMB billion)		446.8	
Rural loans		26.45	
Registered loan applicants (RMB million)	60		
Borrowers with a credit line (RMB million)	34		7.3
Client outreach	Up to 567 cities in 31 provinces		

Sources: Annual Report of WeBank, 2017; annual report of MY Bank, 2017; xwbank.com.

beauty shops, small textile shops, mini-supermarkets, and domestic services providers.[50] WE Bank has developed two loan products: microconsumer loans and auto loans. More recently, the bank has piloted microloans to MSEs in Shenzhen, where the bank and TenCent are located.

The use of large datasets and a credit risk model have been the keys to instant loan processing and delivery by e-banks and others in China. For example, MY Bank has created a large dataset by combining the Alibaba and Alipay data with

TABLE 14-3. Selected Loan Products of Digital Banks in China

	WeBank	*MY Bank*	*XW Bank*
Major loan products	Auto loans, other consumer loans, and micro and small enterprise (MSE) loans	MSE loans to Taobao users[a]	Individual loans
Selected loan product	Consumer loans	MSE loans	Consumer loans
Loan amounts and terms	RMB500–300,000, up to 36 months	Up to 500,000 and 24 months	Up to RMB1 million, 6–36 months
Collateral or guarantee	None	None	None
Annualized interest rates (%)	7–18	5.84–17.15	7–8
Time needed to evaluate a loan application after online submission	3 minutes, fastest 1 minute	3 minutes	15 minutes
How to apply	Through WeChat and qq.com website	Through Alipay	Through WeChat
Other products		WMPs[b] to 6.5 million MSEs	

Sources: Annual report of WeBank, 2017; annual report of MY Bank, 2017; xwbank.com.

a. Taobao is one of the major internet shopping sites of Alibaba.

b. WMPs = wealth management products.

the external dataset from customs, taxation offices, electricity suppliers, and others to establish a credit scoring model and other models for instant loan processing and delivery with zero human intervention. The bank has collected over 100 variables of data from Taobao and Tmall (online shopping sites) and Alipay, including data on trade transactions and related cash flows, credit records, sales data, inventory turnover, and disputes. Moreover, both traditional statistical computation as well as the latest artificial intelligence (AI) technology with machine learning have been applied to the credit scoring and other models for instant loan processing and delivery.[51]

The development of e-banks has serious cost and time implications for financial inclusion in China and around the globe after the credit scoring and risk management models are tested and elaborated. First, the new technology makes lower lending rates possible by reducing costs and shortening loan processing and approval time. E-banks have potentially changed a number of benchmarks for microloans around the world. As shown in table 14-3, first, the loan processing and delivery time has been slashed from two to three days for repeat borrowers to less than fifteen minutes (three minutes for MY Bank and WeBank). Next, e-banks have slashed the loan processing costs by removing branches and loan officers from the processing procedures, the two major costs in traditional microfinance. For example, MY Bank has fewer than 400 staff who handle about 5,000 each. Of those 400, two-thirds are technicians working on large datasets, computation, internet interface, and risk management. Third, the average cost per loan has fallen to RMB2.3, of which RMB2 is the cost of computation and using digital hardware and software whereas the transaction cost per loan for traditional microfinance has been 8–12 percent of the loan portfolio.[52] Fourth, geographic location and distance are less important for expanding inclusive financial services, similar to local knowledge. Finally, the e-bank model has the potential to grow exponentially, given its huge savings in loan processing and delivery time, in financial costs, and in costs to borrowers. It has the potential to revolutionize financial inclusion in China and around the world.

The e-bank model is likely to spread to other banking and nonbanking financial institutions in China soon. In June 2018, MY Bank released a plan to share its instant loan processing and delivery technology (three-minute loan processing + one-second loan delivery + zero human intervention) to all interested financial institutions in China. The bank proposed to collaborate with 1,000 financial institutions to provide microloan services to over 30 million microentrepreneurs around China.

Ant Financial and MY Bank have already transferred some of their microloan models and technologies to CFPA MF by working together on suitable credit models for reaching rural clients. Ant Financial became a shareholder of CFPA MF at the end of 2016; since then the former has made a great effort to upgrade technologies for the latter by sending an AI expert team to CFPA MF to improve credit risk analysis and management using large data analysis and internet technology. Since introducing a mobile phone app of its own making in August 2018,[53] CFPA MF has the technology to do microloan processing and delivery to its rural clients in ten minutes. From August to December 2018, using the mobile app, CFPA MF provided RMB577.6 million credit lines to 277,812 loan applicants, with an average amount of loans at RMB7,323, and the portfolio at risk for the microloans with monthly repayment is at 0.17 percent. CFPA MF plans to provide all its microloans up to RMB20,000 by using the instant payment app in near future. CFPA MF is also using internet and other digital technologies for its micro-insurances, micro WMPs, and internet shopping services.

Despite all the progress on internet lending achieved, China's e-banks still confront numerous challenges ahead for expanding their financial services. First and foremost, the ability of the e-banks, like other private banks, to organize savings deposits has been limited by the regulation that the regional banks are not allowed to open long-distance bank deposit accounts on the internet. Private banks also face restrictions on cross-regional operations.[54] Moreover, the instant microloan processing and delivery methods developed by e-banks can be used mainly for those clients about whom the banks have collected sufficient information, such as the microentrepreneurs who have used Alibaba's internet shopping sites or payment and other services provided by TenCent. E-banks will be challenged to extend their services into rural areas where similar data are not available for village residents and migrant workers in peri-urban areas. The efforts by Ant Financial to work with CFPA MF to develop models jointly for those in the rural and peri-urban areas should be encouraged. Finally, more time is needed to test the costs and repayment rates for the instant loan processing and delivery technologies developed by e-banks.[55]

The new digital microloan models developed by e-banks and others in China raised serious questions about financial inclusion and about social and economic development in China. First, after the model is tested further and extended from consumer loans and MSE lending to SME lending, sweeping changes are likely to occur. Millions of jobs in loan application, processing, monitoring, and collection will be replaced by machines, similar to what happened to bank front office jobs in deposit taking, remittances, and payments. Second, the monopolistic position of a few big internet service providers such as Alibaba/Ant Financial and TenCent will likely be further enhanced, especially when WeBank and MY Bank begin collaborating with other financial institutions in China. Using the advantage created by big data, the existing internet service network, new cloud technology, and AI on the one hand, Alibaba/Ant Financial and TenCent will be able to expand their financial services at diminishing costs (with marginal costs close to zero), making it hard for other banks and financial institutions to compete. On the other hand, if microentrepreneurs and SMEs in the real economy are forced to use internet services (such as payments and money transfers) and internet shopping sites of Alibaba and TenCent in order to access the loan services provided by WeBank and MY Bank, then the banks will be in a position to collect even more information to improve their credit models. Finally, the new developments in internet banking will also present challenges to economic theories on the importance of local and soft knowledge and whether small banks are more suitable for the delivery of small and microloans.

Conclusions

The development of inclusive finance started with the Grameen model of rural microcredit programs for poverty reduction in China's poor areas in the early and middle 1990s. Next, rural financial institutions in China, including the Agricultural Bank of China and rural credit co-operatives, began similar programs, supported by subsidized poverty loan programs and agricultural support on-lending from China's central bank. The pilot rural microfinance programs indicated that poor people were able to repay microloans without providing physical collateral. International donors and emerging social organizations, such as county-level NGOs, also played an important role in rural microfinance pilot programs in the 1990s.

Since the beginning of the twenty-first century, Chinese government agencies and financial regulators have undertaken several major policy shifts to strengthen market competition and provide incentives for formal financial institutions to provide more services to rural households and MSEs in both rural and urban areas. Following a partial liberalization of loan interest rates and entry of microcredit companies and other new players, three significant changes took place: more local commercial banks, mainly city commercial banks and rural commercial banks, started to do rural household and MSE lending; after China's urbanization process, inclusive finance began targeting more MSEs in urban and peri-urban areas; and more commercially oriented and financially sustainable inclusive financial institutions and programs emerged, including CFPA MF and MSE lending programs.

The rapid development of fintech in China, including the application of internet, artificial intelligence, and large data, has changed the landscape for payments, deposits, and money transfer services. Mobile banking has become the major means for more and more people to do banking in China. Since the emergence of the e-banks and instant lending programs, fintech has the potential to bring formal lending services to hundreds of millions of clients for consumer lending and to a large number of MSEs through data collected from value chains. Fintech has slashed the costs of operating bank branches and loan assessment, two major costs for financial institutions in servicing MSEs and low-income earners.

E-banks and the rapid development of online instant processing and delivery of microloans can be attributed to a number of factors: (1) the development of microfinance models and technologies, piloted by NGO microfinance and refined by the IPC model of MSE lending with the microfinance downscaling programs; (2) Chinese government policies to support technological innovations for economic upgrading, including IT and internet, automation, big data, and artificial intelligence, as well as regulatory changes to permit entry of e-banks initiated by giant internet service providers Alibaba/Ant Financial and TenCent in particular; (3) the development of infrastructure for internet and mobile uses; (4) lessons learned by policymakers, financial regulators, and e-bank service providers from the development of P2P related to models, regulation, the application of technologies, and e-bank policy.

Many challenges remain, however. First, microinsurance services and wealth management products for low-income earners are scarce. Second, it remains difficult for urban youth, privately owned MSEs, and rural households to access institutional finance because the large state-owned commercial banks and joint stock banks have not been motivated to do more MSE and microlending. Third, the use of technology has been uneven. Many rural populations, especially the elderly in more remote areas, are still excluded from the formal financial system.

Policy Recommendations

1. *Improve regulations to strengthen local financial supervision and market competition.* Competition is perhaps the most important driving force for the downscaling of rural financial services to micro and small enterprises (MSEs) and small farmers. The recent permits issued for private banks have gone to large private capital in China's large cities where there is more competition among financial institutions. More small-bank permits should be issued to private capital and others for operation in rural counties and in China's western regions, where formal rural financial services have been dominated by rural credit co-operatives (RCCs). Moreover, well-performing non-deposit-taking institutions such as microcredit companies (MCCs) and NGO microfinance institutions (MFIs) that have provided substantial support to MSEs and to rural households, could be granted banking licenses to enhance competition and to demonstrate the effects for others. Poorly performing formal rural financial institutions (RFIs) should be pushed to exit the market through mergers and acquisitions and other means, following the establishment of a deposit insurance facility in China. Meanwhile, the offices of the China Banking and Insurance Regulation Commission (CBIRC) at the prefecture and county levels should be strengthened to provide effective and adequate supervision to rural financial institutions. Following the creation of MCCs, China's local government offices, mainly the financial offices of provincial governments, have been primarily responsible for the supervision of MCCs, credit guarantee companies, and some other local financial institutions. Some local governments have neither sufficient staff nor the necessary expertise to carry out financial regulation. It is recommended that the government set up a formal provincial-level financial regulation and supervisory framework with accountable authorities,

clear responsibilities, and sufficient resources for financial regulation and the supervision of local financial institutions. Moreover, the local financial supervisory body could be responsible for the supervision of co-operative financial institutions to be piloted and created, village community funds, and at least two of the three new types of RFIs—that is, loan companies and rural fund co-operatives.

2. *Accelerate the reform of formal rural financial institutions and expand the services to microenterprises and rural households.* The reforms of the RCC system have been ongoing for more than a decade. Further reforms are required to clarify the relationship between the RCCs and local governments, especially the provincial governments and their agencies, the provincial RCC federations. The corporate governance of RCCs needs to be improved further, including the rights of the shareholders and the board in the appointment of managerial staff. Poorly performing RCCs should be allowed to exit the market. The Chinese government has encouraged RFIs to provide loans to MSEs and agriculture by providing formal financial institutions tax concessions for their loans under RMB50,000. It is recommended that the same tax concessions, in the form of subsidies and tax concessions, should be applied to all financial institutions in China, including MCCs, registered NGO microfinance institutions, and other registered lending institutions. The importance of the credit bureau system has grown over time following the development of communication and internet banking. The credit bureau services have, however, been limited to deposit-taking financial institutions and a few selected MCCs and one or two NGO microfinance institutions. It is recommended that the PBOC shall extend the credit bureau system to all the legally registered financial institutions, including all the MCCs and NGO MFIs, on a fee paying basis.

3. *Increase the supply and improve the operation of agricultural support on-lending.* The PBOC has provided agricultural support on-lending to rural financial institutions, mainly RCCs, at low rates of interest to increase the supply of institutional credit in China's rural areas. Given the direct impacts of such on-lending on credit supply to MSEs and rural households, it is recommended that the People's Bank of China (PBOC) increase its supply of agricultural support for on-lending. Moreover, well-performing non-deposit-taking rural financial institutions, such as microcredit companies and NGO microfinance institutions, should be eligible to receive such on-lending support as well.

4. *Allow the use of land-use rights and farmhouses as collateral for bank loans and widen the scope of collateral for banks.* First, relevant laws regarding loan collateral and guarantee should be modified. Second, the governments should set up farmland and farmhouse registration offices to register land-use rights and farmhouses, to issue rel-

evant certificates, and to register the land-use rights and farmhouses as collateral. The government should facilitate the development of markets for land-use rights and farmhouses at the county and township levels. Third, China's financial regulators, mainly the China Banking and Insurance Regulatory Commission (CBIRC) and the PBOC, shall allow the formal financial institutions in China to take the land-use rights (not the land operation rights) and the second farmhouses as collateral for loans, provided that there are local markets for the transfer of land-use rights and farmhouses. The first farmhouse (or the minimum space of rooms resided in by the household members) shall not be allowed to be used as loan collateral. However, for households that have resettled permanently in urban areas, the first farmhouse could be used as collateral. Pilot programs can be undertaken to streamline the processes for assessment, evaluation, and registration of farm assets as collateral and to train loan officials in the field so as to increase the access of rural smallholders to formal financial services. Local governments are in a position to facilitate such a process by improving the registration system for farm machines, greenhouses, and other relatively large farm assets. Crops and livestock could be used as collateral as well, provided that those crops and livestock have sufficient insurance policy coverage.

5. *Promote innovations for agricultural insurance, value chain, and community-based financing.* Pilots for weather- and price-indexed insurance have been conducted in different parts of China to mitigate adverse selection and moral hazard problems with agricultural insurance schemes. The government is encouraged to learn the lessons from the current pilot programs within and outside China and to provide support for the commercial financial institutions and donors to replicate the pilots on a larger scale and implement indexed insurance schemes for the major crops and animal products. To be financially viable, the insurance schemes should reach certain scale, for which support from the government is crucial. The government and insurance regulators should also promote catastrophe insurance by undertaking research and learn lessons from other countries. In addition to agricultural insurance services, the government should provide support to companies that lease farm machines and equipment.

6. *Remove territorial restrictions on microcredit company operations.* In some provinces, such as Inner Mongolia, well-performing MCCs have been granted a larger operational area. The borrowing limit for MCCs can be raised. In other countries, the leverage for lending-only institutions is between 300 percent and 400 percent. In China, the leverage could be raised to 100 percent–200 percent. The actual leverage for many MCCs in China is below 50 percent. They borrow from banks up to around 10 percent of their equity capital—far below the borrowing limit for similar institutions in other countries.

Notes

1. See People's Bank of China (PBOC), "China Inclusive Finance Analysis Report 2018," at the People's Bank of China website (www.pbc.gov.cn).

2. Asli Demirgüç-Kunt and others, "The Global Findex Database 2017: Measuring Financial Inclusion and the Fintech Revolution (Washington: World Bank, 2018).

3. Ibid.

4. The decline of MSE lending in China in 2017 was partly attributable to the economic slowdown and a reduced demand for loans. Here, MSE loans refers to loans to MSEs in urban areas only.

5. PBOC and China Banking and Insurance Regulation Commission (CBIRC), "China Inclusive Financial Report 2019," at the People's Bank of China website (www.pbc .gov.cn).

6. The regulated nonbanking financial institutions in China include the insurance companies (regulated by the then China Insurance Regulation Commission), financial leasing companies (regulated by the Ministry of Commerce), and financial institutions regulated by the China Security Regulation Commission. Note that China Insurance Regulation Commission was merged with China Banking Regulation Commission (CBRC) in April 2018; after the merge, CBRC was renamed CBIRC.

7. Enjiang Cheng, Jennifer Isern, and Xu Zhong, "Supply of Financial Services in China: A Study of Domestic Money Transfers," *Asia Pacific Journal of Finance and Banking Research* 1, no. 1 (2007) (https://papers.ssrn.com/sol3/papers.cfm?abstract_id=1535573).

8. On RCC reforms in China, see L. Zhang and others, "Responding to Financial Crisis: Bank Credit Expansion with Chinese Characteristics," *China Economic Review* (SSCI), October 2018, DOI: 10.1016/j.chieco.2018.09.014.

9. Zhu Xiujie and Li Yucui, "Report about the Situation of Finance Serving Rural Economy, Farmers, and Agricultural Development," China Banking Regulatory Commission, 2014.

10. Y. Huang, "The New Direction of China's Rural Finance," *The Paper*, 2018 (in Chinese) (www.thepaper.cn).

11. PBOC, "Quarter 1 Statistical Report on China's Microcredit Companies (2018)," April 28, 2018 (http://www.pbc.gov.cn/).

12. See China's Poverty Alleviation Office (LGOP) and the Ministry of Finance, "An Announcement for Conducting Pilot Village Mutual Help Funds," August 8, 2006 (www .China.com.cn/law/flfg/txt/2006-08/08/content_7056240.htm).

13. "The Monitoring Report for VCFs by the Foreign Capital and Project Management Centre under LGOP," unpublished report, 2015.

14. See the website of the Credit Reference Centre of the PBOC at www.pbccrc.org.cn.

15. For a more detailed discussion of donors' contributions to inclusive finance in China, see Enjiang Cheng, "International Agencies and the Microfinance Movement in China," in *From Microfinance to Inclusive Finance: Collected Papers for the 25th Anniversary of Microfinance in China*, ed. Xiaoshan Du and Wenpo Liu (Beijing: China Social Science Press, 2018), pp. 101–07.

16. Xiaoshan Du divides the development of inclusive finance in China into three stages: stage 1 (1993–96): pilot microfinance programs by informal financial institutions funded by

international donor agencies; stage 2 (1997–2005): acceptance and promotion of microfinance by China's central bank and formal financial institutions; stage 3 (2006–): from microfinance pilots to inclusive finance. See Xiaoshan Du, "From Microfinance to Inclusive Finance: Some Reflections," in *From Microfinance to Inclusive Finance*, ed. Xiaoshan Du and Wenpo Liu, pp. 19–33.

17. Author's interviews with CFPA and UNDP's microfinance pilot program directors; see also Wenpo Liu, "Reflections on the Introduction of the Grameen Model of Microfinance in China in the Early 1990s," in *From Microfinance to Inclusive Finance*, ed. Xiaoshan Du and Wenpo Liu, pp. 34–47.

18. The financial sector in China has been highly regulated, and individuals and institutions have been prohibited from engaging in deposit-taking and lending activities without permission from the financial regulators.

19. The 300 or so microcredit programs based on the Grameen model, using donor funds and TA, were implemented mainly by the MFIs set up by the county-level LGOP, the Women's Federation, the Bureau of Agriculture, the Bureau of Civil Affairs, and the Federation for the Disabled. See Enjiang Cheng, "International Agencies and the Microfinance Movement." So those county-level MFIs were government organized and controlled NGOs (GONGOs), organizations registered as social organizations but initiated and to some extent directed by government agencies.

20. Du Xiaoshan and Wenpo Liu, "From Microfinance to Inclusive Finance."

21. Z. Xu and Y. Lei, "A Review of Microfinance in China and the Prospects for Future Development," in *From Microfinance to Inclusive Finance*, ed. Xiaoshan Du and Wenpo Liu, pp. 48–56.

22. Since the mid-1980s, one major obstacle for rural households and MSEs in China in gaining access to institutional finance has been the requirement that they provide banks with physical collateral for loans. Farmland and houses in the villages could not be used as collateral.

23. Another challenge faced by RCCs in providing microloans to households was that RCC loan officials were not properly trained to disburse microloans to rural households and therefore had little incentive to do so.

24. Z. Xu and others, "Access to Finance—Microfinance Innovations in the People's Republic of China" (Manila: Asian Development Bank, 2014).

25. In December 2006, the China Banking Regulatory Commission issued a document titled "Certain Opinions about Adjustment to Lift the Control over Banking Financial Institutional Permits for Entry in Rural Areas to Effectively Support New Agricultural Construction" (in Chinese). Significant changes in the entry permits eased the entry of VTBs, finance corporations, and rural mutual funds. See ibid.

26. E. Cheng and D. Wang, "Report on Best Practices for Sustainable Models of Pro-Poor Rural Financial Services in China," APRACA RuFBeP Publication 2014-2015-2, funded by the International Fund for Agricultural Development (IFAD) (Bangkok, 2014).

27. See E. Cheng and and G. He, "A Report on China's Poverty Reduction Loans Submitted to LGOP, unpublished report, 2011. It is hard to judge whether such loans have contributed to inclusive financial development in China because the poverty loans are obviously not sustainable. Moreover, if a poor person fails to repay a poverty loan, the credit bureau system will record this and the person will be denied any additional poverty loans.

28. This clause does not apply to loan companies and rural fund co-operatives.

29. Minor changes were introduced in April 2014. To be eligible for the subsidies, the new types of RFIs need to lend 70 percent of their total portfolios for agricultural uses (mainly loans to rural households) and for use by MSEs.

30. Ministry of Finance, "Management Rules for Cash Subsidies to the County-Level RFIs for Their Increase in Agricultural Loan Portfolios" (in Chinese) (Beijing, 2009).

31. The usual corporate tax rate is 27 percent; see Ministry of Finance, "An Announcement on the Taxes for Rural Financial Institutions," MOF Document 4 (Beijing, 2010).

32. To encourage RFIs to provide more loans for rural development, China's central bank (PBOC) provides RFIs with agricultural support for on-lending at a low rate of interest (about 2 percent per year).

33. The primary source of the information in this section is the author's interviews with CFPA management staff. The author also worked as a consultant for the World Bank Poverty Projects in China, including the Southwest Poverty Reduction Project and Qianba Mountain Poverty Reduction Project; and on an International Finance Corporation technical assistance project with CFPA MF.

34. Cheng, "International Agencies and the Microfinance Movement in China."

35. CFPA MF was transformed from a microfinance program piloted under the World Bank's Qianba Mountain Poverty Reduction Project in China's Sichuan and Shaanxi provinces in the mid-1990s; DF Micro-loan Co. was transformed from a county-level MFI initiated and funded by the China Aid Foundation and the county government in 1996; and Chifeng MFI started as a UNDP microfinance pilot project in 1997.

36. G. Hao, "NGO Microfinance in China—Current Development, Problems, and Strategies for Moving Forward," in *From Microfinance to Inclusive Finance*, ed. Xiaoshan Du and Wenpo Liu, pp. 305–18.

37. See CFPA Microfinance Ltd. Annual Report, 2019 (http://en.cfpa.org.cn/index.php ?file=article&cmd=list&cid=21).

38. See CFPA MF website at www.cfpamf.com.cn.

39. A typical UNDP MFP in a poor county of China had US$200,000 to fund its microfinance operation, plus technical support. It was unlikely for such programs to achieve operational and financial sustainability in a poor county on their own, especially after the TA support from UNDP/CICETE was phased out. One primary reason for Chifeng's survival was an influx of money from KfW.

40. In field investigations by the author around 2010, CFPA MF's average funding costs were around 6.5 percent, and operating costs (mainly staff salaries) 9–10 percent of its loan portfolio. CFPA MF had to charge an interest rate on loans of at least 17 percent in order to cover its costs and any losses from bad loans. The low rates of interest charged (10–12 percent on average) are perhaps the most important reason for the failure of most NGO MFPs in China.

41. CFPA Microfinance has three standard loan products: group (joint liability) loans, usually below RMB12,000; individual loans, usually below RMB50,000; and microenterprise loans, from RMB50,000 to about RMB100,000.

42. When the joint venture was set up in 2011, IFC and Sequoia each had about 20 percent of the shares and CFPA remained the majority shareholder, controlling 40 percent of the shares.

43. See website of CD Finance at www.cdfinance.com.cn.

44. The other two institutions are CASS, which had pilots in three poor counties of China, and JUNDP/CECITE, which had pilots in over 33 counties of China. In September 2016, CASS and Grameen Trust signed an agreement with CFPA MF to entrust CFPA MF to manage its MFIs in Nanzhao and Yucheng counties of Henan Province and Laishui county of Hebei Province.

45. This section draws heavily on an unpublished consultant report prepared by the author for CDB in China, titled "The Project Completion Report for the Microfinance Downscaling by China Development Bank" (2010).

46. For commercial banks in China, including the small-scale banks at the county level, it is common for the loan applicants to apply in person at the bank branches.

47. The State Council, The People's Republic of China, "Opinions on Several Policies and Measures to Vigorously Promote Mass Entrepreneurship and Innovation," June 11, 2015 (http://english.www.gov.cn/policies/infographics/2015/06/16/content_281475128482059.htm).

48. This section draws on a draft report prepared by the Inclusive Finance Institute of Renmin University in China, "Digital Finance for Poverty Reduction in China," October 2018.

49. Wang Dai Zhi Jia, "China P2P Lending: Number of Platforms," P2P Lending Network, 2018 (https://www.ceicdata.com/en/china/p2p-lending-number-of-platform).

50. Haifeng Li, "The Credit Scoring System of MY Bank," 2019 (in Chinese) (www.dooland.com).

51. Duaguang Bei and Yan Li, *The New Era of Digital Inclusive Finance in China* (Beijing: Zhonxin Publishing House, 2017), p. 107 (in Chinese).

52. See Annual Reports of MY Bank and WeBank for 2017 through 2019 at https://www.mybank.cn/ and https://www.webank.com/en/.

53. The CFPA MF app includes a large dataset with credit scoring and loan collection models, face recognition, machine learning, and other technologies.

54. Li, "The Credit Scoring System of MY Bank."

55. In addition more research is needed on how the data collected by the internet service providers affect privacy.

FIFTEEN

The Future of Microfinance in Africa

Differentiating East and West

RENÉE CHAO-BEROFF AND KIMANTHI MUTUA

East Africa

KIMANTHI MUTUA

It is difficult to predict the future of microfinance in East Africa considering the changes that have taken place over the past thirty years. These changes have affected conventional microfinance institutions in many ways and are already shaping the future of microfinance in the region. Changes in the regulatory regimes have caused many traditional microfinance institutions to alter their institutional form as well as their ownership and governance models. When combined with technological advancements such as mobile banking innovations, the changes have also brought in competition from nontraditional microfinance players and expanded the microfinance product range considerably.

Traditional microfinance institutions (MFIs) in the region were established between the mid-1970s and mid-1980s. They all started as small projects that were initiated by donor organizations and run by different forms of development organizations. Their main aim was to alleviate poverty through financial intervention. Their main activity was to provide very small loans to low-income and

poor people who operated businesses, as a way to generate income and employment opportunities. The businesses that they financed were also very small and
were known globally as microenterprises. Mobilizing savings was part of the lending methodology, rather than a stand-alone effort. In many cases the services were
combined with some form of training and technical assistance, at no cost to the
beneficiaries.

These microfinance projects were all funded through grants from donors. Their
success, or lack thereof, was largely based on how many poor people—or beneficiaries, as they were known then—a project had supported or reached. Financial performance parameters, such as the quality of the loan portfolio, profitability, or the
extent to which the projects were financially sustainable, were not considered crucial
at this early stage. Apart from the beneficiaries, the public, regulators, mainstream
financial institutions, and other institutions took very little notice of these projects.
They were considered charitable services.

This original model changed in the 1990s. Concerted efforts by donor organizations and successful new models, dubbed the "financial systems approach," from
other parts of the world influenced MFIs in the region to change their business model.
First, the microfinance projects were institutionalized and became registered nongovernmental organizations (NGOs). The rationale for this change was that projects lacked continuity, which is essential for organizations that provide financial services. Second, MFIs began to be judged on financial indicators as well as the size of
the operation. Third, the funding model began to change. Although donor grants
continued to play an important role, many MFIs started relying on borrowed funds
from local banks and international development finance organizations. This 1990s
model also came with a new feature—the provision of microfinance services, that is
loans and savings—known as the minimalist approach. Provision of training and
technical assistance was either dropped completely or transferred to another related
organization, leaving MFIs to focus on financial services. Savings became an important stand-alone product as opposed to being linked to loan products. Last, the model
included a proven group-based method of lending to low-income and poor people: it
effectively reached a large number of people and leveraged peer pressure to enforce
repayment of loans.

The MFIs that adopted this model were very successful in providing microfinance
services. Those that failed to adapt to change either died or remained small and ir-
relevant. The large ones caught the attention of regulators and policymakers, who
started monitoring their operations but showed no intention of regulating MFIs. Conventional commercial banks remained unwilling or unable to serve the microfinance market, despite efforts by donor organizations to get them to introduce mi-

crofinance loan products. Increasingly, though, banks began funding MFIs, mostly because they were custodians of the MFI funds and had good insight into the quality of their lending process and growing cash reserves.

From the mid-1990s to the early 2000s, therefore, the provision of microfinance services was dominated by the traditional microfinance institutions. Most low-income and poor people had limited access to conventional financial institutions. They relied largely on MFIs and co-operative societies, although those organizations did not reach deeply into rural areas. Their operations were concentrated in cities, towns, and market areas. Despite their success in lending to poor people, a large proportion of the poor remain unserved by financial institutions.

MFIs and co-operative societies were the only types of institutions that could serve the poor at this point. MFIs had a competitive advantage in know-how, a unique lending methodology, and service delivery channels embedded in their business model that promised access to all poor people. Co-operatives had a good system that had served poor people for many years. But they faced many challenges that are ingrained in that age-old system, which limited their growth potential. As membership organizations, they could only serve those who met their common-bond membership criteria. Further, unlike MFIs who continued to get grants and loans from varied sources, co-operatives relied on members' contributions to their share capital and borrowed funds from the co-operative banks.

At this juncture, during the 1990s and early 2000s, it was widely believed that MFIs were the only institutions appropriate to provide financial services to poor people. This view was reinforced by several factors. Their legacy focus on the social mission of poverty alleviation endeared MFIs to policymakers, politicians, and donors, as well as to many development organizations and pundits. The demonstrated success of lending to large numbers of poor people convinced many that MFIs had solved the problem of providing access to financial services. Spirited campaigns to popularize microfinance by donors, microfinance associations, and international organizations fortified that view.

The success of the 1990s and the preceding hype led to spirited campaigns and advocacy for new laws, or amendments to existing ones, to license and regulate MFIs. This, it was argued then, would introduce order and discipline to the sector; legalize deposit mobilization; develop microfinance savings products; create a funding stream; and most important, bring institutions that serve poor people to the center of the policies, laws, and regulations that govern the financial system, as opposed to having them operate on its periphery. It took time to convince the regulatory bodies, but when they conceded, one country after another enacted laws to regulate MFIs, beginning in about 2003.

Before the enactment of the new laws, MFIs such as the Kenya Rural Enterprise Program (K-Rep) opted to transform into commercial banks under existing laws but focus on microfinance. Other regulated housing finance companies, such as Equity and Family, also based in Kenya, also transformed into commercial banks and targeted the microfinance market. Some banks, such Centenary in Uganda, also focused on microfinance. The main difference between those banks and MFIs is that the banks also targeted small and medium-sized enterprises (SMEs) and corporate entities, while the MFIs were solely focused on microfinance.

At the point when microfinance laws proliferated in the region, the future of microfinance was clear, or so it was thought. Microfinance was synonymous with MFIs because it was still believed that they would remain the dominant players. Many romanticized the notion of a microfinance industry in the belief that the microfinance market segment would predominantly be served by MFIs. MFIs continued to have a competitive advantage, and their social mission was considered essential. The few commercial banks were more of an exception than the rule because of their background. What followed were three waves of change that altered this view considerably.

The first wave of change followed the introduction of the new regulations. Although only a few of the traditional MFIs transformed, many were expected to follow. Among the traditional MFIs that transformed immediately after the laws were enacted were three in Kenya, one in Tanzania, and three in Uganda, and one was taken over by Equity Bank soon after. New products and services emerged, such as savings not linked to loans, money transfer, and investment clubs. Funding from grants and a small amount of borrowed funds was replaced by deposits, equity investments, and large volumes of borrowed funds from development finance institutions and microfinance funding vehicles.

MFIs continued to be the dominant players and key drivers of changes in policies and regulations. Most regulators required MFIs to have prior experience before being licensed. But the number of regulated MFIs remained small, except in countries where it was mandatory to be licensed, like Ethiopia, which in the 1990s was the first country to introduce regulations for MFIs.

The second wave was ushered in by a global focus on financial inclusion policies. This shifted the drivers of change in policies and regulations from the microfinance community to regulators and policymakers. Financial inclusion policies were aimed at ensuring access to financial services to all (the poor included) by mainstream institutional players. This change in policy ushered nontraditional players into the regulated MFI sector. The prior experience requirement was no longer relevant. Newly formed MFIs that did not necessarily subscribe to the social mission aspect of microfinance entered the sector. Some saw microfinance as a profitable market segment; others capitalized on the lower barriers to entry in the financial system (regulatory arbitrage). For example, in Kenya, of the thirteen regulated microfinance banks, only three came from the traditional MFIs that prevailed in the 1990s. In Uganda, of the five regulated microfinance deposit-taking institutions (MDIs), three were newly established. Of the initial three that transformed from NGO to MDI, one was taken over by Equity Bank. In Tanzania, of the five regulated microfinance banks, almost all are "greenfield" (newly established) banks. It is important to note, though, that in Uganda and Tanzania many of the newly formed MFIs have a development background.

Many of the new entrants were funded by private capital, with little or no reliance on development finance institutions or microfinance funds. The myth that traditional MFIs with a social mission were the most appropriate providers of microfinance waned fast. It became clear that institutions driven by a profit motive were just as appropriate as the traditional ones. This view was reinforced by the fact that the characteristics of customers or beneficiaries served by the new players were the same as those served by the traditional social-oriented MFIs.

Further, a lot of innovations in service delivery took place in this wave of change. For example, the group-lending method was replaced by a focus on individual borrowers. As a result, the competitive advantage enjoyed by traditional MFIs began to erode quickly.

Then came the game changer: the third wave of change, which was spurred by an enabling policy and regulatory environment, improved infrastructure, and technological advancement. It started with mobile phone money transfer services but evolved to three areas of innovation that are shaping the future of microfinance in the region.

The first area is *financial technology* (fintech): the use of technology and innovations in business models to provide financial services. Fintech introduced new business models that challenged the traditional methods of microfinance service delivery. It gave all types of institutions—conventional commercial banks, mobile network operators, and companies that develop or acquire appropriate computer and phone applications—greater access to the microfinance market segment.

The second area of innovation was further development in the use of mobile phones to access financial services: *mobile banking.* Mobile phones created a new channel for accessing financial services and broadened outreach to areas that the regulated MFIs could not reach. Mobile banking improved the efficiency and accuracy of records, and it reduced the cost of service provision considerably. Banks and

FIGURE 15-1.   Use of Mobile Bank Accounts vs. Traditional
Banking Services, by Age Percent

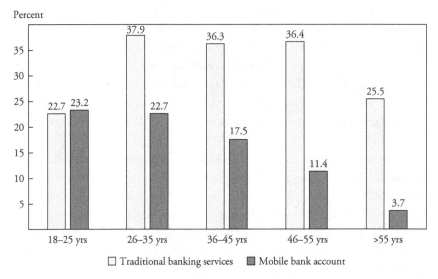

Source: FSD Kenya, 2016 FinAccess Household Survey (https://fsdkenya.org/dataset/finaccess-household-2016/).

mobile network operators (MNOs) no longer needed to work with MFIs to serve the microfinance segment.

The third area of innovation was in *digital financial services*: financial services that are accessible through digital channels. Many new target products and services that are crucial to low-income and poor communities (impact financing) were introduced. For example, utility payments solutions made it possible for poor people to pay for clean water and power services. Insurance services and affordable premium payments, short-term loans for small and microenterprises, money transfer to any individual or bank account in any financial institution, agriculture loans, and other features were introduced and continue to be developed.

These developments lead to several observations. The first is that the younger generation is increasingly using digital banking channels to perform their banking activities and visiting bank branches less often than ever before (see figure 15-1).

The behaviors and preferences of this generation are shaping the future of banks and the relationship between banks and their customers. Commercial banks too are under threat as nonbank third-party organizations such as mobile network operators, social media, and mobile app developers are providing financial and related services.

FIGURE 15-2.   Use of Financial Service Providers by Wealth Quintile

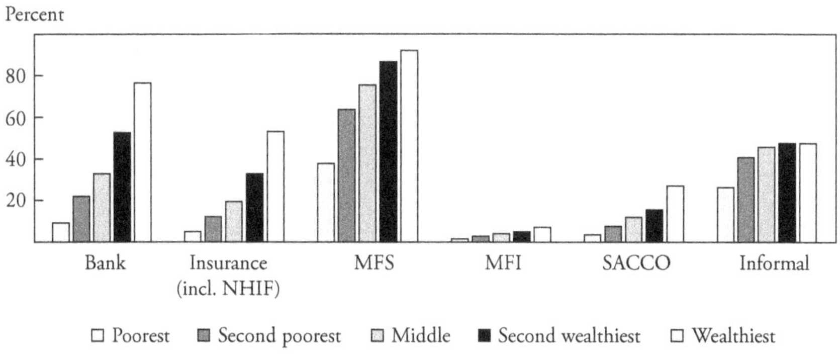

Percent

Source: FSD Kenya, 2016 FinAccess Household Survey (https://fsdkenya.org/dataset/finaccess-household -2016/).
NHIF = National Hospital Insurance Fund
MFS = mobile financial service
MFI = microfinance institution
SACCO = savings and credit cooperative organization

Second, commercial banks demonstrated the importance of a large capital and funding base, which MFIs are less endowed with. The fintech innovations were available in the market looking for takers. MFIs could easily have taken advantage of the innovations and retained their competitive advantage but were constrained by lack of access to funds. Commercial banks, which were previously unwilling or unable to serve the microfinance market segment, snatched the opportunity. They have invested a large amount of money, developed solutions, and are now the largest providers of services to the microfinance market segment. It is likely that funding capacity is what led MNOs to prefer partnering with commercial banks and less with MFIs, even though the latter were their initial partners of choice.

A third observation is that low-income and poor people are comfortable using mobile financial services (MFS) platforms. Figure 15-2 shows MFS to have the highest volume of use by the poorest and second poorest. MNOs provide their own mobile financial services, especially money transfer, payment systems, and electronic wallets. Commercial banks, whose distribution channels are provided by MNOs, are the biggest providers of mobile financial services. They have a wide range of products and services, with loans and savings being the most popular. For example, one commercial bank in Kenya has over 25 million MFS customers. Most of these customers come from the poorest and second-poorest wealth quintile, which is what MFIs target.

Although different countries in the region are at different stages of fintech development, there are clear signs that the trend visible in Kenya will spread to all countries. In the very near future most of the population in the region will have access to formal financial institutions. Mobile financial services will more than likely be the preferred channel for accessing financial services, and commercial banks will be the dominant players in mobile financial services.

These waves of changes have affected microfinance institutions and the microfinance market segment in the region fundamentally. MFIs have lost their competitive advantage in the delivery of services to the microfinance market segment. They are neither the custodians of the microfinance know-how nor the dominant players in the microfinance sector. Although many are working hard to innovate, change myths, and adapt fintech innovations, it is unlikely that they will regain the competitive advance they once had.

Competition has increased significantly and is coming from different types of organizations that are well endowed financially. Other players, such as co-operative societies, community banks, and village banks, are also competing in this space. Today microfinance is no longer synonymous with microfinance institutions. The former is considered a retail banking market segment, which can be served by any institution that is able to do so. Fintech innovations have provided solutions to problems that prevented many from venturing into this market segment: high-cost operations, inappropriate service distribution channels, and lack of know-how.

The future of the microfinance market segment is therefore very bright. Low-income and poor people in this market segment will have a wide choice of institutions from which to access financial services. The range of products and services, cost, and quality of service are also expected to improve as competition increases. Of course, there are concerns being raised, among which are indebtedness, the cost of services, fraud, and others. It is likely that the market, policy, and regulatory interventions will gradually address them. Initiatives on consumer education, consumer protection, and credit reference bureaus are being implemented in all countries in the region. The most powerful of these interventions is consumer education, which unfortunately takes a long time to have the desired effect.

As for microfinance institutions, the future is likely to be very challenging. It is not clear whether the number of regulated MFIs will grow beyond the current level, as many possible candidates are reconsidering the option. Their reluctance is informed by what they see as challenges faced by those who have transformed, including an inability to attract large amounts of capital and a large volume of deposits. Capital-raising challenges have led a couple of the regulated MFIs to change their ownership structure from NGOs to large commercial entities. There are also indications that some are considering becoming commercial banks, since the regulatory regime allows the provision of a broader range of services, which in turn can help mobilize deposits. Finally, because the earlier notion of creating a microfinance industry is no longer a reality, becoming a regulated MFI is not necessarily the most appropriate institutional form for providing services to the microfinance market.

Box 15-1 illustrates the evolution of a microfinance project in Kenya, K-Rep, to an NGO, from there to a regulated microfinance bank (the first in Africa to attract

---

BOX 15-1.   The Transformation of the Kenya Rural Enterprise Program (K-Rep) into an MFI

Background: K-Rep was founded in 1984 by a U.S. NGO and was subsequently funded by the U.S. Agency for International Development, which provided funding to existing NGOs involved in microfinance and small-business development in Kenya. In 1990, K-Rep established its own MFI and introduced peer-group lending to microentrepreneurs. By 1994, K-Rep had decided to transform into a microfinance bank and focus on its own operations. This was the first NGO-to-bank conversion in Africa. It took K-Rep several years to transform, partly because of the unfamiliarity of Kenya's central bank with microfinance and how best to supervise such an entity.

Ownership Structure: After careful consideration of its options, the board of K-Rep decided to establish a holding company to manage its various activities, which included the bank (K-Rep Bank Ltd.), the NGO (K-Rep Development Agency), and a consulting company (K-Rep Consulting Services). Initially, K-Rep Holdings sought to own 51 percent of the bank, but the central bank limited ownership concentration to 25 percent. K-Rep attracted several like-minded investors that would allow the bank to retain its mission.

Management and Employee Incentives: With the support of the Consultative Group to Assist the Poor (CGAP), K-Rep set up a form of employee stock ownership plan as a co-operative, the K-Rep Welfare Association (KWA), so that existing and future directors, managers, and employees could purchase shares in the bank with a view that the bank would eventually undertake an IPO on the Nairobi Stock Exchange. CGAP funding allowed the KWA to retain liquidity so that shares could be sold and purchased by employees, including

(continued)

BOX 15-1.   The Transformation of the Kenya Rural Enterprise Program (K-Rep) into an MFI (continued)

future employees. The KWA retained a 10 percent interest in the bank but was not allocated a board seat.

Management Capability: Senior management of the NGO remained with the bank; in particular, the long-serving CEO, Kimanthi Mutua, who was well known and highly respected in the microfinance sector. In time, employees with specialized knowledge were recruited from the banking sector.

Growth and Performance: K-Rep Bank grew steadily and strongly as a bank: between 2000 and 2007, the number of clients grew from 15,000 to 153,961, savers from 2,724 to 16,701, the gross loan portfolio from US$4.6 million to US$110 million, and return on equity from 13.4 percent to 22.3 percent. In 2007, the bank began to experience delinquency problems: its portfolio at risk (PAR) jumped from 3.6 percent to 12.6 percent. K-Rep's problems increased partly because of the bank's diversification into small-business loans and a failed effort at management succession. Investors provided the bank with more liquidity in the form of a rights offering. In time, a new managing director was brought in when Kimanthi Mutua retired after some twenty-five years at the helm. He remained chair of the holding company, and the bank was restored to health.

Purchase of a Majority Interest: On April 4, 2016, K-Rep Bank was renamed Sidian Bank, reflecting the acquisition of a majority interest in the bank by Centum Investment Company, a Kenyan financial group, at the end of 2015. K-Rep Holdings and the KWA continued to hold a minority share in the bank.

Source: Pasquale di Benedetta, Ira W. Lieberman, and Laura Ard, "Corporate Governance in Microfinance Institutions" (Washington: World Bank, 2015), pp. 24-25.

commercial investors), to the adoption of digital financial technology (mobile banking), and finally to its sale to an external financial investor.

Box 15-2 illustrates the evolution of a failed savings and loan institution to a commercial bank, Equity Bank, its rapid growth and branch expansion within Kenya, its listing on the Nairobi Stock Exchange, its expansion within East Africa as a multinational bank, and its adoption of digital financial technology (mobile banking).

BOX 15-2.   The Evolution of Equity Bank Limited

Background: Equity Bank Limited (EBL) was founded as the Equity Building Society (EBS) in Nairobi in 1984 and initially focused on providing term loans and mobilizing deposits. The high risk of term loans, a stagnant deposit base, undercapitalization, poor management, and a difficult macroeconomic and political environment took the bank to the brink of collapse. In 1993, the central bank of Kenya declared EBS insolvent with more than 50 percent of its loan portfolio at risk of default.

Restructuring the Bank: Under the leadership of James Mwangi, EBS began a major restructuring effort that focused on the economically active poor. The bank also began a marketing campaign aimed at mobilizing savings deposits. The vision was to become the leading retail bank in East Africa by providing a full range of financial services to the economically active poor. Loyal savers were gradually converted into borrowers on the basis of their savings patterns. As a result, the company incurred few additional marketing costs while building its loan portfolio. The company invested significant funds and effort in management information systems (MIS) data and software to manage credit risk, to comply with changing banking regulations in Kenya, and perhaps more important, to tighten its control over its portfolio performance.

Managing Explosive Growth: The organization's new strategy, new management team, external technical assistance, and investors paid off. In 2004, EBS was given a full banking license, and following its turnaround and initial takeoff phase, the bank began to grow dramatically. By 2006, when the bank decided to list on the Nairobi Stock Exchange, Equity Bank Limited, as the bank was renamed, was benchmarked against other Kenyan banks. From 2003 to 2006, the number of borrowers increased from 59,000 to 240,000 at an annual average rate of 66 percent. The portfolio grew from US$15 million in 2002 to US$158 million at year-end 2006—an annual average growth rate of 82 percent. At the same time, the number of savings accounts increased from 156,000 to just over a million, an average growth rate of 61 percent; deposit balances grew from US$28 million to US$236 million, an annual average growth rate of 72 percent. Portfolio at risk remained a problem throughout this period, at 12.2 percent at end-2006. EBL sought to address the problem

(continued)

BOX 15-2.   The Evolution of Equity Bank Limited
(continued)

with a significant investment in MIS and with technical assistance on credit risk management supported by CGAP. At the end of 2006, the bank's return on assets (ROA) was 4.85 percent, its return on equity (ROE) 40.36 percent, its profit margin 31.53 percent, its capital adequacy 11 percent, and its debt-to-equity ratio 8.10 percent. Throughout this period of explosive growth, the bank continued its outreach to poor clients, with an average loan balance of US$444, or 65.64 percent of gross national income (GNI) per capita. The bank also continued to offer savings to the working poor, which reached US$165 on average, or 36.73 percent of GNI per capita, in 2006.

Listing on the Nairobi Stock Exchange: The bank went from being traded over-the-counter (OTC) to being listed on the Nairobi Stock Exchange on August 7, 2006. The purpose of the listing was "to offer shareholders and the Bank the benefits of the stock market liquidity and price discovery."

Attracting a Major Investor: On November 14, 2007, EBL and Helios EB Investors, LP (Helios) subscribed to 90.5 million new ordinary shares in the bank at 122 Kenyan shillings (KES) (US$1.94 per share, with 63 KES equal to US$1). The investment substantially increased EBL's capital, and Helios became the largest shareholder in EBL at 24.99 percent.

International Expansion: EBL subsequently purchased a transformed microfinance bank in Uganda and has expanded into other countries in Africa, such as Rwanda.

Technology Adoption: EBL has also entered into a joint venture with M-Pesa/Safaricom to extend mobile banking to its client base for payments, loans, and savings products.

Source: Pasquale di Benedetta, Ira W. Lieberman, and Laura Ard, "Corporate Governance in Microfinance Institutions" (Washington: World Bank, 2015), p. 21.

West Africa

RENÉE CHAO-BEROFF

Since the late 1990s, the microfinance sector in West Africa has grown significantly, not only in outreach numbers but also in diversification (products and client segments) and commercialization. Delivery channels have also changed (nascent digital finance, payments, from back to front office transformation).

In West Africa, eight countries share the same currency, the CFA franc (XOF), and are supervised by one regional central bank, the Banque Centrale des Etats de l'Afrique de l'Ouest (BCEAO). In the 1980s, BCEAO promulgated a microfinance law to regulate the *mutuelles d'épargne et de crédit* (*mutuelles*), the only legal entities allowed to provide financial services to the poor and excluded populations of West Africa. This regulation has been a strong enabler of financial inclusion in the sense that thousands of small *mutuelles* were created in all eight countries, especially in rural areas where the traditional banks were not interested in operating. However, after ten years, the BCEAO and the ministries of finance of the eight countries in charge of regulating and supervising the sector realized that implementation of the law was almost impossible in countries with widely dispersed populations and hundreds of very small entities mobilizing savings, giving loans in an autonomous manner, and with weak governance structures and weak technical skills.

In 2010, a second-generation microfinance law was promulgated with three main objectives: (1) consolidation: all primary financial *mutuelles* have the obligation to be in a "network"—that is, a union or federation of *mutuelles*, under an umbrella organization that will take responsibility to ensure that internal audits and reporting are completed and will ban and take away the licenses of all isolated entities; (2) better supervision and inspections, especially for larger institutions (with more than 2 billion XOF in assets, equivalent to US$3.4 million), where joint missions were to be performed by the regional banking commission together with the ministries of finance (which are considered weaker and also more politically sensitive) using a risk-based approach to supervision; (3) allowing the entry of private (nonco-operative) entities in the form of share companies (*sociétés anonymes*, or publicly traded corporations), which can individually obtain a license to operate. It was expected that they would target the urban market and micro, small, and medium enterprises. A decade later, very few mergers and acquisitions had taken place or were successful in bringing the numbers of small entities down and building larger and stronger institutions; nor have the ministries of finance successfully closed isolated and unviable *mutuelles* in rural areas. Supervision remains very problematic, especially in fragile states.

Joint supervision and inspections by the Commission Bancaire de l'Afrique Centrale (COBAC) and local ministries have led to putting some very large *mutuelles* under provisional administration and supervision (for example, Crédit Mutuel du Senegal), very few of which have been able to recover full financial health and operate normally, even after five years or more under this status. Governance issues and fraud are the primary reasons.

The microfinance institutions (MFIs) under corporate status are mostly doing well. They focus on urban clients and compete for the same segment of the market. However, their more aggressive methods are leading to a risk of over-indebtness. Overall, the portfolio quality in all MFIs in West Africa has deteriorated far below the standards in the industry and those of the central bank. The figure for portfolios at risk (PAR) has risen to more than 7–8 percent, leading to poor performance and capital adequacy issues.

Here I look at all of these growth trends and try to analyze how each of them has contributed to the next generation of microfinance in West Africa.

Maintaining a Client-centric Environment

As in many geographic regions where the rural population still constitutes a majority, the microfinance sector that started up at the end of the 1970s and early 1980s was initiated by rural-development-driven NGOs and co-operative mutualist actors from the North (Canada, Germany, France, Ireland, the United States). The two major models implemented in West Africa were the *mutuelles* (*caisses populaires*, *caisses mutuelles*, and Crédit Mutuel) and the CBFOs (*caisses villageoises d'épargne et de crédit autogérées*—CVECAs, or village banks).

Still today, in outreach and coverage, these participatory forms of finance, which are physically very close to their "members," represent a vast majority of institutions in the sector and also in market share (60 to 80 percent). However, if one looks more carefully into performance, many of them have difficulty retaining clients and maintaining portfolio quality, profitability, and ultimately, capital adequacy.

A few years ago, a large *mutuelle* network in West Africa commissioned a large-scale client satisfaction survey, which was considered bold and innovative for players in this category. To the surprise of the top managers and governance bodies, the participating *mutuelles* received very negative reviews of their performance in client service, innovation, and most of all, governance and participation. The large *mutuelles* were losing members because members wanted to be treated like clients and not like owners, users, or beneficiaries.

All the rules and principles of financial mutualism (saving first, permission to borrow three times what is in your savings account, no remuneration on savings (due to overliquidity of the majority of them) had become so rigid and outdated that the *mutuelles* no longer attracted the younger generation; even conservative farmers who wanted to move to more market-led agriculture found it difficult to find a loan product that fit their cash flow. This survey made it clear that the *mutuelles* in West Africa, although physically and historically close to their members, were no longer perceived by their members as client-centric, able to listen to their needs, or adapt products to their aspirations and life projects. Their governance, which is supposed to represent the participation of the members in decision making, was far too disconnected from its base to provide feedback to the management about the members' sentiments. The *mutuelles* were not performing because they had lost the deep connection with their base members, owners, and clients.

The rising model for MFIs in West Africa is definitely more commercial. Many are registered under the BCEAO law as share companies. These are mostly greenfields, heavily supported by development finance institutions (DFIs) through technical assistance grants, well capitalized (capital adequacy), and potentially with easy access to concessional loans. They are growing quickly, but only or mostly in large cities, where they serve traders and businesses. Some also take aggressive approaches in human resources and client acquisition. They tend to create new products and propose a larger range of products, especially loan products, and disburse large amounts to attract larger businesses in the formal and informal sectors. Some of the larger players in this category are MicroCred/Bambou, Advans, ACEP, Première Agence de Microfinance (PAMF; Cote d'Ivoire, Senegal, in the francophone zone), ProCredit, Opportunity International (in Ghana, for instance).

Are greenfield institutions more client-centric? The answer is not clear, since they all offer largely the same range of products and, because they seek profitability, tend to put more pressure on loan officers for high performance, which in general is not synonymous with providing client care and high-touch attention to clients.

Since the mid-2010s, a new breed of player has emerged in West Africa: an all-African investment group that has set up a financial holding company to promote greenfields focusing on the SME market in francophone countries. The partners are African financial professionals who have credible records as top managers of either microfinance institutions or commercial banks, and have invested their own money in the holding company as well as in affiliate microfinance banks.

At this writing in 2020, five such banks are operating and profitable, including COFINA Senegal and CAC Cote d'Ivoire; others are still very young and operating in Mali, Guinea, and Gabon.

They are in urban areas, sometimes only in the capital city, but use money transfer facilities to acquire clients and test markets elsewhere. Clients can be planters, businesses, and processors in-country; the bank sends officers to work with them where they are. Digital platforms reduce the need for brick-and-mortar branches, especially for these SME clients. The banks also create clusters to facilitate support and monitoring. The ambition of the COFINA Group is to become the Equity Bank of West Africa, and it has shown signs of progressing in this direction.

Unlike the two first categories of microfinance players that come from a development background or are supported heavily by DFIs and grant money, this third player is privately funded and led; surprisingly, it is also the most client-centric, probably because, in order to mitigate risks and be profitable, it needs the clients to succeed in their businesses and to be satisfied with the services they receive. The founder, Jean Luc Konan, a former investment banker, has a well-conceived business model and has noted that SME financing needs a paradigm change in client-centricity.[1]

It seems that client-centricity is a matter of leadership, not an ideology or a legacy.

The Decline of the Financial *Mutuelles*

Mutuelles became outdated because they have neglected to listen to their members' needs and aspirations, by simply thinking that being owned by their members leads automatically to being close to them. This belief has been proved wrong, and the price for that is very high dropout rates and dormant accounts.

In the same vein, the leaders of the *mutuelles* took it for granted that their members and owners would not "betray" them by looking to competitors for financial services, especially loans. The reality is that competition is widespread, and younger generations are highly connected to the urban surroundings where all kinds of players advertise all kinds of services with new and simpler platforms and less administrative hassle. The younger clients can make the comparison quickly between the old *mutuelles* and the new entrants. They tend to be more individualistic and interested in what will help them seize opportunities and earn more money; they are less inclined to hold "old-fashioned" values like loyalty, solidarity, and sharing.

Governance is seen as being in the hands of a few powerful people in the communities, and annual meetings of the *mutuelle* are not truly informative or transparent. This is very strong criticism of the essence of the system, which is based on the democratic principle of "one person, one vote." The *mutuelles* are no longer as democratic as they once were. These factors are the reason for their decline, as viewed from the clients' perspective.

The competitors to the *mutuelles* in West Africa are the greenfield microfinance banks. They are seen by potential clients as providing faster services, having fewer prerequisites, and promoting access to loans (without savings). They offer confidentiality, staff discipline, and creative branding, which are seen as more modern and professional. These greenfield microfinance banks are also able to invest in information technology and provide services using tablets, mobile banking, and agent banking. Their interest rates may be a bit higher, but clients value the fast service and the range of products and services.

Hence, even if these microfinance banks seem to occupy only a minority of the market share, the trend is positive for them, and they will be able to compete favorably if they can improve their outreach.

The key factor in this market divide is the regulatory authority, the BCEAO, which is the promoter of the microfinance law that has favored the *mutuelles*. It still refuses to reconsider the law and allow some very large *mutuelles* to transform into share companies to improve their governance structure and raise equity from private investors.

If this bottleneck could be removed and the landscape of *mutuelles* could change naturally, leading to a total restructuring of the ecosystem, what kind of exclusion would the disappearance of the *mutuelles* lead to in West Africa?

The *mutuelles* are emblematic of the values of solidarity and social bonds that are valued in the local and rural communities. With the weakening of the *mutuelles*, will financial inclusion still be able to mobilize those values to integrate the most vulnerable and hard-to-reach people and use them to exercise discipline and social pressure for repayment of loans?

In fact, the past two decades or so have witnessed a rapid transformation of societal behavior in West Africa. In addition to urbanization, migrations have brought individualism and consumerism to the rural societies. Monetization has replaced the barter system in exchanges of products and services, leading to less concrete expressions of solidarity at the village level. These traditional values have now by-and-large disappeared and been replaced by a modern society in which money is the basis for relationships between people. In such a society, therefore, we see a long-term but steady trend of *mutuelles* decline in West Africa (as occurred in East Africa many decades ago), except in weak-state countries and fragile economies (Sierra Leone, Liberia, Gambia) where people have few options other than a system based on a form of self-help.

This observation is confirmed by the reduced influence of large technical promoters such as DID, Crédit Mutuel, and the World Council of Credit Unions. It is said that this is the era of the triumph of capitalism, that the mutualist spirit is dying globally, and that Basel III—the international regulatory accord intended to strengthen the regulation, supervision, and risk management of banks, especially on capital adequacy—may instead create the conditions that lead to the decline of the model.

The Market for Digital Finance

In West Africa, hundreds of thousands of young men migrants (and sometimes young women) play a very important role in their families' welfare by sending revenues back home. Their migrations take different directions: from rural areas to cities within the country; from struggling regions to more productive regions and more prosperous countries; and to European countries looking for a better future.

Some ten years ago, the strongest players in the field of money transfer were Western Union and MoneyGram. These were the main formal remittance channels for sending money home to families in need. More recently, telecommunications companies (telcos) started exploring this lucrative market, and in just a few years have taken the place: these include Orange Money, MTN Mobile Money, Tigo, Airtel, and others. The telcos have captured the market for payments and remittances. Besides topping up airtime, the range of financial services available is still limited. The reason is that, at the regulatory level, BCEAO is reluctant to let telcos enter the banking sector, especially in microfinance, where many of the potential clients are still illiterate.

Therefore, telcos still depend on banks to deliver financial services, as BCEAO requires. Because this partnership with banks has not been smooth, the telcos would prefer to create their own banks, as Orange Bank has done in France. The two competing models are (1) telcos becoming or acquiring banks and (2) banks creating their own digital finance platforms. Banks believe that they have a strong advantage in financial skills and knowledge of the market, especially in urban areas. Telcos believe that their model better reflects the realities of Africa, and they already have wider coverage than traditional banks inside the countries. Orange Money says it has 110 million users in seventeen countries in Africa; Middle East and North Africa (MENA) claims to handle 2 billion euros per months in transactions. Large companies use it to pay salaries, and inhabitants use it to pay school fees and utility bills.

Some greenfield MFIs have developed some use of digitization, mostly for back office improvements—for example, Microcred in Senegal. Another greenfield in Cote d'Ivoire, Advans, has tested digitizing payments by small farmers in the cacao value chain and created a savings facility for them. But these developments are still very limited. Marketing and education are essential before any large uptake can take place. It is notable, however, that these two limited innovations are supported heavily by grants from donors.

The megatrend that we are observing in West Africa is for progressive but irresistible financial inclusion through digitization. The market is there, and the demand for rapid, flexible, and confidential access to financial services is huge. The battle to capture the business is between fintechs, telcos, and banks: should it be a competition or a collaboration? There will be a lot of further evolution before we see the emergence of clearer and more stable models. In this battle the regulators will have a key role to play as they consider the need for both financial inclusion and client protection. The region is also sensitive to preventing money laundering and terrorism in financial services.

The microfinance institutions, even the tier 1 and 2 (stronger) institutions, may be able to develop digital financial services in-house, far from the radar of banks, fintechs, and telcos that they will need to partner with when regulations are eventually in place. Delays in negotiating partnerships between MFIs and telcos are getting longer and longer because of the low priority that they represent in the expansion strategy of telcos.

Microfinance institutions in rural areas that can develop high-tech, high-touch products—by integrating digitization in their services and delivery channels, empowering clients, and achieving sustainable growth—will bring a new dynamism to the mission of inclusive finance. It is very uncertain, however, that this category of actors will have any influence on the future of financial service delivery at the bottom of the pyramid in West Africa in the years to come.

Financing Agricultural Value Chains and Smallholders

The key question for inclusive finance in West Africa going forward is who will replace the *mutuelles* in serving the rural clients and the small farmers as they decline. It appears that the new generation of commercial MFIs (shareholder companies) is well positioned to take up this role. They have been crowded out by the banks that are occupying the urban market and higher-end clients (employees and professionals); they will have to go to secondary towns and rural areas for expansion and growth, where dynamic local entrepreneurs are emerging, especially in profitable agricultural value chains; and the wider use of technology will allow them to acquire clients and test the markets in land.

The COFINA Group mentioned earlier is emblematic of the new players who may be able to bring financial services in the agricultural value chain to farmers through a well-organized and skilled organization equipped with technology to reduce infrastructure and transportation costs. Focusing on SMEs, these second-generation MFIs have the potential to pursue the inclusive finance revolution using high-tech to bring client relationship and services to accompany the sustainable growth of rural clients in West Africa.

On the other end, community-based financial organizations such as CVECAs and village savings and loan associations (VSLAs) will probably remain, especially in fragile states and hard-to-reach areas where vulnerable populations still need to build their financial management skills based on trust and solidarity. For these, it is likely that some limited and targeted grants will still be needed to maintain the

> **BOX 15-3.   Resilient CBFOs in Fragile States: The CVECA**
> **Pays Dogon experience in Mali**
>
> The *caisse villageoise d'épargne et de crédit autogérées* (CVECA) of Pays
> Dogon in the northern part of Mali is a regulated village-based microfinance
> institution created by the Centre International de Développement et de Re-
> cherche (CIDR), a French NGO, with the support of the German Develop-
> ment Bank (KFW) in the 1980s. The region covered is very poor and drought
> affected. It was designed to mobilize all the social assets of the local
> population—mainly honesty, hard work, and solidarity—to make up for the lack
> of financial resources. CVECA Pays Dogon has sustainably served 25,000 ac-
> tive rural clients since its break-even year in the 1990s. Its success has at-
> tracted more traditional microfinance institutions to the region, creating
> sound competition among them. However, when Al Qaeda invaded these
> localities and spread terror everywhere, all the MFIs retreated to the south.
> CVECA Pays Dogon is the only MFI remaining and pursuing its financing of
> agriculture and other productive activities for farmers.
>
> Since 2015, its performance has been stable in outreach, savings mobi-
> lized, and loans distributed; and most admirably, its portfolio at risk (PAR) has
> remained under 10 percent in difficult circumstances.
>
> The people say: this is our bank, this is our savings, we have to use the
> loans well and repay because if this bank fails, no one else will replace it. We
> put our honor and pride in making it work.

financial inclusion mission. To illustrate this statement, we can refer to the CVE-
CAs of Pays Dogon in Mali, which have been operating since the 1980s in a poor
and remote region that was invaded in 2019 by Al Qaeda (see box 15-3).

In the future in West Africa, there will be banks using technology as distribution channels in developing economies, and CBFOs like CVECA operating in fragile states.

Note

1. Leaders League, "Jean-Luc Konan (Cofina): 'The Originality of the Mesofinance System is that It Asks for a Complete Change of Paradigm,'" September 6, 2015.

The Future of Microfinance in Africa

RENÉE CHAO-BEROFF

Microfinance has long been considered insignificant in Africa in comparison with its achievements in the rest of the world, especially Latin America and South Asia (5 percent of the client outreach and 8 percent of the loan portfolio of Latin America and Asia). Demography and the density of population are among the most serious barriers, together with poor infrastructure (roads, electricity, telecommunication) and low levels of education. The fact that 70 to 80 percent of the population live and work in rural areas in agriculture and in raising livestock is another important obstacle to rapid economic development in this subregion.

Mobile or Digital Finance

The recent but revolutionary history of M-Pesa, a mobile-phone-based banking service, which dates back to 2007 in Kenya, has totally changed the development paradigm. It has blown up all the traditional barriers to financial inclusion based on brick-and-mortar bank agencies by bringing services to rural populations living in remote places. After someone realized that African people value communication (with friends and family) more than (m)any other goods, mobile phones spread like wildfire in Kenya and in every part of Africa (there are now more cell phones connected than

403

there are adults in the population). Even illiterate men and women adopted cell phones immediately even in very remote places—or especially in very remote places—where people were cut off from communication with others if there were no connections. These remote regions are also very poor and home for the majority of migrant workers. In Mali, in the region of Kayes, the country's migrants in France have chipped in money to pay for satellite connections for their villages and cell phones for their parents so that they can stay connected. In a remote village in southern Tanzania, women who were asked about their energy needs for their villages first cited the need for cell phone chargers so they do not miss calls from their sons abroad.

Using cell phones to get banking services is indeed a huge leap forward to financial inclusion for governments, but it is even more so for poor people who use them to receive remittances, transfer money from cities home to their villages, help family members pay for doctors and medicine, pay school fees, and more. The list is long. Solidarity and social links are the true value of mobile money in Africa and a key factor in its fabulous success.

Toward Financial Inclusion and Client-Centricity

Nevertheless, the economic and social circumstances in Africa have also changed tremendously over the past two decades. Among the most important features are the emergence of a middle class, urban and educated, in which both men and women live and work separately from their extended families. This middle class has good purchasing power, shops in modern supermarkets, has global food preferences, and wants quality and is willing to pay for it. The rise of a middle class has created a viable market for agricultural products, both fresh and processed, which was almost nonexistent just a decade ago.

Modern distribution channels have also been improved to address these new demands. Domestic agriculture value chains are a recent phenomenon in Africa, a direct link with the change of life style and habits of a new generation.

In the late 1980s and 1990s, the major challenge that pioneers of microfinance wanted to address was poverty alleviation and sustainability of livelihoods for the billion people living below poverty. The microfinance concept, tools, and methodologies were about achieving those things at scale, which can be called "inclusive finance"—that is to say, finance that is not only about managing money, loans, or even savings, but about building an ecosystem that supports economic and social inclusion.

Governments and regulators also saw the power of financial inclusion for bringing those who are excluded by the formal financial system into it. Since 2010, financial inclusion has been the goal of microfinance in the form of economic policies that would regulate financial transactions and fight fraud, money laundering, and terrorism. It was easy to get the buy-in of governments and central banks on those issues, but they are not the sort of goals that include economically and socially excluded populations. In a nutshell, financial inclusion may not be inclusive at all, particularly if it does not incorporate client-centricity.

To say it differently, if we want financial inclusion to include the goals of the early days of microfinance, it will have to put the client at the center of its efforts, both in the design of products and services and in distribution channels. For this reason a high-tech, high-touch approach makes sense for inclusive finance.

What Is High-Tech, High-Touch?

A few years ago at a MasterCard Foundation symposium in Turin there was a very interesting debate between two brilliant players in the field of financial inclusion: the debate compared and contrasted the high-tech, low-touch approach of the early days of fintechs with the low-tech, high-touch field-based NGO approach. It also compared a more urban approach with a more rural- and farmer-oriented mission. The audience was skeptical about these comparisons that high tech and low touch would effectively compete with MFIs offering low tech and high touch. A few years later, at the same symposium in Africa, the debate became more specific, comparing fintechs and telecommunication companies with the more traditional banks with branches and client services. Microfinance institutions (MFIs) had disappeared from the debate because in this fight they were simply not relevant. Even among the leading development organizations that together constitute the Consultative Group to Assist the Poor (CGAP), for example, microfinance and MFIs have not been the central topic for several years.

The change occurred because financial inclusion (achieving a high number of "connected" individuals and enterprises) has been given priority over including the poor (achieving a better and sustainable quality of life).

The current controversy (and hype) is over whether what fintech and mobile money players are bringing to the world is "finance for the poor" or "finance for Sustainability."[1]

In this battle, what should be the posture of financial intermediaries who do not want to miss the (high-speed) train of digital technology while still remaining client-centric? I defend the mantra of high-tech, high-touch, which means that technology is used to reduce internal and external costs, accelerate client acquisition by making service easy, fast, and affordable (including making payments in very small installments), data analytics is used to learn about clients' patterns of spending and saving, and credit scoring is used to pre-process small-loan applications for repeat clients and reduce the administrative work of loan officers. High-tech not only reduces infrastructure and operational costs but is transformational in the sense that it eliminates the routine work for thousands of loan officers and staff. High-tech will make financial institutions competitive in the eyes of clients.

High-touch comes in when the costs saved are allocated to financial education, client services, and client relationships, including linking clients with opportunities that will make them more successful or find solutions to their constraints. As clients grow to become micro, small, and medium-sized enterprises (MSMEs), we find that only financial institutions that are attentive to their clients as they grow are successful. High-touch is needed more than ever, as we shift from group lending to individual SME-type lending.

In What Sectors Will High-Tech, High-Touch Make the Most Impact?

In sub-Saharan Africa, agriculture is the main income producer for a vast majority of households. The conditions for agriculture to move beyond subsistence to become more commercial are now in place, especially with the existence of a viable domestic and regional market.

Upstream, high-tech and high-touch could reach millions of small farmers who constitute a very large supply group. At the processing level, there is the opportunity to create jobs for hundreds of thousands, from low-skill but labor-intensive jobs to more high-skilled jobs in quality assurance, certification, and machine operations of all kinds. At the distribution level, there is also a high potential for good jobs, from marketing to transport and sales. Agricultural value chains that are starting to be organized for a number of food crops truly have the potential to spur inclusive economic growth in Africa.

Digitizing agricultural value chains and integrating them with financial services and products in an ecosystem approach is where the high-tech, high-touch approach will work best for inclusive finance and have the most impact for several of the Sustainable Development Goals (SDGs), such as zero hunger, no poverty, gender equality, climate action, and sustainable cities and communities.

It is also a way to bring people from very different fields (agridealers, distribution channels, fintechs, the private sector) into partnerships (goal 17) linked to sustainable climate practices.

For microfinance banks that care about impact at the clients' level, being a stakeholder in this platform and ecosystem can be a differentiation factor that makes them more competitive and attractive to clients. Similarly, agribusinesses can count on the value addition of the platform to secure the higher-quality supplies and deliver the goods that the market demands.

Sectorwide, this vision can be supported by impact investors and impact investment vehicles that invest in ecosystem financing, in financial institutions, in SMEs, and in fintechs while providing all of them with up-to-date technical assistance to build strong and fair contractual relationships in value chains.

PAMIGA as a Case Example

The Participatory Microfinance Group for Africa (PAMIGA) is a young but agile and knowledge-based player that has been in a privileged position to analyze, capitalize on, draw lessons from, and advocate for innovation in the wider community in sub-Saharan Africa. It has built an innovative technical assistance tool and an organization that provides cutting-edge counseling to rural financial intermediaries (RFIs) in rural Africa to help them diversify, mitigate risk, innovate, protect clients, and modernize governance and management. It has also created various impact investment vehicles to bring adapted financing solutions for RFIs to address challenges of growth and regulatory compliance. It is currently creating and fundraising to establish an equity fund for SMEs in an ecosystem approach.

PAMIGA believes in integrating technical assistance with financing to build sustainable growth for investees (the MFIs) and impact for beneficiaries (clients). It is using technology to make virtuous progress for the financial sector, help it achieve impact, and contribute to the SDGs.

Over the next five to ten years, PAMIGA plans to work in close partnership with key players in digital finance and agrifood supply chains to promote regional marketplace platforms for key value chains. By pursuing an ecosystem approach, it hopes to invest in and support these chains in meaningful and sustainable ways.

It is hoped that a high-tech, high-touch approach to finance and technical assistance will produce a more sustainable and just world for sub-Saharan Africa. If carefully implemented, it should contribute to more inclusive growth for small farmers, women's employment, and youth employment by bringing sustainable basic services (renewable energy, adapted productive water systems, agricultural extension techniques) that will have a significant impact in Africa.

Thirty years after the "microfinance revolution" that disappointed many by failing to deliver fully on its promise of ending poverty, this holistic and ecosystem approach for green growth and sustainable goals can be a more realistic and multisector partnership-oriented way to foster inclusive development. Many African entrepreneurs and startups share the same perspective.

Note

1. See Graham Wright, "Can Fintech Really Deliver on Its Promise of Financial Inclusion?," *Banking and Finance Post*, January 8, 2018 (https://bfsi.eletsonline.com/can-fintech-really-deliver-on-its-promise-for-financial-inclusion/).

SIXTEEN

Latin America and the Caribbean

The Journey, the Gap, and a Vision of the
New Microfinance Revolution

JOSE RUISANCHEZ

This chapter looks at the background and current status of microfinance in Latin America and the Caribbean and its future trends and outlook. The "microfinance revolution" started in Bolivia in 1992 when a nongovernmental organization (NGO) became a bank and demonstrated that microfinance could operate on a commercial basis and without a need for donations. Emulating this innovation, microfinance institutions (MFIs) in the region and the world massively scaled up the provision of sustainable financial services to the working poor. While much has been achieved, there remains a substantial and persistent gap in financial inclusion in Latin America and the Caribbean. The region's MFIs face the challenge of bridging this gap, likely by using new financial technologies and rededicating themselves to the mission, in order to expand inclusion sustainably. A new revolution in the making, perhaps?[1]

The Numbers

There were 404 financial services providers (FSPs) from twenty-one countries in Latin America and the Caribbean (LAC) posting their information on the MIX website in late 2018.[2] The FSPs (MFIs and other institutions such as banks, finance companies, co-operatives, and NGOs) provide loans and other services such as savings, payments, and remittances to both microenterprises and low-income individuals. Their combined client outreach and money indicators are summarized in table 16-1, along with those for other world regions, which appear on the MIX website.

The magnitude of the loans and deposits of the 404 FSPs in Latin America and the Caribbean that reported to the MIX compares favorably with that of the FSPs in the other regions. In addition, Latin America and Caribbean's client outreach leads the other regions when considering the number of clients as a percentage of the adult population (see table 16-2).

Penetration varies widely across countries in LAC: the 12.9 percent average for the LAC region includes countries such as Brazil, where only 2.4 percent of the population aged 15–64 were clients of FSPs reporting to the MIX; and Bolivia, where the FSP clients reached 97 percent of the population aged 15–64. Andean countries generally evidence a higher percentage of clients than their respective populations aged 15–64. In contrast, Brazil has significant coverage by its largest banks, such as Bradesco and Banco do Brasil, which provide financial services to a large portion of the country's small businesses yet do not report to the MIX.

TABLE 16-1.   Financial Services Providers (FSPs) Reporting
to the MIX, by Region

Region	No. of FSPs	No. of clients (millions)[a]	Deposits (billions of US$)	Gross loan portfolio (billions of US$)
Latin America and the Caribbean	404	54	42.9	53.6
Africa	312	31	14.5	10.7
South Asia	230	144	14.5	36.7
East Asia and Pacific	178	47	11.3	21.1
Eastern Europe and Central Asia	161	8	8.3	10.2
Middle East and North Africa	35	3	0.5	1.6

Source: Mid-November 2018 MIX website at www.themix.org/mixmarket/countries-regions/latin-america-and-caribbean.

a. No. of clients = number of depositors plus number of active borrowers.

TABLE 16-2.   Number of Clients in the MIX and as a Share
of the Adult Population, by Region

Region	No. of clients (millions)[a]	Share of the adult population (%)[b]
Latin America and the Caribbean	54	12.9
Africa	31	6
South Asia	144	12.4
East Asia and Pacific	47	3.4
Eastern Europe and Central Asia	8	4
Middle East and North Africa	3	1.9

Sources: November 2018 MIX and World Bank websites.

a. No. of clients = number of depositors plus number of active borrowers.

b. Adult population = persons aged 15–64.

The existence of LAC FSPs that do not report to the MIX is confirmed by the Inter-American Development Bank, whose Latin American and Caribbean database for 2015 contained 847 financial institutions with a microcredit portfolio. Of those institutions, 340 were banks, financial companies, and others under official bank supervision; and the remaining 507 were NGOs and other institutions, such as co-operatives, which had no or alternative regulators. The region's 2015 microcredit portfolio amounted to US$44.5 billion, corresponding to 18.5 million borrowers. In some countries, virtually all financial institutions in the database had microcredits in their loan portfolios.[3]

The Types

Latin America and the Caribbean's microfinance institutions vary widely in the number of clients, type of institution, affiliation, ownership, funding, philosophy, and other factors, as follows:

Client outreach. The leaders are Mexico's Compartamos Banco with over 2.9 million active borrowers and Colombia's Banco de la Caja Social with over 4.6 million depositors. Both are national institutions covering the whole of their respective countries. At the other end are numerous and very small FSPs that provide their services to a handful of clients in their immediate communities. (The figures are from the MIX, November 2018.)

Type of financial institution. The various types of financial institutions include banks (such as ADEMI in the Dominican Republic); nonbank financial institutions (regulated, such as FDL in Nicaragua and FINSOL in Honduras; and unregulated, such as ENLACE in El Salvador and ACME in Haiti); savings and loan co-operatives (such as Jesús Nazareno in Bolivia); municipal and rural *cajas* (such as, respectively, Arequipa and Credinka in Peru); and foundations and other NGOs that do not take deposits (such as Fundación Paraguaya, Genesis in Guatemala, and ESPOIR in Ecuador). In some countries the official regulations extend to foundations and NGOs even though they do not take deposits from the public. In most countries, one can find financial services providers that are not regulated.

Affiliation. FSPs are in many instances a single entity. In other instances, however, FSPs are part of a specialized network that includes sister FSPs in other countries, such as Accion International, FINCA, Opportunity, ProMujer, and Women's World Banking of the United States; ACCESS and ProCredit of Germany; PAMIGA, PlaNet, and SIDI of France; responsAbility of Switzerland; Vision Fund of the United Kingdom; and BBVA Microfinance Foundation of Spain.

Ownership. Ownership ranges widely as well. For example: BanEstado is owned by the government of Chile; CrediAmigo is controlled by Banco Nordeste do Brasil, a regional official development bank; Banco PRODEM of Bolivia is controlled by Venezuela's National Development Bank; Crediscotia of Peru is controlled by Canada's Bank of Nova Scotia; MiBanco is controlled by the leading private, locally owned Banco de Crédito del Peru; Pichincha Microfinanzas is controlled by Ecuador's leading private, locally owned domestic bank of the same name; Compartamos Banco is publicly owned (listed); Banco Visión in Paraguay and Optima in El Salvador are controlled by their respective local investors. And many others are controlled by the local foundation that launched them, such as Banco FIE in Bolivia, Banco W in Colombia, FAMA in Nicaragua, and Integral in El Salvador.

Funding. FSPs that are regulated institutions rely on deposits from the public as their main source of funding. Other FSPs sell their bonds in the local capital market or receive loans from foreign and local financial institutions. Share capital is often from local and foreign investors, including from investment vehicles (funds) that focus on MFIs and financial inclusion. However, the main source of equity capital over time has been the FSPs' own retained earnings. Donations, which once dominated MFI funding, have been losing relevance as commercial microfinance has surged.

Methodology. Some MFIs use Grameen-like group-lending methods, where the individual loans are co-guaranteed by all the members of a solidarity group. In most instances, however, the loans are now made individually and without a group. Some MFIs use both methods, with the group approach often being better suited to first-time borrowers with low incomes, frequently women.

Philosophy. Most MFIs provide financial services only or, in addition, provide enterprise support and advice and other services. For example, ProMujer provides women's health services to its clients in several countries, and Bolivia's CRECER provides educational services.

The Journey

Modern Latin American MFIs rose in the mid-1980s following decades in which savings and loan co-operatives provided limited financial services to low-income persons. The co-operatives declined with the rise of inflation and the region's recurring macroeconomic crises, as well as the limitations of their governance model (one member-client, one vote).

The MFIs arose as NGOs mainly in response to the surge in the number of informal workers, often just arrived in the city from the countryside and lacking the skills needed to find formal employment. Informality was also fueled by the loss of jobs that resulted from deep macroeconomic and debt crises in Latin America during the 1980s, as well as the closing of many state-owned enterprises.

The MFIs were often launched as NGOs by locals and by the specialized networks for the purpose of helping the poor who lacked access to the formal financial system. The NGOs and the networks received funding from corporate and individual donors and from official development agencies. The latter often increased their support after a sovereign debt crisis, of which there were many harsh examples in Latin America.[4] The networks would partner with local entrepreneurs and bankers who, on a pro bono basis, provided management oversight and donated part of the funding, which was used for microcredits.

Church-related groups also played a role in the origins of a number of FSPs, such as the Caja Popular Mexicana, Colombia's Caja Social, Bolivia's Diaconía, and Ecuador's Maquita. Other institutions were sponsored by foreign donors, and many others by municipal leaders, as in the case of Caja Municipal de Arequipa and similar *cajas municipales* and *cajas rurales* and co-operative institutions in other Peruvian cities and rural areas.

The MFIs made microloans in support of entrepreneurial initiatives. The enterprise usually consisted of the informal business of one person who was sometimes aided by family members. Most of the microcredits were provided individually to the members of a solidarity group who would cross-guarantee each other's loans. The innovation was simple but powerful: to look at the informal businessperson, often a woman, not as a poor person seeking charity, but rather as an entrepreneur deserving credit and, perhaps most important, respect. While demand was high, the MFIs' growth was limited by their NGO nature and small scale, which resulted from their dependence on philanthropic donations.

The large demand for microcredits, along with donor fatigue, encouraged Bolivia's PRODEM Foundation to transform its microcredit business into Banco Sol in 1992, the first commercial bank dedicated to serving microenterprise. Banco Sol demonstrated that several things were possible: to provide credit and savings services to microenterprises and be sustainable; to fund continuing expansion with deposits from low-income persons; to expand the types of services to low-income persons and increase their quality; and to grow in scale, improve efficiency, lower unit (loan) operating costs, and lower the interest rate on loans while still yielding a good return for investors.[5]

Once it became clear that it was possible both to keep the mission of helping the poor and to operate sustainably as a formal financial institution, many NGOs decided to become banks or other regulated, deposit-taking institutions. The result was an enormous surge in the number of financial institutions providing low-income persons with financial services. Competition among these institutions fostered innovative, efficient, and high-quality services. However, many NGOs preferred to stay away from profit and remained dependent on donations.[6]

In many countries the leading MFIs now operate in partnership with service providers, agents, and correspondents, such as commercial banks, gas stations, and convenience stores, which channel deposits from the MFI clients and disburse the loans.

Unreported are the myriad loans still made by informal lenders, who dominated the market before the MFIs and who continue with their activities. Their volume is likely smaller in scale among those microenterprises that have prospered following the growth of regulated microfinance institutions in LAC over the past three decades.

The path to excellence in MFI performance, and to financial sustainability, usually started with a small NGO that expanded and improved its operations and eventually became, as in the case of Bolivia's Banco Sol, a bank or similar deposit-taking regulated institution. As of 2007, CGAP counted eighty-four of these transformations worldwide, of which twenty-nine were in Latin America and the Caribbean.[7]

Many of the region's FSPs have reached top levels of quality in the variety and suitability of the services they provide their clients; they are meeting the standards of oversight by official regulators, as well as achieving favorable financial results, social impact, and risk ratings. These attributes have endeared Latin American MFIs to foreign equity investors and lenders, starting in 1995 with PROFUND, the first fund for investing in the share capital of microfinance institutions in Latin America and the Caribbean. More than seventy funds followed PROFUND's example the world over, among them Fondo Próspero de Microfinanzas, which was launched in 2010 to invest in smaller MFIs in the region.[8] In one instance, Mexico's Compartamos Banco completed a successful initial public offering (IPO) of its shares on the local stock exchange.[9]

The Regulators

The region's regulators have demonstrated good judgment and a constructive approach. In the beginning, microcredit was not an issue for the regulators of the country's financial system because the lending NGOs were for the most part small and took no deposits from the public. The generally accepted view was that, because lending to the poor could not be sustainable, it made sense for microcredit to be funded with donations. If the NGO failed, it was the donors' problem rather than the financial authority's responsibility.

The challenge to the regulators started when PRODEM Foundation asked the Bolivian authorities for a banking license to create Banco Sol and take deposits from the public to fund its loans. After lengthy negotiations, a bank license was obtained subject to numerous conditions, including: the majority of the share capital being local and also private; the board of directors relying on well-known local bankers and businesspersons; the bank's leverage being lower than for the regular commercial banks not doing microfinance; it being demonstrated that the solidarity guarantee was as effective a form of collateral for the loans as other means of security; and the oversight requirements (for example, for the banking processes, information systems, portfolio, and staff qualifications) being as demanding for the new bank as for the other (nonmicrofinance) banks. In addition, the Inter-American Investment Corporation of the IDB Group took a significant equity position and role both on the bank's board and as a creditor. This combination of flexibility and rigor by the regulator was emulated and improved upon, and it facilitated the incorporation of other regulated MFIs in Bolivia and elsewhere.[10]

The Women

Women have played a key role in the development of microfinance. They are responsible for the success of the Latin American and Caribbean MFIs, given that the bulk of the clients in many leading MFIs have been women and their loan repayment and savings performance have been generally excellent. Women have rejected complacency about poverty and have endeavored to make their microenterprises, and their families, prosper. And MFIs that are managed by women have distinguished themselves throughout the region.

In Bolivia in 1985, when five male bankers founded the PRODEM Foundation for microcredit (later Banco Sol), five women professionals had already been making microloans at the FIE Foundation (today, Banco FIE) for a few weeks. From its outset, FIE innovated by making individual rather than solidarity loans, reflecting its trust in women's entrepreneurship and creditworthiness.[11]

In Colombia the majority of the top MFIs are affiliated with the Women's World Banking (WWB) global network, which also helped found Banco ADOPEM in the Dominican Republic and has partnered with fourteen MFIs throughout the region. WWB's studies, along with others, have shown that loans to women-led businesses result in the greatest spending on child health and education.[12]

Reflecting the importance of women for the Latin American and Caribbean MFIs in its network, Spain's BBVA Microfinance Foundation appointed an equal number of women to its board of trustees. It has also elected a woman as board chair, as Accion International did earlier. The foundation has received an award from the Organization of American States for its commitment to offering economic opportunities to women in the region.[13]

Latin America and the Caribbean is the worldwide leader in the portion of fintech (financial technology) startups with at least one woman among the founders (35 percent); globally the figure is 7 percent. Their success reflects progress in overcoming the traditional social, educational, and business barriers faced by women in the region.[14]

In summary, the progress of microfinance in Latin America and the Caribbean since the early 1990s has been driven by:

- a strong demand for financial services among microenterprises, which were not being served by the traditional banks;

- strong MFI owners that provided responsible governance to their institutions and kept a sound balance between mission and profit;

- the constructive approach of the regulators, which facilitated the setting up and development of the for-profit MFIs under prudent guidelines and official supervision;

- the turn to sound macroeconomic management in the region, which has avoided crises and provided a favorable context for microfinance in many countries;

- the good repayment performance of the women borrowers and the example set by many women-led MFIs; and

- vibrant competition among many MFIs that innovated "from the bottom up" and managed to expand outreach, increase scale and productivity, lower interest rates, and improve service quality while maintaining sound financial performance.

The Gap

Even with the impressive client outreach of the 404 FSPs from Latin America and the Caribbean that reported to the MIX, and despite the region's leadership in market penetration, there is still a major gap in financial inclusion in Latin America and the Caribbean, as table 16-2 shows. The database of the Inter-American Development Bank further shows that the number of the region's adults estimated to be in the informal sector (that is, microenterprises) is five times the number of microcredit borrowers. This means 80 percent of the region's informal workers lack access to microcredit.[15]

Beyond microfinance, and with regard to the broader concept of financial inclusion, the World Bank's Findex Report shows the large portion of the population of Latin America and the Caribbean that still lacks access to financial services. Account ownership by adults ranges from 81 percent in Trinidad and Tobago to 12 percent in Haiti, with the average being about 55 percent. Only 3 percent of adults have a mobile phone account, even though almost 90 percent of adults in the region own a mobile phone. The World Bank Group's "Doing Business Report" ranks the ease of getting credit in 190 countries; the region's countries range from Colombia at number 3 to Haiti at number 178.[16]

The gap in financial services provision persists despite the widespread commitment of the countries in the region to increase their level of financial inclusion. This commitment was stimulated by the G-20 Partnership for Financial Inclusion and the UN Sustainable Development Goals and has generated official policies and support for financial inclusion in virtually all the countries in the region. Notably the region's countries have attained eleven of the top twenty positions in the ranking of the 2018 Global Microscope on Financial Inclusion. This report provides valuable insights into the magnitude of the gap and the factors that contribute to it, as for instance:

- In Argentina, an estimated 4 million microenterprises lacked access to financial services. This compares with the meager 27,000 active borrowers from the Argentine MFIs that reported to the MIX for 2017.

- In Bolivia, government-mandated interest rates (a ceiling for loans and a floor for deposits) may be restricting the continuing expansion of financial services for those persons at the bottom of the economic pyramid.

- In Brazil, the lack of definitive regulations for digital financial services makes their ongoing development and future performance vulnerable.

- Colombia heads the ranking among the fifty-five countries reviewed in the 2018 Microscope report, and yet there remain barriers that hinder the access to digital accounts by consumers and a preference by many persons to continue doing business with informal lenders and unregulated MFIs.

- Mexico's new law for financial technology has not yet produced the expected impact on financial inclusion.

- Peru has a national digital payment system, but it is little used.

- In the region as a whole there are far fewer mobile money accounts than in many countries in Africa and Asia. Even when the local telephone company has implemented mobile wallets, their use is modest in comparison with the uptake in many countries outside the region. The use of mobile phones for loans and investments is lower still.[17]

In 2006, CGAP presented several scenarios for the future of financial inclusion. CGAP identified mobile phones as the technology most likely to facilitate access to finance for excluded persons. This has occurred in Africa and other regions but not yet in Latin America and the Caribbean. The promise of mobile wallets to facilitate payments and otherwise foster financial inclusion remains unfulfilled in the region. For instance, the central bank of Bolivia reported in 2017 growing but still modest use of mobile wallets for payments, even though they have been available since 2013. The use of mobile wallets in other countries of the region is not reported as different from Bolivia's.[18]

Why the Gap?

Given the progress that has been made in the provision of financial services to the poor, and the high quality of the leading MFIs, it is difficult to understand the reasons for the persistent gap in microfinance penetration and, more generally, in the access to financial services by the poor in Latin America and the Caribbean. Following are possible explanations:

- Many people in Latin America and the Caribbean do not trust their telephone company enough to keep their money in a mobile wallet. Even those who do have mobile wallets tend not to use them.

- Unlike in other countries, the region's phone companies appear to have been reluctant to compete with the banks (compare, for example, Telenor Microfinance Bank in Pakistan).

- Regulators prefer telephone companies not to operate as banks. They also seem content with the slower pace of technical innovation among many financial institutions than in other regions.

- Informal workers seem to like informality more than access to formal financial services. For them the benefits of access to formal finance are perceived as being less important than the costs of formality.

- Contrary to the premise of Muhammad Yunus (founder of Grameen Bank), not everyone can be a creditworthy entrepreneur.

- In a number of instances, the larger and well-funded MFIs see a saturated market among the upper echelon of the micro enterprises at the bottom of the pyramid (BOP). They prefer to move upscale and expand their financial services among small and medium-sized enterprises (SMEs) rather than scale down to the next level of micro enterprises at the BOP.

- MFIs incur higher risks and diminishing returns when they try to extend their services to less entrepreneurial and poorer clients.

- The leading MFIs have become more conservative. They see themselves as banks that ought to be prudent and protect their deposits and ratings, rather than as pioneers burning to innovate and to try out new ways to extend finance to the poor beyond the present frontier.

- Dividends trump mission.[19]

In order rapidly to bridge the gap in financial inclusion, a breakthrough is needed.

Fintech to the Rescue

Fintech (financial technology) holds the promise of accelerating financial inclusion and helping to reduce poverty. The main argument is that fintech facilitates reaching the poor while lowering the transaction costs. The expected result ought to be a new and swift wave of access to sustainable finance for poorer clients not previously served. Following are four notable examples of fintech initiatives for expanding access to finance:

- The United Nations Economic Commission for Africa is partnering with the World Bank Group's International Finance Corporation and China's Ant Financial (Alibaba) to bring the latter's digital payment and credit services from China and promote digital financial inclusion in Africa.

- The Bill and Melinda Gates Foundation is introducing the MojaLoop project in Africa, India, Indonesia, Bangladesh, and Pakistan. MojaLoop is an open-source software that can be used to build national digital payment platforms.

- India's Unified Payment Interface (UPI) is a new payment system backed by the government that makes a mobile wallet redundant by directly connecting the mobile phone to a bank account. It has the potential to extend consumer credit and replace the credit card.

- The Application Programming Interface Exchange (APIX) has been launched by the ASEAN Financial Innovation Network (AFIN) "to connect companies to financial institutions globally and become a banking solution for two billion people without bank accounts worldwide." AFIN is an initiative of the Monetary Authority of Singapore, the ASEAN Bankers Association, and the International Finance Corporation.[20]

These four examples of fintech initiatives have several things in common: they are all large scale; their sponsors have very deep pockets; and they are all from and for outside Latin America and the Caribbean. They also appear to follow a top-down approach to the dissemination of technology for financial inclusion. And there may be elements of competition among them and with other large fintech initiatives hoping that each particular technology becomes the industry's dominant standard to which everyone else adheres and pays tribute.

In contrast to these examples, the majority of fintech initiatives are bottom-up in the form of small startups targeting specific financial services, such as mobile payments, currency exchange, remittances, direct and person-to-person loans, wealth management, compliance with regulations, the management of the financial function, and digital banking.

Introduced by a phone company, Kenya's M-Pesa is viewed as the original fintech business enabling mobile phones as digital wallets that replace cash. M-Pesa set the example and stimulated the global development of mobile applications for financial services. Some financial regulators have set up "sandboxes" to encourage fintech trials, while others have been more cautious given concerns about cybersecurity, fraud, and other risks to financial system stability.

Fintech has spread rapidly the world over, and the biggest outreach has been attained in China, where the dominant fintechs are Ant Financial and WeChat (TenCent), both involved in consumer payments and buyer and seller credits for the e-commerce businesses. India seems to have the greatest variety of fintech initiatives. In many countries the large banks have invested in fintech startups or partnered with them.

The bulk of the fintech initiatives are independent from the large banks and are run by young and dynamic entrepreneurs. Their funding comes largely from venture capital-type sources. There is a constant flow of regional and country contests, labs, bootcamps, and festivals in which startups compete for awards and support from investors. Universities collaborate with fintechs and teach the new magic. Many a startup aims at being acquired by a well-established fintech or a large financial services company or bank.

The LAC region is actively participating in the global fintech rush. An IDB-Finnovista report counted 1,166 fintech initiatives in eighteen countries in 2018, up from 703 fintechs in fifteen countries the previous year. There are an estimated 20,000 fintech companies worldwide. The region's most prolific fintech countries in 2018 were Brazil (380), Mexico (273), Colombia (148), and Argentina (116). The services most targeted by these fintech initiatives were payments, remittances, loans, and corporate financial services for SMEs. All eighteen countries now have a fintech association that engages with the local regulator to identify obstacles and search for solutions. Accomplishments in 2018 included the passage of Mexico's fintech law; a new regulation for crowdfunding in Colombia; and public consultations by the central bank of Brazil with regard to electronic banks. The report noted vigorous growth and enthusiasm for technological innovation throughout the region, along with substantial venture capital ready to invest in startups.[21]

While the promise is substantial, it is still early to identify major fintech contributions to financial inclusion in Latin America and the Caribbean. There are many initiatives that seem intent on providing services to high- and middle-income consumers, such as those related to payments for e-commerce. In some instances, the region's large commercial banks are developing or investing in financial technology, sometimes in collaboration with small startup initiatives. The latter sometimes compete with, and gain market share from, the banks. Here are four examples of fintech initiatives that show promise for accelerating financial inclusion in the region:

- Brazil's Nubank, founded in 2013 as an e-bank, has issued 5 million credit cards to clients, half of whom have opened digital bank accounts. In processing the card applications, Nubank identified 20 million people who did not meet its credit threshold. Nubank is now testing a debit card to be gradually introduced to reach those 20 million people plus the 100 million Brazilians who still lack a bank account.[22] China's TenCent is an investor in Nubank.

- Creditas is a Brazilian online platform that makes collateralized (auto and housing) consumer loans. The International Finance Corporation (IFC) and Naspers of South Africa have been early investors, along with several venture capital firms.[23]

- Mercado Pago is a payment platform similar to PayPal. It originated in Argentina to facilitate payments for e-commerce purchases on the Mercado Libre platform, which is similar to Amazon in Latin America. Today Mercado Pago operates in Argentina, Brazil, Chile, Colombia, Mexico, Peru, Uruguay, and Venezuela. It has expanded into online loans to enterprises that sell their goods through Mercado Libre.[24]

■ SEMPLI is a Colombian online lending platform that provides working capital to SMEs. Digital algorithms are used in the process of assessing the prospective borrower's creditworthiness. IDB LAB (formerly the Multilateral Investment Fund of the Inter-American Development Bank) and Oikocredit have provided funding to SEMPLI.[25]

These fintechs cater to the more technically savvy and affluent consumers, and also to SMEs. A smaller number of the region's fintechs do target microenterprises as clients—for example:

■ Tienda Pago of Mexico and Peru has received an equity investment from Accion International through one of its funds for investing in fintechs at various stages of technology and enterprise development. Tienda Pago makes one-week mobile loans to small shops for payment of deliveries of high-volume consumer merchandise.[26]

■ Kubo Financiero of Mexico is affiliated with the Endeavor network. It builds financial communities where microenterprises are linked to investors (peer-to-peer, or P2P). Its founder is the former CEO of local MFI Fincomún.[27]

■ FINCA Forward is a two-year pilot to develop and launch a platform to facilitate collaboration among early-stage fintechs and MFIs seeking to expand financial inclusion and, in particular, support women entrepreneurs, in both microenterprise and fintech.[28]

■ Gentera, the holding company that controls Mexico's Compartamos Banco and other MFIs in Guatemala and Peru, has launched FINLAB to foster alliances with, and investments in, fintech startups seeking digital innovations that have the potential to eradicate financial exclusion. FINLAB has invested in, among others, Avante, a Brazilian microlender using mobile technology. In turn, Avante has acquired Sling, an Israeli startup that enables micro-merchants to collect from customers by tapping into mobile payment technologies.[29]

This list illustrates the variety and vibrancy of the initiatives in the region in pursuit of innovation by means of financial technology. Although the initiatives are modest in number and size in comparison with those in China and India, there is abundant talent and dedication in the region's startups, whose contribution to financial inclusion will blossom with time. Some estimate that financial inclusion will double over the next decade.[30] Despite the fintech investments, fintechs have managed to gain a very small share of the financial market.[31]

The next section looks at the trends that are likely to shape the continuing development of microfinance in Latin America and the Caribbean in the coming years.

Trends and One View of the Future of Microfinance in LAC

Several trends will likely shape the continuing development of microfinance and financial inclusion in the region:

- The sustained growth of microfinance and the good performance of the leading FSPs over the past three decades provides a solid base for the continuing expansion of financial inclusion in the region.

- The entrance of the large commercial banks into the microfinance market strengthens the prospects of accelerating financial inclusion.

- Acquisitions of MFIs and investments in them further reinforce those prospects.

- Quality regulation in the region provides a solid anchor for expanding financial inclusion.

- Too much, too fast might be expected from fintech initiatives.

- Mission (helping the poor) is considered the ultimate likely driver of a breakthrough in financial inclusion. The right balance between mission and profit might even foster a new microfinance revolution in Latin America and the Caribbean.

Each of these trends deserves deeper coverage than this chapter permits. Following are some brief observations on these six trends.

Sustained Growth and Returns of the Leading Microfinance FSPs

The leading microfinance institutions in Latin America and the Caribbean have continued to grow and generate good returns, both financial and social, for their clients and investors, providing a strong base for the future. Growth has resulted mainly from the region's favorable macroeconomic performance in this century, along with generally good governance at the MFIs and effective official regulation. Table 16-3 shows the continuing growth in outreach for the leading FSPs in the region.

Profitability of the self-sufficient MFIs in Latin America and the Caribbean has been good. On average, however, it was exceeded by those of other regions, according

TABLE 16-3. Number of Microcredit Borrowers from the Leading Financial Services Providers (FSPs) in Latin America and the Caribbean Reporting to the Database Sources, 1999, 2013, and 2017

FSP	1999	2013	2017
Compartamos Banco Mexico	40	2,537	2,913
CrediAmigo Brazil	35	1,793	2,074
AgroAmigo Brazil	N/A	773	1,117
Fundación Mundo Mujer Colombia	N/A	466	561
Fundación de la Mujer Colombia	N/A	459	280
Bancamía Colombia	N/A	434	326
Edyficar Peru	5	379	(a)
CAME Mexico	7	331	273
Banco Caja Social Colombia	55	286	735
Pichincha Microfinanzas Ecuador	N/A	276	262
Banco WWB Colombia	N/A	267	206
MiBanco Peru	38	241	958
BancoEstado Chile	15	231	223
Banco Sol Bolivia	77	194	260
Banco Solidario Ecuador	10	194	277
Banco FIE Bolivia	24	184	211
Compartamos Financiera Peru	2	171	477
Crecer Bolivia	15	170	185
Financiera Confianza Peru	1	164	212
Financiera Independencia Mexico	N/A	150	740
Total for 20 FSPs	324	9,700	12,290
Total for the region	1,520	13,842	54,000
FSPs reporting to database	205	214	404

Sources: For 1999: Robert Christen, "Comercialization and Mission Drift. The Transformation of Microfinance in Latin America" (Washington: CGAP, 2000) (www.cgap.org/sites/default/files/researches/documents/CGAP-Occasional-Paper-Commercialization-and-Mission-Drift-The-Transformation-of-Microfinance-in-Latin-America-Jan-2001-Spanish.pdf). For 2013: The top 100 MFIs in 2014 (http://idbdocs.iadb.org/wsdocs/getDocument.aspx?DOCNUM=39174911). For 2017: The MixMarket database in November 2018 (www.themix.org/mixmarket/countries-regions/latin-america-and-caribbean).

a. Edyficar's 2017 borrowers postmerger are included under MiBanco.

to a 2004 review.[32] Table 16-4 shows recent results for several MFIs. Financial returns have been affected by official interest rate constraints (floor on deposits, ceiling on loans to clients) and sector loan requirements in some countries of the region. The leading MFIs are well capitalized for future growth.

The leading MFIs have access to low-cost funding mainly from deposits, and they seem capable of continuing this trend of growth and profitability in the future. As

TABLE 16-4. Return on Equity (ROE) and Price-to-Book Ratio (PB) for Several Leading Financial Services Providers (FSPs) in Latin America and the Caribbean

FSP	ROE (%)	PB
Compartamos Banco Mexico	22.4	1.3
CrediAmigo Brazil	19.3	N/A
AgroAmigo Brazil	(a)	N/A
Fundación Mundo Mujer Colombia	22.8	N/A
Fundación de la Mujer Colombia	N/A	N/A
Bancamía Colombia	6.3	N/A
Edyficar Peru	(b)	N/A
CAME Mexico	23.8	N/A
Banco Caja Social Colombia	15.9	N/A
Pichincha Microfinanzas Ecuador	45.6	N/A
Banco WWB Colombia	6.9	N/A
MiBanco Peru	5.4	N/A
BancoEstado Chile	8.3	N/A
Banco Sol Bolivia	20.5	N/A
Banco Solidario Ecuador	7.9	N/A
Banco FIE Bolivia	10.7	N/A
Compartamos Financiera Peru	25.5	N/A
Crecer Bolivia	9.8	N/A
Financiera Confianza Peru	5.6	N/A
Financiera Independencia Mexico	5.3	0.3
ASA Financial Group Bangladesh	36	5
BRAC Bank Bangladesh	22.1	N/A
SATIN India	Loss	1.1
EQUITAS India	1.4	1.7
Minsheng Banking Corp. China	12.4	0.6
Bank Rakyat Indonesia	18	2.8
Banco Supervielle Argentina	20	1.7

Source: FSP websites in February 2019.

a. Included in CrediAmigo.
b. Merged into MiBanco.

noted earlier, there is plenty of room to grow at the bottom of the pyramid. The main challenge to the MFIs is likely to come from the commercial banks as they become comfortable doing business with the best-performing microenterprises and using the new technologies.

Competition for Clients from the Large Commercial Banks

Many of the large commercial banks in the region now compete with the MFIs for clients. Usually the commercial banks prefer to serve the former microenterprises that have grown to become small, formal businesses. In addition, the banks provide consumer services (for example, debit cards and remittances) to low-income clients through the use of financial technology and in partnership with commercial agents. Here are three examples of this trend from Mexico:

- BBVA Bancomer, the largest commercial bank in the country, has a special business credit card for SMEs and for persons with their own business enterprise.[33]

- Santander Mexico, the country's second-largest commercial bank, has a financial inclusion program that uses digital accounts to provide financial services to underserved businesses.[34]

- Citi Banamex, the third largest commercial bank in Mexico, reported at FOROMIC 2018, in Barranquilla, that it has accumulated over 10 million low-income clients through a program of digital accounts in partnership with convenience store chain OXXO and with Inbursa, a financial company in the Carlos Slim Group. The latter is the controlling shareholder of the country's largest telecom business.[35]

The large commercial banks in other countries of the region are in tune with the interests of their Mexican counterparts in microfinance. The MFIs are responding to the banks' challenge mainly by continuing to target the clients at the bottom of the pyramid with their traditional "high-touch" model of services to microenterprises, and by modernizing and competing with their own digital financial products. An example of a leading MFI is Compartamos Banco, also in Mexico, which offers its traditional group-lending product, mainly for women borrowers, as well as individual loans and digital financial services (including a debit card) that are complemented by correspondent financial services via a network of over 2,000 agents (such as convenience stores and gas stations) all over the country.[36]

So far the leading MFIs seem capable of holding their ground in the competition with the commercial banks for client market share. And the smaller NGOs appear, so far, to be holding on to their traditional markets as well.

Acquisitions of and Investments in MFIs

The favorable conditions for microfinance throughout the region and the good institutional performance of many MFIs have led to acquisitions of, and investments in, MFIs by large banks and investors. Here are salient examples:

- Banco de Crédito del Perú acquiring Edpyme Edyficar and the control of MiBanco, both in Peru

- Banco Mercantil Santa Cruz acquiring the microfinance portfolio of Germany's Banco Los Andes/ProCredit in Bolivia

- Gentera of Mexico (holding company for Compartamos Banco in that country) acquiring the control of Financiera CREAR in Peru

- BANDES (Banco Nacional de Desarrollo Económico y Social de Venezuela) acquiring Fondo Financiero Privado FFP (now Banco) PRODEM in Bolivia

- Bank of Nova Scotia of Canada acquiring Banco del Trabajo in Peru and Crédito Familiar in Mexico

- Acción Comunitaria del Peru acquiring Banco Forjadores in Mexico

- Te Creemos acquiring CAME in Mexico

- OPTIMA acquiring FINCA in El Salvador

- Banco Atlántida of Honduras acquiring Procrédito in El Salvador

- ACCESS Holding of Germany acquiring the control of Accion Microfinanças in Brazil

- BBVA Microfinance Foundation of Spain acquiring the control of:

    ○ Corporación Mundial de la Mujer Colombia and Corporación Mundial de la Mujer Medellín to form Bancamía

    ○ Caja Nuestra Gente and Financiera Confianza in Peru

    ○ Fondo Esperanza and Emprende in Chile

    ○ Banco ADOPEM in the Dominican Republic

    ○ Microserfin in Panama

In addition, there have been numerous minority investments in the region's MFIs by local and foreign investors. It is estimated that two-thirds of the twenty leading MFIs in the region, listed in appendix 16-1, have received equity capital from foreign investment vehicles (funds) and specialized microfinance networks. The latter have special relevance given that they provide both capital and sector knowledge, along with sharing know-how and insights with the other MFIs in the network. In other instances the investors are impact or environment, social, and governance (ESG) investment funds, or funds that specialize in financial institutions. Notably, there have been few commercial MFIs started from scratch in the past two decades.[37]

In contrast with other regions, only Compartamos Banco among the Latin American and Caribbean MFIs has had an initial public offering of its shares on the stock exchange; the other MFIs typically experience investor exit by means of private sales of shares. At the other extreme, in terms of size, there are hundreds of small MFIs that focus operations in a small region and have mostly local ownership, funding, and culture. Many of the latter are NGOs dependent on donations for their funding and are not under the supervision of the country's monetary authorities.

The region's MFIs seem capable of retaining the interest of investors in the future, which ought to permit their continuing access to the necessary capital for expansion.

Regulation

Regulation by country authorities is expected to continue to promote financial inclusion while preventing damage to the integrity of the financial system, especially with regard to new financial technologies. Not expected, however, is a government stimulus of fintech as in India and China. Latin American and Caribbean countries have shown steady regulation much in line with the Bali Agenda and Bank for International Settlements (BIS) counsel with regard to fintech development. It is hoped that the limits on interest rates, along with portfolio quotas in some countries, will not drive clients toward the traditional money lenders or inhibit MFIs in their search for the innovations needed to accelerate financial inclusion.[38]

Financial Technology

The expectation has been that the vigorous investment in technology and the many startups everywhere in the region will provide the breakthrough that is needed for the rapid acceleration of financial inclusion. So far, however, there is substantial inspiration, enthusiasm, investment, and sweat, but no breakthrough. Progress will likely accelerate, but its timing is largely unpredictable.

In one scenario, a financial technology permits a bank or MFI to provide a combined mobile wallet and savings and payments mechanism at near-zero cost, so that everyone can have a bank account and it is possible to say the immediate goal of financial inclusion has been met. Such a mechanism, in the form of a mobile phone wallet, already exists, and millions of people in the region have it but do not use it. And those who still lack it seem not inclined to get it. This situation presents a sharp contrast with many countries outside Latin America and the Caribbean where mobile wallets have gained acceptance and use for a multiplicity of financial services.

In a better scenario, the mentioned technology makes financial inclusion both massive and profitable, attracting investments by competing or collaborating FSPs.

Neither scenario has materialized, perhaps because insufficient time has elapsed for the fintech initiatives to result in a major breakthrough for financial inclusion. So far it seems that most of the investments in technology either support e-commerce or target the financial services that are provided to the affluent clients, but not so much the delivery of financial services to the poor. This may be because the former tend to be more tech-savvy, while the latter need more time and effort to understand and trust the new technology.

The main obstacle to attaining a breakthrough in financial inclusion by means of technology seems to be a reluctance by the incumbent FSPs to make substantial investments in innovation, because doing so may lower their profit and increase the risk of being hacked. The easy path for an established bank or MFI is not to rock the boat and to delay major investment until there is more certainty of results and of a lower risk.[39]

When the breakthrough comes, the MFIs that lag behind will be vulnerable to losing market share to the banks, to fintech startup companies, and to other MFIs, especially those that invest in technology or that wait for the pioneer to innovate and then swiftly copy and improve on the new model.[40] It is likely that all of the leading

MFIs are digitizing and laying the groundwork for the future breakthrough; but none so far seems confident enough to commit resources for massive expansion beyond the pilot stage.

In addition to time for the pilots to demonstrate the new technologies, this situation calls for further research in order to understand better which are the remaining barriers to financial inclusion and how to remove them, whether through fintech or other tools. It also calls for a more open mindset on the part of the MFIs' management, boards, and shareholders.

Risk, Profit, and Mission

For the leading MFIs, it makes sense to move incrementally into new technologies and ensure that the risks have been managed with care. There are, after all, client services to deliver, hackers to avoid, debt ratings to preserve, and dividends to be paid. The MFIs' old information technology systems may not be as productive as the new technologies, but they are reliable and well known, and they require maintenance instead of new investment. It is easier for a (now) traditional MFI management team to lean toward prudence than to challenge itself to take on the startup-like risks of the new technologies. Regulators likely reinforce this more conservative approach toward progress in technology adoption for financial inclusion, given their priority to maintain the integrity of the financial system.

From the clients' standpoint, what is important is not the adoption of the new technology but using it in a way that reduces their costs and increases their income. Such improvement often comes primarily from how the new financial services are used, and this in turn is a function of each client's financial education, of the advice, training, capacity building, and other non-financial services that have much more to do with the MFI's mission (of helping the poor) than with the profit objective and desire to keep risks low. Rewards and risks move into a more challenging dimension as the MFI reaches deeper for clients into the bottom of the pyramid. The main obstacle appears to be the uncertainty that comes from such a dive.

The leading MFIs focus on the sustainable provision of financial services. In many instances, they also provide financial literacy courses to their clients and design products and services that are sensitive to women's special needs. In other instances, business training and advice might be arranged for SMEs, but seldom for microenterprises. All sorts of factors combine to make it easier and safer for the leading MFIs to move up the pyramid toward SMEs as clients, rather than downward toward the poorer and less-business-capable clients. Yet the SME market segment is where the large banks and the new fintech companies are likely to compete most effectively with the leading MFIs.[41]

Lacking, it seems, is an MFI prepared to invest in or target, as its priority clients, those persons at the bottom of the pyramid—an MFI that will use the solidarity-group-lending method (or whatever other lending method works) to reach the underserved, particularly those who are less educated and less familiar with modern technology; or an MFI willing to provide or arrange the non-financial services that will help improve those people's capacity to become good MFI clients and to use the financial services to generate prosperity. Outside Latin America and the Caribbean, a best-practice example of this approach is provided by BRAC, originally from Bangladesh but now expanding into other parts of Asia and in Africa. BRAC provides education and health services along with financial services. In Latin America and the Caribbean, the ProMujer network and CRECER are notable users of this high-touch approach.[42]

For a breakthrough in financial inclusion to take place, there is a need for substantial research and development investment in the technologies and methodologies that incorporate more of the poor as successful clients of the FSPs. It matters not that the initiative be taken by a bank or an MFI, or that the means used be high-tech or high-touch, as long as it is deployed vigorously and resolutely beyond the pilot stage. And it matters for such an initiative to gain in scale, turn a profit, and engender competition from other FSPs. When that happens, we may well have another revolution in microfinance in Latin America and the Caribbean.

Notes

I am grateful to colleagues, investors, and practitioners in microfinance for reading and providing comments on an earlier draft of this chapter.

1. The origins of commercial microfinance, how Bolivia's PRODEM Foundation and its partners founded Banco Sol, and how global microfinance achieved financial self-sufficiency are recounted in Marguerite Robinson, *The Microfinance Revolution: Sustainable Finance for the Poor* (Washington and New York: World Bank and Open Society Institute, 2001). Robinson identifies the leaders of the microfinance revolution as the microbanking division of Bank Rakyat Indonesia (BRI); Bank Dagang Bali; India's SEWA; Bangladesh's Grameen Bank; and many others (pp. 3 and 35). Robinson first heard the term microfinance revolution from Maria Otero and Elisabeth Rhyne (pp. 3 and 35). On the status of the region's microfinance at different times, see Robert P. Christen, "Comercialization and Mission Drift: The Transformation of Microfinance in Latin America" (Washington: Consultative Group to Assist the Poor [CGAP], 2000), which cites data for 1999 (www.cgap.org/sites/default/files/researches/documents/CGAP-Occasional-Paper-Commercialization-and-Mission-Drift-The-Transformation-of-Microfinance-in-Latin-America-Jan-2001-Spanish.pdf); and MIX, "Microfinance in Latin America" (Washington: CGAP, November 2012). For a 2005 look into the future of microfinance in Latin America and the Caribbean, see

Beatriz Marulanda and Maria Otero, "The Profile of Microfinance in Latin America in the Next 10 Years: Vision and Characteristics" (Washington: Accion International, 2005) (www.microfinancegateway.org/sites/default/files/mfg-en-paper-the-profile-of-microfinance-in-latin-america-in-ten-years-vision-characteristics-apr-2004_0.pdf).

2. The MIX (Microfinance Information Exchange) was founded by CGAP (originally the Consultative Group to Assist the Poorest) with World Bank support in 2002 to gather and report financial and operating data and analysis on microfinance institutions in developing countries. The MIX database contains information on institutions that work for financial inclusion, even when they are not MFIs, and hence the broader FSP designation. The MIX database contains information and insights on over 1,300 FSPs from all over the world. This number is a fraction of the total FSPs, which is estimated to be in the tens of thousands. Most of those FSPs do not report to the MIX database. See the websites of MIX (www.mixmarket.org) and CGAP (cgap.org). A reference to the estimated number of MFIs appears in Tomás Miller, "Sharing Lessons on Financial Inclusion between China and Latin America and the Caribbean," FOMIN, September 1, 2016 (www.fomin.org/en-us/Home/News/article-details/ArtMID/18973/ArticleID/11595/Sharing-Lessons-on-Financial-Inclusion-between-China-and-Latin-America-and-the-Caribbean.aspx).

3. Verónica Trujillo and Sergio Navajas, "Financial Inclusion and the Development of the Financial System of Latin America and the Caribbean" (Washington: Inter-American Development Bank, 2016) (https://webimages.iadb.org/publications/english/document/Financial-Inclusion-and-Financial-Systems-in-Latin-America-and-the-Caribbean-Data-and-trends.pdf).

4. Most international aid agencies contributing to early microcredit efforts in the region were from North America and Europe. In contrast, China's aid in Latin America and the Caribbean has contributed mostly to large infrastructure projects rather than to the development of microfinance. Margaret Myers and Carol Wise, eds. *The Political Economy of China–Latin America Relations in the New Millennium* (New York: Routledge, 2017), pp. 75–76. A study of debt crises, including in Latin America, appears in Ira W. Lieberman, *In Good Times Prepare for Crisis* (Brookings, 2018).

5. A confirmation of Banco Sol's early performance appears in Claudio González-Vega and others, "BANCOSOL: The Challenge of Growth for Microfinance Organizations," Economics and Sociology Occasional Paper 2332 (Ohio State University, Rural Finance Program, Department of Agricultural Economics, May 1996). For a review of the financial performance of microfinance institutions, see Michael Tucker and Gerard Miles, "Financial Performance of Microfinance Institutions: A Comparison to Performance of Regional Commercial Banks by Geographic Regions," *Journal of Microfinance* 6, no. 1 (2004).

6. Robinson, *The Microfinance Revolution.*

7. CGAP's 2008 review of these NGO-to-regulated institutional transformations appears in Kate Lauer, "Transforming NGO MFIs: Critical Ownership Issues to Consider," Occasional Paper 13 (Washington: CGAP, 2008).

"We are going to make a bank!" Pancho Otero, PRODEM Foundation's and Banco Sol's managing director, remembers the decision to transform from NGO to bank in December 2018 (www.microsave.net/author/pancho-otero/). Otero went on to advise and help found other MFIs. Elisabeth Rhyne remembers him in "Genius in Microfinance—Reflections on

Pancho Otero," Huffington Post, August 12, 2014 (https://www.huffpost.com/entry/genius
-in-microfinance-re_b_5671545). An early account of Banco Sol's transformation appears
in David Hulme and Paul Mosley, "Finance against Poverty," chap. 10 in *Metamorphosis from
NGO to Commercial Bank: The Case of Banco Sol in Bolivia* (London: Routledge, 1996).

On how to align the interests of the various stakeholders at transformation time, along with
relevant case studies, see Brian Busch and others, eds. *Alignment Interests at Transformation*
(San José, Costa Rica, and Washington: Calmeadow and Accion's Center for Financial Inclusion, 2005) (www.calmeadow.com/pdf/aligning.pdf). Encouragement and support for NGOs
to transform into financially sustainable MFIs continues: see Alex Silva, Mohammed Khaled,
and Karen Beshay, "Transforming Microfinance Institutions in the Arab World" (Washington:
International Finance Corporation, May 2018) (www.ifc.org/wps/wcm/connect/1ffc3ec0
-63ac-4426-863c-c7d1b8b0df46/ESOP-Transforming+22-5-2018.pdf?MOD=AJPERES).

8. For the story of PROFUND, as told by Chairman Martin Connell and CEO Alex
Silva, see www.calmeadow.com/pdf/profund.pdf. The investments continue: it is estimated
that 54 percent of the total impact investments in the region (equity, debt, and quasi-equity) in
2016–17 were made in microfinance institutions. See Aspen Network of Development Entrepreneurs and LAVCA, "The Impact Investment Landscape in Latin America Trends 2016
and 2017" (https://cdn.ymaws.com/www.andeglobal.org/resource/resmgr/research_library
/latam_reports/latam_impinv_eng_2018_digita.pdf). Pròspero Microfinanzas fund is managed by Bolivia's BIM and Grassroots Capital of the United States. See Jay Coen Gilbert,
"Putting the Impact in Impact Investing: 28 Funds Building a Credible, Transparent Marketplace," *Forbes*, October 9, 2017 (www.forbes.com/sites/jaycoengilbert/2017/10/09/putting-the
-impact-in-impact-investing-28-funds-building-a-credible-transparent-marketplace
/#2cc469f63e5f).

9. For a review of the issues connected with the IPO, see Richard Rosenberg, "CGAP
Reflections on the Compartamos Initial Public Offering: A Case Study on Microfinance Interest Rates and Profits," Focus Note (Washington: CGAP, 2007) (www.ruralfinanceand
investment.org/sites/default/files/1185353349349_CGAP_Compartamos_case_study.pdf).

10. Robert P. Christen and Richard Rosenberg, "Regulating Microfinance: The Options"
in *Microfinance: Evolution, Achievements and Challenges*, ed. Malcolm Harper (London:
ITDG, 2003).

11. Calmeadow and Accion's Center for Financial Inclusion, "Aligning Interests: Addressing Management and Stakeholder Incentives during Microfinance Institution Transformations" (San José, Costa Rica, and Washington, 2005) (www.calmeadow.com/pdf/aligning
.pdf). Other studies have confirmed FIE's findings.

12. Website of Women's World Banking (www.womensworldbanking.org/about-us
/partnerships/).

13. BBVA Microfinance Foundation, recipient of the Corporate Citizen of the Americas
2018 award from the Organization of American States (www.prnewswire.com/news-releases
/bbva-microfinance-foundation-recipient-of-the-corporate-citizen-of-the-americas-2018
-award-from-the-organization-of-american-states-300761844.html).

14. Inter-American Development Bank and Finnovista, *Fintech in Latin America 2018:
Growth and Consolidation* (Washington, 2018), chap. 2 (https://docs.google.com/viewerng/

viewer?url=http://media.ambito.com/diario/2018/1107/imagenes/pdf_subido_1107011351
.pdf); K. Azar, E. Lara, and D. Mejía, *Inclusión financiera de las mujeres en América Latina.
Situación actual y recomendaciones de política. Políticas públicas y transformación productiva*
(Caracas: CAF—Banco de Desarrollo de la America Latina, 2018) (http://scioteca.caf.com
/handle/123456789/1162).

    15. Trujillo and Navajas, "Financial Inclusion," p. 13.

    16. The World Bank's Global Findex Data Base 2017 is at https://globalfindex.worldbank
.org/#data_sec_focus; the ranking in the "Doing Business Report" is at www.doingbusiness
.org/en/rankings. None of the LAC countries ranked in the top ten for making improvements in access to credit.

    17. Economist Intelligence Unit, "2018 Global Microscope on Financial Inclusion" (www
.eiu.com/public/topical_report.aspx?campaignid=Microscope2018).

    18. CGAP, "Financial Inclusion 2015: Four Scenarios for the Future of Microfinance,"
Focus Note 39 (October 2006) (www.cgap.org/sites/default/files/researches/documents/CGAP
-Focus-Note-Financial-Inclusion-2015-Four-Scenarios-for-the-Future-of-Microfinance
-Oct-2006.pdf); Banco Central de Bolivia, "Informe sobre Pagos" (www.bcb.gob.bo
/webdocs/publicacionesbcb/2018/05/22/SISTEMA_DE_PAGOS_2017.pdf). Bolivia's mobile money transactions are estimated to be about 5 percent of Kenya's (adjusted to account
for the respective gross national income levels of the two countries). Significant is that in
both countries about 88 percent of adults use mobile phones. The information on Kenya
comes from June Okal, "What Does the Data Say? Kenya's ICT Sector Reports," February 9, 2019.

    19. These nine possible explanations are not exhaustive. In addition, MFI boards may no
longer feel an urgency to discuss how to extend outreach and "do more good" for the poor. It
is not clear to what extent this is due to a weaker sense of mission among the shareholders
and board members. Perhaps everyone is waiting for someone else to take the risk of innovation. What is clear, however, is that incremental progress is insufficient and that there is a
need for major breakthroughs in order to rapidly bridge the gap in financial inclusion. A
similar observation from Mexico illustrates that the growth in outreach is slowing down in
other countries as well. See Fernando Gutierrez, "El microcrédito ya no crece como antes,"
El Economista, October 29, 2017 (fernando.gutierrez@eleconomista.mx). The story of how a
telecom has evolved to encompass a microfinance bank is found in https://www.telenorbank
.pk/index.html.

    20. "The Coming UPI Battle in Mobile Payments," *Factor Daily*, January 2018 (https://
factordaily.com/longform/the-coming-upi-battle-in-mobile-payments/); Meha Agarwal,
"PM Modi Launches 'APIX' to Include 2bn People into the Fintech Wave," *Inc42*, November 14, 2018 (https://inc42.com/buzz/pm-modi-launches-apix/); "How Chinese Companies
Are Planning a Global Fintech Coup," *Factor Daily*, December 2018 (https://factordaily
.com/chinese-fintech-goes-global/).

    21. Inter-American Development Bank and Finnovista: "Fintech in Latin America 2018."
A comprehensive review of how countries (including in Latin America) are working to promote technology and innovation for financial inclusion appears in J. Villaseñor, D. M. West,
and R. J. Lewis, "The 2015 Brookings Financial and Digital Inclusion Project" (Brookings, 2015)

(www.findevgateway.org/library/2015-brookings-financial-and-digital-inclusion-project
-report-measuring-progress-financial).

22. Angelica Mari, "Brazilian Fintech Nubank Launches Debit Card to Reach 120
million Clients," *Forbes*, December 11, 2018 (www.forbes.com/sites/angelicamarideoliveira
/2018/12/11/brazilian-fintech-nubank-launches-debit-card-to-reach-120m-clients/). In contrast to upstart Nubank, Brazil's largest commercial bank, Itaú Unibanco, reports that 11 million persons are using the bank's digital financial services. "Itaú Unibanco mira 11 mi de pessoas
físicas em canais digitais" (https://economia.estadao.com.br/blogs/coluna-do-broad/itau-unibanco
-mira-11-mi-de-pessoas-fisicas-em-canais-digitais/).

23. Jonathan Schieber, "Brazilian Startup Creditas Is Revolutionizing Credit in the
World's Third Largest Lending Market," *Techcrunch*, December 12, 2017 (https://techcrunch
.com/2017/12/12/brazilian-startup-creditas-is-revolutionizing-credit-in-the-worlds-third-largest
-lending-market/).

24. The Latin America e-commerce giant Mercado Libre is nowhere near the level of market penetration of similar e-commerce Chinese companies, such as Ant Financial (Alibaba)
and TenCent. A recent review of the role played by these Chinese e-commerce companies in
bringing financial services to the two-thirds of Chinese consumers lacking credit histories appears in Institute of International Finance, "A New Kind of Conglomerate: Big
Tech in China," November 1, 2018 (https://www.iif.com/Publications/ID/16/A-New-Kind
-of-Conglomerate-Bigtech-in-China).

25. "Sempli Raises $5.7 Million to Support Colombia's Small Businesses," *ImpactAlpha*,
November 2, 2018 (https://impactalpha.com/colombian-fintech-firm-sempli-raises-5-7-million
-from-oikocredit-and-bid-lab/).

26. Tienda Pago reports it uses a combination of technology and traditional personal
engagement with small shop clients in Mexico and Peru to provide one-week mobile loans to
pay for high-volume consumer goods (for example, Coca-Cola) that the small shops carry in
their inventory for sale to the public. "The Tech Touch Balance: How the Best Fintechs
Startups Integrate Digital and Human Interaction to Acclerate Financial Inclusion," *Accion
Insights*, October 2018 (https://content.accion.org/wp-content/uploads/2018/10/1122_TechTouch
-RO6-Singles.pdf).

27. Ximena Leyva, "Kubo Financiero, la plataforma que invierte en otras personas," *My-
Press*, December 13, 2018 (www.mypress.mx/negocios/kubo-financiero-plataforma-invierte
-personas-3460).

28. "Fintechs Can Tap Microfinance Clients with New FINCA International Platform,"
Ventureburn, October 8, 2018 (http://ventureburn.com/2018/10/finca-usaid-finca-forward/).

29. Edgar Juárez, "Fintech que generen alianzas con bancos tendrán un crecimiento más
rápido," interview in *El Economista*, December 3, 2018 (www.eleconomista.com.mx/sector
financiero/Fintech-que-generen-alianzas-con-bancos-tendran-un-crecimiento-mas-rapido
-20181203-0157.html); Silvia Rosa, "Avante, the Microcredit Startup, Receives Major Funding," *Valor*, July 10, 2017 (www.avante.com/single-post/2017/07/10/Avante-the-Microcredit
-Startup-receives-major-funding); Abigail Klein Leichman, "18 Israeli Firms Rocking Financial Technology," *Israel21c*, February 27, 2017 (www.israel21c.org/18-israeli-firms-rocking
-financial-technology/).

30. From 2001 to 2017, Mexico increased financial inclusion from an estimated 5 million persons to 15 million. A local fintech entrepreneur estimates that the new fintech law, and the many startup initiatives under way, will likely double client outreach thanks to fintech in the next seven to ten years. Fernando Gutiérrez, "Industria fintech sumará a 15 millones de personas al sistema financiero," *El Economista*, May 24, 2018 (www.eleconomista .com.mx/sectorfinanciero/Industria-fintech-sumara-a-15-millones-de-personas-al-sistema -financiero-20180524-0114.html).

31. An example from Brazil: it is estimated that fintechs currently hold about 2 percent of the financial services market in Brazil, where the commercial banks continue to dominate. Roberta Prescott, "Microfinanzas: fintechs brasileñas crecen pero bancos continuan dominando el mercado," *Iupana*, October 1, 2018 (http://iupana.com/2018/10/01/microfinanzas -fintechs-brasilenas-crecen-pero-bancos-continuan-dominando-el-mercado/). The dominance of Brazilian commercial banks is attracting competition from fintech startups and from nonfinancial companies, which are inspired by China Alibaba's success. An example is Cosan, a leading sugar-alcohol-energy company seeking to compete with banks and credit card companies. "Brazilian Sugar-Cane Mogul Is Creating the Alipay of Brazil," Bloomberg, January 16, 2019 (https://finance.yahoo.com/news/brazilian-sugar-cane-mogul-creating-142127832.html).

32. The majority of MFIs are small nonprofits that depend on donations. A growing number of MFIs have reached financial self-sufficiency (revenues cover operating expenses, risk provisions, and a return on capital), and of these, a select number are regulated. Tucker and Miles, "Financial Performance of Microfinance Institutions."

33. BBVA Bancomer website, "Tarjeta de crédito Negocios," November 2018 (www.bancomer .com/empresas/productos/financiamiento/servicios-adicionales-para-empresas/tarjetas -empresariales/tarjeta-negocios.html).

34. Santander Mexico website, Sala de Prensa 2018: "Santander Comprometido con la Inclusión Financiera en México: Ana Botín," October 22, 2018 (www.santander.com.mx). Santander's chairperson, Ana Botín, is a member of the CEO Partnership for Financial Inclusion. The partnership is chaired by Queen Maxima of the Netherlands. The queen is the United Nations Secretary General's Special Advocate for Inclusive Finance for Development (UNSGSA). See "CEOs and UN Special Advocate Launch Private Sector Partnership for Financial Inclusion," UNSGSA, January 31, 2018 (www.unsgsa.org/resources/news/ceos -and-un-special-advocate-launch-private-sector-partnersh/).

35. "Miradas globales de inclusión financiera," Sala Plenaria, FOROMIC Barranquilla, October 30, 2018 (https://livestream.com/accounts/4699050/events/8422324/player).

36. Compartamos Banco website, "Canales Digitales Compartamos," November 2018 (www.compartamos.com.mx/wps/portal/compartamos/canales-digitales).

37. Accion International is a leading global microfinance network and fintech investor. It runs MFIs in several countries, including in Latin America, and it manages or oversees several investment funds, among which are: Accion Global Investments, which invests in established MFIs; the Accion Frontier Inclusion Fund, managed by Quona Capital and investing in technology for the underserved; and the Accion Venture Lab, which provides seed capital for fintech startups aiming to accelerate financial inclusion. Although these funds invest globally, they include investments in MFIs in Latin America and the Caribbean. In addition,

Accion International founded the Center for Financial Inclusion, which operates as a think tank and R&D center. Other examples of network investors are: FINCA, also of the United States and operating globally through its wholly owned MFIs; and ACCESS of Germany. Among the equity funds that invest in MFIs are: BIO and INCOFIN of Belgium; Oikocredit of the Netherlands; and the Danish Microfinance Partners Fund. In addition, the bilateral and multilateral finance institutions regularly invest in the equity of and make loans to MFIs, including in Latin America and the Caribbean.

38. Regulation in Latin America and the Caribbean has provided a context for sound fintech activity. The region has avoided precipitous fintech deposit and credit expansion and surges in fraud and defaults as in China, which has led the Chinese authorities to cap P2P financing and shut down many tech-based nonbank financial services providers. The LAC region's varied credit bureau infrastructure has been saved from court disruption, as in India, where credit disputes are often litigated through the courts. Latin America and the Caribbean's regulators appear in tune with the Bali Fintech Agenda presented to member countries in 2018 by the IMF and the World Bank and are seeking a balance between promoting fintech and maintaining the integrity of the financial system. See "The Bali Fintech Agenda," IMF Policy Paper (Washington: International Monetary Fund, October 2018); Jitendra Gupta, "3 Major Setbacks for Fintech Industry," *Livemint,* December 22, 2018 (https://www .livemint.com/Money/jxepdJVODLb6fGDfhue6qI/3-major-setbacks-for-fintech-industry .html). The Bali Agenda is at www.findevgateway.org/sites/default/files/publication_files /pp101118-bali-fintech-agenda_1.pdf. In line with the Bali Agenda, the BIS sees the need for a balance between fintech and development. See Agustín Carstens, "Harnessing the Fintech Revolution," *Livemint,* January 1, 2019 (www.livemint.com/Opinion/LsDm0HkPjRclv7OAH4CN8H /Opinion—Harnessing-the-fintech-revolution.html). For an example of stimulus from India's government, see Anthony Peyton, "Fintech Firm WB21 Caught in Storm of Allegations," *Fintech Futures,* January 7, 2019 (https://www.fintechfutures.com/2019/01/fintech-firm -wb21-caught-in-storm-of-allegations/). It appears that India's initiatives have inspired both Mexico's new government and Amazon Inc. to cooperate in the introduction of a new mobile payments system, as reported in "Amazon Mexico: Gov't Explores Mobile Payments Play," Pymts.com, March 5, 2019 (www.pymnts.com/amazon/2019/mexico-mobile-payments -banxico/). An example of the more common catalytic approach to financial inclusion that is seen among governments in Latin America and the Caribbean is found in Colombia's Banca de las Oportunidades, which facilitates initiatives by private institutions. See the website of Banca de las Oportunidades at http://bancadelasoportunidades.gov.co/.

39. The risk of hacking and of reputation loss hinders fintech development. When a bank as well regarded as HDFC, in a country as tech-capable as India, pulls its new mobile banking app off the air, other banks can probably feel justified in their cautiousness about bringing the latest in digital innovation to the market; and so do regulators. "Tech Snag Has HDFC Bank Pulling Out Its New Mobile Banking App," Bloomberg, December 3, 2018 (www .bloombergquint.com/business/tech-snag-has-hdfc-bank-pulling-out-its-new-mobile -banking-app#gs.BrEnOtg). There are numerous other instances of alleged fraud that make MFIs wary of adopting new technology too quickly. For example, see Peyton, "Fintech Firm WB21 Caught in Storm of Allegations." On the other side, there are entities that encourage

sound digitization as a means of reducing financial exclusion; the United Nations–sponsored "Better than Cash Alliance" is an example (see www.betterthancash.org/).

The region's cautious progress concerns some microfinance leaders that Latin America might be lagging too far behind other world regions and losing its leadership in innovation. See, for instance, Diana Taylor, "Latin American Microfinance Must Embrace Innovation " (blog) April 13, 2016, Center for Financial Inclusion (http://progresomicrofinanzas.org/wp -content/uploads/2016/06/latin-american-microfinance-must-embrace-innovation-to-help -build-better-lives-_-center-for-financial-inclusion-blog.pdf).

40. This MFI vulnerability to technology-using fintech startups and banks is evident in Kenya, where some MFIs are reported to be losing market share and returns. Dominic Omondi, "Fintech Is Driving Local Microfinance Institutions to an Early Grave," *Standard Digital*, January 15, 2019 (www.standardmedia.co.ke/article/2001309493/mobile-lenders -drive-microfinance-entities-to-early-grave).

41. The original mission of many an MFI in the region was to promote enterprise and create employment so as to lower poverty. Most of the original MFI clients were microenterprises. Over time, some of these clients have grown into small enterprises. In this context, supporting SMEs is not MFI mission drift. The question still remains what to do about the excluded. Christen, "Comercialization and Mission Drift."

42. The poor in Latin America and the Caribbean in the past two decades have proved to be a moving target, fortunately in the right direction (shrinking in number). Yet some of the leading MFIs might have weakened their "relationship to the poor" as they have moved upward toward the SME clients. This approach might make sense in order to put the money behind the SMEs, which are generally more productive than microenterprises. But it also brings to mind the timeless admonition to keep the focus on the end of reducing poverty and not just the means—that is, the financially sustainable MFI. Maria Otero, "Bringing Development Back into Microfinance," *Journal of Microfinance* 1, no. 1 (1999).

Other MFIs, however, continue to work toward finding ways of reaching the underserved, such as Colombia's Banco W, which has found that as many as half the low-income persons still borrow from informal lenders and is developing ways to get them as its clients. Jose David Castilla, "Proponen crear banca de microfinanzas para eliminar el gota-a-gota," *La República*, December 31, 2018 (www.larepublica.co/finanzas/banco-w-propone-crear-banca-de-microfinanzas -para-eliminar-el-gota-a-gota-2810684). The expectation is that mobile finance can rival the informal lenders in serving the poor. Thomas Dichter, "Is Universal Financial Inclusion for the Third World's Poor Achievable?," *Forbes*, January 17, 2019 (www.forbes.com/sites/thomasdichter /2019/01/17/is-universal-financial-inclusion-for-the-third-worlds-poor-achievable/). Still other MFIs are trying to reach the unbanked by starting with services other than finance, such as off-grid solar energy by FINCA-related companies in Uganda. Stefan Grundmann and Thibault Lesueur, "Opinion: Reaching the World's Unbanked," Devex News, January 25, 2019 (www .devex.com/news/opinion-reaching-the-world-s-unbanked-94193).

Appendix: What the Data Tell Us

BLAINE STEPHENS AND NIKHIL GEHANI

Despite the lack of regulatory reporting requirements or mandatory public disclosures for MFIs in many countries, the global microfinance sector—investors, associations, microfinance institutions (MFIs), and others—responded to the demand for basic business data in order to connect capital to financial services providers.[1] MIX, in close participation with other sector stakeholders, built a hub—MIX Market—to collect, manage, and analyze key financial, operational, and social performance data that included reporting standards and agreement on the key indicators. In addition, in response to demand from investors and MFIs alike, MIX delivered benchmarks to help actors analyze sector development, including growth in the number of clients, accounts, and loan portfolios, along with measures of efficiency, portfolio risk, and returns. Together, the data would enable the microfinance sector to categorize MFIs across various attributes, measure and compare performance, and evaluate these providers—and the industry—in light of their social missions.

As a result of these developments in the information market of microfinance, we know that women make up 89 percent of total borrowers in South Asia but only 49 percent of borrowers in Eastern Europe and Central Asia.[2] We know that most borrowers in Latin America and the Caribbean live in urban areas, and that 79 percent of borrowers in East Asia and the Pacific live in rural areas. The data also show that 75 percent of the loan portfolio in the Middle East and North Africa is made up of microenterprise loans, and 64 percent of the loan portfolio in East

441

Asia and the Pacific consists of household loans. And we can see that the number of depositors and deposits is growing more rapidly than the number of active borrowers.

We also know that the data helped improve the flow of capital to MFIs, with microfinance investment vehicle (MIV) portfolios growing at a compound annual growth rate of 22 percent, totaling US$12 billion by the end of 2017.[3] This vast body of basic business data helped the sector and individual MFIs grow through greater market transparency, comparable benchmarks—which have been and continue to be the single most downloaded materials from MIX Market—and a better understanding of MFI performance. But the supply-side data are augmented by a growing body of data on the consumers of these services, and to some extent, on the impact of these services.

Global Findex provides comparable longitudinal data on the behaviors of low-income consumers of financial services, including access and usage of various formal and informal services. As a result, we have good evidence of the increase in access to basic accounts: 515 million people obtained an account between 2014 and 2017. We can also see the role that digital financial services are playing in access in regions like sub-Saharan Africa, where the percentage of adults with mobile money accounts increased from 11.6 percent in 2014 to 20.9 percent in 2017. Randomized controlled trials and a growing body of research—led in part by Innovations for Poverty Action—are helping to delineate impacts and, importantly, identify which methods work and which do not. Together, these demand-side data have spurred improvements to products, processes, and measurement.[4]

Looking Back: How We Added to the Data over the Years

During the rapid growth of microfinance in the mid-2000s, a series of crises in several countries, including Bosnia, India, Nicaragua, and Morocco, shed light on the downside and risks of microfinance, as well as on standard operating practices at the time. The industry responded by developing and adopting consumer protection standards, metrics, and a framework for analyzing how an MFI translates its stated mission into practice.

The Social Performance Task Force and the Smart Campaign were born from these efforts, and together with sector actors crafted a framework and data standards for social performance.[5] To enable the adoption of these standards, and to ensure that they became central to the business of microfinance, MIX integrated the data into regular reporting processes through the MIX Market platform.

As the body of evidence from social performance data grew, the sector was able to look at the synergies and trade-offs between financial and social performance. Analysis of the data enabled the measurement of these tensions and supplemented our understanding of microfinance performance.[6] For example, we have evidence that, while there is a trade-off in efficiency for MFIs that explicitly target "poor clients," there is no measurable effect on portfolio quality. Efforts like this, as well as by Global Findex and in randomized controlled trials, are examples of how the sector has filled gaps in our understanding of the customer experience by analyzing the impacts of these financial services and informing better business practices.

Looking Ahead: What Data Gaps Exist

As the industry evolves and expands around the digitization of financial services, there are renewed calls for new data to better understand these products. We are already seeing a growing fact base in areas like how brick-and-mortar MFIs are digitizing their product delivery—including data on digital delivery access points[7]— as well as mobile money, which counted more than 866 million registered accounts in 2018.[8]

But this approach, grouped by provider type, is less useful today as digitization generates opportunities for new business models. The traditional MFI model is now one of many methods for reaching financially underserved people and businesses, and the rate of innovation demands new data to assess performance and impact. New and old entrants alike are unbundling various pieces of the financial services value chain (client acquisition may rely on agents) and combining them with other goods and services (pay-as-you-go off-grid energy products, for instance). As a result of the changing dynamics in financial services, nascent efforts are beginning to address this new reality, particularly from the vantage point of investors and operators. For example, the pay-as-you-go industry is developing data standards and benchmarks to help operators better understand their businesses and to bring capital to the sector through a better understanding of risk.[9] Similarly, MIX is creating data standards for inclusive fintech to help unlock capital for cross-cutting digitization of financial services, whether it is a service such as credit or insurance, or an infrastructure component supporting those services. In building these standards, the sector is looking to categorize fintechs, measure performance, and evaluate fintechs from an inclusivity angle. If these objectives sound familiar, well, that is because they are.

Over the course of two decades, the MIX Market platform matured alongside the microfinance market. Now, as the universe of financial services for the poor expands through new delivery channels, product types, and technologies, MIX is working to help investors understand these new models. And, just as before, basic business data are needed to connect capital to financial services providers.

Notes

1. Tillman Bruett, ed., *Measuring Performance of Microfinance Institutions: A Framework for Reporting, Analysis, and Monitoring* (Washington The SEEP Network and Alternative Credit Technologies, Ltd., 2005) (www.onekerato.com/uploads/7/9/4/8/7948160/seep_framework_manual.pdf).

2. MIX, "Global Outreach & Financial Performance Benchmark Report: 2017–2018" (https://www.themix.org/sites/default/files/mix_market_global_outreach_financial_benchmark_report_2017-2018.pdf).

3. Symbiotics, "2018 Symbiotics MIV Survey Market Data & Peer Group Analysis, 12th edition" (http://symbioticsgroup.com/wp-content/uploads/2018/10/Symbiotics-2018-MIV-Survey.pdf).

4. Innovations for Poverty Action, "Evidence on Microcredit: Rethinking Financial Tools for the Poor: Using Results" (https://www.poverty-action.org/impact/evidence-microcredit-rethinking-financial-tools-poor).

5. "The Universal Standards for Social Performance Management" (https://sptf.info/universal-standards-for-spm/universal-standards).

6. MIX, "Where Good Intentions Meet Good Business Practice," August 17, 2016 (https://www.themix.org/publications/where-good-intentions-meet-good-business-practice).

7. MIX, "Measuring the Performance of Alternative Delivery Channels," March 2017 (https://www.themix.org/publications/measuring-the-performance-of-alternative-delivery-channels).

8. Francesco Pasti, "State of the Industry Report on Mobile Money 2018" (London: GSMA, 2019) (https://www.gsma.com/mobilefordevelopment/resources/2018-state-of-the-industry-report-on-mobile-money/).

9. "Key Performance Indicators for PAYGo PERFORM: How Far We Have Come" (London: GSMA, 2019) (https://www.gogla.org/resources/paygo-perform-webinar-presentation).

Glossary

Accion International	Nonprofit focused on financial inclusion.
assets under management (AUM)	Total market value of all the financial assets that a financial institution manages on behalf of its clients and itself.
Consultative Group to Assist the Poor (CGAP)	Institution created by the World Bank and other donor institutions; de facto secretariat for the microfinance industry. Center of knowledge management.
downscaling	Commercial banks entering the microfinance sector.
financial inclusion	Financial solutions for the economically underprivileged.
Findex	Financial inclusion dataset published every three years by the World Bank.
Grameen Bank	Prominent Bangladeshi microfinance institution.
greenfield MFI	Newly created microfinance institution, usually a subsidiary of a holding company.
impact investing	Investing intended to generate measurable social or environmental impact in addition to financial return.
informal sector	Untaxed, unmonitored sector of an economy.
International Finance Corporation (IFC)	Financial institution offering investment, advisory, and asset management services to encourage private sector development in less-developed countries.
M-Cril	Ratings agency for financially inclusive and developmental organizations in Asia.

MFX   Social investment hedging and risk management
                                 organization.

microcredit   Small loans with low interest rates provided to
                                 businesses in the developing world.

microfinance   Financial services for individuals and small
                                 businesses that lack access to conventional banking
                                 and financing opportunities.

microfinance institution (MFI) Organization offering financial services to
                                 low-income populations through loans, insurance,
                                 deposits, and other financial services.

microfirm   Also known as a microenterprise; a firm employing
                                 fewer than ten people.

microinsurance   Risk management tool for individuals living in poverty.

MicroRate   Ratings agency for microfinance institutions.

microsavings account   Deposit account used to provide incentives for
                                 low-income individuals and families to save.

mission drift   The pull of business needs such as revenue generation
                                 and return away from a socially conscious
                                 organization's core objectives.

MIX Market   Microfinance Information Exchange, an online data
                                 resource on the financial and operating performance
                                 of some 2,000 MFIs supporting financially inclusive
                                 and developmental investing. See appendix.

neobanks   Banks operating exclusively through digital applications.

social investor   An investor seeking to foster social or environmental
                                 good in addition to earning a financial return.

Symbiotics   Investment fund focused on "investable" MFIs in
                                 developing and emerging economies.

United Nations Sustainable   Seventeen global goals intended to address challenges
Development Goals (SDGs)   related to poverty, inequality, climate and environment
                                 degradation, prosperity, peace, and justice.

upscaling   Microfinance institutions transforming into regulated
                                 entities.

World Bank Group   International financial institution that provides loans
                                 and grants to the governments of poorer countries for
                                 the purpose of pursuing capital projects.

Contributors

Momina Aijazuddin is Global Head of Microfinance Financial Inclusion with the International Finance Corporation (IFC) and works also as Principal Investment Officer in IFC's Financial Institution Group. She covers IFC's microfinance investment and advisory activities globally, which exceed cumulative investments of US$6 billion worldwide with over 300 microfinance institutions, in addition to advisory services worth US$63.7 million in sixty-eight projects across thirty countries. She is also leading IFC's efforts to scale up private sector commitments with strategic partners in the digital finance, microfinance, and fintech space committed to achieving the World Bank Group's Universal Financial Access goals by 2020. She was also a core member of the drafting team for the G-20 Digital Financial Inclusion Principles.

Matthew Brown is a microfinance banking specialist with over fifteen years of experience in management, consulting, training, and research. He is currently a senior microfinance specialist with the Micro and Digital Financial Services practice groups at the International Finance Corporation. He was formerly the Chief Executive Officer of Fonkoze Financial Services in Haiti and led its successful restructuring and turnaround. He has also worked with Mennonite Economic Development Associates, Opportunity International, and the Consultative Group to Assist the Poor. He has field experience in Afghanistan, the Democratic Republic of Congo, Ghana, Liberia, Myanmar, Nicaragua, Sierra Leone, Syria, and Yemen. Brown has served as a faculty member of the Boulder Institute of Microfinance and School of African Microfinance. He holds a master's degree in international relations and international economics from the Johns Hopkins University's Paul H. Nitze School of Advanced International Studies.

Greta Bull is CEO of the Consultative Group to Assist the Poor (CGAP) and a director at the World Bank Group. She has eighteen years of experience in development finance, primarily focused on small and medium-sized enterprise finance, microfinance, and digital financial services. She has worked with both financial services providers and policymakers in Latin America, Central and Eastern Europe, sub-Saharan Africa, and South Asia. Her clients have included banks, microfinance institutions, mobile network operators, and fintechs. Before joining CGAP, Bull was a manager for Financial Institutions Advisory Services at the International Finance Corporation. She has served as director of the Finance, Banking, and Enterprise Division at DAI Europe and in senior-level positions at the Eurasia Foundation. Bull has a master's degree in public policy from Harvard University's John F. Kennedy School of Government and an undergraduate degree in international studies from the University of Washington.

Lory Camba Opem is Global Lead for Responsible Finance, Microfinance, and Digital Finance Practices in the Financial Institutions Group of the International Finance Corporation (IFC). She has over twenty years of private and financial sector expertise across advisory and investment operations in emerging markets. She represents IFC as a co-founding member of the Responsible Finance Forum and co-leads IFC's strategy and implementation of the Investor Guidelines for Responsible Investing in Digital Financial Services.

Renée Chao-Beroff is the General Manager and Founder of the Participatory Microfinance Group for Africa (PAMIGA) and Managing Director of PAMIGA Finance SA, an impact investment vehicle for rural microfinance in sub-Saharan Africa. She holds a Ph.D. in economics and finance. Chao-Beroff has worked in economic development and microfinance for thirty years. She developed the self-managed village saving and loan bank model (*Caisse villageoise d'épargne et de crédit autogérées,* or CVECA), which has brought sustainable microfinance to remote rural areas across West and Central Africa. She regularly advises donors, governments, national networks, and MFIs and teaches microfinance at the Center for Finance, Economics, and Banking Studies in France as well as in the Boulder Institute's microfinance training program. Chao-Beroff was a member of the Policy Advisory Group from 1995 to 1999 and also served on the Executive Committee of the Consultative Group to Assist the Poor for years.

Enjiang Cheng is a Program Officer in the Ford Foundation's Beijing office developing programs on China's development finance in countries of the Global South. Before joining the foundation in 2016, he was an Associate Professor at the Victoria Institute of Strategic Economic Studies at Victoria University in Melbourne, Australia, where he focused on China's economic structural change and energy use transformation, development finance, and poverty reduction. Earlier, he served as Fellow and Chief Research Coordinator at the International Poverty Reduction Center of China and then spent a year as Vice President and Senior China Economist at Citibank in China.

Craig Churchill is Chief of the Social Finance Programme and the Team Leader of the International Labour Organization's Impact Insurance Facility. He has more than two decades of microfinance experience in developed and developing countries. In his current position, he focuses on the potential of financial services and policies to achieve social objectives. He serves on the governing board of the Access to Insurance Initiative and was the founding chair of the Microinsurance Network. He has written and edited over forty articles, papers, monographs, and training manuals on microfinance topics, including microinsurance, customer loyalty, organizational development, governance, lending methodologies, regulation and supervision, and financial services for the poorest of the poor.

Gerhard Coetzee leads the customer value team at the Consultative Group to Assist the Poor (CGAP) and is also responsible for Gateway Academy, a digital learning platform. He is an Extraordinary Professor at the University of Stellenbosch Business School. Before joining CGAP, Coetzee was Head of Inclusive Banking at Absa Bank (South Africa), responsible for its branchless banking proposition; founder and Director of the Centre for Inclusive Banking in Africa; Professor of agricultural economics at the University of Pretoria; and technical lead and CEO of a consulting firm (owned by DAI). He has also held several senior roles at the Development Bank of Southern Africa. His areas of specialization are development finance, financial inclusion, agricultural finance, and rural development. He is published widely and has worked in several countries, the majority in Africa. Coetzee holds a Ph.D. in agricultural economics from the University of Pretoria, South Africa.

Aparna Dalal is a Senior Research Officer with the Impact Insurance Facility of the International Labour Organization (ILO). She leads the facility's Research and Innovation Initiative, which supports practitioners in developing valuable risk management solutions for low-income and emerging customers. She has a decade of technology and business management experience in the public and private sectors. Before joining the ILO, Dalal was the Director of Special Projects for the Financial Access Initiative at New York University, where she led microinsurance research projects.

Paul DiLeo is the founder of Grassroots Capital Management PBC. He has over three decades of experience in development finance and twenty years of experience in the microfinance sector. DiLeo has worked in Russia, Nicaragua, India, Argentina, Bosnia, and many other countries. He led equity investments in microfinance institutions in India and Bangladesh as early as 2001 and to date has managed or advised funds that have invested equity in thirty-five microfinance companies. DiLeo started his career with the U.S. Treasury and Federal Reserve Bank of New York. He holds a B.A. from the University of Massachusetts, an M.S. in economics from Boston University, and a certificate in business accounting and finance from New York University.

Roland Dominicé is an expert in microfinance investments and international finance and development. He studied social sciences and international relations both at the University of Geneva's Graduate Institute of International and Development Studies, where he wrote his master's thesis on state-building and the stages of modern political development, and at the University of Chicago's Committee on International Relations, where he wrote his master's thesis on globalization strategies and organizational development theory. Dominicé started his career in finance in wealth management at UBS and in corporate finance as a management consultant at PricewaterhouseCoopers. He then joined the founding team at BlueOrchard Finance to launch the first private wealth manager dedicated to microfinance investments, where he served as the CFO for three years. He helped the firm gain an international reputation by leading the launch of the first microfinance structured bonds in the capital markets in 2004, in cooperation with J. P. Morgan and the U.S. Overseas Private Investment Corporation. He then co-founded Symbiotics, where he initially served as a business development manager before becoming CEO in 2008.

Nikhil Gehani is the Director of Marketing and Communications at MIX, the leading global data resource for socially responsible investors and businesses focused on inclusive finance. Gehani has over a decade of experience as a marketing, communications, and branding specialist, working for global agencies where he led the digital strategy for several Fortune 500 brands. He holds an M.A. in international development from the George Washington University and a B.A. in marketing from Michigan State University.

Claudio Gonzalez-Vega is Professor Emeritus at the Ohio State University. Since 2008 he has been a member of the Board of Trustees of the BBVA Microfinance Foundation, which he chaired from 2015 through 2018.

Jennifer Isern has over thirty years of experience in development in more than sixty-five countries. She is the founder and CEO of Catalyze Global Impact LLC, advising and investing in initiatives to achieve sustainable impact for households and businesses globally. Previously, Isern served in senior roles for the World Bank and the International Finance Corporation (IFC) for twenty-three years. During this period, Isern served thirteen years as Lead Financial Specialist with the Consultative Group to Assist the Poor (CGAP), leading several global initiatives including payments and remittances, training for banks and funders, and policy advocacy focusing especially on sub-Saharan Africa and China. As Senior Manager for IFC and the World Bank, she led the financial sector development team in South Asia for seven years while based in New Delhi, India, and the financial and private sector development team in East Asia and the Pacific for three years while based in Hanoi, Vietnam. Before joining the World Bank Group, Isern worked for five years with CARE International to launch and manage new microfinance institutions while based in Niger and Togo. She enjoys speaking on finance and global development issues, and taught for two years at the Wilson School at Princeton University and for five years at the Boulder Microfinance Program. A CFA Charterholder, Isern holds a doctorate with double specialization in finance and international business from Nova Southeastern University, an M.P.A. from the Wilson School at Princeton University, and B.A. from the University of Montana.

Anna Kanze is a Managing Director of Grassroots Capital Management PBC, where she supports the creation of impact investment funds in India and Latin America. She is also a board member of the Social Performance Task Force (SPTF) and has been a co-chair of the SPTF's Social Investor Working Group since 2017.

Ira W. Lieberman is the Chairman and CEO of Lipam International. He started the Consultative Group to Assist the Poor Secretariat at the World Bank in 1995 and managed it for some five years. Thereafter he continued to work in the sector for the Open Society Institute (Soros Foundation) and on numerous boards of directors of microfinance institutions funding the sector in Africa and Latin America.

Kimanthi Mutua has over thirty years of experience in microfinance, financial inclusion, and development finance. He founded K-Rep in 1999 and led the first transformation of a nongovernmental organization into a commercial bank in Africa, where he served as CEO until 2010. He serves as a board member and chair of several organizations, including Sidian Bank, K-Rep Group, K-Rep Development Agency, the Participatory Microfinance Group for Africa (PAMIGA), ECLOF International, and others. Mutua has devoted over three decades to diverse initiatives on microfinance and financial inclusion. Currently he is involved in advising regulatory bodies, microfinance institutions, and commercial banks. He also serves as a faculty member of the Boulder Institute of Microfinance and a guest lecturer at L'Université Libre de Bruxelles. His hands-on experience in areas such as leadership, governance, transformation, and policy formulation have made him a widely sought out public speaker.

Timothy N. Ogden is Managing Director of the Financial Access Initiative, a research center focused on financial services for low-income households around the world, and an Adjunct Professor at New York University–Wagner. He is also a Senior Fellow of the Aspen Institute's Economic Opportunities Program, serves as a Director of Sona Partners, Chairman of GiveWell, and President of the Bardet Biedl Syndrome Foundation. He was previously Managing Director of the U.S. Financial Diaries Project; Chief Knowledge Officer of Geneva Global, a philanthropy advisory firm; and Vice President at Gartner. Ogden writes and speaks frequently on topics related to financial inclusion, poverty, economic development, financial services innovation, social investment, and philanthropy, and he produces *The faiV*, a widely read and influential weekly newsletter on financial inclusion, global development, and social investment. He has developed and edited more than twenty books and is co-author of *Toyota under Fire*. His most recent book is *Experimental Conversations*, a collection of interviews of leading economists on the use of randomized control trials in development economics. He is currently working on *Financial Inclusion: What Everyone Needs to Know* (Oxford University Press) and *Automated Conversations* (interviews on how artificial intelligence, machine learning, and big data are changing the field of economics).

Jose Ruisanchez is a consultant to companies, development organizations, and financial institutions. Based in Washington, he is originally from Cuba. He has advised the founders of several microfinance institutions and funds that invest in MFIs. Ruisanchez is a former Manager of Esso-affiliated companies in Spain and a former Vice President for Latin America and the Caribbean of the International Finance Corporation of the World Bank Group.

Alejandro (Alex) Silva is the founder and partner of OMTRIX, a fund management and financial consulting company. He has been involved in or has managed multiple initiatives related to microfinance, including ProFund, Antares, Short-Term Liquidity Fund, Risk Management Facility, Emergency Liquidity Fund, and Higher Education Finance Fund.

Blaine Stephens is the COO at MIX, the leading global data resource for socially responsible investors and businesses focused on inclusive finance. Since the launch in 2002 of MIX's first online platform, MIX Market, Stephens has worked with global and national stakeholders and a team of analysts to further industry development through reporting standards, benchmarks, rankings, and other information products, ranging from microfinance and agrifinance to digital financial services and fintech. He has more than twenty years of experience in the sector, having previously helped develop the startup operations for a Moroccan microfinance institution, Al Amana, and collaborated with the United Nations Capital Development Fund on the development and rollout of an online microfinance training course for donors and practitioners. He holds a B.A. from Claremont McKenna College and an M.I.A. from Columbia University's School of International and Public Affairs. He speaks English, French, and basic Arabic and German.

Todd A. Watkins is Professor of economics and Executive Director of the Martindale Center for the Study of Private Enterprise at Lehigh University. His research and teaching focus on the intersection of microfinance, economic development, innovation, entrepreneurship, and public policy. He is the author of more than seventy-five related publications, including *Introduction to Microfinance* (World Scientific, 2018), and co-editor of the book *Moving beyond Storytelling: Emerging Research in Microfinance* (Emerald, 2009). Watkins founded and directs Lehigh's Microfinance Program and was a founding member of the advisory Faculty Council for Accion International's Center for Financial Inclusion, which seeks to promote innovation and growth of commercial microfinance worldwide. He serves as a board member and past President of the Rising Tide Community Loan Fund, which targets the business development credit needs of low-to-moderate-income communities in eastern Pennsylvania.

Index

Boxes, figures, and tables are indicated by b, f, and t following the page number.

CPSIA information can be obtained
at www.ICGtesting.com
Printed in the USA
JSHW022155290520
5971JS00001B/1